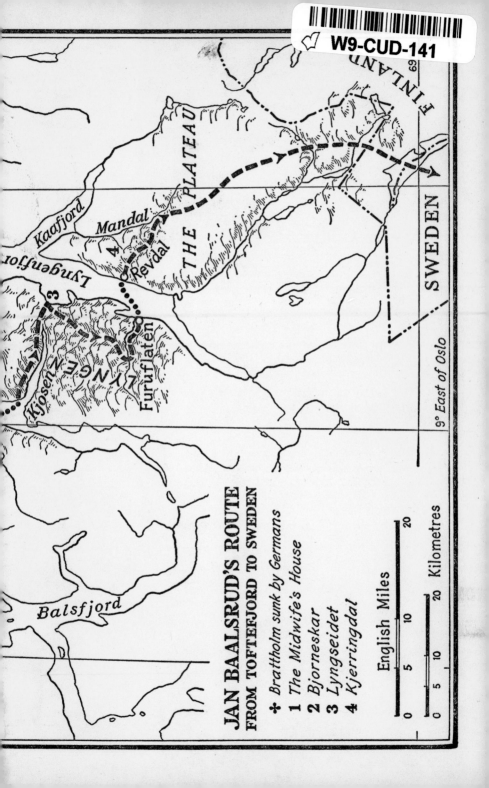

W9-CUD-141

JAN BAALSRUD'S ROUTE
FROM TOFTEFJORD TO SWEDEN

✛ *Brattholm sunk by Germans*
1 *The Midwife's House*
2 *Bjorneskar*
3 *Lyngseidet*
4 *Kjerringdal*

English Miles

0   5   10   20

0   5   10   20   Kilometres

9° East of Oslo

FINLAND

SWEDEN

THE PLATEAU

Kaafjord

Mandal

Revdal

Lyngenfjord

LYNGEN

Kiosen

Furuflaten

Balsfjord

WE DIE ALONE

THE MACMILLAN COMPANY
NEW YORK • CHICAGO
DALLAS • ATLANTA • SAN FRANCISCO
LONDON • MANILA

DAVID HOWARTH

WE DIE ALONE

New York
THE MACMILLAN COMPANY
1955

On mourra seul

PASCAL
1623–1662

CONTENTS

CONTENTS

ILLUSTRATIONS

ILLUSTRATIONS

AUTHOR'S NOTE

I HEARD the bare bones of this story during the war, soon after it happened, and I mentioned it briefly in my book *The Shetland Bus*. All that I knew about it then was based on a report which was written in a Swedish hospital by a man called Jan Baalsrud. It was a graphic report, but Baalsrud was very ill when he wrote it, and it left a lot unsaid. One could see that there was much more in the story, some things which Baalsrud had forgotten and others he had never known, although he played the main part in it. But it was not until ten years later that I had a chance to talk it all over with him, and persuade him to come with me to the far north of Norway where it happened, to try to find out the whole truth of it.

Now that I have found it out and written it down, I am rather afraid of being accused of exaggeration. Parts of it are difficult to believe. But I have seen nearly all the places which are mentioned in this book, and met nearly all the people. Not one of the people knew the whole story, but each of them had a most vivid recollection of his own part in it. Each of their individual stories fitted together, and also confirmed what Baalsrud himself remembered. Some minor events are matters of deduction, but none of it is imaginary. Here and there I have altered a name or an unimportant detail to avoid offending people; but otherwise, I am convinced that this account is true.

CHAPTER ONE

LANDFALL

EVEN AT the end of March, on the Arctic coast of northern Norway, there is no sign of spring. By then, the polar winter night is over. At midwinter, it has been dark all day; at midsummer, the sun will shine all night; and in between, at the vernal equinox, the days draw out so quickly that each one is noticeably longer than the last. But the whole land is still covered thickly with ice and snow to the very edge of the sea. There is nothing green at all: no flowers or grass, and no buds on the stunted trees. Sometimes there are clear days at that time of year, and then the coast glitters with a blinding brilliance in the sunlight; but more often it is swept by high winds and hidden by frozen mist and driven snow.

It was on that coast, on the 29th of March, 1943, that this story really began. On that day a fishing-boat made landfall there, six days out from the Shetland Islands, with twelve men on board. Its arrival in those distant enemy waters in the third year of the war, within sight of a land which was occupied by the Germans, was the result of a lot of thought and careful preparation; but within a day of its arrival all the plans which had been made were blown to pieces, and everything which happened after that, the tragedies and adventures and self-sacrifice, and the single triumph, was simply a matter of chance; not the outcome of any plan at all, but only of luck, both good and bad, and of courage and faithfulness.

That particular day was sunny, as it happened, and the

twelve men watched it dawn with intense excitement. It is always exciting to make the land after a dangerous voyage; the more so when one's ship approaches the land at night, so that when daylight comes a coast is revealed already close at hand. In that landfall there was an extra excitement for those men, because they were all Norwegians, and most of them were about to see their homeland for the first time since they had been driven out of it by the German invasion nearly three years before. Above all, here was the supreme excitement of playing a dangerous game. Eight of the twelve were the crew of the fishing-boat. They had sailed it safely across a thousand miles of the no-man's-land of ocean, and had to sail it back when they had landed their passengers and cargo. The other four were soldiers trained in guerrilla warfare. Their journey had two objectives, one general and one particular. In general, they were to establish themselves ashore and spend the summer training the local people in the arts of sabotage; and in particular, in the following autumn they were to attack a great German military airfield called Bardufoss. In the hold of the boat, they had eight tons of explosives, weapons, food and arctic equipment, and three radio transmitters.

As the day dawned, they felt as a gambler might feel if he had staked his whole fortune on a system he believed in; except, of course, that they had staked their lives, which makes a gamble even more exciting. They believed that in a Norwegian fishing-boat they could bluff their way through the German coast defences, and they believed that with their plans and equipment they could live ashore on that barren land in spite of the arctic weather and the German occupation; and on these beliefs their lives depended. If they were wrong, nobody could protect them. They were beyond the range of any help from England. So far, it had all gone well; so far, there was no

sign that the Germans were suspicious. But the gleaming
mountains which they sighted to the southward, so beautiful
and serene in the morning light, were full of menace. Among
them the German coast watchers were posted, and soon, in the
growing light, they would see the fishing-boat, alone on the
glittering sea. That morning would put the first of the theories
to the test, and that night or the next would bring the boat and
its crew to the climax of the journey: the secret landing.

At that time, in 1943, that remote and thinly populated
coast had suddenly had world-wide importance thrust upon it.
Normally, in time of peace, there is no more peaceful place
than the far north of Norway. For two months every summer
there is a tourist season, when foreigners come to see the
mountains and the Lapps and the midnight sun; but for the
other ten months of the year, the people who live there eke out
a humble livelihood by fishing and working small farms along
the water's edge. They are almost cut off from the world outside, by the sea in front of them and the Swedish frontier at
their backs, and by bad weather and darkness, and by the vast
distance they have to travel to reach the capital of their own
country or any other centre of civilisation. They live a hard
life, but a very placid one. They are not harassed by many of
the worries which beset people in cities or in more populous
countrysides. They take little account of time.

But when the Germans invaded Norway in 1940, the thousand miles of Atlantic seaboard which fell into their hands was
the greatest strategical asset which they won; and when Russia
entered the war, the far northernmost end of the coast became
even more important, and even more valuable to Germany.
The allied convoys to the Russian arctic ports, Archangel and
Murmansk, had to pass through the narrow strip of open sea
between the north of Norway and the arctic ice; and it was

from north Norway that the Germans attacked them with success which had sometimes been overwhelming. Bardufoss was the base for their air attacks and their reconnaissance, and the coast itself provided a refuge for submarines and a safe passage from German harbours all the way to the Arctic Ocean.

As soon as the Germans had installed themselves on the northern coast, their position was impregnable. It was a thousand miles from the nearest allied base, and the country could not have been better for defence. A screen of islands twenty miles wide protects it from the sea, and among the islands are innumerable sounds through which defending forces could manœuvre by sea in safety. The mainland itself is divided by a series of great fjords, with mountainous tongues of land between them. Beyond the heads of the fjords is a high plateau, uninhabited and mostly unsurveyed, snow-covered for nine months of the year; and across the plateau, marked by a cairn here and there among its deserted hills, is the frontier of Sweden, which was a neutral country then, entirely surrounded by others under German occupation. To attack the Germans in arctic Norway with any normal military force was quite impossible. Every island and every fjord could have become a fortress; and if the Germans had ever found themselves hard pressed in northern Norway, they could have reinforced their position by occupying Sweden, which would not have been to the advantage of the Allies.

In these circumstances, the voyage which had come to its end on that March morning had a possible importance out of all proportion to the size of the expedition. Great hopes of its outcome were held in London. Only four men were to be landed, but they were quite capable, with a little luck, of putting the air base at Bardufoss out of action long enough for a convoy to have a chance of getting through undetected; and the time was also ripe for the training of local people. The great majority of Norwegians up there would have gladly taken some positive action against the Germans, and would have done it long before if they had had any weapons and any instructions on how to set about it. Once the training was started, it would grow like a snowball.

The only reason why nothing of the kind had been done in Norway before was that it was so difficult to get there. Small parties of men on skis could get over the mountains across the border from Sweden, and a radio transmitter had been taken in that way and was installed in the town of Tromsö. But a saboteur's equipment was much too bulky and heavy to carry across the mountains, or to smuggle past the Swedes. The only way to take it was by sea.

By that time, a great many landings had been made in the southern part of Norway by fishing-boats fitted with hidden armament, which sailed from a base in Shetland, and the resistance movement down there was well supplied and flourishing. But none of these boats, up till then, had tackled such a long and risky journey as the one to the north of Norway. The boat which had just accomplished it had come from the Shetland base. Its name was the *Brattholm*. It was 75 feet long, and had a single cylinder engine which gave it a speed of eight knots. Its appearance had been carefully preserved, so that it looked like any Norwegian fishing-boat, and it had false registration numbers painted on its bows. But it was armed with seven machine-guns hidden on mountings on deck, and each of its passengers had his own spare machine-gun stowed somewhere where he could get it in a hurry.

The date when it sailed from Shetland, in the third week in March, had been a compromise which was not entirely satisfactory for anybody. The skipper and crew of the boat had to make up their minds between sailing in the depth of winter, when they would have the cover of the arctic night but would also have to weather the arctic storms, or in the late spring or early autumn, when the weather would probably be rather more moderate but the German defences, and their air patrols in particular, would have the advantage of daylight. On the whole, from the skipper's point of view, it would have been better to go earlier than March, because his boat was sound and fit to stand up to any weather. But the passengers also had to be considered. If they had been landed in the worst of winter weather they might not have been able to keep themselves alive after they got ashore.

But still, the choice of March had been justified in so far as the voyage had been a success. The weather had not been bad. The little boat had felt very conspicuous to the people on board it as it slowly steamed northwards day after day, but it had only been sighted once, by a German aircraft about three hundred miles from land; and this aircraft, which was probably on a weather reconnaissance flight and not really concerned with stray fishing-boats, had only circled round and then flown away.

So it seemed that whatever happened when they were sighted from the shore, at least the shore defences could not have been warned about them, and would have no reason to guess that the humble boat they saw in front of them had crossed a thousand miles of the Atlantic. But it still remained to be seen whether the coast watchers would be deceived by *Brattholm's* innocent appearance. It had worked often enough farther south, but on a new bit of coast there was always the risk of infringing some local fishing regulation and so giving the game away. For all that the crew or the passengers knew, they might be pretending to fish in the middle of a minefield,

6

or an artillery range, or some other kind of forbidden area, because nobody had been able to tell them before they left Shetland exactly where these kinds of defences were.

At the tense moment of the dawn, all the four passengers were on deck. Wars often bring together people of very different character, and these four were as varied in experience and background as any four Norwegians could have been. Their leader was a man in his middle forties called Sigurd Eskeland. As a young man, he had emigrated to South America, and he had spent most of his adult life in the back of beyond in Argentina running a fur farm. On the day when he heard on the radio that Norway had been invaded, he got on his horse and left his farm in the hands of his partner, and rode to the nearest town to volunteer by cable for the air force. The air force turned him down on account of his age, but he worked his way to England and joined the army instead. He got into the Commandos, and then transferred to the Linge Company, which was the name of the military unit which trained agents and saboteurs for landing in occupied Norway. Long ago, before he went abroad, he had been a postal inspector in north Norway, so that he remembered something about the district he had been assigned to.

The other three men were very much younger. There was a radio operator called Salvesen, who was a member of a well-known shipping family. He had been a first mate in the Merchant Navy when Norway came into the war; but after a time that defensive job had begun to bore him, and when he heard of the Linge Company he volunteered to join it as an agent.

The other two were specialists in small arms and explosives, and they were close friends who had been through a lot of queer experiences together. Both of them were 26 years old. One was called Per Blindheim. He was the son of a master baker in Ålesund on the west coast of Norway, and in his youth he had served his time on the bread round. Superficially, he was a gay and very handsome young man in the Viking tradition, tall and fair and blue-eyed; but hidden beneath his boyish appearance and behaviour, he had a most compelling sense of justice. When the Russians attacked Finland, it seemed to him so wrong that he threw up his job and left home to join the Finnish army. When the World War began and his own country was invaded, he hurried back and fought against the Germans; and when the battle for Norway was lost, he set off for England to begin it all over again, escaping from the Germans by way of Russia, the country against which he had fought a few months before.

The other one of this pair of friends, and the fourth of the landing party, was Jan Baalsrud. To look at, Jan was a contrast to Per; he had dark hair and grey-blue eyes, and was of a smaller build altogether. But he had the same youthful quality, combined with the same hidden serious turn of mind; a depth of feeling which neither of those two would show to strangers, but one which all four of the men must have needed to carry them through the hardships of their training and bring them to where they were.

Jan had been apprenticed to his father, who was an instrument maker in Oslo, and had only just started his career when the invasion came. He had fought in the army, and escaped to Sweden when there was no chance to fight any more. By then he had discovered a taste for adventure, and he volunteered as a courier between Stockholm and Oslo, and began to travel to and fro between neutral Sweden and occupied Norway, in the service of the escape organisation which the Norwegians had founded. Luckily for him, he was caught and arrested by the Swedes before he was caught by the Germans. They sentenced him to five months' imprisonment, but after he had served three months of his sentence he was let out and given a fortnight to leave the country.

This was easier ordered than done; but he got a Russian visa and flew to Moscow, where he landed inauspiciously among Russian celebrations of German victories. However, the Russians treated him well and sent him down to Odessa on the Black Sea; and it was while he was waiting there for a ship that he first met Per Blindheim, who was on the same errand. The two travelled together to England by way of Bulgaria, Egypt, Aden, Bombay, South Africa, America and Newfoundland. When they got to London, the first of the sights that they went to see was Piccadilly Circus; and while they were standing looking rather glumly at this symbol of their journey's end, and wondering what was going to happen next, Jan saw in the crowd an English officer he had known in Stockholm. This man recruited them both forthwith for the Linge Company, and there they found a job which fulfilled all their hopes of adventure.

These, then, were the four men who stood on the deck that March morning at the climax of a year of preparation. They had trained together in the highlands of Scotland, doing forced marches of thirty and forty miles with packs across the mountains, living out in the snow, studying weapons and underground organisation, doing their quota of parachute jumps, and learning to draw and cock an automatic and score six hits on a half-man-sized target at five yards, all in a space of three seconds; finally learning all the vulnerable points of airfields; and incidentally, enjoying themselves tremendously. They were tough and healthy, and elated at the imminence of danger; and very confident of being able to look after themselves, whatever the dawn might bring.

9

CHAPTER TWO

THE FIGHT IN TOFTEFJORD

ON THAT sort of expedition it was useless to make a detailed plan, because nobody could foresee exactly what was going to happen. The leader always had a degree of responsibility which few people are called upon to carry in a war. The orders he was given were in very general terms, and in carrying them out he had nobody whatever to advise him. His success, and his own life and the lives of his party, were in his own hands alone.

As leader of this party in north Norway, Eskeland had a specially heavy load to carry. From the south, or from any country from which a lot of refugees had escaped to England, a fund of information had been collected about German dispositions and the characters and politics of innumerable people, and the information was always being renewed. The leader of an expedition could be told, in more or less detail, whom he could trust and whom he should avoid, and where he was most likely to meet enemy sentries or patrols. But information about north Norway was scanty. A good many people had escaped from there, but the only route they could follow was across the mountains into Sweden, where they were interned. Many of them were content to stay in internment and wait for better times; and even those who made the effort to escape again, and managed to pass on what they knew to the British intelligence services, had usually been held by the Swedes for a matter of months, so that all that they could tell was out of date. Eskeland had been given the names of a few people who were known to be sound, but beyond that very little could be done to help him. Once he left Britain, he could only depend on his own training and wit and skill.

He had been as thorough as he possibly could be in his preparations. Ever since he had known he was to lead a landing from a fishing-boat, he had pondered in a quiet way over every emergency he could foresee. On the high seas, the skipper of the boat was in command, and out there the problems had been comparatively simple. The boat might have been overcome by stress of weather, which was a matter of seamanship; or its one single-cylinder engine might have broken down, which was a job for the engineers; or it might have been attacked by aircraft, which would have been fought with the boat's own "Q-ship" armament. But now that it had closed the coast, he had to take charge, and now anything might happen and an instantaneous decision might be needed. For the present, the boat's first line of defence was for its guns to be kept hidden, so that it seemed to be innocently fishing. But once they got into the constricted waters of the sounds among the islands, they might meet a larger ship with heavier armament at short range at any moment, and then the boat's armament would be nothing but a hindrance. They might still bluff their way out as a fishing-boat, but they could not hope to fight an action at two or three hundred yards. Apart from anything else, a single shot in their cargo might blow them all to pieces. The only way they could prepare for that kind of encounter, as Eskeland foresaw it, was to hide every vestige of war-like equipment and to lure the enemy ship to within pistol shot. Then, by surprise, there was a chance of boarding it and wiping out its crew.

During the past night, as *Brattholm* approached the coast, Eskeland and his three men had begun to prepare for this possible crisis. They had cleaned and loaded their short-range weapons, Sten guns and carbines and pistols; and they had primed hand-grenades and stowed them in convenient places, in the wheelhouse and galley, and along the inside of the bulwarks, where they could be thrown without warning on board a ship alongside. In case it came to close quarters, he and his three men had all put on naval uniform, although they were soldiers, so that the Germans would not be able to identify them as a landing party.

But even while they made these preparations, they all knew that although with luck they might be successful in that sort of hand-to-hand action, they had very little chance of getting away with their lives. Between themselves and safety there were the thousand miles of sea which they had crossed. They might hope to kill or capture the entire crew of even a larger ship; but unless they could do it so quickly that no radio signal could be sent, and unless it happened in such a remote place that nobody heard the gunshots, all the German defences would be alerted; and then, it was obvious, *Brattholm* at eight knots would not get very far. The only hope of escape then, and it was a small one, was to scuttle the ship and get ashore.

Eskeland had provided for this too. The three radio transmitters in their cargo were a new type still graded top secret, and they also had a few important papers: ciphers, maps, and notes about trustworthy people and German defences. They all understood quite clearly that they had to defend these things with their lives. It went without saying. It was one of the basic rules which they had been taught. Ever since they had entered enemy waters, the papers had been stowed in an accessible place with matches and a bottle of petrol; and a primer, detonators and fuses had been laid in the eight tons of high explosives in the hold. The transmitters were on top of the primer. There were three fuses. One had a five-minute delay, for use if there seemed to be a chance to destroy the ship and cargo and then to get away. The next was thirty seconds, and the last was instantaneous. Each of the twelve men on board was able to contemplate soberly the prospect of lighting the instantaneous fuse, and they understood the circumstances in which they were to do it; if they had tried a hand-to-hand fight with a German ship, for example, and been defeated. The main point was that the Germans should not get the cargo.

Eskeland should have felt satisfied with these preparations as he approached the coast; they were intelligently conceived, and carefully carried out. But on that very day a change of plan was forced upon him, and he was reminded, if there had been any doubt about it, how sketchy his information was. They had intended to land on an island called Senja, about forty miles south-west of the town of Tromsö; but as they approached it, steaming peacefully through the fishing zone, they sighted a trawler coming out towards them. They altered course to the eastward, waiting to see what was going to happen. The trawler reached the open sea at the outer edge of the islands, and then it turned back on its track and went into the sounds again. As it turned, they saw a gun on its foredeck. It was a patrol ship, where no patrol ship had been reported.

At that stage of the expedition, it was their job to avoid trouble rather than look for it, and there was no sense in trying to land their cargo on the one island, from all the hundreds in the district, which they now knew for certain was patrolled. Their disguise had worked so far. They had been seen, and passed as a fishing-boat. The sensible thing to do was to choose another island; and after a discussion, they agreed upon one a

little farther north. It is called Ribbenesöy. It is due north of
Tromsö, thirty miles from the town. On the chart of it, they
found a little bay on the north-east side which seemed to offer
good shelter, and one of the men who had been in that district
before remembered the bay as a remote and deserted spot. At
about midday on the 29th of March, they set course towards it.
Its name is Toftefjord.

It was late in the afternoon by the time they reached the
skerries which lie scattered in the sea for seven miles off the
shore of Ribbenesöy, and began to pick their way among them.
In bad weather the passage which they used is impassable.
There are thousands of rocks awash on either side, and the
whole area becomes a mass of spray in which no marks are
visible. But on that day the sea was calm and the air was clear.
They sighted the stone cairns which are built as seamarks on
some of the biggest rocks, and passed through into sheltered
water. They steamed below a minute island called Fuglö,
which rises sheer on every side to a black crag a thousand feet
high; they skirted the north shore of Ribbenesöy, a steep,
smooth, gleaming sheet of snow which sweeps upwards to the
curved ice-cornice of a hill called Helvedestind, which means
Hell's Peak; and as the light began to fade they crept slowly
into Toftefjord, and let go an anchor into clear ice-blue water.

When the engine stopped, Toftefjord seemed absolutely
silent. After six days of the racket and vibration of a Norwegian fishing-boat under way, the mere absence of noise was unfamiliar; but there is always a specially noticeable silence in
sheltered places when the land is covered thickly with snow.
All familiar sounds are muted and unresonant. There are no
footfalls, no sounds of birds or running water, no hum of in-
sects or rustle of animals or leaves. Even one's own voice

seems altered. Even without reason, in places hushed by snow, the deadening of sound seems menacing.

Yet the appearance of Toftefjord was reassuring. They stood on deck when the work of coming to anchor was finished and looked round them, talking involuntarily in quiet voices. It was almost a perfect hiding-place. To the south and west and east it was shut in by low rounded hills. The tops of the hills were bare; but in the hollows by the shore, the twigs of stunted arctic birch showed black against the snow. To the north was the entrance of the bay, but it was blocked by a little island, so that one could not see into it from outside. *Brattholm* was quite safe there from observation from the sea, and she could not be seen from the air unless an aircraft flew almost overhead.

The beaches showed that the bay was always calm. On the rocks and islands which are exposed to the sea, there is always a broad bare strip of shore where the waves have washed the snow away; but there in the land-locked fjord the snow lay smooth and thick down to the tidemark. There were no tracks in it. Close inshore, the sea itself had been frozen, but the ice had broken up and was floating in transparent lumps around the ship. The air was cold and crisp.

Yet the place was not quite deserted. At the head of the bay, below the hill, there was a barn and a very small wooden house. Close by, on the beach, there were racks for drying fish. There was nobody to be seen, but there was smoke from the cottage chimney.

The first thing to be done, when the ship was at anchor, was to find out who lived in that cottage, and whether they were likely to cause any difficulties or danger. Eskeland and the skipper changed out of their naval uniforms into fishermen's clothes and rowed ashore. Perhaps they wanted to be the first to land in Norway. It was always a moment of unexpressed emotion.

They soon came back, saying there was nothing to worry about. There was a middle-aged woman with her two children, a boy of about sixteen and a girl who was younger. Her husband was away at the cod fishing in the Lofoten islands, and she did not expect him back for several weeks. Eskeland had told her that they had stopped to make some engine repairs. There was no reason why she should be suspicious, and there was no telephone in the house. It would be quite easy to keep an eye on her and the children. She had told him, incidentally, that no Germans had ever been in Toftefjord. In fact, she herself had never seen a German. Her husband had had to hand in his radio set to the authorities, and her nearest neighbours were two miles away. She was quite out of touch with the world and with the war.

The landing party and the crew had dinner in relays, leaving a watch on deck. They were very cheerful. For one thing, it was the first good dinner they had had on board, not only because it is difficult to do much cooking in a fishing-boat at sea, but also because the cook had been seasick and Jan Baalsrud, who had deputised for him, had had rather limited ideas. The landing party were happy also because the voyage was successfully ended, and they could really get to work. For soldiers, a sea voyage is always tedious; they are usually pleased to get out of the hands of sailors.

While they ate, they discussed the coming night. When the four men of the sabotage group had started to prepare themselves for the expedition, they had divided among them the enormous territory they were to cover, and each of them had studied his own part of it in detail. But by changing the landing place from Senja, they had put themselves farther north than any of the districts they knew best. However, Eskeland remembered a little about Ribbenesöy from his days as a postal inspector, and he had taken the precaution of learning the names of a few reliable people in the neighbourhood. One of these was a merchant who kept a small general store on the south side of the island. Eskeland had never met him, but his name was on a list in London of men who could be trusted. His shop was only a few miles away, and they decided to make a start that night by going to see him and asking him about hiding their cargo. Experience in the southern part of Norway had shown that shopkeepers were often more adept than any-one else at providing a temporary hiding-place for stores. Most shops had outhouses and back premises which in war-time were nearly empty. Cases of weapons had often been stacked among cases of groceries. A shopkeeper was also a likely man to tell them where they could get a local boat to take them into Tromsö, where they would find their principal "contacts."

So Eskeland set off, as soon as it was dark, in *Brattholm's* motor dinghy. He took the ship's engineer with him to look after the motor, and another man who had been added to the crew as an extra hand because he knew the district. They steered out of the bay and followed the shore of Ribbenesöy to the eastward, through the sound which separates it from the next island of Hersöy, and then back, close inshore along the south side of the island. They saw the shop and a few buildings near it, and a wooden jetty, silhouetted against the afterglow in the western sky. There was a light in the shop, and another on board a boat which was lying, with its engine running, a few yards off the end of the jetty.

As they approached the jetty, they passed close to the boat. It was a small fishing craft with two or three men on board. It would have seemed strange to pass it without a word, and besides, a small local fishing craft was one of the things they wanted. So they hailed it and told the men the story they had prepared: that they had engine trouble and wanted a lift to Tromsö to get some spare parts.

The men were sympathetic, and only mildly inquisitive, as fishermen would naturally be. They talked all round the subject, in the infinitely leisurely manner of people who live on islands. They asked what make of engine it was, and what horse-power, and what spare parts were needed. They recommended a dealer in Tromsö, and suggested ringing him up in the morning and getting him to send the parts out in the mailboat, which would probably be as quick as going to fetch them, and certainly cheaper. They asked what the herring fishing was like, and where the *Brattholm* was bound for.

Everyone who lives under false pretences gets used to receiving perfectly useless advice with patience and cunning. Eskeland and the engineer, in this unrealistic conversation across the dark water, answered the questions carefully one by one, until a chance came for them to put the one question in which they were interested.

"I suppose you couldn't take us into Tromsö?"

This started a long explanation of how they were waiting there for a man to bring them some bait which they had paid for already, so that they could not afford to miss him, and they said all over again that they could not see any sense in going all the way to Tromsö for spares when there was a telephone up in the shop. But they told Eskeland that if he was really set on wasting money by going there, the shopkeeper had a boat and might take him in.

Eskeland thanked them and left them, understanding perhaps that to a man who lives in the outer islands Tromsö is a very distant city, and a journey there is not a thing to be undertaken lightly. At least, he had learned that the shop at the head of the jetty was really the one he wanted.

The shopkeeper was in bed when they got to the house; but when they knocked he came downstairs in his underclothes and took them into the kitchen. They apologised for coming so late, and told the same story again. But with him, they only told it as a means of introduction, to make conversation till he felt at ease with them and they could tell him the true reason for their visit. While they were talking, they slipped in questions about the Germans. No, he said when they asked him, the Germans had really been no trouble out there on the islands. They had never been ashore. He saw their convoys passing in the channel south of Ribbenesöy, and they had been out laying minefields. And of course they sent out notices which had to be stuck up everywhere: "Contact with the enemy is punished by death." There was one downstairs in the shop. He had heard stories about how they behaved in Tromsö, but as for himself, he had never had anything to do with them.

Carefully feeling his way, Eskeland began to broach the subject of his cargo, and his need to go to Tromsö. The shopkeeper was willing to take one or two men to town in his boat. Eskeland offered to pay him a substantial sum of money for his help. It was the size of this sum which first impressed on the shopkeeper that he was being asked to do more than hire out a boat. He looked puzzled; and then, because it would be unjust to involve a man in what they were doing without giving him an idea of the risks he was running, and because the man had such an excellent reputation, Eskeland told him that they had come from England.

At this, his expression changed. At first he was incredulous. One of them gave him a cigarette, and he took it and lit it; and the English tobacco seemed to convince him that what they said was true. Then, to their surprise, they saw that he was frightened.

He began to make excuses. He couldn't leave the shop. It wasn't fair to leave his wife alone in the house these days. There were the animals to attend to. Fuel for the boat was difficult to come by.

Slowly and reluctantly, they had to admit to themselves that it was useless to try to persuade him. An unwilling nervous helper would be a danger and a liability. Yet they could not understand how a man who had been so highly recommended could be so cowardly in practice. The vast majority of Norwegians, as everybody knew, would have been delighted by a chance to do something against the Germans. They puzzled over his behaviour, and told him they were disappointed in him.

"But why did you come to me?" he asked plaintively. "What made you think I'd do a thing like that?"

They told him they had heard he was a patriot; and then the truth came out, too late, and they saw the mistake which they had made. The man told them he had only been running the shop for a few months. Its previous owner had died. His name was the same, so there had been no need to change the name of the business.

There was nothing left to do then except to impress on him as clearly as they could that he must never tell anyone what they had told him. He promised this willingly, glad to see that they had accepted his refusal. In his relief, he even recommended two other men who he thought would give them the help they needed. Their names were Jenberg Kristiansen and Sedolf Andreasson. They were both fishermen, and they lived on the north shore of the island, beyond Toftefjord. He felt sure they would be willing.

Landfall off Senja: "the coast glittered with a blinding brilliance"

No photograph was ever taken of *Brattholm*. *Andholmen*, shown here at anchor in the harbour of Scalloway, was almost a sister ship

Toftefjord. *Brattholm* lay a little farther in than this fishing boat. The crew landed on the beach on the right, and the agents at the far end of the fjord

The snow gully up which Jan escaped at the head of Toftefjord: on the right, the beach where Jan landed and the mound which gave him cover

Eskeland and his two companions left him then, with a final warning that he must never mention what he had heard that night.

They went back to their dinghy, annoyed and slightly uneasy. There was no reason to think that the shopkeeper was hostile, or that he would do anything active to harm them. Not one man in a thousand would go out of his way to help the Germans. But many Norwegians of the simpler sort were prone to gossip, and any man whose own safety was not at stake was potentially the nucleus of a rumour. It was a pity, but the risk, so far as they could see, was small, and without entirely recasting their own plans there was nothing much they could do about it. It was sheer bad luck that the one man they had selected from the lists in London should have died, and even worse luck that another man with the same name should have taken his house and business. But it could not be helped. At least, he had given them new contacts.

They set off back towards Toftefjord, to tell the rest of the party what had happened. On the way, they were overtaken by the fishing-boat which had been lying off the jetty of the shop. Its crew had got their bait and were on their way to the fishing-grounds. They took the dinghy in tow; but just before they came to the mouth of Toftefjord the skipper shouted that they had forgotten a rope, some part of their fishing gear, and that they had to go back to the shop to fetch it. He cast the dinghy off. Eskeland went on into Toftefjord, and saw the fishing-boat turn round and steam away.

What happened when the skipper and crew of the fishing-boat got back to the shop will never exactly be known. The shopkeeper had gone back to bed, but they called him out again, and this time his wife joined them to hear what was going on. He said he was feeling sick and giddy. He thought it was due to the cigarettes the strangers had given him. His brother was one of the crew, and he and the skipper plied him with questions about the strange boat and the three unknown men. Before very long, the shopkeeper had told them everything.

It was probably during this conversation that a new and appalling fear struck him. Was it possible that the three men were German agents sent to test him? He had heard people say that the Germans sent men about in the islands, dressed in civilian clothes, to do that very thing: to say that they came from England, and then to report anyone who offered to help them. What was more likely than that they should pick on him, a merchant, a man with a certain standing in the community, and one who had only recently set up in business? He was thankful, now he came to think of it, that he had refused to help them. And yet, had he been careful enough? He racked his brains to remember exactly what he had said about Germans. He felt sure he had been indiscreet. There had been something about minefields. That was probably secret. Of course, he said to the others, the only way to make sure of his position, the only safe thing to do, was to report what the men had told him. Supposing they were German agents, it would not be enough only to have refused to help them. They would be waiting now to see if he reported them. If he didn't, they would get him anyhow.

The three men discussed this dilemma for an hour. The shopkeeper's wife listened in distress at his agitation. His brother was in favour of doing nothing. It would be a bad business, he admitted, if the men were Germans; but on the other hand, if he reported them and it turned out that they had really come from England, it would be far worse. The trouble was, it was impossible to be sure; but on the whole, he thought it was right to take the chance.

With this decision, after a long confusing argument, the skipper and the shopkeeper's brother left for the fishing again. The shopkeeper himself went back to bed, still feeling sick and dizzy. He could not sleep. He knew what it meant to be disloyal to the Germans, or rather, to be caught at it: the concentration camp for himself and perhaps for his wife as well; the end of the little business he had begun to build up; the end of everything. He lay there imagining it all. But to make sure of his safety was so easy. There was the telephone downstairs in the shop. And yet, if they were really Norwegians, and had really come from England, and the neighbours got to know he had told the Germans, he knew very well what they would say, and he knew what his customers would do. Those men had sounded like Norwegians: not local men, but they spoke Norwegian perfectly. But of course there might be Norwegian Nazis, for all he knew, who would do a job like that for the Germans. And was it possible to come in a fishing-boat in March all the way from England? That sounded an unlikely story. Perhaps the best thing would be to get up and go over to Toftefjord and speak to them again and see if they could prove it. But then the Germans were too clever to do anything by halves; they would have their proofs all ready. How could he tell? How could he possibly find out?

The shopkeeper lay all night, sick with fear and confusion. Towards the morning, the last of his courage ebbed away. About seven, he crept down to the shop, and picked up the telephone. He had thought of a compromise. He asked for a man he knew who had an official post in the Department of Justice.

In Toftefjord, when Eskeland had told the others about the two merchants with the same name, they agreed that there was nothing to be done. The man had promised not to talk, and short of murder they could not think of any way of making more sure of him than that. So Eskeland set off again, not very much discouraged, to see the two fishermen the shopkeeper had recommended.

This time he got the answer he expected. There was no point in telling these men the story about spare parts. By then, it was about three o'clock in the morning, and even in the Arctic, where nobody takes much notice of the time of day, people would not expect to be woken up at such an hour with any ordinary request. He did not ask them to go to Tromsö either. Most of the first night was already gone, and the most urgent need was to get the cargo ashore so that *Brattholm* could sail again for Shetland.

The two fishermen agreed at once, enthusiastically, to hide it in some caves which they knew. Eskeland did not tell them the whole story. He did not mention England, but left them with the impression that he had brought the cargo from the south of Norway, and that it contained food and equipment for the home forces to use when the tide began to turn. But the two men did not want to be told any more about it. If it was anti-German, that seemed to be good enough for them. They said they would come to Toftefjord at half-past four on the following afternoon to pilot *Brattholm* out to their hiding place, so that everything would be ready for unloading as soon as it was dark.

It was daylight by the time the dinghy got back to Toftefjord. Eskeland and the men who were with him were tired, not merely by being out all night, but by the long hours of careful conversation. When they came aboard, they found that

Jan Baalsrud, the only one of the landing party who had not been either to the shop or the fishermen, had been at work all night checking over their small arms again. As an instrument maker, Jan loved the mechanism of guns and always took particular care of them; and like Eskeland, he had been a little worried about the shopkeeper.

They made breakfast, and talked about the shop again. It was only two hours' steaming from Tromsö, somebody pointed out, for any kind of warship; so if they had really had the bad luck to hit upon a Nazi and he had reported them, they would surely have been attacked by then. Dawn would have been the obvious time for the Germans to choose. But dawn was past, and Toftefjord was as quiet and peaceful as before. They agreed in the end that the landing party should stay on watch till ten o'clock. If nothing had happened by then, it really would look as if that particular danger was over; and then the landing party would turn in and leave some of the crew on watch till the fishermen came at half-past four.

The morning passed. The only thing which was at all unusual was the number of aircraft they could hear. There was the sound of machine-gun fire too, from time to time. It was all out at sea. But none of the aircraft flew over Toftefjord. It sounded as though there was a practice target somewhere beyond the islands, and that seemed a possible explanation. The air forces at Bardufoss must have somewhere for training, and the sea or the outer skerries would be a likely place. As the day went by, the men began to relax. By noon, they were reassured. Eskeland and his party went below to sleep, leaving half of the crew on deck.

A shout awoke them: "Germans! Germans!" They rushed for the hatch. The men on watch stood there appalled. Two hundred yards away, coming slowly into the fjord, there was a German warship. As the last of the men reached the deck, it opened fire. At once they knew that the aircraft were on patrol stopping the exits from the sounds. There was no escape for *Brattholm*. Eskeland shouted "Abandon ship! Abandon ship!"

That was the only order. They knew what to do. Somebody ran up the naval flag to the mizen head. The crew leaped down into one of the boats and cast off and rowed for shore. The German ship stopped and lowered two boats. Troops piled into them and made for the shore a little farther north. Jan Baalsrud and Salvesen poured petrol on the cipher books and set them all on fire, and cast off the second dinghy and held it ready in the lee of the ship out of sight of the Germans. Eskeland and Blindheim tore off the hatch covers and climbed down among the cargo and lit the five-minute fuse.

With her boats away the German ship began to approach again. It was firing with machine-guns and a three-pounder, but the shots were going overhead. The Germans meant to capture them alive: they were not expecting much resistance. Eskeland called from the hold: "Jan, hold them off!" Jan took a sub-machine gun and emptied the magazine at the German's bridge. The ship stopped for a moment, and then came on again. Eskeland jumped up from the hold, calling to the others "It's burning," and all of them climbed down into the dinghy, and waited. They knew the drill: to wait till the last possible minute hidden in *Brattholm*'s lee before they started to try to row away.

Eskeland sat looking at his wrist-watch, with his arm held steadily in front of him. One of the others held on to the side of *Brattholm*'s hull. Two were ready at oars. One minute had gone already. They could not see the German ship from there. They could hear it approaching the other side of *Brattholm*, firing in bursts at *Brattholm* and at the crew in the other dinghy. Per Blindheim said: "Well, we've had a good time for twenty-six years, Jan." Eskeland said: "Two minutes," Jan could see the crew. They had got to the shore. Two were still in the dinghy with their hands up. Three were on the beach. One was lying in the edge of the water. One was trying to climb the rocks, and machine-gun bullets were chipping the stones above him and ricocheting across the fjord. Eskeland said: "Three minutes." The German landing party came into sight, running along the shore towards the place where the crew had landed, jumping from rock to rock. When they got near, the firing stopped, and for a few seconds there was no sound but the shouts of German orders. "Three and a half," Eskeland said. "Cast off."

They began to row, keeping *Brattholm* between them and the Germans. In that direction, towards the head of the fjord, it was two hundred yards to shore. But the German ship was very close, and it was much bigger than *Brattholm*. Before they had gone fifty yards they were sighted, and at this point-blank range the Germans opened fire. The dinghy was shot full of holes and began to sink. But the German ship was slowly drawing alongside *Brattholm,* and the last quarter of a minute of the fuse was burning down, and the fascination of watching the trap being sprung blinded them to the miracle that so far they had not been wounded.

The ship and *Brattholm* touched, and at that very moment the explosion came. But it was nothing, only a fraction of what it should have been. Only the primer exploded. The hatch covers were blown off and the front of the wheelhouse was wrecked, but the German ship was undamaged. There were shouts and confusion on deck and for a few seconds the firing stopped. The ship went full speed astern. *Brattholm* was burning fiercely. In that momentary respite, the men in the dinghy rowed for their lives, but the ship swung round till its three-pounder came to bear. Its first shot missed the dinghy. And then the whole cargo exploded. *Brattholm* vanished, in the crack of the shock wave, the long roar in the hills, the mushroom of smoke streaked with debris and blazing petrol. Eskeland was blown overboard. Jan leaned out and got him under the arms and hauled him on to the gunwale, and the German gunner recovered and a shot from the three-pounder smashed the dinghy to pieces. They were all in the water, swimming. There were seventy yards to go. The Germans brought all their guns to bear on the heads in the water. The men swam on, through water foaming with bullets, thrusting the ice aside with their heads and hands.

All of them reached the shore. Jan Baalsrud stumbled through the shallows with his friend Per Blindheim beside him. As they reached the water's edge Per was hit in the head and fell forward half out of the water. With a last effort, Jan climbed a rocky bank and found cover behind a stone. As he climbed he had been aware that his leader Eskeland had fallen on the beach and that Salvesen, either wounded or exhausted, had sunk down there unable to make the climb. He shouted to them all to follow him, but there was no answer. A bullet hit the stone above his head and whined across the fjord. He was under fire from both sides. He looked behind him, and saw the Germans who had landed. Four of them had worked round the shore and crossed the hillside fifty yards above him to cut off his retreat. He was surrounded.

At the head of the fjord there is a little mound, covered with small birch trees. Behind it the hills rise steeply for about two hundred feet. A shallow gully divides them. Within the gully the snow lies deeply, a smooth steep slope only broken by two large boulders. The patrol came floundering down the hill, pausing to kneel in the snow and snipe at Jan with rifles. Caught between them and the fire from the ship he could find no cover. But to reach him the patrol had to cross the little dip behind the mound, and there for a moment they were out of sight. He got up and ran towards them. He could not tell whether they would come over the mound, through the birches, or skirt round it to the left. He crept round it to the right. He had been wearing rubber sea-boots, but had lost one of them when he was swimming, and one of his feet was bare. He heard the soldiers crashing through the brittle bushes. Soon, as he and the patrol each circled round the mound, he came upon their tracks and crossed them. It could only be seconds before they came to his. But now the foot of the gully was near, and he broke cover and ran towards it.

They saw him at once, and they were even closer than before. An officer called on him to halt. He struggled up the first part of the gully, through the soft sliding snow. The officer fired at him with a revolver and missed, and he got to cover behind the first boulder in the gully and drew his automatic.

Looking back down the snow slope, he watched the officer climbing up towards him with three soldiers following close behind. The officer was in Gestapo uniform. They came on with confidence, and Jan remembered that so far he had not fired a shot, so that they possibly did not know that he was armed. He waited, not to waste his fire. Beyond the four figures close below him, he was aware of uproar and confusion, shouting and stray shots in the fjord. As he climbed, the officer called to Jan to surrender. He was out of breath. Jan fixed on a spot in the snow six yards below him. When they reached there, he would shoot.

The officer reached it first. Jan squeezed the trigger. The

pistol clicked. It was full of ice. Twice more he tried, but it would not work, and the men were within three paces. He ejected two cartridges, and it fired. He shot the Gestapo officer twice and he fell dead in the snow and his body rolled down the slope over and over towards the feet of his men. Jan fired again and the next man went down, wounded. The last two turned and ran, sliding down the snow to find cover. Jan jumped to his feet and began the long climb up the gully.

For a little while, it was strangely quiet. He was hidden from the fjord by one side of the gully. The snow was soft and deep and difficult, and he often slipped with his rubber boot. With all his strength, he could only climb slowly.

Above the second boulder, for the last hundred feet, the gully opened out into a wide snow slope, perfectly clean and white and smooth, and as soon as he set foot on it he came into sight of the German ship behind him.

In his dark naval uniform against the gleaming snow up there he was exposed as a perfect target for every gun on the warship and the rifles of the soldiers on the beaches. He struggled in desperation with the powdery snow, climbing a yard and slipping back, clawing frantically with his hands at the yielding surface which offered no hold. The virgin slope was torn to chaos by the storm of bullets from behind him. Three-pounder shells exploding in it blew clouds of snow powder in the air. He could feel with sickening expectation the thud and the searing pain in his back which would be the end of it all. The impulse to hide, to seek any refuge from this horror, was overwhelming. But there was nowhere to hide, no help, no escape from the dreadful thing that was happening to him. He could only go on and on and on, choking as his lungs filled with ice crystals, sobbing with weariness and rage and self-pity, kicking steps which crumbled away beneath him, climbing and falling, exhausting the last of his strength against the soft deep cushion of the snow.

He got to the top. There were rocks again, hard wind-swept snow, the crest of the hill, and shelter just beyond it. He dropped in his tracks, and for the first time he dared to look behind him. The firing died. There below him he could see the whole panorama of the fjord. Smoke hung above it in the sky. The German ship was at the spot where *Brattholm* had been anchored. On the far shore, a knot of soldiers were gathered round the crew. Nearer, where he had landed, his companions were lying on the beach, not moving, and he thought they were all dead. All round the fjord there were parties of Germans, some staring towards him at the spot where he had reached the ridge and disappeared, and others be-ginning to move in his direction. In his own tracks before his eyes the snow was red, and that brought him to full awareness of a pain in his foot, and he looked at it. His only injury was almost ludicrous. It was his right foot, the bare one, and half his big toe had been shot away. It was not bleeding much, be-cause the foot was frozen. He got up and turned his back on Toftefjord and began to try to run. It was not much more then ten minutes since he had been sleeping in the cabin with his friends, and now he was alone.

CHAPTER THREE

HUNTED

IF JAN had stopped to think, everything would have seemed hopeless. He was alone, in uniform, on a small bare island, hunted by about fifty Germans. He left a deep track, as he waded through the snow, which anyone could follow. He was wet through and had one bare foot, which was wounded, and it was freezing hard. The island was separated from the mainland by two sounds, each several miles wide, which were patrolled by the enemy, and all his money and papers had been blown up in the boat.

But when a man's mind is numbed by sudden disaster, he acts less by reason than by reflex. In military affairs, it is at moments like those that training is most important. The crew's training had been nautical, the sea was their element, and when their ship disappeared before their eyes and they were cast ashore without time to recover themselves and begin to think, their reaction was to lose hope and to surrender. But Jan had been trained to regard that barren hostile country as a place where he could live and work for years. He had expected to go ashore and to live off the land, and so, when the crisis came, he turned without any conscious reason to the land as a refuge, and began to fight his way out. If his companions had not been wounded or overcome by the icy water, no doubt they would have done the same thing, although none of them knew then, as they learned later, that any risks and any sufferings were better than surrender.

For the moment, his thoughts did not extend beyond the next few minutes. He thought no more than a hunted fox with a baying pack behind it, and he acted with the instinctive cunning of a fox. It served him better, in that primitive situation, than the complicated processes of reason. On the southern slopes of the island there was less snow. Here and there, where the rocks were steep, he found bare patches, and he hobbled towards them and crossed them, leaving no track, laying false trails, doubling back on the way he had come, jumping from stone to stone to leave the snow untrodden in between. But there was no cover. Wherever he went, he could be seen from one part of the island or another; and as the shock of the battle faded and his heart and lungs began to recover from the effort of his climb, he began to believe that although he had escaped, it could only be minutes before the Germans ran him down.

Running blindly here and there among the hills, hampered by his wounded foot, he had no idea how far he had come from Toftefjord, and before he expected it he found himself facing the sea again. Below him on the shore there were some houses and a jetty, and from Eskeland's description he recognised the shop. He had crossed the island already. He remembered that the shopkeeper had a boat, and he thought of trying to steal it. But the water in front of him was wide and clear, and the Germans would be over the hill behind him at any moment. He knew he could not get out of sight in a boat before they came.

He went on, down to the shore a little way from the jetty. There at least was a narrow strip of beach which was free of snow, and he could walk along it, slowly and painfully, without leaving any tracks at all. He turned to the left, away from the shop, back towards Toftefjord. He felt intolerably lonely.

There were two little haysheds by the shore. He wanted to creep into one and hide there and burrow in the hay and get warm and go to sleep. They were obvious hiding places. But even as he began to think of it, he knew they were too obvious. They were isolated. He pictured himself hidden there in the dark, hearing the Germans coming along the beach, and their expectant shouts when they saw the sheds, and himself trapped in there while they surrounded him. The very uselessness of the haysheds impressed upon him that there really was no hiding place for him in that dreadful island. If he stayed on the island, wherever he hid he would be found.

As he scrambled along the beach he was coming nearer, though he did not know it, to the sound which Eskeland and the others had passed through on their way to the shop. It is called Vargesund, and it is full of rocks, in contrast to the wide open waters to the north and south. The largest of the rocks is about half an acre in extent. As soon as Jan saw this little island, he knew what he had to do, and for the first time he saw a gleam of hope. He hurried to the edge of the water, and waded in, and began to swim again.

It was only fifty yards to the rock, and in spite of his clothes and his pistol and his one sea-boot, he had no difficulty in swimming across. But when he dragged himself out of the mixture of ice and water, and climbed over to the far side of the rock, the effect of this second swim began to tell on him. He had to begin to reckon with the prospect of freezing to death.

There was a minute patch of peat on top of the islet, and someone had been cutting it. He got down below the peat-bank and started to do exercises, keeping an eye on the hills of

34

the main island. His bare foot was quite numb, although running had made an unpleasant mess of the raw end of his toe. He took off his sea-boot and moved his one sock from his left foot to his right. It seemed a good idea to have a boot on one foot and a sock on the other. He stamped his feet, crouching down below the bank, to start the circulation and try to ward off frostbite.

It was only a very short time before the Germans came in sight, and for the next two hours he watched them, at first with apprehension, and then with a growing sense of his own advantage. They came slowly, in straggling line abreast, pausing to challenge every stone, with a medley of shouts and orders and counter-orders; and Jan, watching them critically in the light of his own field training, remembered one of the many things he had been told and had only half believed: that the garrisons of that remote part of Norway were low-grade troops whose morale was softened by isolation and long inactivity. Gradually, as he watched their fumbling search, he began to despise them, and to recognize beneath that formidable uniform the signs of fallibility and even fear. They were probably clerks and cooks and batmen, dragged out unwillingly at a moment's notice from comfortable headquarters billets in the town. He could guess very well what they would think of having to hunt a desperate armed bandit among ice and rocks and snow.

It was dusk when the first party of them came along the beach, but he could see them clearly because they were using torches which they flashed into dark crevices. They passed his island without a glance behind them out to sea. So far, it seemed not to have crossed their minds that he might have swum away.

When it was dark, the confusion increased. They were

scattered in small groups all over the hills. Each group was signalling to others with its torches. Men were shouting their own names, afraid that their friends would mistake them for the bandit. Now and then a single shot echoed from hill to hill. That could only mean that nervous men were firing at fancied movements in the dark. Slowly it dawned on Jan, with a feeling of intense elation which gave him new strength and courage, that for all their numbers, they were afraid of him.

That opportunity to study the German army at its worst was worth months of military training, because after it he never again had the slightest doubt that he could outwit them till the end.

At the same time, he was becoming more aware of the dangers of his natural surroundings. A human enemy, however relentless and malevolent he may be, has human weaknesses; but nobody can trifle with the Arctic. In immediate terms, Jan knew that if he stayed where he was in his wet clothes, he would be dead before the morning.

Of course, there was only one alternative: to swim again. He could swim back to Ribbenesöy, among the Germans, or he might conceivably swim across the sound, to Hersöy, the next island to the eastward. One way or the other, he had to find a house where he could go in and get dry and warm. He had only seen two houses on Ribbenesöy, the shopkeeper's and the one in Toftefjord, and both of them were out of the question. He knew from the chart that there were others farther west, but by that time they were probably full of Germans. Across the sound, on Hersöy, he had seen a single lonely house, but he had no idea who lived there.

He looked at Vargesund, and wondered if it was possible. In fact, it is 220 yards across, but it was difficult for him to guess its width in the darkness. The far shore was only a shadow between the shining water and the shining hills. The surface of the sound was broken here and there by eddies: the tide had begun to set. In health and strength he could easily swim the distance; but he could not judge the effects of the tide and the cold and his own exhaustion. He stood for a long time before he made up his mind. He did not want to die either way, but to drown seemed better than to freeze. He took a last look behind him at the flashing torches of the soldiers, and stumbled down the rocks and waded in and launched himself into the sea again.

It is a mercy that the ultimate extremes of physical distress often get blurred in memory. Jan hardly remembered anything of that third and longest swim, excepting an agony of cramp, and excepting the dreadful belief that he was just about to die; an experience most people encounter once or twice in a lifetime, but one he had had to face so many times on that single day. It was after he had given up any conscious struggle, and admitted his defeat, and was ready to welcome his release from pain, that some chance eddy swept him ashore on the farther side and rolled his limp body among the stones, and left him lying there on his face, groaning and twisted with cramp, and not able to move or to think of moving.

Seconds or minutes later, in the mists of half-consciousness, there were voices. There were footsteps on the beach, and the clink of stones turning. He wondered with a mild curiosity whether the words he could hear were German or Norwegian, and from somewhere outside himself he looked down with pity on the man who lay beaten on the shore and the people who approached him; because if they were German, the man was too weak to get away. But slowly his dim enfeebled brain began to accept a fact which was unforeseen and strange on that day of death and violence. They were children's voices. There were children, coming along the beach and chattering in Norwegian. And suddenly they stopped, and he knew they had seen him.

He lifted his head, and there they were, two little girls, holding hands, wide-eyed with horror, too frightened to run away. He smiled and said: "Hullo. You needn't be afraid." He managed to turn round and sit up. "I've had an accident," he said. "I do wish you could help me." They did not answer, but he saw them relax a little, and he realised that when they had seen him, they had thought that he was dead.

Jan loved children; he had looked after his own young brother and sister after his mother died. Perhaps nothing in the world could have given him strength of mind just then, except compassion: the urgent need to soothe the children's fear and make up for the shock which he had given them. He talked to them calmly. His own self-pity and despair had gone. He showed them how wet he was, and made a joke of it, and they came nearer as their fright gave way to interest and wonder. He asked them their names. They were Dina and Olaug. After a while he asked if their home was near, and whether they would take him there, and at the idea of bringing him home and showing their parents what they had discovered they brightened up and helped him to his feet. The house was not far away.

Two women were there, and the rest of their children. They exclaimed in horrified amazement at the frozen, limping, wild dishevelled man whom the little girls led in. But the moment he spoke to them in Norwegian their horror changed to motherly concern and they hurried him into the kitchen, and took him to the fire and brought him towels and put the kettle on.

Of all the series of acts of shining charity which attended Jan in the months which were to come, the help which these two women gave him on the first night of his journey was most noble, because they knew what had happened just across the sound, and they knew that at any moment, certainly by the morning, the Germans would be pounding on their door. They knew that their own lives and the lives of all their children would hang on a chance word when they came to face their questioning. Yet they opened their door at once to the stranger in such desperate distress, and cared for him and saved his life and sent him on his way, with no thought or hope of any reward except the knowledge that, whatever price they paid, they had done their Christian duty. Their names are Fru Pedersen and Fru Idrupsen.

The first thing Jan did was to warn them all that the Germans were after him, and that when they were questioned they must say that he came in carrying a pistol and demanded their help by force. He brought out his pistol to emphasise what he said. As soon as he had made quite sure that they understood this, and that even the children had a clear idea of what they should do and say, he sent two of them out as sentries, and told them to warn him at once if they saw a boat coming into the sound.

Fru Idrupsen, it turned out, was the woman from Toftefjord. She had run to the hills with her children when the shooting started, and she had seen most of what happened from the top of the island. She had rowed across the sound to take refuge with her neighbours. Fru Pedersen had a grown-up son and daughter and two young children. Her son was out fishing, but she expected him back at any minute. Her husband, like Fru Idrupsen's, was away for the Lofoten fishing season and would not be home till it ended.

All the time Jan was talking, the two women were busy with the practical help which he needed so badly. They gave him food and a hot drink, and helped him to take off his sodden clothes. They found him new dry underclothes and socks and a sea-boot Herr Pedersen had left behind, and they hung up his uniform to dry, and rubbed his feet and legs till the feeling began to come back to them, and bandaged the stump of his wounded toe.

Twice while they worked to revive him, the sentries came running in to say that a boat was coming. Each time Jan pulled on his steaming jacket and trousers and the sea-boots, one his own and one Herr Pedersen's, and gathered together everything which belonged to him and ran out of the house and up into the hills. But each time the boat passed by.

Between these alarms, he rested and relaxed. That humble Norwegian kitchen, with the children gathered round him speaking his native tongue, was more homely than any place he had seen in the three years he had been abroad. The warmth, and the sense of homecoming, and the contrast of family life after the fearful tension of the day, made him drowsy. It was difficult to remember that outside in the darkness there still were ruthless men who would shoot him on sight, and wreck that home if they found him there, and carry the children off to captivity and the mothers to unmentionable torment. Such violence had the quality of a dream. And when he dragged his mind back to grapple with reality, Jan found himself faced with a doubt which often came back to him later: ought he to let such people help him? Was his own life worth it? Was he right as a soldier, to let women and children put their lives in such terrible danger? To save them from the consequence of their own goodness, ought he not go out, and fight his own battle alone? But for the moment, these questions went unanswered, because he was not fit to make any such decision. Fru Pedersen and Fru Idrupsen had taken him in hand, and they treated him as an extra child.

When he had been there half an hour or so, the eldest son of the Pedersen family came home. He had heard the explosion in Toftefjord, but did not know what had happened. They told him the story, and as soon as he had heard it he took it as a matter of course that a wounded survivor should be sitting in his mother's kitchen while the Germans scoured the islands round about. As his father was not at home, it was up to him to get Jan away to safety. He began to debate the question of how to do it.

The first thing was to rest. For one thing, there was no knowing when Jan might get another chance, and for another it would be madness to go out in a boat while the Germans were still there. And after that, the boy said, when he had rested, he ought to get away from the islands altogether, to the mainland. Any island, however big it was, might be a trap, not only because you might find your retreat cut off, but also because everyone on an island knew everyone else's business. If he stayed another day in Hersöy, everyone would know he was there. But on the mainland, if they did come after you, you could always go on a stage farther; and gossip did not spread there quite so fast. Altogether, he would be safer there. Besides, that was the way to Sweden.

This was the first time Jan had paused to think of an ultimate escape. Up till then, it had only been a matter of dodging for the next few hours, and he had still thought of north Norway as his destination. That was where he had set out for, and he had arrived; and although he had lost his companions and all his equipment, he had not admitted to himself that the whole expedition was a failure. He still hoped to do part of his job there, at least, as soon as he had got his strength back and shaken off the Germans. But the people who lived there, as he now began to see, all thought at once of Sweden for a man in such serious trouble. It was a difficult journey, but not a very long one; about eighty miles, in a straight line; if you could travel in straight lines.

The trouble was, the boy went on, he only had a rowing-boat himself, and they could never row to the mainland. Just south of them was the sound called Skagösund, which was two miles wide. On the other side of that was Ringvassöy, an island about twenty miles square, and south of that again you had to cross Grötsund itself, which was the main channel into Tromsö from the north and was four miles wide and full of patrol boats. The best he could do himself was to row Jan across to Ringvassöy before the morning. But he knew a man there called Jensen who was all right, and he had a motor-boat and was meaning to go into Tromsö some day soon. His wife was the midwife over there, and he had a permit and was always moving about with his boat. He could easily put Jan ashore on the mainland.

Jan listened gratefully as this plan unfolded. He was glad for the moment to have everything thought out for him, and was ready to fall in with any idea which would take him away from Toftefjord.

When it was all decided, and he was resting, the eldest son of the Toftefjord family went out in his boat to see what had happened at his home, and to find out for Jan if there was any sign of the rest of his party. He was away for a couple of hours. When he came back, Jan knew for certain that of all the twelve men, he was the only one who was not either killed or captured. Toftefjord itself was quiet. There were still parties of Germans searching the distant hills. The slopes of the fjord were littered with scraps of planking. The boy had found the remains of a petrol barrel, and seen an ammunition belt hanging in a tree. But there was no one, alive or dead, on the beaches. The German ship had left. It was steaming slowly up the north side of the island, using a searchlight. Jan's friends, or their bodies, must have been taken aboard it. Eskeland and Per Blindheim and all the others were gone, and he could never expect to see them again. There was nothing he could do except to go on alone.

He left the house on Hersöy very early in the morning, well before it was light. Fru Pedersen and Fru Idrupsen watched him go and brushed aside his thanks, which could certainly not have been adequate for what they had done. The boy took him down to his boat and they got aboard and pushed her off into the sound. Jan felt fit again and ready for anything. They turned to the southward and began to row, past the place where he had landed from his swim, past the shop, and then out across the open water, heading for Ringvassöy, with Toftefjord astern. Everything was peaceful.

CHAPTER FOUR

SEA-BOOTS IN THE SNOW

IN MOMENTS of calm, Jan often thought about his family, as all soldiers of all armies think in war. So far as he knew, they were still in Oslo: his father, and his young brother Nils, and his sister. His sister's name was Julie, but none of them ever called her that because they thought it was old-fashioned; they had always gone on calling her Bitten, which was the nickname he had invented for her when he was eight and she was a baby. When his mother died, he had been sixteen, Nils ten, and Bitten only eight; and so he had suddenly had to be very much more grown up than he really was; he had had to take care of the children when his father was at work, and even shop and cook and wash for them for a time till his aunt could come to the rescue.

They had always been a closely united family, both before and after that disaster, until the morning just after the invasion when his orders had come and he had left home on an hour's notice. But somehow a special affection had grown up through the years between himself and Bitten. Young Nils was a boy and an independent spirit who had always been able to stand on his own feet; but Bitten had turned to him more and more for advice, and he had become very fond of her, and proud of her, and deeply interested in her growing-up.

Perhaps this big-brotherly affection had been the deepest emotion in Jan's life, when fortune landed him in Toftefjord

44

when he was twenty-six. At any rate, leaving Bitten had hurt more than anything when the time came. He had tried to make the break as quick and painless as it could be when he knew he had to do it. He had waited around that morning till he knew she would be coming home from school, and he had met her in the street on his way to the station just to tell her he was going. She was fifteen then, and he had never seen her since. For the first few months, while he was in Norway and Sweden, he had been able to write to her sometimes, using a false name so that if the letters got into the wrong hands she would not get into trouble for having a brother who was still opposing the Germans after the capitulation. In his letters he had begged her to stay on at high school, not to be in a hurry to get a job; but he had never known if she had taken that advice. While he was in prison in Sweden he had a few letters from her, sending him press cuttings about netball games she had played in. It had made him smile to think that she wanted him to be interested in netball when he was just beginning a prison sentence; but it had also made him very homesick. Since he had left Sweden and started his journey to England, he had never heard of her at all. That was nearly three years ago. She would be eighteen now: grown up, he supposed. He sorely wished that he knew if she was happy.

Sitting in the boat that early morning, as the boy from Hersöy rowed him across the sound, Jan had every reason to think of his family. It had always been on his mind since he started to train as an agent that he would have to be careful to protect them from reprisals if anything went wrong. Now that capture and death were so close to him, he had to remind himself of the one and only way he could protect them: to refuse to be captured, and to die, if he had to die, anonymously. He had nothing on him to identify him or his body as Jan Baalsrud,

45

and that was as it should be: if the worst came to the worst, the Germans would throw him into a grave without a name. His father and Nils and Bitten would never know what had happened to him. He would have liked them to know he had done his best; but to leave them in ignorance was the price of their safety.

Something the boy said brought this forcibly to his mind. The boy meant to take him to Jensen's house and introduce him and make sure that he was safe; but Jan had to ask him to put him ashore out of sight of the house and leave him. He explained the first principle of any illegal plan: that nobody should know more than he needs. It was a pity that the boy and his family knew Jan was going to Jensen, but there was no need for Jensen to know where he came from. You might trust a man like your brother, he said, but it was no kindness to burden him with unnecessary secrets, because no man alive could be certain he would not talk if he was caught and questioned. What your tongue said when your brain was paralysed by drugs or torture was not a mere matter of courage; it was unpredictable, and beyond any self-control. Jan himself would be the only one who knew everyone who helped him; but he had his pistol, and he solemnly promised this boy, as he promised more people later, that he would not let them catch him alive. So the two of them parted on the shore of Ringvassöy, and the boy backed his boat off and turned away into the darkness, leaving Jan alone.

Jan owned nothing in the world just then except the clothes he was wearing, and a handkerchief and a knife and some bits of rubbish in his pockets, and his pistol. He had navy blue trousers and a sweater and Herr Pedersen's underclothes, and a Norwegian naval jacket, a warm double-breasted one with brass buttons and a seaman's badges, though he had never been a seaman, and was not even very sure if he could row. The jacket had the Norwegian flag sewn on its shoulders, with the word NORWAY in English above it. He had lost his hat. He was amused at the odd footprints which his two rubber boots left in the snow, one English and one Norwegian. There was something symbolic there, if you cared about symbols.

There were a dozen houses in that part of Ringvassöy, but he easily picked out Jensen's. The lights were on, and there were voices inside. He hoped that might mean that Jensen was making an early start on his trip to Tromsö. He went to the back door, and hesitated a moment, and knocked. A woman opened the door at once, and he asked if Jensen was at home. No, she said, he had left for Tromsö the morning before, and would not be back for two or three days.

At this disappointing news Jan paused for a moment uncertainly, because he did not want to show himself to people who could not help him. He would have liked to make an excuse and go away; but he saw surprise and alarm in her face as she noticed his uniform in the light of the lamp from the doorway.

"I'm in a bit of trouble with the Germans," he said. "Have you got people in the house?"

"Why, of course," she said. "I have my patients. But they're upstairs. You'd better come inside."

That explained the lights and the voices so early in the morning. He had not made allowances for what a midwife's life involves. He went in, and began to tell her a little of what had happened, and what he wanted, and of the danger of helping him.

Fru Jensen was not in the least deterred by danger. She had heard the explosion in Toftefjord, and already rumours had sprung up in Ringvassöy. The only question she asked was

47

who had sent Jan to her house, and when he refused to tell her and explained the reason why, she saw the point at once. She said he was welcome to stay. She was very sorry her husband was away, and she herself could not leave the house at present, even for a moment. But there was plenty of room, and they were used to people coming and going. He could stay till the evening, or wait till Jensen came home if he liked. He would be glad to take him to the mainland. But she could not be sure how long he would be away, and perhaps it would be risky to try to ring him up in Tromsö and tell him to hurry back.

"But you must be hungry," she said. "Just excuse me a moment, and then I'll make your breakfast." And she hurried upstairs to attend to a woman in labour.

Jan felt sure he would be as safe in her hands as anyone's. He could even imagine her dealing firmly and capably with Germans who wanted to search her house. If you were trying to think of a hiding-place, there could hardly be anywhere better than a labour ward, because even the Germans might hesitate to search there. And yet it would be so impossibly shameful to use it. It might fail; it might not deter the Germans. Jan had all a young bachelor's awe and ignorance of childbirth; but he had a clear enough vision of German soldiers storming through that house, and himself forced to fight them there, and failing perhaps, and having to blow out his brains. If it came to that, he was ready to face it himself; one always knew it might happen, one could think of it calmly. But to involve a woman in something like that at the very moment of the birth of her baby, or perhaps to see a new-born infant shot or trampled underfoot—that was too appallingly incongruous; it could not bear to be thought about at all.

Besides this, there was another practical, strategic consideration. He was still much too close to Toftefjord. If the Germans really wanted to get him, it would not take them long to turn Ribbenesöy inside out: they had probably finished that already. And the obvious place for them to look, when they were sure he had left the island, was where he was now, on the shore of Ringvassöy which faced it. Their search would gradually widen, like a ripple on a pond, until they admitted they had lost him; and until then, at all costs, he must travel faster than the ripple.

When Fru Jensen came back and began to lay the table, he told her he had decided to move on. She did not express any feeling about it, except to repeat that he was welcome to stay if he wanted to; if not, she would give him some food to take with him. She began to tell him about useful and dangerous people all over her island. There were several ways he could go: either by sea, if he happened to find a boat, or along either shore of the island, or up a valley which divides it in the middle. But if he went up the valley, she warned him, he would have to be careful. People in those remote and isolated places were inclined to take their politics from the clergyman or the justice of the peace, or the chairman of the local council, or some other such leader in their own community; they had too little knowledge of the outside world to form opinions of their own. In the valley there happened to be one man who was a Nazi, or so she had heard; and she was afraid a lot of people might have come under his influence. If a stranger was seen there, he was certain to hear of it; and although she could not be sure, she thought he might tell the police. Of course, most of Ringvassöy, she said, was quite all right. He could go into almost any house and be sure of a welcome. And she told him the names of a lot of people who she knew would be happy to help him.

It was still early when Jan left the midwife, fortified by a good breakfast and by her friendliness and fearless common sense. He wanted to get away from the houses before too many people were about; but it was daylight, and it was more than likely someone would see him from a window. It was a good opportunity to be misleading. He started along the shore towards the west. In that direction, he might have gone up the valley or followed the coastline round the west side of the island. But when he was out of sight of the last of the houses, he changed his direction and struck off into the hills, and made a detour behind the houses to reach the shore again farther east. He had made his plans now a little way ahead. The next lap was to walk thirty miles to the south end of the island.

It looked simple. He remembered it pretty clearly from the map, and during his training it would have been an easy day. He knew that maps of mountains are often misleading, because even the best of them do not show whether a hill can be climbed or not; but he was not prepared for quite such a misleading map as the one of that part of Norway. In the normal course of events, nobody ever walks far in the northern islands. The natural route from one place to another is by sea. The sea charts are therefore perfect; but the most detailed land map which existed then was on a scale of about a quarter of an inch to a mile, and it made Ringvassöy look green and smoothly rounded. No heights were marked on it. There were contours, but they had a vague appearance, as if there had been more hope than science in their drawing. One might have deduced something from the facts that the only houses shown were clustered along the shores, and that there was no sign of a single road; but nothing on the map suggested one tenth of the difficulty of walking across the island in the winter.

Jan had arrived there in the dark, and if he had ever seen the island at all, it was only in that momentary glimpse when he had come over the hill from Toftefjord with the Germans close behind him. So he set off full of optimism in his rubber boots; but it took him four days to cover the thirty miles.

He was never in any immediate danger during that walk. The only dangers were the sort that a competent mountaineer can overcome. Once he had disappeared into the trackless interior of the island he was perfectly safe from the Germans until he emerged again. But it was an exasperating journey. It had new discomfort and frustration in every mile, and the most annoying things about it were the boots. Jan was a good skier; like most Norwegians, he had been used to skiing ever since he could walk: and to cross Ringvassöy on skis might have been a pleasure. Certainly it would have been quick and easy. But of course his skis had been blown to pieces like everything else; and there can hardly be anything less suitable for deep snow than rubber boots.

He had started with the idea of following the shore, where the snow would be shallower and harder and he would have the alternative of going along the beach below the tidemark. But on the very first morning he found it was not so easy as it looked. He soon came to a place where a ridge ran out and ended in a cliff. He tried the beach below the cliff, but it got narrower and narrower until he scrambled round a rock and saw that the cliff face ahead of him fell sheer into the sea. He had to go back a mile and climb the ridge. It was not very steep, but it gave him a hint of what he had undertaken. The wet rubber slipped at every step. Sometimes, where the snow was hard, the climb would have been simple if he could have kicked steps; but the boots were soft, and to kick with his right foot was too painful for his toe. He had to creep up slowly, one foot foremost, like a child going upstairs. But when the snow was soft and he sank in it up to his middle, the boots got full of it, and came off, and he had to grovel and scrape with his hands to find them.

At the top of the ridge, when he paused to take his breath, he could see far ahead along the coastline to the eastward; and there was ridge after ridge, each like the one he was on, and each ending in a cliff too steep to climb.

He started to go down the other side, and even that was painful and tedious. Down slopes which would have been a glorious run on skis, he plodded slowly, stubbing his toe against the end of the boot, and sometimes falling when the pain of it made him wince and lose his balance.

But still, all these things were no more than annoyances, and it would have been absurd to have felt annoyed, whatever happened, so long as he was free. He felt it would have been disloyal, too. He thought a lot about his friends as he floundered on, especially of Per and Eskeland. He missed them terribly. Of course he had been trained to look after himself, and make up his own mind what to do. In theory he could stand on his own feet and was not dependent on a leader to make decisions for him. But that was not the same thing as suddenly losing Eskeland, whom he admired tremendously and had always regarded as a bit wiser and more capable than himself, someone he could always rely on for good advice and understanding. And still less, in a way, did his training take the place of Per, who had shared everything with him so long. Jan knew his job, but all the same it was awful not to have anyone to talk it over with. As for what was happening to his friends, he could not bear to think about it. He would have welcomed more suffering to bring himself nearer to them in spirit.

In this mood, he forced himself on to make marches of great

Jan Baalsrud

The post office at
Bjorneskar

Bernhard Sörensen of
Bjorneskar and his wife

duration: 24 hours, 13 hours, 28 hours without a rest. But the distances he covered were very short, because he so often found himself faced with impassable rocks and had to go back on his tracks, and because of the weather.

The weather changed from one moment to another. When the nights were clear, the aurora glimmered and danced in the sky above the sea. By day in sunshine, the sea was blue and the sky had a milky radiance, and the gleaming peaks of other islands seemed light and insubstantial and unearthly. The sun was warm, and the glitter of snow and water hurt his eyes, though the shadows of the hills were dark and cold. Then suddenly the skyline to his right would lose its clarity as a flurry of snow came over it, and in a minute or two the light faded and the warmth was gone and the sea below went grey. Gusts of wind came whipping down the slopes, and clouds streamed across the summits; and then snow began to fall, and frozen mist came down, in grey columns which eddied in the squalls and stung his face and hands and soaked him through, and blotted out the sea and sky so that the world which he could see contracted to a few feet of whirling whiteness in which his own body and his own tracks were the only things of substance.

In the daytime, he kept going in these storms, not so much for the sake of making progress as to keep himself warm; but when they struck him at night, there was no question of keeping a sense of direction, and one night he turned back to take shelter in a cowshed which he had passed four hours before.

He stopped at two houses along the north shore of the island, and was taken in and allowed to sleep; and oddly enough it was the wounded toe that served him as a passport to people's help and trust. Rumours had gone before him all the way. It was being said that the Germans had started a new search of every house, looking for radio sets, which nobody was allowed to own. Everyone had already guessed that this search had something to do with what they had heard about Toftefjord, and as soon as they learned that Jan was a fugitive, they jumped to the conclusion that the Germans were searching for him. And indeed, if the search was a fact and not only a rumour, they were probably right. This made some of them nervous at first. Like the shopkeeper, they were frightened of agents provocateurs, and Jan's uniform did not reassure them; it was only to be expected that a German agent would be dressed for his part. But the toe was different. The Germans were thorough, but their agents would not go so far as to shoot off their toes. When he took off his boot and his sock and showed them his toe, it convinced them; and he slept soundly between his marches, protected by men who set faithful watches to warn him if Germans were coming.

Always they asked who had sent him to them, and some of them were suspicious when he would not tell them. But he insisted, because he was haunted by the thought of leaving a traceable series of links which the Germans might "roll up" if they found even one of the people who helped him. Such things had happened before, and men on the run had left trails of disaster behind them. To prevent that was only a matter of care. He never told anyone where he had come from, and when he asked people to recommend others for later stages of his journey, he made sure that they gave him a number of names, and did not tell them which one he had chosen. Thus nobody could ever tell, because nobody knew, where he had come from or where he was going.

The last stretch of the journey was the longest. Everyone he had met had mentioned the name of Einar Sörensen, who ran the telephone exchange at a place called Bjorneskar on the south side of the island. All of them knew him, as everybody knows the telephone operator in a country district, and they all spoke of him with respect. Bjorneskar is opposite the mainland, and if anyone could get Jan out of the island, Einar Sörensen seemed the most likely man. But if he refused, on the other hand, or if he was not at home, it would be more than awkward, because the south end of the island was infested with Germans, in coastal batteries and searchlight positions and patrol boat bases, defending the entrance to Tromsö. Bjorneskar was a kind of cul-de-sac. The shore on each side of it was well populated and defended, and Jan could only reach it by striking inland and going over the mountains. It would be a long walk, and there was no house or shelter of any kind that way; if there was no help when he got to the other end, it was very unlikely that he could get back again. But some risks are attractive, and he liked the idea of descending from desolate mountains into the heart of the enemy's defences.

It was this stretch of the march which cost him 28 hours of continuous struggle against the wind and snow. Up till then, he had never been far from the coast, and he had never been able to see more than the foothills of the island. The sea had always been there on his left to guide him. But now he entered a long deep valley, into the barren wilderness of peaks which the map had dismissed so glibly. Above him, especially on the right, there were hanging valleys and glimpses of couloirs, inscrutable and dark and silent, and of snow cornices on their crests. To the left was the range of crags called Soltinder, among which he somehow had to find the col which would lead him to Bjorneskar.

Into these grim surroundings he advanced slowly and painfully. Here and there in the valley bottom were frozen lakes where the going was hard and smooth; but between them the snow lay very deep, and it covered a mass of boulders, and there he could not tell as he took each step whether his foot would fall upon rock or ice, or a snow crust which would support him, or whether it would plunge down hip deep into the crevices below. Sometimes a single yard of progress was an exhausting effort in itself, and he would have to pause and rest for a minute after dragging himself out of a hidden hole, and look back at the ridiculously little distance he had won. When he paused, he was aware of his solitude. The whole valley was utterly deserted. For mile upon mile there was no trace of life whatever, no sign that a man had ever been there before him, no tracks of animals, no movement or sound of birds.

Through this solemn and awful place he walked for the whole of a night and the whole of a day, and at dusk on the third of April he came to the top of the col in the Soltinder. four days after Toftefjord. Below him he saw three houses, which he knew must be Bjorneskar, and beyond them the final sound; and on the other side, at last, the mainland. He staggered down the final slope to throw himself on the kindness of Einar Sörensen.

He need never have had any doubt of his reception. Einar and his wife and his two little boys all made him welcome, as if he were an old friend and an honoured guest. Their slender rations were brought out and laid before him, and it was not till he had eaten all he could that Einar took him aside to another room to talk.

To Einar's inevitable question, Jan answered without thinking that he had heard of his name in England, though he had really only heard it the day before. At this, Einar said with excitement, "Did they really get through to England?" Jan knew then that this was not the first time escapers had been to that house. He said he did not know whether they had reached England or only got to Sweden, but at least their report had got through.

After this, there was no limit to what Einar was willing to do. Jan felt ashamed, when he came to think of it later, to have deceived this man on even so small a point. But the fact is that a secret agent's existence, whenever he is at work, is a lie from beginning to end; whatever he says is said as a means to an end, and the truth is a thing he can seldom tell. The better the agent is, the more thorough are his lies. He is trained with such care to shut away truth in a dark corner of his mind that he loses his natural instinct to tell the truth, for its own sake, on the few occasions when it can do no harm. Yet when, through habit, he has told an unnecessary lie to a friend, it would often involve impossible explanations to put the thing right. So Jan left Einar with the belief that whoever it was he had helped had got somewhere through to safety.

They sat for an hour that night and talked things over. Einar thought Jan should move at once. His house was the telegraph office as well as the telephone exchange, and people were in and out of it all day; and there were German camps within a mile in two directions. As for crossing the sound, there was no time better than the present. It was a dirty night, which was all to the good. The patrol boats ran for shelter whenever the weather was bad, and falling snow played havoc with the searchlights. The wind was rising, and it might be worse before the morning.

About midnight, Einar went to fetch his old father who lived in the house next door; he thought it would take two of them to row over the sound that night. Before he went out, he took Jan to the kitchen to wait. The two boys were still there with their mother, though they should surely have been in bed. They asked Jan to tell them a story, and he sat down by the fire and the younger one climbed on his knee. He was deadly tired, and he was sick at heart because the boys' father had just told him the terrible story of what had happened to Per and Eskeland and all his other companions. He put out of his mind this story of murder and treachery, and put his arm round the boy to support him, and tried to think back to his own childhood.

"Well, once upon a time," he began slowly, "in a far away country, long ago . . ."

CHAPTER FIVE

THE TRAGEDY IN TROMSÖ

EINAR HAD come back that afternoon from a visit to Tromsö. Everyone there had been talking of Toftefjord and its sequel; and although the people were used to brutality, they were aghast at the pitiless drama which had reached its grim climax in their town. In fact, what Einar told Jan that night is a sombre story of inhumanity. It is told here not because there is pleasure in telling it, but because without it the full contrasting picture cannot be drawn of the compassion and kindliness of the people who helped the only survivor; for all of them were familiar with the German technique of occupation and knew quite well what punishment they would suffer if they were caught.

Although Einar, and everyone else in north Norway, knew the outline of the story a day or two after it happened, it was not till the end of the war that its details were discovered. They were given then in evidence in trials in Norwegian courts.

When the shopkeeper made the fateful decision after his sleepless night and telephoned to his friend the official, the official himself was faced with a dilemma. He was a member of the Norwegian Nazi party, whose leader Quisling had been appointed head of the puppet government by the Germans; but this fact did not mean in itself that he had Nazi inclinations. Soon after the occupation of Norway began many people in minor Government posts received a circular letter from the

Germans simply saying that unless they joined the party they would be dismissed from office. In the south, a lot of them were able to consult each other when they got this ultimatum, and they agreed to reject it. So many refused to join that they succeeded in calling the Germans' bluff and retained their offices. But in the scattered districts of the north, where it might be two days' journey for one of them to visit another, each of them had to face this problem on his own; and a great many of them decided, or persuaded themselves, rightly or wrongly, that if they did sign on as members they would be able to protect the interests of the people, whereas if they refused they would be replaced by a German nominee. The man the shopkeeper knew was one of these.

In any case, Nazi or not, it was certainly his nominal duty, as a Government servant, to report any story so strange as the one which the shopkeeper told him that morning. Perhaps he did it unwillingly. Perhaps he argued that already a dozen people had heard it, and that now the shopkeeper had begun to talk there was nothing to stop him telling everyone. Moreover, the shopkeeper had told it to him on the telephone, and most of the telephones there were on party lines. Anyone could listen to interesting conversations, and everyone did. The story was bound to spread, and the Germans were bound to hear it; and then the official himself would be the first to suffer.

At all events, as soon as the shopkeeper had rung off, the official put in a call to Tromsö. With what feelings he did it, nobody but himself will ever know.

First he rang the police station, but it was still early in the morning and the constable on duty wrote down the report and said he would show it to his chief at half-past nine. He also rang a friend of his in Ribbenesöy, to ask him if he had seen any strangers, and if there was really a boat in Toftefjord. This friend had not seen anything himself; but the shopkeeper had just rung him up and told him all about it. Then the official, feeling perhaps that things were moving too quickly for him, put in a call to police headquarters. He was given another rebuff. They told him to take his own boat and go over to Toftefjord to see if the story was true.

This idea did not attract him in the least, so he called his assistant and told him to do it. The assistant went off to borrow a boat from a neighbour, but as he had not had his breakfast he sat down to a cup of coffee with the neighbour before he embarked. In the meantime the official was struck by a better idea, and rang up his friend in Ribbenesöy again and asked him to go overland to see if there was anything in Toftefjord. The friend said he was too old to go climbing at that time in the morning. But he sent a small boy; and some time in the forenoon, unknown to the *Brattholm*'s crew, the boy peered over the crest of the hills and saw the top of a mast in Toftefjord, and did not dare to go nearer, and ran home to confirm the story.

When he heard this, the official rang the police headquarters again. He could assure them now that the boat had really been seen, and he hoped they agreed that there was no point in his going unarmed to investigate. He thought they should tell the Gestapo. But they rang off without giving him any definite answer; and some time in the morning, he rang the Gestapo himself.

It seems clear when one reads this story, with its incongruous elements of inefficiency and farce, that all the Norwegian police prevaricated on purpose. No doubt they hoped that if they delayed the report for an hour or two it would help the strangers in Toftefjord, whoever they were, to make good their escape. But as the crew of the *Brattholm* did not know

they had been betrayed, this effort to help them was wasted. It
is said that at the very moment when the German ship was
sighted off Toftefjord two rowing boats were entering the
fjord to warn the *Brattholm*. One of them was probably
manned by the two fishermen who were going to hide the
cargo, but nobody knows who was in the other one. In any
case, they were too late. Both of them stopped when the German ship bore down on them, and the men in them put out
lines and pretended to be fishing.

The people of Tromsö knew nothing of the fight till the
German ship got back there. Then they saw prisoners being
landed, and men carried ashore on stretchers. Within a few
hours, the story was whispered throughout the town, and
some hundreds of citizens were in fear of their safety.

Tromsö claims to be the biggest town in the Arctic, and it
is the metropolis of an enormous area; but for all that, it is
not very big: about the size of an average English market
town. It is so far from other towns that it is more than usually
self-contained. It would be an exaggeration to say that everyone knows everyone else; but certainly everyone knows its
more prominent people. Its interests are fishing and whaling
and arctic furs, and the general business of a small seaport.
During the occupation, its modest and peaceful affairs were
swamped by the demands of a German headquarters, and its
society was riven by the chasms of political beliefs. It had its
few traitors, despised and ostracised by everybody else; and it
had a new form of society, in which money counted for very
little, united by an implacable loathing of Germans which was
never experienced in England or America.

By the time that the *Brattholm* landed, the town had already organised itself to combat the effects of the occupation as

well as it could. Active opposition had been out of the question without direct help from England; there were probably more Germans than Norwegians in north Norway. But some things could be done, and at least preparations could be made for the end of the occupation. Eight of the leading citizens had combined to build up an organisation to collect intelligence and make plans to administer the town and the surrounding country on the day of the Germans' defeat. They expected this day from season to season throughout the five years; each Christmas they believed it would come in the spring, and each spring they looked forward to the autumn. They had sent messengers to Sweden and got into touch with the free Norwegian embassy in Stockholm, and through Stockholm with their government in London. They had been sent a radio transmitter and it was installed in the loft of the state hospital in the town.

Apart from sending a radio message from time to time when the Germans did anything which seemed of particular interest, perhaps the most important thing which an organisation of this sort could do was to befriend people who got into serious trouble. Many men who would have opposed the Germans when they found they had a chance, or when a decision was forced upon them, had had to give in, in the early days, for fear of what would happen to their wives and children if they were arrested. It strengthened their will to resist if they knew there was somebody who would see that their families did not starve if they themselves were imprisoned or banished to Germany. The organisation in Tromsö had this matter extremely well arranged. It could call on funds from all the rich people and business houses in the town. The family of a man who suffered at the hands of the Germans was cared for without any question. When the crisis of the capture of *Brattholm*

63

broke upon them, they were actually disbursing £2000 a week in secret to widows and orphans and the dependents of local men who had been arrested by the Germans or forced to flee the country.

It was never intended that the sabotage organisation which the *Brattholm* party was to found should have any connection with this existing spontaneous intelligence and relief organisation. The two things were always kept separate in Norway, so that if one was broken open, the Germans could not necessarily penetrate the other. But the names of the two men in Tromsö which had been given to Eskeland and his party as their principal contacts were Thor Knudsen and Kaare Moursund. These men had been chosen, without their knowledge, merely because they were known to be patriotic; but they were actually two of the eight leaders of the Tromsö organisation.

As soon as Jan heard from Einar in Bjorneskar that some of his companions were alive and in the Gestapo's hands, he knew that Knudsen and Moursund ought to be warned. He could not possibly go into Tromsö himself without any papers, so he asked Einar if he would do it for him. Einar agreed; but whether he ever went there is not known. If he did, he would have been too late; because both men had already been arrested.

These two arrests set Tromsö in a ferment of excitement and apprehension. Both the men were well-known in the town. Knudsen was the managing editor of one of the two local papers, and Moursund the office manager of the coastal shipping line. Knudsen was the actual man who distributed money for the organisation in secret charities. Several of his colleagues in the newspaper office were involved in his illegal activities, notably the editor, whose name is Sverre Larsen, and the owner, Larsen's father, whom the Germans had already dismissed from his own paper for his views. The arrests were totally unexpected. No one believed that Knudsen or Moursund had known the *Brattholm* was coming, but it seemed only too clear that the *Brattholm*'s men had known these two names and were then, at that very moment, under Gestapo pressure. How many other names did they know? Would Knudsen and Moursund be put to torture? There was not a man in Tromsö that night with any pretentions to patriotism who did not know that his own hour might be at hand. Those who were closest to the two arrested men went home to prepare their own wives for a parting which it was useless to pretend would not be final, and to prepare themselves for the sudden imperious hammering on the door, and for the crippling pain which had to be borne in silence.

Meanwhile, the shopkeeper and the official were called to town and courteously fêted by the Germans. Neither of these somewhat simple men was any match for the questioning at which the Gestapo were so remarkably skilful whether they used torture or threats or flattery. It is very unlikely that they hid anything which they knew, whether they wanted to or not. They were thanked by the Germans, and congratulated on their excellent work, and rewarded with money and food and cigarettes and two dozen bottles of brandy. It may be supposed that there in the town they first felt the depth of the wrath of their neighbours against them. The gifts of the Germans perhaps had a bitter taste.

The next people to be arrested were, unexpectedly, the two fishermen who had promised to hide the cargo. Nobody ever discovered who had given their names to the Germans. The shopkeeper denied it. There is a possibility that the names were extracted from the crew, or that the two men were caught and questioned when they were rowing into Toftefjord, and gave themselves away. It was hard that these men were taken, because they did not even know that the cargo had come from England.

The state of tension in Tromsö did not last very much longer. While it lasted, it was in all truth hardly bearable, and it could not have been sustained for very long. During the day after the first arrests, the men who had every reason to expect to be among the next to go went on with their business as usual, because to have done anything else would have focused suspicion on themselves. The newspaper had to be written and printed, to take a single example. But it was hardly possible for them to give the appearance of normal living, or to keep their thoughts or their eyes away from the shuttered windows of the great grey Gestapo building in the middle of the town, where they knew their own names might be shouted aloud when agony went at last beyond endurance.

On the third day the news became known that the *Brattholm* men were dead and Knudsen and Moursund deported. It seems callous to say that the news of these deaths was heard with relief, and it is true that the thought of the barbarous deeds which had been done in their town shocked the townspeople profoundly; but the men themselves could only have wished that their end would come quickly.

Exactly what was done with them did not become known till after the war was over, when their bodies were exhumed for Christian burial and their executioners were put on trial.

Of the twelve men of the expedition, Jan had escaped, and one man had been killed in the fight in Toftefjord. The other ten were all brought to Tromsö alive, although several of them were wounded. Eight of them were shot chained together on the outskirts of the town, and thrown into a common grave. The other two were tortured to the point of death and then put in the Catholic hospital, where they died.

The details of these executions are known, but they are not a thing to be written or read about. Two men were selected for torture in the hope that they would talk; but the shooting of the other eight was accompanied by acts of ferocity which were absolutely aimless. Countries which are civilised and yet have recourse to execution have evolved the convention of the firing-squad and the one or two blank rounds. This protects the conscience of people whose duty compels them to act as executioners. The method the Germans used in Tromsö was the very opposite of this. Yet it was done in strictest secrecy. There was no question of making use of cruelty as a deterrent to other people. It can only have been done as it was for one possible reason: to amuse the executioners. The Germans made it an orgy of hideous delight.

It is not known whether one of the men who were tortured gave Knudsen's and Moursund's names to the torturers. It would not be surprising if they did, and no one would have the right to blame them. But it is equally possible that the activities of these two men were already known to the Germans, and that they were arrested on mere suspicion of complicity in the *Brattholm* affair. Both of them died in concentration camps in Germany, and so did the two fishermen Andreasson and Kristiansen.

So when the shopkeeper played for safety, and the official did what he afterwards claimed was his duty, their actions cost fifteen lives. Yet it is not for an Englishman, who has never lived under the rule of the Germans, to pass judgment on what they did. Their own countrymen judged them hardly.

In a few moments of panic, they both threw away their peace of mind for ever. For the rest of the war, their lives were made a misery by their neighbours, and after it ended, the shop-keeper was sentenced by a Norwegian court to eight years' hard labour, and the official to fourteen.

CHAPTER SIX

THE AVALANCHE

WHEN EINAR left Jan in the kitchen at Bjorneskar and went
to fetch his father, Bernhard Sörensen, the old man was in bed.
Einar called to him from the bottom of the stairs, and when he
woke up and asked what the matter was, he said, "Come out,
Father. I want to talk to you." He was not sure if he ought to
tell his mother.

Bernhard, who was 72 at that time, came down and listened
to Einar's story, leaving his wife upstairs. When he had heard
it all, he went back to his bedroom and began to put on his
clothes. Fru Sörensen asked him where he was going.

"We've got to take the boat out," the old man said. "There's
a man who wants to cross the sound."

"But now, at this time of night?" she asked him.

"Yes," he said.

"It's a terrible night."

"So much the better. We'll go down to Glomma and cross
with the wind. Now, don't worry. He must get across, you see.
It's one of those things we mustn't talk about."

When he was ready he left her, with no more reassurance
than that, to the traditional role of women in a war. She spent
an anxious night at home, waiting for Bernhard, to whom she
had then been married for fifty years.

But he was enjoying himself. Jan had been worried at asking a man of his age to cross the sound on such a night of wind

and snow. It was a row of ten miles across and back. But Bernhard laughed at his fears. When he was a young man, he had rowed to the Lofoten fishing and back every year, and that was two hundred miles. He did not think much of the rising generation. "In my day," he used to say, "it was wooden ships and iron men, and what is it now? Iron ships and a lot of wooden men. Why, do you know," he said, as they went down to the boathouse at the water's edge, "do you know, there was a young fellow taken to hospital sick only the other day. And do you know why he was sick? Because he'd got his feet wet. Yes," he chuckled, "taken to hospital because he'd got his feet wet. I've had my feet wet for over seventy years. Come along, boy. Across the sound is nothing. We'll swindle the devils out of one corpse, eh?"

The old man's good humour was catching, and Jan himself was elated at the prospect of reaching the mainland. The news of the fate of his friends had not shocked him very deeply in itself. Like everyone who took part in that kind of operation, they had all left England with a small expectation of life, and death loses its power to hurt when it is half-expected. Besides, he had thought of them as dead ever since he had seen them lying on the beach in Toftefjord. It distressed him more to learn they were captured alive and had lived for another three days, because for their own sakes and from every point of view it would have been better if they had been killed in action.

But apart from the matter of emotion, the story had a minor lesson to teach him. Hitler himself had just issued an order that everyone who took any part in this kind of guerrilla action was to be shot, whether he was in uniform or not. They had all known this before they left England; but if the order was meant to be a deterrent, it was accepted as a compliment. So far as Jan knew, this was the first time since the order was made that a crew had been captured, and he had still had a half-formed belief that a uniform might give some protection. He was still dressed as a sailor himself; but now it seemed rather absurd, on the face of it, to try to cross Norway in such a conspicuous rig. But to change it was easier thought of than done. It had been simple enough to swap underclothes with the Pedersen family, but it was different to ask someone to give him a whole civilian outfit when he had nothing to give in exchange and no money to offer. But anyhow, when he came to think of it carefully, it could not make very much difference. The Germans knew he was still at large, and he could never pass himself off as a local civilian without his civilian papers. If he kept out of sight of the Germans, his uniform did not matter, and if he came to close quarters with them, he would have to fight it out whatever clothes he was wearing. In the middle distance, the uniform might be a disadvantage; but on the other hand, he thought to himself, it was warm.

But at the particular moment when they got into the boat and took up the oars, the naval uniform was an embarrassment, because Einar and Bernhard took it for granted that he was a naval rating, and he felt that he ought to offer to row. He had rowed before, but only on lakes when he was trout fishing; and when he tried one of the heavy sweeps in the high sea which was running off Bjorneskar, all he managed to do was to knock the tops off the waves and splash the old man who was sitting astern. He had to make the lame excuse that he was too tired, and Bernhard took over, probably not surprised to find that the navy was not what it had been.

Bernhard referred to the Germans as devils. Devil is one of the few serious swear words in the Norwegian language, but he used it with a lack of emphasis that made it rather engaging. It was as if he could not bring himself to utter the word

German. "You see the point of land over there?" he would say to Jan. "That's Finkroken. There are seventy devils there. They've some damned great cannons, and searchlights. We'll give them a wide berth. And down there ahead of us, that's Sjursnes. That's where the patrol boats lie. A whole company of devils there too. But don't you worry. They won't get you this time, boy. We'll swindle them. We'll steer between them." And he chuckled with joy, and heaved on his massive oar.

Jan was more than content to leave it to Einar and Bernhard to get him across the sound. This was the second consecutive night he had been without sleep, and he had been on the go all the time. He was too tired to take any notice of the flurries of snow and spindrift, or the steep seas which bore down on them out of the darkness to starboard, or of the searchlights which endlessly swept the sound and sometimes appeared as a dazzling eye of light with a halo round it when a beam passed over them. Einar and his father were sure they would not be seen, so long as the snow went on falling, and they were not bothered about the patrol boats, although they were crossing their beats. "No devils at sea on a night like this," the old man said. "There's not a seaman among them."

Jan did not care. The mainland was close ahead, and Einar had given him the things which he coveted most in the world just then: a pair of ski-boots and skis. In an hour or so, he would finish with boats and the sea, and enter a medium where he would feel at home. Among the snow mountains on skis he would be confident of outdistancing any German. He could go where he wished and depend upon no one. Even the Swedish frontier was only sixty miles away: two days' journey, if all went well; and the Germans had lost his trail. He needed one good sleep, he thought, and then he would be his own master.

It was about three in the morning when Bernhard and Einar

beached the boat on the southern shore. Jan jumped out thankfully. The others could not afford to wait. To take advantage of the wind on the way back home, they would have to row close under the devils' gun battery at Finkroken. They thought they could bluff it out if they were seen, so long as they were not too far away from home, but it would be better not to have to try. So as soon as Jan was ashore with his skis, they wished him luck and pushed off and disappeared: two more to add to this list of chance acquaintances to whom he owed his life.

There were small farms along the water's edge just there, with houses spaced out at intervals of two hundred yards or so. The people who owned them pastured sheep and cattle on the narrow strip of fertile land between the sea and the mountainside, and eked out a living by fishing. The Sörensens knew everyone who lived there, and had said he could go safely to any of the houses. They had specially mentioned a man called Lockertsen. He lived in a farm called Snarby, which was a little larger than the rest, and he had a thirty-foot motor-boat which might come in useful.

Jan would gladly have set off there and then without making further contacts. He felt guilty already at the number of people he had involved in his own predicament; and besides, this series of short encounters, each at a high pitch of excitement and emotion, was exhausting in itself. He longed to be able to sleep in barns without telling anyone, and take to the hills again each morning. But before he was fit to embark on a life like that, he had to have one long sleep whatever it cost him, and that night he could only count on a few hours more before the farms were stirring. He reluctantly put his skis on his shoulder and went up through a steep farmyard to the house which was nearest. He crept quietly round the house till

73

he found the door, and he tried the handle. It opened. As it happened, this was Snarby.

Fru Lockertsen said afterwards it was the first night she had forgotten to lock the door since the occupation started. In ordinary times, of course, nobody thought of keys in a place like that; it was not once in a year that a stranger came to the door. But now, when you could always see a German patrol ship from the front windows of Snarby, you felt better at nights behind a good lock; and when she was woken by blundering footsteps in the kitchen, the first thing she thought was that some German sailors had landed. She prodded her husband and whispered that there was somebody in the house, and he listened, and dragged himself out of bed, and went to see what was happening.

Lockertsen was a big heavily-built man like a polar bear. He was a head taller than Jan and looked as though he could have picked him up and crushed him; and probably that is what he felt inclined to do. He was intensely suspicious. Jan told him his story, and then told it all over again, but every time he told it Lockertsen had thought of new doubts and new questions. He simply refused to believe it, and Jan could not understand why. But the fact is that Jan was so sleepy that he hardly knew what he was saying. His explanation was muddled and unconvincing, and the way he told the story made it sound like a hastily-invented lie. The only thing that was still quite clear in his head was that he must not say where he had come from. Somebody had brought him across from Ringvassöy, he insisted; but he refused to say who it was and could not explain why he refused to say it. To Lockertsen one naval uniform was probably much the same as another, and Jan had obviously landed from the sound; and the only navy in the sound was German. It seemed much more likely that he was a German deserter. Even the toe would have fitted that explanation. Everyone had heard of self-inflicted wounds.

The argument went on for a solid hour, and it only ended then because Jan could not talk any longer. His speech had got slow and blurred. He had to sleep. It was a pity, and he was resentful that the man did not believe him. But he was finished. He had taxed his endurance too much, and left himself without the strength to get away. Let him report him if he liked; there was nothing more to be done about it. He lay down on the rug in front of the kitchen stove. He heard Lockertsen say: "All right. You can stay there till half-past five." At that, he fell deeply asleep.

Lockertsen spent the rest of the night pacing up and down the kitchen and trying to puzzle things out, and stopping from time to time to look down at the defenceless, mysterious creature asleep on his floor. Many of the doubts which had afflicted the shopkeeper came to him also, and they were strengthened for him by the fact that the stranger had come from a place where he knew there were Germans. But Lockertsen was a man of different calibre. He had plenty of courage. He was only determined to get the truth out of Jan, if he had to do it by force. He was not going to act one way or the other until he was sure.

Some time while Jan was sleeping the big man went down on his knees on the hearthrug and searched through his pockets. There was nothing in them which gave him a clue, and Jan did not stir.

He had said he could sleep till 5.30, and at 5.30 he shook him awake. The result of this surprised him. Jan was subconsciously full of suspicion, and leapt to his feet and drew his automatic and Lockertsen found himself covered before he could move.

"Take it easy, take it easy," he said in alarm. "Everything's all right." Jan looked round him and saw that the kitchen was empty, and grinned and said he was sorry.

"You can't lie there all day," Lockertsen said. "The wife'll be wanting to cook. But I've made up my mind. You can go up in the loft and have your sleep out, and then we'll see what's to be done with you."

Jan gratefully did as he told him; and when he woke again in the middle of the day, refreshed and capable of explaining himself, Lockertsen's distrust of him soon disappeared. Fru Lockertsen and their daughter fed him and fussed over him, and Lockertsen himself grew amiable and asked him where he was going. Jan answered vaguely, "Over the mountains," and Lockertsen offered to take him part of his way in the motor-boat if that would help him.

Jan's idea of where he was going was really rather vague. By that time, by a process of subconscious reasoning, he had decided to make for Sweden. He knew he ought to tell London what had happened. At headquarters they would soon be expecting signals from his party's transmitter, and they would already be waiting for *Brattholm* to get back to Shetland. In a week or two they would give her up as lost, and when no signals were heard they would probably guess that the whole party had been lost at sea. No one would ever know, unless he told them, that he was alive, and sooner or later, in the autumn perhaps, they would send another party. It would really be stupid for him to try to work on alone when nobody in England knew he was there. Any work he could do might clash with a second party's plans. The proper thing for him to do, he could see, was to get into Sweden and fly back to England and join the second party when it sailed.

To go to Sweden was a simple aim. If he kept moving south,

he would be bound to get there in the end. But nobody he had met had had a map, even of the most misleading sort, and he could only plan his route from recollection. He was now on the very end of one of the promontories between the great fjords which run deep into the northern mountains. To the west of him was Balsfjord, and to the east Ullsfjord and then Lyngenfjord, the greatest of them all, fifty miles long and three miles wide. All the promontories between these fjords are high and steep. The one between Ullsfjord and Lyngenfjord in particular is famous for its mountain scenery: it is a mass of jagged peaks of fantastic beauty which rise steeply from the sea on either side. Away from their shores, these promontories are not only uninhabited, they are deserted, never visited at all except in summer and in peace time by a few mountaineers and by Lapps finding pasture for their reindeer. Along the shores there are scattered houses, and roads where there is room to build them.

Jan's choice of route was simplified by the fact that Tromsö lay to the west of him, and the farther he went that way the thicker the German defences would become. Apart from that, he had to decide whether to keep to the fjords and make use of roads when he could find them, or to cut himself off from all chance of meeting either friend or enemy by staying in the hills.

Lockertsen's advice was definite. On the shores of the fjords he would run the risk of meeting Germans, which would be awkward; but to cross the mountains alone at that time of year was, quite simply, impossible and suicidal, and nobody but a lunatic would try it.

They talked all round the subject several times. Jan listened to everything that Lockertsen suggested, intending as usual to take the advice which suited him and forget about the rest. In the upshot, Lockertsen said he would take him in his motor-boat that night as far as he could up Ullsfjord, and land him on the far shore, the eastward side. There was a road there which ran up a side fjord called Kjosen and crossed over to Lyngen-fjord through a gap in the mountains. Then it ran all the way to the head of Lyngenfjord; and from there there was both a summer and a winter road which led to the frontier. It was true that the road itself might not be much use to him. It ran through several small villages on the fjord, which would be sure to have garrisons. Beyond the end of the fjord, the sum-mer road of course would be buried in snow and the winter road, which crossed the frozen lakes, was certainly blocked and watched by the Germans. But at least this was a line to follow, and it skirted round the mountains.

Jan hated the thought of putting to sea again, but the lift he was offered would put him twenty miles on his way, and he accepted it. When it was dark, he said good-bye to Fru Lockert-sen and her daughter and went down to the shore again. Lock-ertsen rowed him out to the motor-boat, which was lying at a buoy, and a neighbour joined them. There was fishing gear on board, and Lockertsen and the neighbour meant to use it, when they landed Jan, to give themselves a reason for the journey. They started her up and cast off, and put out once more into the dangerous waters of the sound.

Jan made them keep close inshore, so that if they were sud-denly challenged by a German ship he could go over the side and swim to land. So they crept up the sound under the shadow of the mountains. But nothing happened; they slipped safely round the corner into Ullsfjord, and in the early hours of the morning put Jan ashore on a jetty at the mouth of Kjosen.

Neither Lockertsen's warning, nor the maps and photographs he had studied, nor even the fame of the Lyngen Alps had quite prepared Jan for the sight which he saw when he landed at Kjosen. It was still night, but ahead of him in the east the sky was pale; and there were the mountains, a faint shadow on the sky where the rock was naked, a faint gleam where it was clothed with snow. Peak upon peak hung on the breathless air before the dawn, immaculate and sublime. Beneath their majesty, the enmity of Germans seemed something to be despised.

He saw the road, beside the shining ribbon of the fjord; it was the first road he had seen in all his journey. He put on his skis with a feeling of exaltation and turned towards the frontier. The crisp hiss of skis on the crusted snow and the rush of the frosty air was the keenest of all possible delight. He knew of the danger of garrisons in the villages on the road, and he knew that the largest of them was only five miles ahead, but at that time and in that place it seemed absurd to cower in fear of Germans. He determined to push on and get through the village before the sun had risen or the people were awake.

The name of the village is Lyngseidet. It lies in the narrow gap between Kjosen and Lyngenfjord. In peace, it is a place which cruising liners visit on their way to North Cape. From time to time in summer they suddenly swamp it with their hordes of tourists; the people of the village, it is said, hurriedly send lorries to Tromsö for stocks of furs and souvenirs, and the Lapps who spend the summer there dress up in their best and pose for photographs. In war time it was burdened with a garrison of more than normal size, because it is the point at which the main road crosses Lyngenfjord by ferry.

Jan expected to find a road block on each side of it, and probably sentries posted in the middle, but on skis he felt sure he could climb above the road to circumvent a block, and to pass the sentries he relied on his speed and the remaining darkness.

He came to the block, just as he had foreseen. It was a little way short of the head of the fjord at Kjosen. There was a pole across the road, and a hut beside it which presumably housed a guard. He struck off the road up the steep hillside to the left. As he had thought, on skis it was quite easy; but it took longer than he expected, because there were barbed-wire fences which delayed him. One of his ski bindings was loose as well, and he had to stop for some time to repair it. When he got down to the road again a couple of hundred yards beyond the block, it was fully daylight.

He pushed on at top speed along the road. He knew it could not be more than two or three miles to the village, and he ought to be through it in ten or fifteen minutes. It was getting risky, but it was worth it; to have stopped and hidden where he was would have wasted the whole of a day, and the thought of the distance he might cover before the evening was irresistible. There was a little twist in the road where it rounded a mass of rock, and beyond it he could already see the roofs of houses. He turned the corner at a good speed.

Fifty yards ahead was a crowd of German soldiers. They straggled across the road and filled it from side to side. There was not time to stop or turn and no place to hide. He went on. More and more of them came from a building on the left: twenty, thirty, forty. He hesitated for a fraction of a second but his own momentum carried him on towards them, and no challenge came, no call to halt. They were carrying mess tins and knives and forks. Their uniforms were unbuttoned. He shot in among them, and they stood back to right and left to let him pass, and for a moment he looked full into their faces and saw their sleepy eyes and smelled the frowsty, sweaty smell of early morning. Then he was past, so acutely aware of the flag and the NORWAY on his sleeves that they seemed to hurt his shoulders. He fled up the road, expecting second by second and yard by yard the shouts and the hue and cry. At the turn of the road he glanced over his shoulder, and they were still crossing the road and going into a house on the other side, and not one of them looked his way. A second later, he was out of sight.

The road went uphill through a wood of birch, and he pounded up it without time to wonder. After a mile he came to the top of the rise. The valley opened out, and ahead he saw the village itself, and the spire of the church, and the wide water of Lyngenfjord beyond it, and the road which wound downhill and vanished among the houses. He thrust with his sticks once more, and began a twisting run between the fences of the road. He knew he would come to a fork at the bottom, in the middle of the village. The left-hand turning ran a little way down Lyngenfjord towards the sea and then came to an end; it was the right-hand one which led to the head of the fjord and then to the frontier. He passed the first of the houses, going fast. The church was on the right of the road and close to the water's edge. There was a wooden pier behind it, and down by the churchyard fence where the road divided a knot of men was standing.

A moment passed before he took in what he saw. Two or three of the men were soldiers, and one was a civilian who stood facing the others. Behind them was another pole across the road, and one of the soldiers was turning over some papers in his hand.

About five seconds more would have halted him among them at the roadblock, but there was a gate on the right which led to a garage in a garden and it was open. He checked and turned and rushed through the gate and round the garage and up the steep garden and headed for some birch scrub behind it. There were shouts from the crossroad, and as he came out into view of it again beyond the garage two or three rifle shots were fired, but he reached the bushes and set himself to climb the mountainside.

In Toftefjord when the Germans were behind him, he had been afraid, but now he was elated by the chase. With a Norwegian's pride in his skill on skis, he knew they could not catch him. He climbed up and up, exulting in the skis and his mastery of them, and hearing the futile shouts grow distant in the valley down below. He looked back, and saw a score of soldiers struggling far behind him up his trail. He passed the treeline and went on, up onto the open snow above.

Up there, he met the sunshine. The sun was rising above the hills on the far side of Lyngenfjord. The water below him sparkled in its path, and in the frosty morning air the whole of the upper part of the fjord was visible. On the eastern side and at the head he could see the curious flat-topped hills which are the outliers of the great plateau through which the frontier runs; and far up at the end of the fjord, fifteen miles away, was the valley called Skibotten up which the frontier road begins. To see his future route stretched out before him added to the joy he already felt at having left the valleys and the shore: he was almost glad of the accident which had forced him to grasp the danger of taking to the hills. And seeing the fjord so beautifully displayed below him had brought back his recollection of the map. There had been a dotted line, he now remembered, which ran parallel to the road and to the shore. This marked a summer track along the face of the mountains; and although it was the same map as the one of Ringvassöy, and the track had probably been put in from hearsay and not surveyed, yet if it had ever been possible to walk that way in summer, it ought to be possible now to do it on skis in snow. At least, there could not be any completely impassable precipice, and so long as the fjord was in sight he could not lose his way.

He stopped climbing after about 3000 feet, and rested and looked around him. The pursuit had been given up, or fallen so far behind that he could not see or hear it; and up there everything was beautiful and calm and peaceful. At that height he was almost level with the distant plateau, and he could see glimpses here and there beyond the fjord of mile upon mile of flat unbroken snow. But on his own side, close above him, the mountains were much higher. He was on the flank of a smooth conical hill with the Lappish name of Go-alesvarre, and its top was still 1500 feet above him; and behind it the main massif of the Lyngen Alps rose in a maze of peaks and glaciers to over 6000 feet.

It was not until he rested there that he had leisure to think of his fantastic encounter with the platoon of soldiers. At first it had seemed incredible that they should have taken no notice of him and let him pass; but when he came to think it over, he saw that it was typical of any army anywhere. It was like the search in Ribbenesöy: one expected the German army to be more fiendishly efficient than any other, but it was not; or at least, not always. He could imagine a British or Norwegian platoon, or an American one for that matter, shut away in a dreary post like that, with nothing whatever to do except guard a road and a ferry where nothing ever happened. With one section on guard at the roadblock, the others, to say the least of it, would never be very alert, and just after reveille they would not be thinking of anything much except breakfast. If someone in a queer uniform came down the road, the guard must have let him through, they would say, and that was the guard's funeral. The officers would know all about it, anyway, whoever he was. Nobody would want to make a fool of himself by asking officious questions. And the uniform itself, Jan reflected, would have meant nothing to them in a foreign country. Probably none of them knew that the word NORWAY was English, any more than you would expect an English soldier to know the German word for Norway. For all they knew or cared, he might have been a postman or a sanitary inspector on his rounds; anything was more likely, far inland, than meeting an enemy sailor on skis. Sooner or later, one of them might mention it to an n.c.o., who might pull the leg of the corporal of the guard next time he saw him, and by the evening perhaps it would come to the ears of the platoon commander, who certainly would not want to report it and would spend a lot of time questioning his men to prove to himself that it was really nothing important.

But of course the guard on the roadblock in Lyngseidet was a more unfortunate encounter. They certainly knew he was up to something illegal, because he had run away, and they knew fairly exactly where he had gone. That incident was bound to be reported, at least to battalion headquarters. He could not be sure if they had seen the uniform, or whether headquarters would put two and two together and guess that the man who had been seen in Lyngseidet was the one who had escaped in Toftefjord. It depended how many other people in the district, for one reason or another, were on the run. At the worst, it meant they had picked up his trail again, and if they thought it was worth it, they might put extra patrols in the country he had to pass through. He wondered how badly they wanted to catch him.

In any case, the best thing, as ever, was speed: to travel faster than they would think he could possibly travel. And now he had the means to do this, because people who do not

Kjosen: by the buildings on the right, a party of German soldiers crossed the road

The Lyngen Alps above Kjosen

Lyngseidet

know much about skis can often hardly believe the distance an expert can go on them in the course of a day. The Germans would not know much about them unless they were Bavarians; and even people who ski in the Alps are inclined only to think of ski-ing downhill, and going uphill by lifts or even railways. Cross-country ski-running, uphill and down, is a particularly Norwegian activity, and a Norwegian skier on holiday, or merely on a journey, thinks nothing of fifty miles a day.

So Jan set off with confidence, and even with a certain amount of pleasure, in anticipation of the run. He imagined himself staying at about 3000 feet, following the contour along the fjord and keeping the water in sight. But of course no mountainside, even the side of a fjord, is quite so regular and simple. He had only gone a few miles along the slope of Goalesvarre when he found a side valley in front of him which ran deep into the mountains. As he approached it and the head of it opened up, he saw the smooth snow surface of a glacier in it, and even the glacier was below him. Rather than try to cross it, he went right down to the valley bed below the ice and climbed up it again on the other side.

Beyond the valley there was another minor hazard of a different kind. The side of the fjord became steeper, and finally sheer. To get past this cliff he might have gone over the top; but it was very high, and to the right of it, on the inland side, there was a col which seemed a more sensible line for the summer track to follow. It looked as though it would lead back to the fjord five miles or so beyond. So he headed for the col, and very soon he lost sight of the fjord.

By then it must have been about eleven o'clock in the morning, and he had covered something like twenty miles since he left the boat at Kjosen. It was good going, and everything looked promising; but it was just before he reached the col that the weather changed again.

It came over the high summits on his right, first the white wisps of clouds like flags on the highest peaks, and then the stray gusts of wind and the darkening of the sky. The sun went in, and the snowfields lost their sparkling clarity and detail and became monotonous and grey, and the air at once struck chill. And then the snow began to fall, softly at first but more heavily minute by minute as the wind increased and the clouds descended. With the same abruptness that he had seen in Ringvassöy, the storm swooped downward and enveloped him in a whirling white impenetrable wall.

It had happened before, and it gave him no cause to be alarmed, because all the sudden storms he had seen in the last few days had been short, and had ended as suddenly as they had begun. It was annoying, the more so now that he had skis. In his rubber boots the storms had not made much difference to his speed. He had plodded on all through them. But now he could not make use of his extra speed. He could hardly see five yards in front of him, and any slight downward grade might lead to a sudden drop. He had to be able to stop at any moment, and on slopes which he might have run at full speed he now had to check, and creep down circumspectly. It was not only slow, it was twice as tiring.

Nevertheless, he pressed on, hoping and still expecting to see the lightening of the cloud which would be the sign that the squall was passing and that a few minutes more would bring sunshine again with the snowcloud whirling away towards the fjord.

But no sign came. On the contrary, the wind went on increasing. It was getting worse than anything he had experienced before, and as hours passed he had to admit to himself

86

that this was not merely a squall. It was useless to rely upon its ending. He ought to act as though it might last for days. That meant that he must find shelter, and to find it he must get down to the fjord again.

But before he had come unwillingly to this decision, a new aspect of storm began to be manifest. The surface of the lying snow began to creep, first in whorls and eddies, and later in clouds which forced him to shut his eyes and put his hand over his mouth to keep the driving snow-powder out of his throat and lungs. When the very surface he stood on began to move, there was nothing stable left for his eyes to be fixed upon; when he stood still, the snow silted into the tracks which he had made, and then it was only by the wind that he could have any idea which direction he had been going. Each little slope which faced him then became a new problem in itself. Each one which he saw from the bottom vanished into the shifting mists a few feet above his head, and each of them might be the foot of a great mountain or the whole of a tiny mound. From the top of a slope he could not tell whether it was five feet in height or a thousand. He only knew that some-where about him the surface plunged down in sheer chasms to the fjord waters three thousand feet below, and that some-where it rose three thousand feet above him to the soaring crags he had seen in the light of the dawn.

He guided himself by the wind, keeping it on his right. The right side of his body was coated with ice; it matted his hair and his week-old beard, and his right hand grew numb. He had tried to keep on in the direction he had been going when the storm came down, because he believed it would lead him to lower ground. But after some hours he began to doubt even the wind. He would sometimes have sworn that he had travelled for fifty yards in a straight line, and yet the wind which had been on his right swooped down on him from ahead. It seemed to be eddying down from the higher mountains, perhaps following valleys which he could not see. He stood still to test it, and even while he stood still it changed direction. Without the wind to guide him, he was lost.

Some time during that day he stopped and tried to dig himself into the snow to wait for the abatement of the storm, because he despaired of finding the way out of the mountains. But as soon as he crouched down in the little hollow he scraped out, the cold attacked him with such violence that he knew he would die here if he rested. He had often read that if you lie down and sleep in a blizzard you never get up again. Now he knew it was true: it would not take very long. He got up and put on his skis and struggled onwards, not caring much any more which way he was moving, but moving because he did not dare to stop. Towards the end of the day his wandering became quite aimless and he lost all sense either of time or space.

One cannot say whether it was the same day or the next that he first perceived a continuity in the slope of the mountain. He was going downhill. By then he had devised a plan for descending slopes which had probably already saved his life. When he came to a void, he gathered a big snowball and kneaded it hard and threw it in front of him. Sometimes, above the sound of the wind, he heard it fall, and then he went on; but more often it vanished without any sound at all, and he turned aside and tried another way. Now, edging cautiously down a slope and throwing snowballs, he saw rock walls both to right and left of it. It was a watercourse. He knew it was possible, or even likely, that it led to the top of a frozen waterfall and that he was running a serious risk of stepping on to the ice of the fall before he could see it. But at last it was something to follow which must lead in the end to the sea. He crept

down it with infinite caution, testing every step for hidden
ice. He saw little bushes and knew he was getting low. And
then, directly below him, there was a square block which
loomed dark in the snow. He ran joyfully down the last few
yards towards it, because he thought it was a house. But it was
not. It was only an enormous isolated rock. But it had a hollow underneath it, like a cave, and he squeezed in there, lying
down because it was not high enough to crawl. As soon as he
lay down, in shelter from the wind and snow, he went to
sleep.

That rock is the first identifiable place which Jan came to
on that journey. It stands in a narrow valley called Lyngdalen.
It is only about ten miles in a perfectly straight line from
Lyngseidet, where the roadblock was: but nobody knows
where or how far he had been before he got there.

At the rock he made a mistake which was nearly fatal. There
is an acute bend in the valley just there. As he approached it,
down the northern side, the valley led on in two directions,
one only a little way to the left and the other equally little to
the right. Downstream was to the left, and that way the valley
ran without any hazard straight down to Lyngenfjord, five
miles below. To the right the valley led gently up to the foot
of the highest mountain in north Norway, the peak of Jaeggevarre, 6200 feet high. In clear weather, the choice is obvious; in fact, Jaeggevarre towers over the upper valley and
closes it with a sheer bastion 3000 feet high and three miles
long. But in storm, when neither the mountain nor the valley
walls were visible, the place was a trap. A great moraine nearly
closes the valley at that point. The summer river passes it
through a gorge. But in winter the gorge is full of snow, and
the immediate foreground of the valley floor slopes down to
the right, upstream. When Jan woke up and crept out of the

crevice below the rock, the storm was still raging. He saw nothing except the foreground, and he put on his skis again and set forth, downhill, towards the right, away from Lyngen-fjord and all possible help or safety, into the very heart of the highest hills.

He was beginning to suffer from exposure by then, and one cannot deduce how long he had been stormbound, or whether it was night or day. When one's body is worn by a long effort at the limit of its strength, and especially when its function is dulled by cold, one's mind loses first of all its sharp appreciation of time. Incidents which are really quite separate become blended together; the present and the immediate past are not distinct, but are all part of a vaguely defined present of physical misery. In a person of strong character, hope for the future remains separate long after the past and present are confused. It is when the future loses its clarity too, and hope begins to fade, that death is not far away.

Jan's mind was certainly numbed and confused by then, but so far he had not the slightest doubt about the future, and he was still thinking clearly enough to use the common sense of the craft of mountaineering. Now that he had found what he knew was a river valley of considerable size, he did not expect any trouble in following it to the sea; and so he was astonished and baffled when he found the ground rising in front of him again. He had come to what he thought was a frozen lake, though in fact it is only a level part of the valley floor, and he followed what seemed to be the shore of it, with the valley wall above him on his right. He came to the end of it expecting to find its outflow; but there was still a steep slope above him, and he could not see the top. He went right round the lake till he came back to the moraine where he had started; and there for the second time he missed the snow-filled gorge.

Search as he might, he could not find the outlet. He seemed to be in the bottom of a bowl, with the lake on his left as he circled round it and unbroken snow-slopes always on his right. There was nothing for it except to give up the hope of going on downhill. He had to start climbing again.

His choice of direction then, if it was not at random, was probably governed by the light. In the thickest of cloud and snow one sometimes has an impression of greater darkness where a steep rock face is close above. The sides of Lyngdalen may have thrown extra darkness, and so may the sharp bend downstream in the narrow valley. But upstream Jaeggevarre stands farther back, and in that direction there is less to obscure the light. Jan may have concluded that this was south, or that it was really the lower reaches of the valley. At all events, he began to climb that way. He went up diagonally, hoping and expecting all the way to find an easing of the gradient and a sign that the valley went on beyond. Very soon he lost sight of the bottom, but although he climbed on and on, he could not see the top. He was on a slope of snow which in his restricted vision seemed eternal; on his left it vanished into invisible depths, and on his right it merged in the cloud above. In front of him and behind him, it was exactly the same: his ski tracks across it disappeared a few seconds after he had made them. It was a world of its own, dizzily tilted on edge, full of the tearing wind, with himself for ever at the centre and the farthest edges diffuse and ill-defined.

Suddenly with lightning speed the snow slope split from end to end and the snow below his feet gave way. He fell on his side and snatched at the surface, but everything was moving, and the snow fell upon him and rolled him over and over. He felt himself going down and down, faster and faster, fighting with roaring masses of snow which were burying him alive. It wrenched and pounded his helpless body, and choked him and battered him till he was unconscious. He fell limply in the heart of the avalanche and it cast out his body on the valley floor below. Down there he lay still, long after its thunder had echoed away to silence.

CHAPTER SEVEN

SNOWBLIND

THE NEXT summer, somebody passed that way and found the broken pieces of Jan's skis, among the massive blocks of melting snow which were all that was left of the avalanche. They were at the foot of the icefall of the unnamed glacier under the east face of Jaeggevarre. One can guess what he had done. He had started his final climb up the valley wall, but had traversed on to the icefall without knowing it. When one can see a little distance, the snow on ice looks different from the snow on rock; but if one can only see a yard or two one cannot tell what is underneath. The snow on the steep ice at that time of year would have been very unstable, ready to fall by itself within a week or two, and Jan's weight and the thrust of his skis were enough to start it. The scar of the avalanche stretched from top to bottom of the icefall. Jan himself must have fallen at least three hundred feet.

To start an avalanche is apt to be fatal, but it did not kill Jan. Luck was extraordinarily kind to him again. Of course nobody knows how long he lay there unconscious; but when he came to, his head was out of the snow, so that he could breathe, and most of his body was buried, which had possibly saved him from freezing to death; and none of his bones were broken. To be alive was far more than he had any right to expect, and so the other results of his fall can hardly be counted as bad luck. One of his skis was lost and the other was broken

93

in two places; and the small rucksack with all his food had disappeared; and he had hit his head and could not remember where he was trying to go. He dug himself out of the snow and stood up, and unfastened the broken bit of ski and dropped it there, and wandered away on foot, utterly lost, with no plan and no notion of where he was going; in fact, without any coherent thoughts at all, because he had concussion of the brain.

After the avalanche, Jan had no sense of time, and hardly any awareness of the reality of what happened. He never stopped walking, but as his body froze slowly and ice formed in the veins of his feet and hands and crept inch by inch up his legs and arms, his mind became occupied more and more by dreams and hallucinations. But the length of this ordeal is known: he was four days and four nights in the mountains from the time when he passed through Lyngseidet. The storm lasted for nearly three days, and then the snow stopped and the clouds lifted and the mountains were clear; but Jan knew nothing of that, because by then the glare of the snow had scorched the retina of his eyes and he was blind.

One has to imagine him, both in the dark and the daylight, and both in the mists of the storm and the clear air which followed it, stumbling on unable to see at all. He never stopped because he was obsessed with the idea that if he lay down he would go to sleep and die; but all the time he was in snow between knee-deep and waist-deep, and towards the end of the time he fell down so often full length on his face in the snow that he might be said to have crawled and not to have walked.

His movements were totally aimless. This is known because his tracks were found here and there, later on in the spring. For the most part, he probably stayed in the valley of Lyngdalen, but at least once he went over a thousand feet up the side of it, and down again in the same place. He was deflected by the smallest of obstacles. There were boulders sticking up out of the snow, and when he ran into them head-on he turned and went away; not round the boulder and on in the same direction, but away at an angle, on a totally different course. There were birch bushes also, in the bottom of the valley, and among them he wandered hither and thither for days, crossing his own tracks again and again and blundering into the bushes themselves so that he got tangled in them and scratched his face and hands and tore his clothes. Once he walked round and round a small bush for so long that he trod a hard deep path in the snow, which was still to be seen in the summer: one can only suppose that he thought he was following somebody else's footsteps.

But he himself knew almost nothing of this. Because he was blind, he believed that the mist and falling snow went on all the time, and he could not reckon the nights and days which were passing. All that he knew of reality was pain in his legs and arms and eyes, and cold and hunger, and the endless, hampering, suffocating wall of snow in front of him through which he must force his way.

On one of the mountains he came to, there were hundreds of people, marching with bare feet which were frozen and they were afraid of breaking them, because they were quite brittle.

He knew it was a dream, and he wrenched himself awake because he was terrified of falling asleep, but when Per Blindheim began to talk to him it was more real than reality, and he swung round joyfully and called "Per, Per," into the darkness because he could not see where he was. But Per did not answer him, he went on talking to Eskeland. They were talking together somewhere, and a lot of the others were with them too, but they were not listening to him. He shouted louder, "Per! Eskeland!" and began to run after them, afraid that they would miss him in the night. And then they were close, and he was thankful to be with them all again. But they were talking together among themselves, quite cheerfully as they always did, and they never spoke to him. He called them again and again to tell them he could not see, but he could not make them hear him. They did not know he was there. And it came back to him that all of them were dead. Yet they had been talking together before he lost them, and he was the one who could not make himself heard. He began to believe that the dream was reality, and that he was the one who was dead. Stories of death came back into his mind. It seemed likely that he had died.

But in the same thought which made it seem so likely, he knew it was fantasy and he was still determined not to die, and to this end he must keep going, on and on, until something happened: something. He could not remember what it was that he had hoped would happen.

As he was going through the woods, he came to a trapdoor in the snow, and he tried to open it by the iron ring. But he was feeling very weak, and it was too heavy for him. It was a pity, because of the warm fire inside it, but he had to give it up. But whenever he turned his back on it to go away, somebody slipped out of the forest and opened it and got inside and shut it again before he had time to stop him. It was unfair that they kept him shut out in the cold and darkness while they all enjoyed the lights and gaiety inside. They always waited till he turned away, and then they were too quick for him. They must have been watching him and waiting for their chance.

It was the same when he found the mountain with windows in it, except that that time he never saw them go in. But they all climbed up to the door at the top so easily. Nobody would help him, and he tried and tried but always slipped down again to the bottom so that he was the only one left who could not do it. But perhaps it was nobody's fault; perhaps the explanation was that they could not see him. That would be logical if he was dead. But he shouted I am still alive and alone out here in the snow, it's all a mistake. The windows went away and the mountain turned into a little mound of snow, and he was scrabbling feebly at its sides.

It was the same too when he came to the log cabin. Stupidly, he was not looking where he was going, and he hurt himself again when he blundered into it. But as soon as he put out his hands and felt the rough logs he knew what it was although they never told him, and he started to feel his way along the wall, round the corner, hoping they would not see him before he found the door. It seemed a long way to the door, but he found it, and felt for the latch. But that time it opened, and he fell inside.

CHAPTER EIGHT

MARIUS

HANNA PEDERSEN was having dinner with her two boys, Ottar and Johan, when the door burst open and the dreadful thing stumbled into the room and groped blindly towards the table. They jumped to their feet and backed away in horror. She nearly screamed, but she put her hand to her mouth and stifled the impulse because of the children. She managed to whisper "Ottar, go and fetch your uncle," and the elder boy slipped out of the room.

"What do you want?" she said. "Who are you?" But Jan's answer was incoherent, and he collapsed on the floor. She overcame her terror and revulsion enough then to creep near him and look at him closely to see if he was somebody she knew.

It would have been hard to tell. When he lay still like that on the floor, one would have thought he was a corpse dug out of the snow. He was caked with ice and frozen dirt and dried blood. His hair and his beard were solidly frozen and his face and hands were bloated and discoloured. His feet were great balls of compacted snow and ice. His eyes were tight shut, screwed up with the pain of snowblindness. He tried to speak again as he lay there, but she could not understand anything he said. Distracted with fright she took the smaller boy and ran to the door to meet her brother.

Her brother's name was Marius Grönvold. He lived in the

next house, and when he heard the boy's anxious frightened story he ran across to see what had really happened. He pushed past his sister and took a single look at Jan. It was enough to show him that they would have to take measures quickly, whoever this man was, if they were to save his life. He had two other sisters who lived nearby, Gudrun and Ingeborg, and he sent the children to fetch them. They both hurried in, and between them all they set to work to bring Jan back to life. They built up the fire, and fed him with hot milk from a spoon, and got off the worst of his clothes and wrapped him in blankets, and lifted him on to a bed. Marius took a sharp knife and carefully cut his boots to pieces and peeled them off. His socks also had to be cut up and taken off in strips, revealing horrible feet and legs in an advanced stage of frostbite, with the toes frozen stiffly together in a solid block of ice. Everyone there knew the first-aid treatment for frostbite: to rub it with snow. The three sisters started then and there to try to save his feet, taking the ice-cold limbs between their hands and kneading the brittle flesh. Jan paid no attention to what they did, because he could not feel anything in his legs at all. He seemed to be slipping off into sleep or unconsciousness.

When the ice began to thaw on the jacket, Marius saw, to his amazement, that it was some kind of uniform, and he had also seen that Jan was armed with a pistol. That meant he was either a German or some sort of Norwegian Nazi, or else someone so actively anti-German that his presence in the house was like dynamite. Whether Jan was going to live or die, Marius simply had to know who he was: everything he did to try to save him, or even to dispose of his body if he failed, would depend on that answer. He asked him where he came from, and when he bent down to hear what Jan was trying to say, he heard the name Overgaard, which is a place at the head

99

of the fjord. He knew that was a lie, because he had seen Jan's tracks and they came from the opposite direction; and the fact that he tried to tell a lie was reassuring, because a Nazi would be too powerful to have any need to do so.

Marius had heard about Toftefjord and suspected the truth already. He sent the women out of the room, and when they had shut the door he said: "Listen to me. If you're a good man, you've come among good people. Now, speak out." Jan told him then, in a halting whisper. Marius heard him out, and took his resolve at once. "Don't worry," he said, "we'll look after you. Go to sleep." Jan asked him what his name was, and he told him Hans Jensen, which is the same as to say John Jones. He asked where he was, and this Marius told him truthfully: in the hamlet of Furuflaten, where the valley of Lyngdalen reaches Lyngenfjord. In the three days since the avalanche, all Jan's wanderings had carried him seven miles. Marius also told him that it was the 8th of April, late in the afternoon.

When he was satisfied that he had got the truth, Marius called his sisters in again and told it to them in whispers. They went to work again, looking at Jan with new pity at what they had heard, but with a desperate anxiety for themselves and the children. Nobody whatever must hear of it, Marius had said; and they could hear him saying the same thing, again and again, to the boys.

He came back to the bed when he had made sure that the children understood him, and looked down at the ghastly face on the pillow. He was trying to think ahead. He was also beginning to see the explanation of some strange events which had happened since the storm. The Germans had suddenly searched every house in Furuflaten. They had been through his own house and his sister's from top to bottom. They were looking for radio sets, they had said; but everyone had thought at the time there was something more behind it, because the place had been searched thoroughly enough for radio sets before. And for the first time, in the last few days, there had been motor-boats patrolling on the fjord, which did not fit in with the radio story. Now, Marius knew what they were searching for. There was the object of all the activity, lying at his mercy on his sister's children's bed.

Jan's luck was still good when it took him to that door. Marius Grönvold was a very unusual man. He was in his early thirties then, still a bachelor, a short strong stocky man with the face of a peasant and an extraordinarily alert and well-stocked mind. His occupation in those days was typical of this contrast: he ran a small farm, and also wrote for the Tromsö paper. His hobbies were politics and Norwegian literature. He knew the Norwegian classics well, and could recite in verse or prose for hours together, and often did so to entertain himself or anyone else who would listen; and he was already a leading member of the local Liberal party, and well on his way to becoming the most prominent citizen in those parts: the sort of man, one might say, who was destined from birth to become a mayor or the chairman of the county council. With these politics and his love of Norwegian history and culture, it went without saying that he was a member of the local resistance group in Lyngenfjord, which was a branch of the one in Tromsö.

To speak of a resistance movement in a place like Lyngen-fjord might be a little misleading. There was an organisation, but there was hardly anything it could do. There had never been time when Norway was invaded to call up or train the people in those far-off northern areas. The battle had been fought and lost before they had had a chance to go and take part in it. Ever since then, they had been entirely cut off from the world outside the German orbit. Their radio sets had been confiscated, and the papers they read were censored by the Germans. All that they ever heard of the fight that was going on from England was in occasional whispered scraps of clandestine news passed on from mouth to mouth from somebody who had hidden a radio somewhere or seen a copy of an illegal newspaper. Yet men like Marius resented their country's enslavement as deeply as anyone: even more strongly perhaps because they had not done anything themselves to try to stop it. It lay heavily on their consciences that they had not been soldiers when soldiers were needed so badly, and that brave deeds were still being done while they could not find any way to test their own bravery. Their organisation was really a kind of patriotic club. None of its members had any military knowledge; but at least they could talk freely among themselves, and so keep up each other's resolution, and help each other not to sink into the belief that the Germans could win the war and the occupation go on for ever; and they knew they could count on each other for material help as well if it was ever needed.

This was the background of Marius's thoughts while he worked on Jan's feet and fed him and kept him warm. The problem which Jan had brought with him was not a mere matter of a night in hiding and a little food. Probably Jan still thought, if he thought at all, that after a good sleep he would get up and walk away; but anyone else who saw him could tell he would be an invalid for weeks, and that walking was the last thing he would do. Marius, turning things over in his mind, could see no end to the problem in front of him, except capture. Furuflaten was a tiny compact community of a few hundred people; and it was on the main road and convoys of German lorries passed through it day and night, and it had a platoon of Germans quartered in its school. He could see the German sentries on the road when he looked out of his sister's window. He could not think how he could keep Jan's presence secret. Even to buy him a little extra food would be almost impossible. Much less could he see how he could ever nurse him back to fitness and start him off on his journey again. But there was never the slightest doubt in his mind that he was going to try: because this was his challenge; at last it was something which he and only he could possibly do. If he could never do anything else to help in the war, he would have this to look back on now; and he meant to look back on it with satisfaction, and not with shame. He thanked God for sending him this chance to prove his courage.

Jan was restless and nervous. He kept dozing off into the sleep which he needed so badly, but as soon as he began to relax, he roused himself anxiously. It was a symptom of his feeble mental state. He felt terribly defenceless, because he could not see. He was afraid of being betrayed; but if he had been in his right mind and able to see Marius's honest worried face, he would have trusted him without the slightest qualm.

Marius, in fact, was watching over him with something very much like affection: the feeling one has towards any helpless creature which turns to one for protection. He had already promised his protection in his own mind, and in the best words he could think of, and it upset him that he had not succeeded in putting Jan's fears to rest. He wanted to find some way to soothe him and make him believe in his friendship; and on an impulse, when the women were not listening, he took hold of Jan's hand and said very emphatically and clearly: "If I live, you will live, and if they kill you I will have died to protect you." Jan did not answer this solemn promise, but its sincerity had its effect. He relaxed then, and fell asleep.

He slept so deeply that even the massaging of his hands and legs did not disturb him. His legs were the worst. Marius and his sisters worked on them in turns for the whole of that night and the following day, trying to get the blood to circulate. Quite early, they invented a simple test to see how far up they were frozen. They pricked them with needles, starting at the ankles and working upwards. When they began, the legs were insensitive up to the knees. Above that, the needle made them twitch, although even this treatment did not disturb Jan's sleep. But as they rubbed the legs, hour by hour, they came back to life, inch after inch, and showed a reaction lower and lower down. Jan did not wake at all during the first night and day after he came in. When he did, even his feet were alive, and he woke with a searing pain where they had been numb before. Hanna Pedersen gave him a little food, and then he went to sleep again.

Although their efforts seemed to be succeeding, Marius and his sisters were all afraid that there might be some better treatment for frostbite which they had never heard of; and so it happened that the first time Marius invoked the organisation was to ask for a doctor's advice. He went first of all to Lyngseidet: a journey of twenty minutes by bus, which covered the whole of the distance which had taken Jan four days. His object there was to talk to the headmaster of the state secondary school, whose name was Legland. There were two reasons for seeing him: one was that he was the member of the organisation who had direct contact with the leadership in Tromsö; and the other was that most of the people of Lyngenfjord were in the habit of going to him when they were perplexed or in trouble. Herr Legland was a patriarch, revered by all his neighbours. The more intelligent of them, in fact, had all been his pupils, for he was an old man by then, and his school served the whole of the district. It was from him that Marius had learned his love of literature as a boy, and he regarded him as the wisest man he knew. Besides, he was a patriot of the old uncompromising school of Björnson and Ibsen. To him, the invasion of Norway was a barbarous affront, a new dark age. His school buildings in Lyngseidet had been requisitioned as a billet for German troops: a symbol of the swamping of the nation's culture by the demands of tyranny.

When Marius sought out this shrewd old gentleman and told him his story, he gave his approval of what Marius and his family had done, and he agreed with what he proposed to do. It went without saying that he would give his help. At the bottom of all the ideas which Marius had thought of up to then was the difficulty, and the necessity, of keeping Jan's presence secret from the people of Furuflaten. It was not that there was anyone really untrustworthy there; but there were plenty of gossips. As soon as it leaked out at all, the whole village would know about it as fast as exciting news can travel; and then it would only be a matter of time before the Germans found out about it too. Nobody would tell them; but living right in the centre of the place, in the school, they had a good idea of what went on there. They only had to keep their eyes open; it was a most difficult place for keeping secrets. The houses are widely spaced on each side of the river which runs out of Lyngdalen, and along the road which runs close beside the shore. There are hardly any trees, and from the middle one can see almost every house and most of the ground between them. It would only need a few too many neighbours calling at Marius's house, out of curiosity or with offers of help, for the Germans on watch at the school, or patrolling the road, to notice that something unusual was happening.

From this point of view, to get a doctor to come and look at

Jan would be very risky. Marius's house was the farthest up the valley, and the farthest away from the road. The doctor would have to leave his car on the road and go on skis for half a mile, all among the houses; and of course as soon as he had gone, they would have everyone up there kindly inquiring who was ill. If the worst came to the worst, they would have to try it; but at present all they needed was advice and some medicine, if there was any medicine that was any good.

This meant sending a message to Tromsö. If they asked the local doctor, or got a prescription made up at the local dispensary, they would have to say whom it was for, and have two or three outsiders in the secret; but in Tromsö inquiries like that could be made without anyone knowing exactly where they came from.

Luckily, the road to Tromsö was still open, though as soon as the spring thaw set in it would become impassable for two or three weeks. To send a private car would be difficult, because the driver would have to give a good reason for his journey at every roadblock he came to; but people had noticed that the Germans never bothered much about a bus. If it was one which ran a regular service on the road, so that they knew it by sight, they usually let it through without questioning the driver. One of the local bus drivers was a member of the organisation. Marius and Legland asked him to do the job and he agreed. One of the bus company's buses was put out of action, and the driver set off in another to fetch a spare part to repair it.

The arrival of this man in Tromsö was the first indication the leaders had had that there was any survivor from Toftefjord. Legland sent the driver to Sverre Larsen the newspaper editor, whose right-hand man Knudsen had been deported. Naturally, his message was only verbal. Larsen did not know the driver, and the organisation was still more than usually wary and on edge. Larsen refused to commit himself, and told the driver he could come back later in the day. But as soon as he had gone, he set about checking the man's credentials through the organisation's chain of command; and by the time he came back he had made sure that he was not a German agent, which he very well might have been, and had already consulted a doctor and a chemist about frostbite. Both of them said there was nothing to be done which had not been done already except to alleviate the pain, and the chemist had made up a sedative. Jan got the first dose of it that evening.

In the meantime, Marius had moved Jan from his sister's house and hidden him in a corner of his barn. He knew it would not make any difference where he put him if the Germans came up to his farm to search, but at least the barn was safer from casual visitors and family friends. These were a constant worry. Jan had come to the house on a Saturday. On a fine Sunday in spring the people of Furuflaten are in the habit of ski-ing a little way up the valley by way of a constitutional; and that Sunday the valley was full of Jan's tracks, which led in the end, plainly enough for anyone to see, up to Hanna Pedersen's door. For anyone to go about on foot was unheard of, and foot tracks instead of ski tracks were the very thing to set people talking. To forestall inquiries, Marius went out and inspected his farm early that Sunday morning, leaving his skis at home, and mixed up his own footsteps with Jan's. He thought out some story to explain why he had done such an eccentric thing. It was a thin story, but good enough to put people off the idea that the tracks had been made by a stranger. They would merely think that the man of the house had taken leave of his senses.

At that stage, the Grönvold family were the only people in

Furuflaten who were in the know: Marius, his three sisters and the two small boys, and Marius's mother. Hanna's husband was away at the fishing, and Marius had the added worry of having no other man in the family to talk to. His sisters never relaxed their efforts to nurse Jan back to health; but women in the far north are not often consulted by men in matters of opinion, and Marius could not help being aware that Jan's sudden arrival had been a serious shock to them all. His mother, in particular, was far from strong, and he was seriously troubled by the strain which it put on her. In fact, it must be a terrible thing for an elderly woman to know that her family is deeply involved in something which carries the death penalty for them all if they are caught. At one moment near the beginning she was inclined to oppose the whole thing, though of course she had no clear idea of the only alternative; but Jan had told Marius by then about his father and sister in Oslo, and Marius put it to her from Jan's father's point of view. "Suppose I was in trouble down in Oslo," he said, "and you heard that the people there refused to help me." In these simple terms she could see the problem better. It made her think of Jan as a human being, a Norwegian boy very much like her own, and not just as a stranger from a war which she had never quite understood. She gave Marius her consent and blessing in the end. Yet it is doubtful whether she ever quite recovered from the nervous tension of the years after Jan arrived there: for the strain did not end when Jan finally went away. Till the very end of the war the risk remained that some evil chance would lead the Germans to discover what she and her children had done. In the upside-down world of the occupation, the Pharisee was rewarded, and the good Samaritan was a criminal. People who acted in accordance with the simplest of Christian ethics were condemned to the life of fear which is only normally lived by an undiscovered murderer.

The two boys were a further worry. To send them to school every day when they knew what they did was a heavy responsibility to put upon children. Some children often can play a secretive role in a matter of life and death as well as anyone older; but to go on doing it for long will wear them down.

Jan lay for nearly a week in the barn. For four days he was never more than semi-conscious; and that was just as well, because he could not have moved in any case, and when he did rise out of his drugged sleep the pain of his feet and hands and his blinded eyes was bad. But he was certainly getting better. Towards the end of the week his eyesight was coming back. He began to see the light of the barn door when it was opened, and then to recognize the faces of the people who came to feed him. By that time, also, it looked as if his feet would recover in the end, though he was still a long way from being able to stand on them or walk. Most important of all, his brain had got over the concussion, and his power of thought and his sense of humour had come back: he was himself again. He and Marius began to find they had a lot in common. Their experience and background could hardly have been more different within a single nation: one the arctic farmer and country-bred philosopher, the other the town technician; one cut off from the war, the other entirely immersed in military training. But Jan's sense of comedy was never far away, and Marius, though he was a serious-minded man, was irrepressible when he was amused. He listened to Jan's stories of England and the war with the greed of a starving man who has an unexpected feast spread out in front of him, and when Jan told him about the many ridiculous aspects of army life, it made him laugh. When Marius laughed, it was as if he would never stop. It was an odd infectious falsetto laugh which started Jan laughing too; and then Marius, squatting beside him in the hay in the darkened barn, would rock with renewed merriment and wipe away the tears which poured down his cheeks, and they had to remind each other to be quiet, in case anyone heard the noise outside.

But although there were these moments when Marius enjoyed Jan's company, he remained a most serious danger as long as he stayed on the farm. There was an alarm every time someone was sighted climbing the hill from the village, and every time the Germans in the schoolhouse made some slightly unusual move. He had to be taken away from there as soon as he was fit enough to go, and Marius had thought of a place to put him.

The opposite shore of Lyngenfjord is steep-to and uninhabited. There had once been a farm over there: just one in a stretch of eight miles. But it had been burnt down a long time before, and never rebuilt. One small log cabin had escaped the fire and was still standing. It was four miles from the nearest house, either along the shore or across the water, and so far as Marius knew, nobody ever went there. If any safe place could be found for Jan, that seemed the most likely. The name of the farm had been Revdal.

To get Jan across there was more than Marius could manage with only the help of his sisters, because he would have to be carried all the way down to a boat and out of it again at the other side; and so at this stage he began to bring in other members of the organization from the village. He chose them on the principle that no two men from one family should be mixed up in the affair, in case something happened and another family besides his own was entirely broken up. In the end, he let three of his friends into his secret: Alvin Larsen,

Amandus Lillevoll and Olaf Lanes. All of them had known one another since they were children. When he told them about it, one by one, they all offered eagerly to help.

They agreed to make the move on the night of the 12th of April. In the fortnight since Toftefjord, the nights had got quite a lot shorter: uncomfortably short for anything illegal. To avoid disaster, the first part of the journey would have to be planned with care and carried out without the least delay. This was the half-mile from Marius's barn to the shore.

Marius had lived there all his life, but it was a new experience for him, as it would be for most law-abiding people, to plan a way out of his own home which he could use without being seen. It was extraordinarily difficult. Jan would have to be carried on a stretcher, and the two sides of the valley set limits to the routes which could be used, because they were both too steep to climb. On the other hand, the triangle of gently sloping ground between them was in full view of the houses, and the paths which crossed it led from door to door. There were two principal dangers, the German garrison in the school and the sentry who patrolled the road. But what worried Marius almost more than these was the thought of meeting a series of neighbours and having to stop to give endless explanations. To carry a man on a stretcher through one's village in secret at dead of night is a thing one cannot explain away in a casual word or two.

Marius made a reconnaissance, looking at his home from this unfamiliar point of view. There turned out to be only one possible route, and that was the river bed. The river, which is called Lyngdalselven after the valley, runs down through the middle of the village and under the road by a bridge about two hundred yards from the shore. It has a double channel, one about fifty feet wide which carries the normal summer flow, and another much wider flood channel which only fills up during the thaw in spring. That mid-April, the thaw had not yet begun, and the whole of the river was still frozen. The flood channel has banks about fifteen feet high, and Marius found that close below them, on the dry bed of the river, one was fairly well hidden from view. There was one snag about it. The nearest of all the houses to the channel was the schoolhouse where the Germans lived. It stands within three or four paces of the top of the bank. But even so, it still seemed that this was the only way. Looking out of the schoolhouse windows the troops could see almost every inch of the valley mouth. The only place they could not see was the foot of the bank immediately below their windows.

When dusk began on the night which they had chosen, they all assembled in the barn. Two men were to go with Marius and the stretcher. His sister Ingeborg had volunteered to go ahead of it to see that the way was clear. Another man was to climb to the top of a high moraine on the other side of the river, where he could watch the sentry on the road. A rowing-boat with a sail had already been hauled up on the beach at the river mouth. Jan had been wrapped in blankets and tied to a home-made stretcher, and they had a rucksack full of food and a paraffin cooker to leave with him in Revdal. They waited nervously for the long twilight to deepen till it was dark enough to go. It was after eleven when Marius gave the word.

It was a breathless journey. For once, they could not use their skis. To ski with a stretcher down steep slopes among bushes in the dark could only end in disaster, at least for the man on the stretcher. But to carry his weight on foot in the deep snow was exhausting work, even for such a short distance. They started by climbing straight down to the river, and when they got to the bottom of the bank without any alarm they put Jan down in the snow for a few minutes and rested. The lookout left them to cross the river and go up to his point of vantage, and Ingeborg went ahead to see what was happening at the school, and to tread out a path in the snow. It was very quiet, but there was a light southerly breeze which hummed in the telephone wires and stirred the bare twigs of the bushes; it was not much, but it helped to cover the sound of their movements. When they had got their breath they bent down and picked up the stretcher and set off down the channel towards the school.

It soon came in sight. There were lights in some of the windows which cast yellowish beams on the trodden snow outside it. One of them shone out across the river channel, but close in, right under the wall of the building, the steep bank cast a shadow which looked like a tunnel of darkness. The stretcher bearers approached it, crouching as low as they could with their burden, keeping their eyes on Ingeborg's footsteps in front of them in case they should stumble, and resisting the impulse to look up at the lights above them. When they came to the fence of the playground, they crept closer in under the bank. In an upward glance they could see the edge of the roof on their right, and the beam of light lit up some little bushes on their left, but it passed a foot or two over the tops of their heads. The troops in the school were not making a sound, and the men were acutely conscious of the faint squeak and crunch of the snow beneath their tread. The silence seemed sinister. It made the thought of an ambush come into their minds. But in thirty seconds they passed the school: and there was the road, fifty paces ahead of them.

This was the place they had feared. With the school behind them and the road ahead, there was nowhere for four men to hide themselves. It all depended on luck: how long they would have to wait for the sentry, and whether a car came past with headlights. But Ingeborg was there, behind a bush at the side of the road, where she had been lying to watch the sentry, and she came back towards them and pointed to the right, away from the river bridge. That was the way they wanted the sentry to go, the longest leg of his beat. At the same moment, there was a tiny spark of light on the top of the moraine; the watcher there had struck a match, and that was the signal that the sentry was nearly at the far end of the beat and would soon be turning round. It was now or never: they had to go on without a pause. They scrambled up on to the road. For a few seconds they were visible, dark shadows against the snow, from the school and the whole of the beat and a score of houses. Then they were down on the other side, among bushes which gave them cover as far as the shore. The worst of the journey was over.

When they had hauled the boat down the beach and bundled Jan on board it, they rowed off quietly for a couple of hundred yards, and then set the lugsail and got under way, with the breeze on the starboard beam and a course towards the distant loom of the mountains across the fjord, under which was the cabin of Revdal.

CHAPTER NINE

THE DESERTED FARM

WHAT JAN came to know as the Savoy Hotel, Revdal, was not very commodious, but the first two days he spent there were the happiest and most peaceful of the whole of his journey, a short fool's paradise: if one can use the word happy about his state of mind, or the word paradise about a place like Revdal. The hut was ten feet long and seven feet wide, and you could stand upright under the ridge of the roof. It was built of logs, and it had a door but no window. The only light inside it when the door was shut came through chinks in the wall and the roof, which was covered with growing turf. On one side, it had a wooden bunk, and the rest of the space in it was filled with odds and ends which seemed to have been salvaged, long before, from the ruins of the burnt-out farm. There was a small, roughly hewn table, and some pieces of a wooden plough, and some other wooden instruments which Jan could not imagine any use for, and an elaborate carved picture frame without any glass or picture. Everything was made of wood, unpainted, even the latch and hinges on the door, and it was all worn with years of use, and white and brittle with age.

As they carried him up there from the boat, he had had a glimpse of its surroundings. It stands about ten yards back from the shore, in a small clearing which slopes up to the forest of little twisted trees which clings to the side of the mountain. He had seen posts and wires in the clearing, which looked as if someone still came there to cut and dry the crop of hay, which is a precious harvest in the north. But there was no sign that anyone had been there for the past eight months of winter, and it was very unlikely that anyone would come for another three months, until July. Under the towering masses of snow and rock the solitary deserted little hut looked insignificant and forlorn, and even smaller than it really was. From a distance one would have taken it for a boulder, three-quarters covered by snow. There was no landing-place to draw attention to it, only the lonely beach. A stranger might have sailed along the fjord ten times and never seen it.

They put Jan in the bunk, and put the food and the paraffin stove on the table within his reach. Marius hesitated a little while, as if there should have been something else he could do for Jan, but there was nothing. He promised to come back two or three nights later to see him, and Jan thanked him, and then he went out and shut the door and left Jan alone there in the dark. For a few minutes Jan listened, hoping to hear the crunch of the boat on the beach as they pushed it off; but inside the hut it was absolutely silent. When he was sure they had gone away, he spread out his meagre belongings round him, and settled down on the hard boards of the ancient bunk. He was as contented as he could be. He had everything he wanted: time, and a little food, and solitude. He could lie there as long as he liked, not much of a burden to anyone, until his feet got all right again. Very soon he drifted off to sleep.

He had had a capacity for sleep, ever since the avalanche, which seemed to have no limit, and there was nothing to wake for in Revdal except to eat. Sometimes when hunger did wake him there was daylight shining through the holes in the roof: sometimes there was not, and he groped for his matches and

Jaeggevarre and the head of Lyngdalen. The avalanche fell down the ice-fall of the glacier in the middle distance

Marius

Furuflaten: on the right is the school where the German garrison was billeted, and the steep bank of the river channel below it. Jan was carried across the road near the bridge on the left

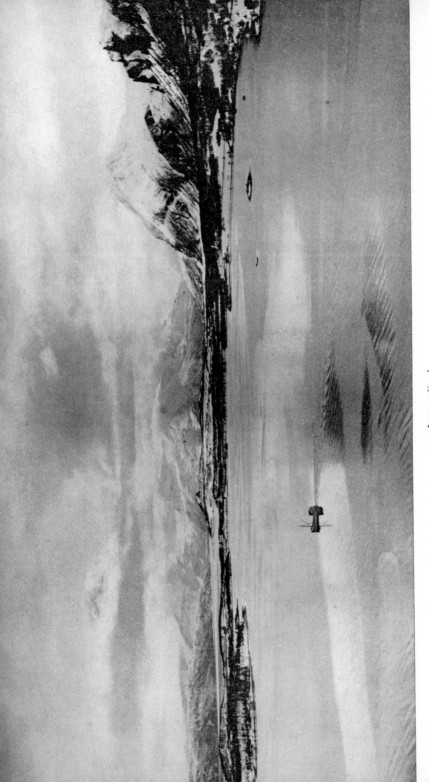

Lyngenfjord

ate by the dim blue gleam of the paraffin cooker. But whether it was day or night outside no longer had any interest for him.

When he was awake, he daydreamed, about Oslo before the war, his family, his football club at home where he had been president, the adventures which he had packed into the three years since he left home, and about his friends in the training camp in Scotland, and about his own ambitions and hopes for the time when the war was over. It had been a long journey and a very strange one all the way from his home and his father's instrument makers' workshop to this bunk and this hut and this desolate arctic shore; but he never thought then that it would end there. Some time, he would get up and go out of the door and begin all over again. And meanwhile, time was passing, and that was all that mattered; because time, he believed, was the only thing which could cure his feet and give him the strength to tackle the last twenty-five miles to Sweden.

But Marius, back in Furuflaten, was not so optimistic. He felt troubled in his mind at having left Jan all alone: he would much rather have hidden him somewhere where he could have kept an eye on him day and night. But he consoled himself by thinking that he had done it more for his family's sake than for his own, and also that it was in Jan's own interest to be in a place which the Germans were very unlikely to search. He believed, just as Jan did, that in time he would get fit again, but he thought it might be a very long time; and he knew, although Jan did not, how difficult it was going to be to keep him supplied with even the barest necessities of life across at Revdal. He would never have grudged him anything, neither time nor danger, nor money while his savings lasted out; but he was very much afraid that keeping things secret, which was so difficult already, would become impossible if it had to go on very long. If people noticed him going off two or three nights a week in a boat towards the uninhabited side of the fjord, there was no credible explanation he could give; and besides, there was always the chance that the Germans might yet make some sudden swoop which would prevent him from crossing at all. They might come and arrest him, and in case they did, he would have to find somebody who could not be connected with the affair but who could take over his responsibilities when he was gone. Otherwise, Jan would be left there till he starved. What it came to, in fact, was that there might be a crisis at any time; and therefore there ought to be a plan to get Jan over the frontier if the crisis came before he could go on his own feet.

Marius went to Herr Legland again, and they had a long discussion. They agreed that apart from being safer in Revdal, Jan was better placed there for an attempt on the frontier. If he had tried to go straight from Furuflaten, there would have been valleys to cross, and the main road; but from Revdal one only had to climb straight up for 3000 feet and one was right on the plateau. Once one was up there, there was no road or habitation whatever before the frontier, and the skiing was straightforward. But if Jan needed help on the journey, it would have to come from one of the settlements on the other side of the fjord.

Marius may have felt disappointed at the idea that he might have to hand Jan over to somebody else, but he had to agree that if it came to a dash for the frontier, he could not be of any help. For one thing, he had never been up on the plateau; and besides, there was no knowing how long the journey might take. It would certainly not be less than four days, and if he was away from home for as long as that, everybody would know it. But on the other hand, there was at least one settlement on the other side where there was no German garrison at all. The men from there would know the plateau, or at least the part of it near at hand, and it would be much easier for them to disappear for a few days.

When Marius had reluctantly agreed with this conclusion, Herr Legland undertook to send a warning to people he knew on the other side that an escort might be needed for the frontier. He meant to arrange a meeting place and a code-word for the operation in case it had to be undertaken in a hurry.

The name of the settlement they had in mind is Mandal. It lies in a deep valley which penetrates for twenty miles into the plateau, and it has a population of six or seven hundred. It is much more cut off from the world than Lyngseidet or Furuflaten. There is no road to it, and not a single pass through the mountains to give access to it by land. It can only be reached by climbs which are always dangerous in winter, or else by a sea voyage of ten miles from Lyngseidet. But even there the organisation had its contacts.

As soon as they began to think about Mandal, it brought them up against a problem which had already been causing both of them some worry, the problem of money. If Mandal had to come into it, the whole business of rescuing Jan was going to cost more than Herr Legland or Marius could possibly find out of their own pockets or their neighbours'. One is apt to forget that this sort of activity needs money, but it does: or at least, it did in north Norway. People like Marius were glad to stretch their own rations to feed Jan, and to sleep with a blanket less on their own beds, and to give him their clothes; but sooner or later he was sure to need something which neither of them possessed themselves. Then there would be only one option: either to go to somebody who could supply it, and let him into the secret so that he would give it for nothing, or else to buy it. The things Jan was most likely to need, the simple necessities of life, were rationed, and a lot of things he might possibly need could not be bought at all except at black market prices; and of course a man who was willing to sell on the black market was the last sort of person one would want to know about Jan. The only safe way to get what was needed would be to pay the price which was asked, however high it was, and not tell anybody. Jan had already had the last of all the brandy and cigarettes that Marius could lay his hands on, and he needed more; or to be accurate, he needed brandy, to keep him going in the cold, and cigarettes were the only luxury he could enjoy. If Mandal came into it too, there was going to be the question of diesel oil for boats. There was a telephone in Mandal, but all telephones were tapped. The only way to tell the Mandal men what was happening would be to get a motor-boat and go there, and if the owner of the boat could not give a proper reason for the journey, the fuel would have to come from the black market too.

There was also the question of paying people for the time they spent on a job of this kind. Marius was his own master and could afford to take time off to look after Jan, and so could the other Furuflaten people. But a lot of men around there, especially in a place like Mandal, lived from hand to mouth, and if they lost a few days' work it really meant less to eat for their wives and children. That might not prevent them from helping, but the organisation's principle was that nobody ought to suffer real financial hardship for anything he was asked to do. The state paid its soldiers, and the organisation expected to do the same. Certainly if anyone had to be asked to take Jan across to Sweden, he would have to have his income made up for the days he was away. One way and another, the whole operation might cost much more than the resources of Lyngseidet and Furuflaten could afford.

Luckily, Herr Legland had to go into Tromsö, and he promised Marius he would take care of this question of finance. Thus for the second time news reached the city of what was happening in Lyngenfjord. Legland went to Sverre Larsen, whose father, the dismissed owner of the newspaper, was an old friend of his. He arrived on a Saturday evening, and told Larsen the whole story from beginning to end, except that he left out all the names of people and places. He had reckoned that he must have a fund of £150 for urgent expenses which he could already foresee. Without it, or the certainty of being able to get it quickly, he would not feel he could ask anyone to go to the frontier.

Larsen accepted the request without any question. It was the kind of thing which the Tromsö merchants expected to pay for. But it was a stern test of his organisation to find the money in cash on a Saturday night. If Legland had come at a time when the banks and offices were open, it would only have taken a few minutes. As it was, Larsen himself put in all the money which he happened to have in the house, and then went the rounds of his friends in the organisation. By Sunday morning he had collected it all, in varying sums from a lot of different people, and Herr Legland took it home, with his money worries set at rest for the time being. But as things turned out, this was only the very beginning of the expense of saving Jan's life. Before the end, it cost £1650 in cash, besides the labour and goods which were given freely by hundreds of people; and the whole of this sum was contributed by business houses and individuals in Tromsö who regarded him as a symbol of the battle against the Germans.

Marius kept his promise to go back and visit Jan. Two nights after he had left him at Revdal, he set off again and rowed across the fjord, taking a new stock of food and some bottles of milk. Jan was still in the bunk, exactly as he had left him. He was cheerful, and the rest was doing him good. He had been amusing himself by pulling out the moss which had been used to caulk the joints between the logs of the wall of the hut, and rolling it in newspaper to make cigarettes. Marius swore that before next time he would find something better to smoke than that. Meanwhile, he cooked up some fish for him, and when he had eaten it they both had a look at his feet. They seemed to be getting on all right, and they talked things over in the hope that Jan would be able to put on skis again before very long.

They had already agreed that Jan ought not to know anything about the organisation. Although his prospects looked a little brighter than they had a week before, both he and Marius knew in their heart of hearts that so long as he could not walk his chance of avoiding being captured in the end was really very small. So Marius still called himself Hans Jensen, and Jan did not know any names at all for the other people he had seen, or anything about the activities in Lyngseidet or Tromsö. He had to be content not to know who was helping him, but just to be grateful for the help when it arrived.

However, Marius did tell him that night, in order to keep his spirits up, that people in Mandal were being asked to stand by in case their help was needed; and he explained the geography of the surrounding mountains and the plateau, so that Jan would have it clear in his head if they had to take sudden action. It is not very far across the mountains from the hut at Revdal into the valley of Mandal: only about five miles on the map, though it involves the climb of 3000 feet up to the plateau level and down again. If Jan needed help when the time came, Marius meant to come to Revdal and lead him up the climb; and he would arrange for the Mandal men to come up from the other side and meet them on top, so that they could take over there and escort Jan southwards across the plateau till he came to the frontier.

It was encouraging for Jan to know that some positive plans had been made to get him away, and Marius left him that night in good humour, and quite contentedly resigned to another two days of solitude and darkness.

It was soon after Marius left, not more than a few hours, that Jan's feet began to hurt. It was nothing much at first, only a slight increase in the pain which had been going on ever since they were thawed. It came and went, and sometimes, that early morning, he thought it was imagination. But by the time when sunlight began to come through the holes in the roof, he was sure that something was happening. He struggled out of his blankets, when it was as light as it ever got in the hut, and unwrapped his feet. The sight of them alarmed him. They had changed visibly since the night before when Marius was with him. Now, his toes seemed to be grey, and although his feet as a whole were more painful than they had been, the ends of his toes were numb and cold, as if he had pins and needles. He rubbed them, but it only made them hurt more, and the skin began to peel off them. The toe which had been wounded had begun to heal, but the scar had a dark unhealthy look.

He rolled himself up again in the blankets and lay there uneasily, wondering what it meant. He did not know what had gone wrong, or what he ought to do to try to stop it. For the first time since he had met Marius, he began to feel lonely. It had seemed so easy to say he would wait for another two days alone, but now he regretted it. He wanted very much to have someone to talk to about his feet. He knew that the thirty-six hours he still had to wait before he could hope to see Marius were going to pass very slowly.

They turned out to be infinitely worse than he expected. The pain grew with appalling quickness, hour by hour. It grew so that sleep became out of the question and he could only lie there staring into the darkness and counting every minute till Marius might arrive, moving his legs in hopeless attempts to find a position which would ease them. The pain spread up his legs in waves, and sometimes seemed to fill his whole body like a flame so that when it receded it left him sweating and trembling and breathless.

In the second dawn, when the light was strong enough, he unwrapped his feet again. After the night he had just survived, what he saw then did not surprise him. His toes were black and swollen, and a foul-smelling fluid was oozing out of them, and he could not move them at all any more.

He was shocked and bewildered, with nobody to appeal to for advice or comfort. When the pain was at its worst, he could hardly think at all. When it eased, he lay there, wondering what Marius would do: whether he would take him back to Furuflaten, or whether there was any doctor who would take the risk of coming to Revdal. He wondered whether there was anything that even a doctor could do, without taking him to hospital. He thought he had either got blood poisoning or gangrene. Either of them, he imagined, would spread farther and farther up his legs. If he had been in hospital, he thought, they would have given him injections and stopped it before it got too far; but there in Revdal, without any kind of medical equipment, he could not think of anything to do. He wondered whether he ought to agree to go to hospital if he got the chance, and soon made up his mind that he should not. In hospital, the Germans would certainly get him in the end, and

all kinds of people might get themselves into trouble on his behalf. He knew it might be tempting to agree if the pain went
on, so he took a firm and final decision there and then, in case
he was not in a fit condition to decide when the moment came;
he would not go to hospital whatever happened. He tried to
think of the worst that could possibly happen, so that this resolve would never weaken, and after all, the worst was only
death. He put all his faith in Marius. Marius would know what
to do: he would either take him to a doctor or bring a doctor
to Revdal; or if he could not do either of those things, he
would get advice and borrow medicine and come and doctor
him himself. This thought kept him going all through the
second day.

At long last the evening came. The little shafts of light inside the hut began to fade, and the darkness he had longed for
all day set in. Marius could not begin to row across till it was
dark, so that an hour and a half of night must pass before he
could be expected. But long before that, Jan lay and listened
for the footsteps outside the door, and the cheerful greetings
which Marius always gave him before he came in, so that he
would know it was a friend who was coming. The minutes of
the night dragged on and on till the first light of the dawn, and
Marius did not come.

A period of time began then which Jan remembered, after
it ended, with the utmost horror. It was the first time that he
sank into absolute despair of coming through alive, and he
had not really resigned himself yet to dying; at least, not to
dying the lingering, lonely agonising death which seemed to
be all he could expect. At first, he waited for each night with
the hope of hearing Marius; but as each night passed and
nothing happened the hope slowly died within him. After five
days, he could only believe that Marius and everyone who

knew he was there had been arrested and shot, and that he was quite forgotten by the world, condemned to lie in the desolate hut till the poisoning killed him, or till he wasted away through starvation. Revdal, which they had chosen because it seemed safe, had turned into a trap. He was walled in by the barren mountain which hung over him, and by the sea and the miles of lonely shore on either side. He could not believe any more that he would ever get up and go across to the door and open it and go out into the fresh air to start on his journey again. He knew his own feet would never carry him to the nearest friendly house, and he knew that so much of his strength had ebbed away that he would never be able to swim or even to crawl there.

In his loneliness, he wished he was able to pray, and lying there waiting to die he tried to set his religious beliefs in order. But like so many young men of his generation, he had grown up without the habit of saying prayers. It was not any fault of his. He had been given a technical, scientific education, and there had not been much room in it for religion. It had given him, at the age of twenty-six, a materialistic view of life. He had done his best to live in accordance with Christian ethics, but nothing he had ever been taught could help him to believe in a personal God who watched over him in Revdal. He did not despise that kind of belief, and he knew to the full what a comfort it would be to him; but nobody of a clear and serious turn of mind can change his beliefs to suit his circumstances. After living without prayers, he thought that to pray when he was in such desperate straits would be hypocritical, and an offence to any God he could believe in. Neither did he believe at that time in a future life. He believed he was already forgotten or assumed to be dead by everyone who knew him, except his father and brother and sister, and that when the last painful tenuous thread was broken he would not exist any more, except as a rotten corpse in the bunk where he was lying.

So day followed day, each merged into another by the mists of pain. On one day, he was aware of the sound of wind, and of snow sifting through the holes in the walls and beneath the door. On another, when he put out his hand to feel for the food on the table, he found it was all gone. On all of them, when he fell into a doze, even after the last of all reasonable hope had gone, he dreamed or imagined that he could hear Marius outside the door, and he started awake with a clutch at his heart. But nobody came.

CHAPTER TEN

AFTER THE STORM

IN FACT, there was nothing wrong with Marius. The Germans had not made any new move, and everything was quiet in Furuflaten. What had stopped him coming to see Jan was simply another storm. Just after his previous visit, it had started to blow up from the south, and before the night when he had meant to cross the fjord again there was such a sea running that the crossing was quite impossible.

While Jan was lying groaning in the hut on the eastern side, Marius was fretting impatiently on the west, and between them four miles of furious sea made an impassable barrier. Nobody could get to Revdal. Every day, Marius watched the grey scudding water which was streaked with spindrift, and every evening at dusk he went down to the beach at Furuflaten to make sure that there was really no chance of going; but it was hopeless even to try to launch a boat. At night he lay and listened for any easing of the shrieks of wind.

But he was not really worried. There was no reason why he should be. When he had left Jan, his health had been improving. He had not been able to leave as much food as he would have liked, but he reckoned that if Jan could spin it out, there was enough to keep him from starving for some time yet. He knew Jan would be disappointed and would be wondering what had happened, but he was sure that he would guess it was the storm. He did not realise that inside the log walls of the hut, with the snow banked up all round them, Jan could not hear the howling of the wind. Also, he still thought Jan was some kind of seaman and would imagine for himself the fearsome effect of a southerly gale in those narrow waters with a clear fetch of twenty miles to windward.

So although Marius was naturally upset by the feeling that he was letting Jan down, he had no immediate anxiety, and what worried him most during the storm was the increasing menace of the daylight. So far as his own help was still concerned, the rescue of Jan was becoming a race against the midnight sun. It was the beginning of the last week in April, and already it was twilight all night. While the storm lasted, the nights were dark enough, but when the sky cleared there would not be more than a couple of hours in which he could sneak away from the Furuflaten beach without being seen by the sentry; and if he left the beach at the time when the twilight was deepest, he would have to run the risk of landing again in broad daylight. In a fortnight's time it would be so light all night that anyone with binoculars would be able to watch him the whole way across the fjord, and if the German motor-boat was still patrolling it would be able to pick him up from miles away. Before then, whatever happened, Jan would have to move on from Revdal.

It was exactly a week after Marius's second visit to the hut when the storm began to show signs of ending. During that day, when he and his family could see that the evening might bring a chance of crossing, he collected everything he had to offer Jan and packed it in his rucksack: food, and paraffin, and bottles of milk, and a few cigarettes. At nightfall he put on his skis and went down to the beach again. Two of his friends were there to meet him. There was still some sea running, but not enough to make the passage dangerous; when the wind drops in that landlocked water, the sea calms very quickly. They quietly launched the boat, and began to row away. During the storm, nothing had been seen of the motor-boat, but that made it seem all the more likely that it would be out on patrol again that night.

However, the crossing was peaceful. Marius himself was happy because he had some good news to bring to Jan. He had just heard that Herr Legland had sent a message to the schoolmaster in Mandal, and that a favourable answer had come back. There had evidently been some kind of a meeting in Mandal, and there had been plenty of volunteers who would stand by to come up to a rendezvous on top of the range between Mandal and Revdal where they would take delivery of Jan. Mandal was willing to take over the responsibility of looking after him, and the schoolmaster thought they would be able to escort him to the frontier. Marius imagined, in that brief moment of optimism while he crossed the fjord, that Jan might be in Sweden before a week had passed.

The shock when he got to Revdal was all the worse. Before he opened the door of the hut, he called "Hullo there!" But there was no answer. He went in. It was pitch dark inside, and it stank of decay. In alarm, he called Jan by his name, and stooped over the bunk as the thought flashed through his mind that the Germans had been there and taken Jan away. But he felt the bundle of blankets and then, to his relief, he heard a faint sound as Jan turned his head.

"What's the matter?" he said. "What's happened?"

"There's the hell of a pain," Jan said.

Marius hastily shut the door and lit a lantern. The sight which he saw appalled him. Jan's face was as white as the face of a corpse beneath the dirt and the straggling beard. He slowly and wearily opened his eyes when the light fell on them, and made a feeble movement. The blankets round his legs were dark with blood.

Jan was too far gone to be pleased that Marius had arrived. It had happened to him so often before in dreams. For a few moments he was even unwilling to be dragged up out of his coma and forced to make the effort to live again. But when Marius boiled some water and made him take a hot drink he revived a little. He said that he had not had anything to eat or drink for several days. This puzzled Marius, who thought he had left enough; but the fact was that three or four days before, what was left of the food had fallen off the table, and Jan had been too bemused to realise what had happened. Since then, he had lain there growing weak with hunger, while bread and dried fish were lying on the floor beside him, just out of his sight below the bunk board.

When Jan had come to himself enough to be able to talk coherently, Marius set himself to the unpleasant job of looking at his feet. Even before he saw them, he knew that it was gangrene. It was perfectly obvious that although Jan was alive, the toes of both of his feet had been dead for some time. Most of the blood on the blankets had come from cuts which Jan had made himself. Some days before, while he still had the strength to do it, he had started to operate on his feet with his pocket-knife. In the belief that it might be blood poisoning, he had reasoned that the only thing he could do was to draw off the blood, as people used to do with snake bites; and so he had pulled up his legs in the bunk, one by one, and stabbed his feet with the knife and let them bleed.

Marius washed them as best he could and bound them up again. Both he and Jan knew, without having to say it, that Jan would never walk or ski to Sweden. Marius privately thought there was nothing to be done except to amputate both feet. He did not say so to Jan, for fear of depressing him; but Jan had also come to the same conclusion.

Marius could not stay long that night because of the daylight, but before he left he promised Jan that he would either get a doctor, or else arrange somehow for him to be carried to Sweden, and that in any case he would come back in two or three days. Then he left him again to his solitude. But now that Jan knew that he still had active friends who were trying to help him, he felt he could face another few days in that abominable hut with equanimity. The mere sight of Marius had brought back his will to live. During the days that followed, between the bouts of pain, he began to come to terms with the idea of living as a cripple. At first he dwelt morbidly on all the active pursuits which he would lose, but by and by he began to look forward to the simple pleasures he would still be able to enjoy. The height of his ambition at that time was to get back to London and go into Kensington Gardens in a wheel-chair on a sunny day and watch the children playing.

Marius, rowing back across the fjord in the light of dawn, knew he had just made promises to Jan without any idea of how he could fulfil them; but he had great faith in the idea that if you are ready to give up everything to the solution of any problem, you will always find an answer. He did not know of any doctor who he was sure would risk his life to go to Revdal, and he did not really believe that a doctor could do much without taking Jan to hospital, which Jan had refused to hear of. Still less did he know, at that moment, how Jan could be carried bodily across the mountains to the frontier. But one or other of these alternatives had got to be arranged, not only because he had promised it, but also because without either of them, Jan was obviously going to die.

As soon as he got home, he told all his friends in the organi-

sation about the new and apparently insuperable difficulty
that Jan was absolutely helpless. Herr Legland and the three
Furuflaten men who had carried Jan over to Revdal all discussed it with him. Bit by bit they pieced together a not impossible plan. Messengers were sent to Tromsö and to Mandal and to a valley called Kaafjord even farther east. The news
of the problem spread far and wide, whispered from one to
another of the trusted people who might have help to offer.
The dormant patriotic club went into action, inspired at last
by a situation which was going to test its efficiency to the utmost. During the following evening, the messengers began to
return, one by one, bringing criticisms and new suggestions
and new offers of help back to the main conspirators. The plan
took shape.

The man who had been to Tromsö brought back a message
from Sverre Larsen simply promising financial support, without any qualifications. The one who had been to Mandal had
a more complicated message, but it was almost equally welcome. A party of four of the Mandal men was ready to make
the climb to the plateau at any moment and to take the responsibility of keeping Jan alive. If Marius and the Furuflaten men
could get Jan up there and bring a sledge, they were also
willing to try to haul it to the frontier. But this they regarded
as a last resort. None of them had ever tried to haul a sledge
across the plateau. It might take a long time, and if the weather
broke again it might end in disaster. Furthermore, none of
them knew the Swedish side of the mountains, and they had to
point out that although the frontier was only twenty-five miles
away, a man who did not know the country might easily have
to go another hundred miles down into the forests towards the
Baltic before he found any human habitation. If that happened, the journey would take so long that their absence could

not possibly pass unnoticed, and that would mean that none of them could come back. They would have to go into exile, and this they were most unwilling to do because all of them had dependents. But they had a better proposal: to get the Lapps to make the journey.

The advantage of getting Lapps to go, rather than Norwegians, was obvious at once to Marius and Herr Legland, as it would be to anyone who knew the Lapps and the country. The only surprising thing was that anyone in Kaafjord or Mandal should know any Lapps well enough to have any hope of persuading them to make the journey. The Lapps are very peculiar people at any time, a small primitive race entirely distinct from anyone else in Europe; and during the war they were more peculiar than usual. The kind of Lapps they had in mind are nomads who live by breeding reindeer, and since the beginning of history they have made the same migrations with their reindeer every year. The same families of Lapps come every spring with their herds to Kaafjord and Lyngseidet, always arriving within a day or two of the fifth of May. They spend the summer there, in Norway, and the winter in Finland or Sweden. National frontiers mean nothing to them, because they have been making their journeys since long before the frontiers existed. To stop them would mean that their race would die out, because the reindeer cannot survive without a seasonal change of feeding-ground, and the Lapps cannot survive without their reindeer. Probably the Germans would have liked to stop them, if only for the sake of tidiness, but they wisely never tried; and all through the World War the Lapps wandered unconcerned between Finland, which was fighting on the side of Germany, and Norway, which was fighting as best it could on the Allied side, and Sweden, which was neutral.

One result of this unique situation was that the Lapps themselves naturally had no interest in the war at all. Probably none
of them had any idea of what it was all about. It was no good
appealing to them on any grounds of patriotism or ideology.
They were no more attached to one of the three countries than
another, and they would never have heard of politics. Neither
would the humanitarian grounds for helping Jan have meant
very much to them, because they do not set a high value on
human life. If a Lapp lost the use of his feet, like Jan, he would
know he was useless and expect his family to leave him alone
to die.

All the same, if any Lapps could be persuaded to take Jan
to the frontier, they were much more likely to succeed than any
Norwegian party could possibly be. For one thing, nobody
could check their movements; there was no limit to the time
they could be away. Also, although they knew nothing about
compasses or maps, they knew that uncharted country far better than anyone else. They were able to survive even the worst
of winter weather in the open; and finally, they had reindeer
trained to draw sledges, and could cover much more ground
in a day than a party of men drawing a sledge themselves.
Therefore Marius, Herr Legland and the rest of the conspirators welcomed this suggestion. The first wave of the migration
of reindeer was due to arrive within a week. They would already be somewhere on their way across the mountains. The
message from Mandal had said that the best ski-runner in
Kaafjord was ready to set off, along the migration tracks
towards the Lapp settlement of Kautokeino, a hundred miles
away, to try to locate the herds. A message was sent back, wel-
coming the idea and asking him to go at once.

Meanwhile, the main problem for Marius and the Furuflaten men was to get Jan up to the plateau. The place for

meeting the party from Mandal had already been agreed. It was in a shallow depression on the plateau, half-way between Revdal and Mandal. To get there from the Revdal side was a steep climb for the first two thousand feet, and then a more gentle upward slope across about three miles of the open snow-field. The meeting place itself was at a height of about 2700 feet. Something of the nature of a stretcher which could be carried would be needed to get him up the first part of the climb, and a sledge would be easiest for the last part. They decided to try to combine both functions by building the lightest possible sledge.

All these discussions and the coming and going of messengers had been happening in the midst of the German garrison areas in Furuflaten and Lyngseidet. For building the sledge, the plot was carried even farther into the German camp. The best joiner anyone could think of was the caretaker of Herr Legland's school. The school buildings had been requisitioned and the pupils turned out to make room for the German district headquarters staff, but the caretaker still worked there and still had access to what had been the school workshop. He undertook to build the sledge; and he did so, inside the German headquarters itself. The impertinence of this filled everyone who knew of it with a kind of schoolboyish glee; and the only disadvantage of such an attractive arrangement was that the joiner could not take the risk of putting the sledge together, because the Germans who came in and out while he was working would have been certain to ask what it was for. However, he made each piece to careful measurements, and was willing to guarantee that when the time came to assemble it, everything would fit. It was built on a pair of ordinary skis, and it had a slatted platform about a foot high, eighteen inches wide and six feet long. Events proved that his workmanship was good. The sledge not only fitted together, but stood up to week after week of the hardest possible treatment.

It was ready on the third day after Marius had last been to Revdal, and all the plans were completed on that day too, except that the ski-runner from Kaafjord had not come back from his search for the reindeer. Marius's three neighbours, Alvin Larsen, Olaf Lanes and Amandus Lillevoll, were prepared to go over with him to Revdal that night to make the attempt to haul Jan up the mountain. Herr Legland telephoned to the schoolmaster in Mandal to say in cautiously chosen words, in case the line was tapped, that the parcel he was expecting was being sent at once. Alvin Larsen was going that afternoon to fetch the sledge from Lyngseidet; but that very morning an avalanche blocked the road between Lyngseidet and Furuflaten.

Luckily, the avalanche did not delay him much, and on the whole it was probably an advantage to their plans. It was also the indirect cause of an incident which appealed to what might be called the occupation sense of humour. The local people had been expecting it to happen. The road just north of Furuflaten runs along the shore of the fjord below a cliff a thousand feet high, the same cliff which Jan had been trying to skirt when he got lost in the mountains; and the snow from the gullies in the cliff always falls and blocks the road about the last week in April. It happens with such regularity that a jetty has been built at Furuflaten for a car ferry which provides a way through for traffic till the danger is past in May. Alvin Larsen had already arranged to go to Lyngseidet by boat if the avalanche started before the sledge was ready; but the Germans were not so well prepared for it, and the sudden blocking of the main road diverted their attention at that crucial moment from everything else that was happening.

Alvin got to Lyngseidet without any trouble, and tied up his boat at the pier. There was a German sentry on the pier who took no notice of him at all. He went up to the school and collected the bits of the sledge from the caretaker, together with a bag of bolts and screws, and minute instructions for putting it all together. The bundles of pieces of wood tied together with string and the pair of skis looked reasonably harmless. He carried them down through the village to the pier. But when he got there the tide was very low, and his boat was a long way down. He was afraid to throw the wood down into the boat in case it broke, and if he got down into the boat he could not reach up again to the level of the pier. So he called to the sentry to give him a hand. The sentry came over, and put down his rifle, and kindly handed the skis and the bundles down to Alvin one by one. Alvin thanked him gravely in Norwegian, and started his engine and steamed away.

CHAPTER ELEVEN

THE ASCENT OF REVDAL

THAT EVENING, the sailing-boat which Marius used crossed over the fjord again, laden with the gear for the attempt to climb the mountain: the sledge, still in pieces, a sixty-foot rope, an old canvas sleeping-bag and two fresh blankets for Jan, two rucksacks full of spare clothing and food and a bottle of brandy, and the four pairs of skis of the men who were making the attempt.

The ascent of Revdal was the first of two feats of mountaineering during Jan's rescue which are possibly unique. It often happens after climbing accidents in peace time that an injured man has to be carried or lowered a long way down a mountain; but there must rarely, if ever, have been any occasion before or since to carry an injured man up a mountain for three thousand feet in severe conditions of ice and snow. At the time, spurred on by the knowledge that Jan's life depended on it, the four men who attempted it never dreamed of failure; but ever afterwards, when they looked up in cold blood at the mountain wall of Revdal, they wondered how they could possibly have done it.

When they got to the far shore of the fjord that evening, they walked up to the hut in some anxiety at what they would find inside, afraid of the effect which another three days of isolation might have had on Jan. But they found him more cheerful than he had been the time before. Physically, he was weaker, and those of the party who had not seen him since they had left him there twelve days earlier were shocked at the change in his appearance, for he had lost a lot of weight and his eyes and cheeks were sunken. But he was much clearer in his head than he had been when Marius saw him, and he had even regained the vestige of a sense of humour. He told them his feet were no worse. The toes, of course, could not get any worse, but the gangrene had not spread any farther, so far as he could tell. He said it was still just as painful; but they could see from his behaviour that he could stand up to the pain now that he knew he was not abandoned. All in all, he was a patient whom no hospital staff would have allowed out of bed for a moment, and looking down at him lying there in his filth, all four men wondered whether it could be right to take him out into the snow and subject him to the treatment they intended. All of them thought it would very likely kill him. But they knew for certain that it was his only chance.

While two of them put the sledge together, the others wrapped him securely in two blankets, and then pushed and pulled him into the sleeping-bag. When the sledge was ready, they lifted him out of the bunk where he had lain for nearly a fortnight, and put him on the sledge and lashed him securely down with ropes, so that not much more than his eyes was showing and he could not move at all. They manœuvred the sledge through the door and put it down in the snow outside. While they adjusted their individual loads of skis and ski-sticks, and ropes and rucksacks, Jan had a moment to glance for the last time, without any regret, at the hovel where he had expected to die. Then they took up the short hauling ropes they had tied to the sledge, and turned it towards the mountain. It was a little after midnight; but there was still the afterglow of the sun in the northern sky above the mouth of the fjord, and even beneath the mountain wall it was not very dark. There were roughly fifteen degrees of frost.

The first part of the climb straight up from the hut at Revdal is covered by the forest of birch scrub. It is not steep enough to be called more than a scramble in mountaineering terms, but in deep snow it is the most frustrating kind of scramble, even for a climber not carrying any burden. None of the miniature trees have trunks much thicker than an arm, but they have been growing and dying there unattended since primeval times, and the ground beneath them is covered with a thick matted tangle of rotten fallen logs which gives no foothold. The trees grow very close together, and they are interlaced with half-fallen branches bowed down or broken by the weight of snow. Some trees have died and are still standing, propped up by the others crowded round them, and these break and crumble away if someone incautiously uses them for a hand-hold. When the deep springy mesh of fallen trees, lying piled on one another, is hidden by a smooth deceptive covering of snow, the forest is a place where a climber must go with care. It would be impossible to fall for more than a foot or two, but it would be very easy to break a leg in falling.

Getting Jan up through the forest was mostly a matter of brute strength and endless patience; but strength and patience, of course, were two of the qualities Marius had thought about when he chose his three companions. Alvin Larsen was slight and thin, and only about twenty-one years old, but he had just come back from the tough school of the Lofoten fishing and was in perfect training. Amandus Lillevoll was a little older, a small wiry man with a great reserve of strength, and an exceptional skier. Olaf Lanes was the only big man of them all. He had shoulders like an ox, and he hardly ever spoke unless he had to: the epitome of the strong silent man. As for patience, all four of them had the unending dogged patience which is typical of Arctic people.

Within the steep forest, they quickly discovered the technique which served them best. Two of them would hold the sledge, belayed to a tree to stop it from running backwards, while the others climbed on ahead with the rope, forcing their way through the frozen undergrowth. When the upper pair found a possible stance, they took a turn of the rope round a tree and hauled the sledge up towards them, the lower pair steering it, stopping it when it threatened to turn over, pushing as best they could, and lifting it bodily when it buried itself in drifts. Their progress was very slow. There was seldom a clear enough space to haul the sledge more than about a dozen feet at a time, and each change of stance meant a new belay and a new coiling and uncoiling of the icy rope. The leaders, treading a trail through the virgin snow, often fell through into holes in the rotten wood beneath, and it was difficult to climb out of these hidden traps. Before they had gained more than a few hundred feet, they began to be afraid that they had started something which it would be impossible to finish; not so much because they thought their own stubbornness and strength would be unequal to the job, but because they were more and more afraid that Jan would not survive it. It was going to be a long time before they got to the top; and they had found a new problem which had no answer, and which nobody had foreseen: the simple problem of whether to haul him feet first or head first. When they took him feet first, of course his head was always much lower than his feet, and sometimes in the steep drifts he was hanging almost vertically head downwards. He could not stand this for very long, certainly not for hour after hour; but when they turned him round and took him up head first, the blood ran into his feet and burst out in new hæmorrhages, and his face showed them the pain he was trying to suffer in silence. But as the climb went on, he was more and more often unconscious when they looked at him. This was a mercy, but it made them all the more sure he would not last very long. This urgency, together with the blind faith which he seemed to have in them, made them press on with the strength of desperation. Every few feet of the forest brought them up against a new obstacle which had to be surmounted. They struggled with each one till they overcame it, and then turned to the next without daring to pause, hoping that Jan would last till they got to the top, and that then the Mandal men would be able to whisk him straight over to Sweden.

When they cleared the forest at last, at a height of about a thousand feet, they had to rest. They slewed the sledge round broadside to the hill and dug in one runner so that it stood level, and collapsed in the snow beside it. Jan was awake, and they gave him a nip of brandy, and sucked some ice themselves, and looked down at the way they had come. The climb had already taken nearly three hours, and it was day. The dawn light shone on the peaks above Furuflaten across the water, and Jaeggevarre glowed above them all on the western skyline. The fjord below was still, and there was no sign of life on it. In the shadow of the hill, the air was very cold.

Immediately above the treeline was a sheer face of rock, but to their right it was broken by a steep cleft with the frozen bed of a stream in the bottom of it. Each time they had crossed the fjord they had gazed up at the face as they approached it, and the cleft had seemed the most likely route to the summit. From closer at hand, it still looked possible. To get to the bottom of it they would have to traverse a steep snow slope about two hundred feet high and perhaps a hundred yards across. The slope was clear and smooth at the top, where they would have to cross it, but at the bottom it vanished in the forest. It had a firm crust on it, and there seemed to be no particular danger about it. When they had got their breath they gathered themselves together to attempt it.

This was the first time they had tried to traverse with the sledge; and crossing the slope turned out to be like a nightmare, like walking a tightrope in a dream. Three of them stood below the sledge and one above it. To keep it level and stop it rolling sideways down the hill, the three men below it had to carry the outer runner, letting the inner one slide in the snow. Very slowly they edged out across the slope, kicking steps and moving one man at a time till the whole slope yawned dizzily below them. It was impossible then to stop or go back. The sledge, resting on a single ski, moved all too easily. While they could keep it perfectly level, all was well, but they could feel that if they let it tilt the least bit either way, either down by the head or down by the foot, it would take charge and break away from them, and then in a split second the whole thing would be over. Kicking steps in a snow slope always demands a fair degree of balance because there is nothing whatever to hold on to. It is impossible to resist a sudden unexpected force. If the sledge had begun to slide they could have saved themselves by falling on their faces and digging their hands and toes into the snow; but they could not have stopped the sledge, and when it crashed into the trees two hundred feet below it would have been travelling at a speed which it was horrifying to imagine. Perhaps it was just as well that Jan, lying on it on his back and lashed immovably in position, could only look up at the sky and the rock face above him, and not at the chasm down below. Before they reached the other side of that slope, the men were sweating and trembling with the effort and tension. At the foot of the cleft, where the gradient eased, they stopped again thankfully and anchored the sledge with ski-sticks driven into the snow, so that they could relax till their strength came back. From there, Jan could see the cleft soaring above them.

When they looked up at it, it seemed to be steeper than they had expected. The walls of it were sheer, and it was about thirty feet wide. The snow in the bed of it showed all the signs of being about to avalanche; but it was safe enough on that western slope just after dawn. The cleft curved gently to the left, so that from the bottom they could not see very far up it; but having seen it from the fjord they knew it had no pitch in it too steep for the snow to lie on, and that it led almost all the way to the easier slopes on the upper half of the mountain. It was certainly going to be difficult and it might be impossible, but now that they had come so far there was no alternative.

After a very short rest, two of them began to lead out the sixty-foot rope. They went up side by side, kicking two parallel sets of steps for the second pair to use. Within the cleft, they were able to use the full length of the rope for the first time, and the leaders did not pause till the whole of it was stretched up the snow above the sledge. Then they dug themselves as deep a stance as they could and braced themselves in it and took the strain of the weight of the sledge while the others down below them freed it from its anchors. So the first pitch of a long and heavy haul began.

In some ways, going straight up the slope was not so hard as trying to go across it. The balance of the sledge was not important: it hung at the end of the rope like a pendulum. But the physical effort was greater and more sustained. At each stance the two leaders hauled the sledge up towards them while the two men below followed it up the steps, pushing as best they could. At the end of each sixty feet it was anchored afresh; but the ski-sticks could not be trusted to hold it alone, and even the effort of holding it was so exhausting that they could not afford to pause.

Beyond the bend, the cleft swept smoothly up to a skyline appallingly far above, and there was nothing in it which offered a chance of a rest: no boulder or chockstone, and no break in the vertical walls on either side.

Somewhere in the upper reaches of the cleft, Jan came as near a sudden death as he had been anywhere on his journey. All four of the climbers by then were in that extremely unpleasant dilemma which is experienced sooner or later by every mountaineer, when one knows one has outreached one's strength, and it is too late to go down by the way one has come, so that one must either win through to the top, or fall. It was at this stage, when they knew they could never manage to lower the sledge to the bottom, that what they had dreaded happened. Somebody slipped, somebody else was off balance: in a fraction of a second the sledge shot backwards. But Amandus happened to be below it. It hit him hard in the chest and ran over him, and somehow he and the sledge became entangled together and his body acted as a brake and stopped it, and within the second the others had it under control again. The climb went on, and Jan did not know what had happened because he was unconscious. For the rest of the climb and long afterwards Amandus suffered from pain in his chest, and in retrospect it seems likely that some of his ribs were broken.

They got to the skyline; but it was not the top. The cleft ended, and ahead of them they saw a frozen waterfall. The ice hung down it in smooth translucent curtains. There was no hope whatever of hauling the sledge up there. But at the bottom of it, more welcome than anything else in the world could have been, there was a boulder projecting through the snow, and with a final effort they heaved the sledge on top of it and wedged it there, and were able at last to rest.

They sat down in a group round the sledge, and looked up at the next pitch. It seemed as if it might be the last difficulty, but it looked the worst of all. The boulder was in the middle of a little *cirque* or bowl of rock and ice which enclosed it all round, except for the narrow gap where their own tracks plunged down out of sight into the cleft. This gap framed a distant view of the fjord waters, now gleaming far below, and the sunlit peaks beyond them. Almost all of the rim of the bowl was as steep and inaccessible as the waterfall itself. But just to the right of the waterfall there was one possible way of escape, up a narrow slope which had an ice cornice at the top. The acute angle of this slope suggested that the whole of it was ice, like the fall, and not snow; but it was the only way out of the bowl which was even worth attempting.

As it turned out, this was the only part of the climb which was really rather easier than it looked. Hard ice would have stopped the party altogether, because none of them had ice-axes, and all they could use to cut steps was the toes of their boots and the tips of their ski-sticks. But when the leaders got on to the slope, they found it was made of hard ice crystals which could be dug away without very much trouble and compacted firmly under their weight. They went up it methodically, side by side as before, hacking out two sets of steps. The slope was too long for the sixty-foot rope, and they had to stop when they had taken out all they could, and dig themselves in again to haul the sledge up after them. This was the only dangerous moment. Again, the place was safe enough for the climbers themselves. If they had slipped out of their steps, they would certainly have gone down to the bottom of the bowl without being able to save themselves, but it would not have done very much harm. For Jan, trussed up on the sledge, it was a very different matter. If they had let him go, he would have gone down much faster, head first on his back, and certainly broken his neck at the bottom. But they took the risk and got away with it again. The second pair anchored the sledge about thirty feet below the cornice. The leaders set off once more, and standing below the cornice in their final steps, they hacked at it with their sticks till they brought a length of it crashing down. They hauled themselves through the gap which they had made, and got to their feet and looked around them. They were standing at last on the icy windswept edge of the plateau. Ahead, the slopes were gentle and the snow was firm.

As soon as the sledge was clear of the cornice, the men put on their skis and the climb took on a totally different aspect. On skis they felt far more at home than on their feet, and more able to cope with any new crisis which might face them. The dilemma of which way up was less painful for Jan was also solved at last, and with his usual resilience he soon began to recover from the rough handling they had given him. The main remaining worry on their minds was simply the matter of time: the climb had taken hours longer than they had expected, and with a thousand feet still to go they were late for the meeting with the Mandal men already. Jan was spared from this worry, as he was from so many others. As he had been unconscious on and off ever since they started, he had no idea how long they had been on the way.

The fear of missing the Mandal men made them press on without another rest. All four of them made themselves fast to the sledge with short ropes tied round their waists, and they started at top speed inland across the plateau. They had no

The hut at Revdal

The bunk in the hut at Revdal. Daylight shows through the wall on the right, where Jan picked out the moss between the logs to make cigarettes

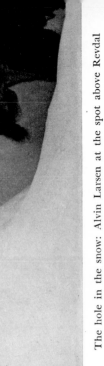

The hole in the snow: Alvin Larsen at the spot above Revdal where Jan lay buried for a week

The top pitch of the ascent of Revdal: a photograph taken when Jan and three of the men who hauled him up Revdal climbed it again ten years later

further doubts about the route. To get to the rendezvous they had to go through a shallow dip which leads up to a chain of small lakes on the watershed between Revdal and Mandal. This dip can easily be seen from across the fjord at Furuflaten, and though none of the four men had ever been up there before, the distant view of the place had been familiar to them all their lives. When they were clear of the dangerous corniced edge, they struck off diagonally to the right up the gently rising ground. The surface was ice, covered here and there by ripples of powdery windblown snow.

Within half an hour the dip in the skyline was in sight. They climbed up into it and entered a little valley among low hillocks of snow. When this valley closed in about them, and cut off the view of the fjord and the distant mountains behind them, they began, each in his own way, to sense for the first time the threatening atmosphere of desolation which oppresses every one of the few people who have ever ventured on to the plateau in winter. The size and the barren loneliness of the plateau appals the least sensitive of travellers. From Lyngenfjord it stretches away into Sweden and Finland, far to the eastward towards the border of Soviet Russia, and then on again beyond the narrow lowlands of Petsamo, to the White Sea and the vastness of Siberia. The valley which they entered that early morning is only on the very verge of it, and yet it is unlikely that any human being will set eyes on that place from one decade's end to the next. Whoever does so, especially when the plateau is under snow, becomes bitterly aware of the hundreds of miles of featureless wilderness beyond him, the endless horizons one after another, and every one the same; the unimaginable numbers of silent ice-bound valleys and sterile, gaunt, deserted hills. Mankind has no business there. It is a dead world, where the affairs of the human race are of no account whatever. In war or peace, it is always the same, and always so fiercely inimical to life that one has to think of it, when one is enclosed within it, as an active malignant enemy. One knows that the human body is too frail a thing to defend itself against that kind of enemy, which attacks with hunger and frostbite and storm-blindness. One knows all too well that the plateau can kill a man easily and quickly and impartially, whether he is English or German or Norwegian, or patriot or traitor. Into these dreadful surroundings the little group of men crept silently, dragging the passive, half-conscious body of Jan behind them.

It had not been very easy to decide on a place for the meeting, because hardly any spot on the plateau can be distinguished from any other, and because there was no map which showed anything more than its outline. But from Furuflaten a single steep bluff could be seen in profile on the far horizon, and for want of anywhere better they had told the Mandal men to meet them at the foot of it.

They came on the place almost unexpectedly, as they breasted a little rise in the valley floor. Before them was a level area, a hundred yards or so across, which was probably a lake or a bog in summer. Beyond it the valley rose again to the watershed, which was still out of sight. On the right was the bluff. It was quite unmistakable, the only piece of black, naked vertical rock in sight. On top of it there was a thick snow cornice like the icing on a cake of festive richness, which they had seen with a telescope from the other side. But down below, at its foot, in the valley, nobody was waiting.

They stood there aghast for a moment at this failure of their hopes. Their first thought, of course, when they saw the empty valley, was that in spite of all their efforts they had arrived too late and the Mandal men had gone. But it only needed a minute or two of search to show that there were no ski tracks anywhere in the valley bottom. Nobody had been there at all, certainly since the last storm had abated, and probably for years.

They all jumped to the conclusion then that something had gone wrong with their instructions about the meeting-place, and that the Mandal men were waiting somewhere else. They had a hurried discussion, grouped round the sledge in the valley below the bluff. It seemed extremely queer that the others should have missed the landmark, which had turned out to be even more conspicuous than they expected. A forlorn hope struck them that the men might be somewhere quite close at hand, hidden perhaps in one of the shallow deceptive hollows in the valley. Someone suggested they should raise a shout. They were strangely reluctant to do so. It seemed rash to break the deathly silence of the plateau. They had been so secretive for so long that they all felt the same absurd fear: that if they shouted, they might be heard by someone who could not be trusted. Yet of course they knew it was inconceivable that anyone could be within earshot except people on the same business as themselves. After a moment's superstitious hesitation, they all shouted in unison. But the sound fell dead, muffled by the blanket of the snow; and nobody answered.

After this, each of them set off in a different direction to search for the Mandal men, leaving Jan lying where he was. To hunt for a party of men on the plateau was not such a hopeless project as it might seem. It was not a matter of finding the men themselves, but of looking for their tracks. If the men had been standing still, it would have been perfectly futile, but a party on the move would leave tracks which could be seen from hundreds of yards away; and in fact a search parallel to the Mandal valley could not miss them if they were there at all.

While Jan was left lying there alone, lashed to the sledge and staring at the sky, he had time to get over whatever disappointment he may have felt at the failure of the meeting, and to make up his mind to the worst that could possibly happen. As he had taken no part in the arrangements, perhaps he was not so surprised as the others that something had gone so obviously wrong. He felt it had been too much to hope for all along that there would really be men waiting for him up there, ready to take him at once to Sweden. He had never seriously pictured himself safely across the border within the next day or two. Besides, after the agony he had suffered while he was being pulled up the mountain, to be allowed to lie still was such an acute relief that nothing else seemed to matter. To lie still and rest, and perhaps to doze a little, was all he really wanted. He even felt rather glad that there was going to be some delay, and that he had not got to set off again at once. And one thing was perfectly clear to him; whatever happened, even to save his life, he simply could not face being taken down again.

When they came back, one by one, he could see from the face of each of them before he spoke that there was no sign of the Mandal party. Amandus was the last one to return. He had been right up across the watershed, and down to the head of the tributary valley running up out of Mandal, which was the route they expected the Mandal men to take. There were no tracks leading out of it. To make doubly sure, he had skirted right round the head of it and gone out on to a sheer bastion of rock which divides the side valley from Mandal itself. From there, leaning out over a vertical drop of nearly three thousand feet, he had looked down the whole length of Mandal. He had seen the houses scattered in the bed of the valley. There was no sign of life among them.

Jan knew that the four men had stayed with him already far longer than was safe. They had to get home, quickly, or their absence was perfectly certain to be discovered, and that would be the end of them, and of him as well. Marius and the others, for their part, also knew what Jan had already made up his mind to tell them; that it was out of the question to take him down again. It would take an impossibly long time; they had not enough strength left to do it; and finally, they were quite certain, as he himself was, that he would not get to the bottom alive.

Thus the decision to abandon him on the plateau did not need very much discussion. There was nothing else whatever to be done. It was a bitter decision for them all, especially for Marius, who blamed himself because the meeting had been a failure. He promised Jan he would get a message through to Mandal the moment he got home, and do everything he could to make sure that the Mandal men would come up and find him the next night. But he made this promise with a heavy heart, because he did not really believe that under the open sky Jan would last through to another day. He thought all the efforts he had made were going to end in failure, and that his hopes of redeeming his own inactive part in Norway's war were never to be fulfilled.

They searched for a place to put Jan where he would have a little shelter, and they found a boulder where the wind had scooped out a hole in the snow. The hole was four feet deep, and exactly the size of a grave. They took off their skis, and lowered him down into it, sledge and all, and then untied the lashings which held him down. They gave him what little food they had, and the remains of the bottle of brandy.

After the last of them had climbed out of the hole, they stood grouped round it, looking down at the haggard, bearded, emaciated face which grinned up at them. Jan said he would be all right, and thanked them as best as he could. They hated what they were doing, and illogically hated themselves for doing it. But neither Jan nor Marius nor any of the others felt like being histrionic about it. One by one they said good-bye, and turned away to put on their skis again. Amandus, as it happened, was the last of them to go, and he always remembered the last words that were spoken, because they were so absurd.

"There's nothing else we can give you?" he asked Jan.

"No thanks," Jan said. "I've got everything. Except hot and cold water."

They began the descent, feeling sure they had left him to die.

CHAPTER TWELVE

THE PLATEAU

THE WAR had not had very much effect upon Mandal before Herr Legland's urgent message was delivered. The place had had no interest for the Germans and they had left it alone, so that its placid and rather primitive and impoverished life went on much the same as usual. It is quite difficult for a stranger to see how the Mandal people can manage to make a living and feed and bring up families in such a forlorn and isolated home. There are millions of people, of course, even in Europe, who live happily enough without any road to connect them with civilisation, and a good many of them even prefer it. But the situation of Mandal seems to have nothing in its favour. The men go fishing, but their jetty is far away from either the fishing grounds or the open sea or the markets. They also farm, but their land is snow-covered and frozen for eight months of the year and the valley faces north: on every other side it is so steeply hemmed in by hills that the sun only shines into it when it is high. Only a little distance to the west, the Lyngen Alps attract tourists who provide a rich annual harvest; but Mandal has no spectacular allurements to offer to visitors, and so any stranger who comes there is a nine-days' wonder.

But in spite of all this, between six and seven hundred people do live there, and they do not want to live anywhere else. They are far from rich, but their houses and farms are neat and tidy, and they themselves are not by any means lacking in self-respect. Their houses are scattered all up the valley for a distance of about ten miles from the jetty and shop at the seaward end. There is a road which connects them, and at least one motor truck which runs up and down it in summer but can never go farther afield. A mile and a half up from the jetty is the school; and it was this school which became the headquarters of Mandal's efforts in rescuing Jan.

The schoolmaster, Herr Nordnes, was a local man himself and he had lived there all his life. He was another disciple in learning of Herr Legland, which no doubt was the reason why Legland chose him to organise the rescue. He knew everybody who lived in the valley, and almost everything that went on there, and practically all the young men in the place had received the whole of their education from him and regarded him still as their teacher. He himself was in middle age, but there could not have been a better choice for a job which called for the mobilisation of the valley's youth.

When he got Legland's message and had given himself time to think it over, he went to call on a few of his recent pupils and told them what he had heard and what was needed. They responded eagerly. In spite of the isolation of Mandal, and the fact that most Mandal people had not seen a German soldier or a German ship or even an aircraft, and had heard no authentic news of the world outside for years, there was much of the same feeling there as on the west side of Lyngenfjord: that nobody had had a chance so far to show what he could do to help the war. Nordnes had no lack of volunteers. His only embarrassment, in fact, was to prevent the news spreading too quickly, and to avoid having too many people who wanted to take some part in this novel adventure. Yet their enthusiasm was surprising, because the appeal for help, as it reached them, was quite impersonal. They did not have the incentive of having seen Jan, and had no idea what kind of person he was. The whole story was third or fourth hand. Not even Legland had seen him, and nor had the messenger. The only reason for thinking that he deserved their help at all was that Legland had said so, and had told Nordnes that the man who was in trouble had come all the way from England.

The Mandal men would have been more than human, in these circumstances, if they had not pointed out, as their first reaction, that to take an injured man to Sweden was not so easy as it looked. The people in Tromsö and Lyngseidet, they thought, probably had no real idea of the difficulties of what they were asking Mandal to do. They might have looked at a map and seen the frontier on it, twenty-five miles away, and imagined some kind of fence with Swedish frontier guards who would take care of Jan on the spot. They probably did not realise that there was nothing there whatever, except cairns at intervals of miles, so that you could cross the border without ever knowing you had done it, and plunge down into endless forests on the Swedish side where you might be lost for weeks without seeing a house or a road. There were no defences on the frontier simply because it was so difficult to cross that no defences were needed.

Having registered their protest, and suggested quite rightly that Lapps were better qualified to make the actual journey, they were perfectly willing to try it themselves if it was really necessary; and they were willing in any case to meet the Furu-flaten men at the rendezvous they suggested, and to look after the injured man when he was handed over. They almost certainly felt some satisfaction at being asked to pull chestnuts out of the fire on behalf of a place like Furuflaten, which had always affected to despise Mandal because it was not on the road.

During the week which elapsed after the first message from Legland, while the gale was blowing which imprisoned Jan in Revdal, the Mandal people heard nothing more about what was happening. They went on with the ordinary chores of early spring, and probably their first enthusiasm faded. The whole story only existed for them in the form of a single sudden visit by a messenger. It began to seem likely that the organisation had found some other way of moving their man, or that he had died or been captured, and that they were not going to be asked to do anything after all. It was disappointing, and made them feel a little foolish.

This was the situation when the second urgent message arrived by telephone. It was very obscure: the parcel Herr Nordnes was expecting was being sent at once. It told them nothing of what was happening in Furuflaten, whether the Germans were hot on the trail, or whether the man they were expected to look after was seriously ill or not. They understood, of course, that it was impossible to say more on the telephone, but it did leave them entirely in the dark. The only shade of meaning it conveyed was one of urgency; and urgency, in that context, suggested that the Germans were suspicious.

However, what it asked them to do was clear enough, and Herr Nordnes rounded up his first party of volunteers and told them the job was on again. They were all men in their early twenties, whom he had chosen because they had been intelligent and resourceful at school, and because they were fit and strong. There had never been any question of him climbing up to the plateau himself, partly because he was a generation older than the climbers he had chosen and would only have held them back, and more especially because he was one of the very few people in Mandal who had to be at work exactly on time in the morning. But his volunteers were still willing, and all said they could make the climb that night. There was still no news of the Lapps from the ski-runner who had set off from Kaafjord to find them; but at least they could take charge of Furuflaten's stranger till they heard if the Lapps were coming. Each of them went off to make his preparations: to change his clothes and wax his skis and pack a rucksack, and perhaps to get a little sleep before he started.

It was at this precise moment that a strange boat was sighted approaching Mandal. This was a very rare event, and plenty of people watched the boat, some with telescopes and binoculars, from the houses near the bottom of the valley. As it approached the jetty, they saw something which was to put the whole valley in a state of turmoil and apprehension: there was a party of German soldiers on board it. The boat reached the jetty, and the Germans came ashore; and a number of people who were in the know put on their skis and pelted up to the schoolhouse to warn Herr Nordnes. As the news spread up the valley, all the people he had consulted began to converge on the school to talk about this sinister development.

They all took it for granted that it had something to do with the plot which was afoot. It seemed certain that the organisation in Furuflaten had been broken up, and that the Germans knew that Mandal was involved in it; or else that somebody higher in the organisation, in Tromsö perhaps, had been arrested and that the Germans were planning a simultaneous raid both sides of the mountain. At all events, it would have been crazy to make the climb that night, before the Germans had shown some sign of what they meant to do. Herr Nordnes himself knew that his own name was the only one in Mandal so far which anyone outside could connect with the affair, and he did the only thing he could do: he told all the others to stay at home and say nothing; and for himself, he resolved that if he was arrested he would try not to give them away whatever was done to him.

That evening, the people of Mandal watched every move which the Germans made; but they seemed to be in no hurry to do anything at all. The second wave of news which spread up the valley reported that there were only six soldiers and an n.c.o. This seemed to suggest that they had come to arrest one single individual. But later rumour said that they were taking over a house as a billet, down by the jetty. Nobody knew whether it was for one night or for good, but obviously if there was going to be an arrest, it was not going to happen before nightfall. That night while Marius and his party were hauling the sledge up Revdal and searching the plateau, nobody was sleeping soundly in Mandal, except perhaps the Germans. When Amandus looked down from the top of the buttress in the early morning, the silent houses he saw far down below him were kept silent by anxiety and fear.

But during the night nothing happened at all. The Germans stayed in their billet, and in the morning they sallied forth and began a house-to-house check of all the inhabitants of Mandal. On the whole this relieved the tension. It pointed to a general vague suspicion of Mandal as a whole, rather than something definite against a particular person. But it meant that nobody could go away from home until the check of his own house had been completed, and to judge by the desultory way that the Germans went to work, this would put a stop to any journey to the frontier for several days. It also made it impossible for the present for anyone to go over to Lyngseidet by boat to find out what had happened; and even to ring up Herr Legland would be asking for trouble, in case he had been arrested.

The whole thing remained a mystery all that day. Whatever way Nordnes and the other conspirators looked at it, it was hard to believe that after years without a garrison, the sudden arrival of even a section of Germans on the very evening when the ascent of the plateau was planned could be simply a coincidence. Yet nothing the Germans did, once they had landed, seemed to have any bearing on the plot, or to suggest in any way that they knew what was going on.

This particular mystery, as it happened, was never solved. To this day it still seems incredible that the Germans arrived there by chance; yet there is no reason to think they had any suspicion, at that particular moment, that Jan had been taken across to the east side of Lyngenfjord. The last time they had seen him was when he was ski-ing through Lyngseidet, and that was nearly three weeks earlier. But perhaps the fact that he had slipped through their grasp and disappeared had brought it home to somebody in the local command that the routes to the frontier were not very well controlled. Perhaps somebody else had had a rap on the knuckles. The somewhat pathetic little garrison sent to Mandal, as well as the motor-boats which suddenly appeared on Lyngenfjord, may have been part of a general tightening of the grip on the frontier, an indirect result of Jan's journey rather than a deliberate search for him. If anyone knows the answer to this, it can only be some German officer.

However, the immediate mystery for Herr Nordnes was cleared up to some extent by an urgent message which arrived that night. It had come by a devious route, but it had originated from Marius, and it told Nordnes that Jan had been left at the meeting-place on the plateau and begged him to have him collected without delay. It also told him, by the mere fact that it had been sent, that there was nothing wrong in the rest of the organisation and that they did not even know that the Germans had come to Mandal. He went out to round up his team again, and to see whether they thought it was safe to start at once. But before the point was decided, it began to snow.

Standing outside the schoolhouse in Mandal, one can see almost the whole of the route to the plateau which they intended to use. As Marius and Amandus had expected, it lies up the side valley which leads out of Mandal on its southern side. This lesser valley is called Kjerringdal, the word *kjerring* meaning an old woman or hag, to correspond with the man of Mandal. Kjerringdal rises steeply, in a series of gleaming curved terraces of snow, and in spring almost the whole of it is swept by avalanches; but there is one route up it clear of the avalanche tracks which is known to the local men. It ends in a wide couloir. From Mandal the rim of the couloir stands against the sky, three thousand feet above; and two miles beyond the rim is the place where Jan was lying.

That night, the snow clouds gathered first above the head of Mandal, and then, even as Nordnes and his men were watching them and debating the weather, they swept up from the south across the plateau, and poured over the edge of the couloir and down into Kjerringdal. Minute by minute they grew thicker and nearer, blotting out the high terraces one by one, till the clouds from Kjerringdal joined with the ones from Mandal and swirled round the vertical crag which divides the two valleys. A few moments later they were overhead, and the snow began to fall, softly and thickly, on the floor of the valley where the men were standing. Soon there was nothing but snowflakes to be seen.

None of them liked to think of a man lying ill and unprotected and helpless up there in the heart of the clouds; but falling snow put an end to whatever hopes they had of reaching him for the present. The German garrison might have been avoided, and even in snow the ascent of Kjerringdal might not have been impossible; but to find the meeting-place would have been out of the question. Nobody in Mandal knew exactly where it was. They would have to depend on seeing the steep bluff which the Furuflaten message had described, and to begin to search for it when they could not see more than a few yards in front of them would be futile and suicidal. There was nothing for it but to wait till the snow-storm ended.

It went on snowing all night, and all the morning. Going about their business in the valley the following day none of them had much hope for the man on the top of the mountain. Perhaps they regretted then they had not gone up on the night that the Germans came. As it turned out, they could have done it without being caught; but nobody could have known that at the time. Now, everything depended on the snow. They were ready to go the moment it showed the first sign of easing. It was simply a question of whether the man would survive till then.

The chance came on the third night after Marius had left Jan up there. There were breaks in the cloud that evening, and the local men, with their knowledge of Mandal weather, believed it would be clear before the morning. The party of four volunteers assembled. The Germans had been watched and counted to make sure they were all out of sight in the billet at the foot of the valley. Everything seemed auspicious.

The ascent of Kjerringdal went off without any serious trouble, though under the best of conditions it is not a safe or easy climb at that time of year. From time to time Nordnes caught sight of the men toiling on up the valley, picking their course to avoid the avalanche tracks. After four hours, on skis all the way, they got to the rim of the plateau. The snow had stopped by then, as they had hoped, and they struck off right-handed to make the level trek across the watershed and then down towards Revdal.

They saw the steep bluff well ahead of them. A series of gentle gullies and frozen lakes led down to the foot of it, and they ran down into the shallow valley which Marius and his party had reached three nights before. The fresh snow which had fallen lay thick over everything. The valley seemed just as deserted and still as the rest of the plateau. There were no tracks and no sign whatever that anyone had ever been there. They searched the foot of the bluff, and the whole of the valley bed above it and below, but they could not find anything at all. They scoured the plateau round about, shouting, but there was no answer. For two hours they hunted far and wide; but then they had to give it up and make back for the head of Kjerringdal again, in order to be at home before the Germans began their day's work of checking the houses. The ski-run down Kjerringdal was very fast, and they were back in Mandal by the time the place was stirring.

When they all talked over this night's expedition with Nordnes, the only conclusion they could come to was that the man who had been left up there had gone off somewhere by himself. They still knew very little about him. They had heard he was crippled, but for all they could tell, he might still have been able to drag himself along. It seemed most likely that when the snow had started, he had tried to get down again on the Revdal side to look for shelter. It had also crossed their minds, of course, that he might have died and been buried by the snow. In fact, they thought anyone who had stayed on the plateau for the past three days would almost certainly be dead; but they dismissed the idea that he had died anywhere near the rendezvous, because they thought they would have found his body. There had not been any avalanche up there, and there was very little drifting, and they would have expected a dead man's body to show as a visible mound on the snowfield. Even if he had dug himself in and then been buried, there should have been something to show where he had done it. But there was nothing at all. He had simply disappeared.

For all practical purposes, Mandal just then was entirely cut off from the outside world. The Germans had been making strict inquiries about anyone they found was not at home, and they expected an explanation of where every man was and what he was doing. Until they had finished their slow and laborious progress from house to house up the whole of the valley, it was obvious that they would not let anyone leave it; and Nordnes could not send a messenger over the fjord to tell Herr Legland what had happened. He could not use the telephone, either. It had always been tapped on and off, and it was sure to be tapped, or simply cut off, while the German search was going on; and the whole mystery was too complicated to discuss in disguised language without any pre-arranged code. If Nordnes had been able to have five minutes' conversation with Marius, everything would have been easy, but they might as well have been on different continents; and besides, at that time neither of them knew who was the organiser of the other village's part in the affair. The only way of communication between them was through Legland, and for the present that way was blocked.

Without any help or advice from outside, the only thing the Mandal men could do was to try again. A second party therefore made the long climb on the following night, the fourth since Jan had been abandoned on the plateau. They regarded it as almost a hopeless effort; but Mandal, in the person of Herr Nordnes, had promised it would do its best, and besides, while there was any chance at all that there was a man alive up there, none of them could have slept easily in their beds.

This time, when they got to the valley below the bluff, it was still covered with the ski-tracks from the night before. They extended the search farther down towards the edge of the drop into Revdal, and inland across the plateau. Every few yards they broke the oppressive silence of the plateau with a shout, and listened while it died again to silence.

Somebody had decided on a password which had been given both to Jan and the Mandal men. Presumably as a tribute to Jan's English training, the Mandal men were to identify themselves to him by saying "Hallo, gentleman." People in Norway often suppose that the word gentleman can be used as a form of address in the singular, as indeed it could if there were any logic in the English language. That night the plateau rang with this repeated cry but nobody in either Mandal or Furuflaten spoke any English at all, and so there was nobody there who would have thought it odd or ludicrous; except Jan, and he could not hear it. Towards morning, the party retreated again by way of Kjerringdal without finding anything. As they went down, the weather was worsening.

This second sortie had made it clear that it was no use to search any more without some kind of consultation with Furuflaten. To put a final end to any thought of another expedition, the snow began again, and during the day the wind got up and increased to a blizzard. This was far worse than the calm snowfall of two days before. In the sheltered valley, the temperature fell abruptly and visibility was restricted, and any outside work became impossible. On the plateau, as the Mandal people knew from generations of experience, no search party would have a hope of finding anything; it would be all they could do to move at all against the wind, or in fact, after a very short time, even to keep themselves alive.

But the blizzard did have one helpful consequence, in that it hampered the German troops as much as anyone. They could not keep their eye any longer on the whole of the foot of the valley, even if they did venture out into the blinding snow; and under the unexpected cover of this storm, a skier slipped out of the valley and brought the news of Mandal's plight to friends in Kaafjord. From there, after a day's delay in which a boat was found which could cross the fjord in such wild weather, the news reached Herr Legland, and he sent a message at once to Marius.

This message undoubtedly was a terrible shock to Marius. It reached him in Furuflaten when the blizzard was still at its height and had already been blowing for days. It meant only one thing to him: that after all Jan had suffered, and all that had been risked for him, he was dead. It was exactly a week since Marius had said good-bye to him when he put him in the snow-grave on the plateau. All that time, as he had not heard any more, he had taken it for granted that the Mandal men had found him, and he had even thought of him safe already in a Swedish hospital. It was dreadful for Marius to think that nobody had ever come to take him out of that hole again. His own knowledge of the arctic mountains, and the wisdom he had learned from older people, all made him certain that nobody had ever survived, or ever could survive, a week of snow and storm on the plateau, under the open sky. He could have wept to think of the pitifully inadequate protection Jan had had: two blankets, and a canvas bag which was not even waterproof, and not more than a day's supply of food. He hated to think what Jan must have thought of him when he knew his end was coming.

Marius's imagination would not let him rest on the day when he got the message. He took the news round to all the people he could tell, those who had helped in different ways. They were all of the same opinion: that it was a pity it had to end that way, but after all, everyone had done his best. Nobody even suggested that Jan might still be alive. Yet Marius knew all the time, in the back of his mind, that he would have to go up to the plateau again that night, whatever the weather, and whatever the risk of being seen and arrested by the Germans when it was really too late to matter. Of course he had not forgotten the solemn promise he had made to Jan; and assuming that Jan was dead, the promise had been broken. He had to go, if only to see for himself. He disliked the idea of leaving Jan's body up there where it lay, till the spring thaw exposed the last remains of it. He wondered if Jan would have left him a message, written on paper perhaps, which the thaw would destroy. Perhaps he had some idea, as people do when the death of a friend leaves them remorseful, of making his peace with Jan by going to look at his body. At any rate, whether it was rational or not, and whether it was suicidally dangerous or not, he knew he was going.

It was a question who would come with him. To go alone would have added a lot to the danger: two people on a mountain in a blizzard are always more than twice as safe as one. But of the three men who had been with him before, Alvin Larsen and Olaf Lanes were away again fishing, and probably storm-stayed somewhere down the coast, and Amandus Lillevoll was having such pain with his broken ribs that it was foolish to think of him making the climb again. There were no other men in the village in the know, only women: his own sisters and mother, and families of the men who had come with him.

Olaf Lanes had several sisters, and one of them was called Agnethe. Agnethe knew Marius well, and she was fond of him, and so was he of her. When she heard that he was determined to go that night, she knew quite well that if nobody else would go with him, he would go alone; and rather than let him do that, she went and told him firmly that she was coming too. Probably if any other girl had said the same thing, he would have refused her offer without a second thought. It was certainly not an expedition for a girl. But Agnethe was as good as any man on skis, and she was strong as well as pretty; and, perhaps even more important, she was the only person that day who really understood the whole depth of what he was feeling, and agreed with him that it was right to go. He possibly needed sympathy just then even more than physical help. She offered him both, and he was grateful; and because there was really no sensible alternative, he agreed to let her come.

At dusk, which was all that was left by then of the vanishing nights, these two embarked on what was to be the last crossing of Lyngenfjord to Revdal. Amandus had come with them to help them to handle the boat and to look after it at Revdal. The crossing was wet and wild, and the small boat under sail was beaten down by heavy squalls from the mountains. But at least it was hidden from German eyes as long as the snow went on falling. They reached the other shore drenched and cold but safe, and beached the boat about half a mile south of Revdal. Agnethe and Marius landed.

They took a new route up the mountain. It looked easier

for unladen climbers than the one which Marius had taken
with the sledge, but it included some pitches of simple rock
climbing, in narrow chimneys, on which the sledge would
have been a hopeless hindrance. Marius looked after Agnethe
with affection and admiration, but she needed no help from
him. On rock she was more agile than he was, and perhaps
she was even more anxious to reach the plateau and see the
worst, so that his mind would be set at rest.

They climbed the first steep two thousand feet very quickly.
But on the steep face they were more or less in shelter. When
they had almost got up to the rim of the plateau, they began
to hear a new note in the wind above them, and when they
looked up through the murk they could see the snow blowing
over the edge. It looked like hard grey pellets, and it shot
over in jets with a power and speed which warned them that
the dangerous part of the climb was only beginning.

When they crossed the rim and stood up on the level surface beyond it, the wind snatched at their clothes and threw
them off their balance and drowned their voices. The air
was so full of whirling particles of snow that it took their
breath away and they felt as if they were suffocating. Both of
them, of course, were properly dressed, in windproof trousers
and *anuraks* with hoods; but the snow lashed the exposed
parts of their faces with such violent pain that they could not
bear to turn unprotected into the wind. Marius shouted to
Agnethe, half-persuaded himself that what they were doing
was madness; but she was already untying her skis, which had
been bound together for carrying. She dropped them on the
shifting surface, and bent down to buckle on the bindings.

The way for the last three miles from there to the rendezvous was against the wind. If it had not been so, it certainly
would have been more than foolish to go on, because of the

danger of over-reaching themselves and being unable to return. They pulled their hoods down as far as they would go, and covered their mouths with their hands to ward off the snow and make breathing possible. Marius set off in the lead, because he knew the way, and marched on with his head bent low, snatching a painful glance ahead of him now and then. Agnethe followed close after him in his tracks. Neither of them could see normally or hear anything but the howling of the wind, and their sense of touch was numbed by cold. When the senses are numbed, a mental numbness cannot be avoided. In this state they went on and on, yard by yard into the wilderness, thinking no farther ahead than the next step and the one after that. They climbed with that thoughtless stubbornness, against all reason, which is often the mainspring of great deeds: Marius driven on by his own compelling conscience, and Agnethe by her sympathy and love.

When they came to the bluff they could see the loom of it above them through the snow-mist; but even Marius had to hesitate before he could find the boulder where Jan had been laid. Everything was changed. The fresh snowfall and the high wind had made new drifts, exposed new rocks and hidden others. The boulder which had stood conspicuously clear of the surface was almost buried, and in the lee of it, where the open hole had been, there was now a smooth windswept surface. The puzzle of why the Mandal men had found nothing there was solved: there was nothing whatever to be seen. Yet Marius felt certain of his bearings. He was sure he had found the right boulder, and that Jan could not have moved, and that therefore, his body was buried far down below that virgin surface. He took off his skis and went down on his knees in the soft snow and began to dig. He scratched the snow away with his hands. Agnethe crouched beside him in an agony of cold. She was exhausted.

When Marius had dug away three feet of snow, the rest collapsed into a cavity underneath, and he knew he was right. He cleared it away, and saw Jan's ghastly waxen face below him. The eyes were shut, and the head was covered with rime.

"Don't look," he said to Agnethe. "He's dead."

At the sound of his voice, Jan stirred.

"I'm not dead, damn you," he said, in a feeble voice but with every sign of indignation.

Then he opened his eyes, and saw the astounded face of Marius peering down at him, and he grinned.

"You can't kill an old fox," he said.

CHAPTER THIRTEEN

BURIED ALIVE

NOBODY CAN give an exact account of what happened to Jan during all the weeks he spent lying alone on the plateau. By the time he had leisure to look back on it, his memory was confused. He had the same difficulty that one has in trying to bring back to mind the events and one's feelings during a serious illness; and in fact, of course, he was seriously ill all the time. Some incidents and impressions were perfectly clear to him, but as he remembered them they had no context; they were isolated, like distant memories of childhood, and he had only a hazy idea of what had led up to them, or what followed after. But most of the episodes he remembered were confirmed in one way or another by the people who visited him up there from time to time. In general, oddly enough, he had no impression of being bored. Once when somebody asked him how he had passed the time, he said he had never been so busy in his life. And one thing, at least, which is perfectly certain is the length of time this extraordinary ordeal lasted. He lay in the sleeping-bag in the snow for no less than 27 consecutive days, from the night of the 25th of April, when Marius took him up to the plateau, till the night of the 22nd of May, when they were to carry him down again in despair.

That first week, in the snow grave, was the worst in some respects, partly because he was not so used to that way of living as he became towards the end, and partly because he was forced to believe, for the second time, that his friends had abandoned him, or lost him, or all been killed themselves. He did not think he would ever get out of the grave again.

At first, he had been so relieved to be allowed to lie still that he said good-bye to Marius and the other three men without any fear of another spell of solitude. He settled down in the sleeping-bag on the sledge, with the wall of snow on one side of him and the rock on the other, and the small segment of sky up above, and he thought he would go to sleep. But only too soon this mood of contentment was driven away by the cold. It was much too cold to sleep. During the climb the sleeping-bag and the blankets had got wet, and in the hole in the snow the moisture froze them stiff. They were to remain either wet or frozen for the whole of the time he was there, and he discovered one thing at once which was to plague him through all those weeks: he could never sleep, because the cold always woke him and he had to keep moving inside the blankets to ward off another attack of frostbite. At the best, he could only fall into an uneasy doze.

Apart from the cold, the sledge made a very uncomfortable bed. It had been a mistake to make the top out of narrow slats with spaces in between them. There were only two layers of blanket and one of canvas, besides his clothes, between him and the wooden slats; and because he had to keep moving he soon got sores all over his back and sides which made the discomfort infinitely worse.

During the first two days and night, before it began to snow, he kept imagining that among the occasional whispering sounds of the plateau he heard the hiss of skis. Sometimes he shouted to the people he thought were there. But this was not the kind of hallucination he had had after the avalanche. On the plateau, his brain was quite clear. Perhaps the sounds were

174

made by little snowballs rolling down the snow-covered scree at the foot of the bluff above him.

As soon as it started to snow, on the second night he lay in the hole, he knew that his chance of being found was very small, at least till the snow stopped falling; and there was an extra worry added to this, because at about the same time he finished the few bits of food they had left him, and he was beginning to get very hungry.

By that time his movements and the heat of his body had made a cavity in the snow, and the sledge had sunk deeper than it had been. The fresh snowfall soon covered his body. He could brush it off his face and his head, but in the narrow hole he could not throw it off the rest of him. Slowly it sifted over his trunk and legs till they were encased in a kind of tunnel, bridged over by a thickening layer of snow which he could not move. For some hours he kept a hole clear to the surface above his head, so that he could still see the open air above him. But the snow grew deeper and deeper till he could not reach up to the surface any more even with his arm stretched out above him. Then the snow closed over the opening, and buried him alive.

He was buried for either four or five days. What kept him alive is a mystery. It was not hope, because he had none, and it was not any of the physical conditions which are usually supposed to be essential to human life. Perhaps it is nearest to the truth to put his survival down to a stubborn distaste for dying in such gruesome circumstances.

He lay on his back in a little vault in the snow. At the sides and above his body there were a few inches of space, and above his head there was over a foot, but there was not enough room for him to draw up his knees or reach down to touch his feet. A dim light filtered down from above, like the light below the surface of the sea. He had no trouble in breathing, because the snow above him was fresh and porous, but he lay all the time in fear that the roof would fall in and pin his arms down and cover his mouth and choke him.

He could imagine quite well the change that had taken place on the surface of the plateau in such a heavy snowfall, and he knew that even if the Mandal men did come to look for him, it was very unlikely that they would find him before the summer thaw exposed his body. Of course, he knew he could not live till then, because in the first stages of the thaw the snow would become compacted and impervious and he would be very, very slowly suffocated.

The only vestige of physical comfort he had in all this time was the dregs of the bottle of brandy. There was not very much in it when he was left there, but as he was weak and starving, less than a mouthful of it was enough to make him slightly drunk. He made it last out for some time after the food was gone. When everything became intolerable, he had the bottle to think about. He would put off taking a sip for hours, so that he could enjoy the anticipation of the warmth going down his throat; and when at last he grasped the precious bottle, and wrestled weakly with the cork, and struggled in the confines of the grave to tilt it to his mouth, the spoonful of raw spirit dulled his pains and made the next hour or two slip past more easily. At times he was even struck by the humour of lying buried in one's grave and swigging a bottle of brandy. But of course the moment came when there was only one more spoonful in the bottle. This he kept as if it were his only link with life, and it was still there when Marius relieved him.

There was one benefit of being buried. Certainly it prevented the Mandal men from finding him, and thereby was nearly the end of him; but to compensate for this, it protected him from everything that happened on the surface. If he had been exposed, the blizzard after the snowfall would have killed him; but in his grave he was no more aware of the howling wind than he was of the shouts of the Mandal party. The blizzard blew over him, but down in the vault in the snow it was always perfectly silent and perfectly calm, and the temperature was always steady, a few degrees below zero.

So he lay while the days and nights passed over. He had no inclination by then to indulge himself with daydreams, or to philosophise as he had in the hut at Revdal. His mind was occupied with the minute details of physical existence: to keep moving, to be on the watch for frostbite, to try to ease the pain of his feet and the sores on his back; to try the impossible task of keeping his body in some state of sanitation; to stop the snow roof falling down, to prevent the bottle of brandy falling over. Each of these tasks became an absorbing activity which occupied him for hours on end, and each one of them was an important part of his conscious effort not to die. He added to them, typically, the task of cleaning the revolver which he still wore in its holster. When any of the tasks were accomplished for the moment, he felt he had warded off death for a few more minutes. He sometimes visualised death as a physical being who prowled about him. He parried the lunges this creature made at him, and he was proud of himself when he thrust off another of its attacks. It did not occur to him then that he might have welcomed death's more compassionate advances.

When Marius broke through the snow above him he was dozing, and he heard his voice in a dream, as he often had before. In the dream he was annoyed that the voice said he was dead. It seemed too bad of Marius to suggest that he had lost the battle with death, when he had been trying so hard to win it, so he denied it hotly. Then he opened his eyes and it was real: and Marius looked so surprised that he laughed and, half-conscious, he said out loud the Norwegian proverb which had been running in his head. "You can't kill an old fox, you know. You can't kill an old fox."

This voice from the dead did in fact almost paralyse Marius for a moment while he reorganised his thoughts. A surge of relief made his heart beat faster; but immediately after it came the fore-knowledge of the problems which had come to life again with Jan. Jan himself was beyond being surprised by then by anything that happened: it did not strike him as particularly strange, though it was pleasant, to see a hooded and yet unmistakably feminine and attractive face looking down at him by the side of Marius. Marius and Agnethe scraped away more snow till Marius could climb down into the hole and clear a space round Jan so that he had a little more freedom to move about. He had brought food with him, more as an offering to fate than with any hope of using it. He fed Jan with bread and bits of fish, while he was explaining how the Mandal men had tried to find him. He had also brought more brandy and some tobacco. Jan could not eat much, but he had a craving for a cigarette, and Marius rolled him one and crouched over him to shelter him while he lit it.

Puffing at this cigarette, while the snow drifted into the hole and the wind shrieked overhead in the grey half-darkness, Jan began to feel almost himself again. It was the belief that he was forgotten that always brought him down to his lowest depths. Now his own hardships faded, and he noticed that Agnethe was in terrible distress. By then, in fact, she was so cold that she could hardly speak. As soon as Jan realised what she was suffering, and all on his behalf, he insisted that they should leave him and get down to the fjord again while they were still able to do it.

Marius himself knew he could not do any good by staying. The only useful thing he could do was to go down and make perfectly certain, as quickly as possible, of getting a large enough party up from one side of the mountain or the other to move Jan away from where he was. The message from Mandal had said they would make the climb again as soon as the weather allowed it. Marius told Jan of this, and to help them to find him if they did come he made a flag by tying a piece of cloth to a ski-stick which he stuck in the snow by the side of the hole. So, after staying with Jan for only half an hour, they left him again with this forlorn signal flapping wildly in the storm above him.

As ever, Marius's unrelenting conscience asked him whether he had done all that was humanly possible, and this time he had to admit to himself that he had not. There was still the slight chance that the Mandal men might be on their way up at that very minute. It was true that the weather had not improved at all, but he felt that he ought to be there, just in case they had chosen to come that night, to make sure that they found the flag. He could not afford to waste time by waiting. The only way to make sure of it quickly was to go on towards Mandal and see if they were coming. Accordingly, instead of turning back down the wind and downhill towards Revdal and home, he and Agnethe faced up into the wind again and climbed on towards the watershed.

In those awful conditions, this was a very brave thing to do, and like many brave and admirable deeds it was also foolhardy. Agnethe agreed with it willingly when Marius proposed it, but she very nearly died as a result. They reached the watershed, fighting against the wind for every step. Up there, they lost their way, but were saved by a sudden momentary clearance. They pressed on and got right across to the rim of the couloir at the head of Kjerringdal. Here there is a small isolated rock from which one can see in clear weather right down to the bottom of Mandal. Marius clung to the lee of this rock and peered down into the depths below. This was the point at which the Mandal men would come up out of Kjerringdal on to the plateau. But that night, although it was light by then, he could only see a few yards down the valley through the scudding snow. There was nobody in sight. While he was searching over the edge, Agnethe collapsed by the side of the rock behind him. When he saw her and turned back to her in alarm, he found she was unconscious.

Both their lives depended then on whether he could revive her, because of course he would never have left her. He set about it in the most drastic way. He shook her limp body, and hit her and slapped her face. He believed, he said afterwards, that apart from anything else this would make her angry, and that anger would improve her circulation. Whether this was the way it worked or not, it did bring her back to consciousness, and as soon as she gave any sign of life he dragged her to her feet and started off, half-carrying her, determined whatever happened to keep her on the move.

Luckily, going down-wind was infinitely easier than going against it, and once they had got back the first mile across the watershed the rest of the way was downhill. Luckily also, although the climb and the cold had used up the last of Agnethe's physical strength, she had an unlimited strength of will. Many people who are exhausted by exposure lose even the will to help those who try to rescue them. If Agnethe had resisted the rough treatment Marius gave her as he hauled her and bullied her along, or if she had ever succumbed to the in-

Snowclouds over Mandal: the route to the plateau led up Kjerringdal, on the right

Mandal from the head of Kjerringdal: the route used by the Mandal men to reach the plateau

sidious temptation to give up, neither of them would ever have been seen alive again. But there was a tough arctic quality in the girl which kept her going, and between them they won through to the head of Revdal and staggered down to the shore where Amandus was keeping the boat.

The climb did her no permanent physical harm, but the memory of the sight of Jan lying in the hole was to haunt her for years. It had been such a terrible sight that she thought when she saw him that he had nothing left to live for and would have been better dead.

CHAPTER FOURTEEN

ATTEMPT ON THE FRONTIER

WHEN A message reached Mandal to say that Jan was still up on the plateau and still alive, they began to make final preparations for an all-out attempt on the frontier as soon as the blizzard died down. For the last few days, they had not been expecting to have to try it, because when they looked up towards the loom of the mountains through the wildly driving snow, it was incredible that up there, away beyond the very top of Kjerringdal, there could be a man still living. But the fact that he had survived so far made it seem all the more worth while to try to save him. The preparations were rather grim. They knew they were running a big risk of never coming back, either because of some disaster on the plateau or through getting lost or interned in Sweden. But if a sick man could exist on the plateau, it would have been a disgrace to admit that four fit men could not try to move him across it to safety.

The plan for getting the Lapps to help had fallen through, at least for the time being. The ski-runner who had gone out from Kaafjord to look for them had come back, just missing the worst of the blizzard, but the news he had brought was discouraging. The reindeer were still much farther away than they usually were at that time of year. He had followed their migration track back across the plateau to the south-east for over fifty miles before he sighted the vast herds, halted and digging for the moss beneath the snow. The Lapps he was looking for were camped among them in their deerskin tents.

He was criticised afterwards for not having made allowance for the queer psychology of Lapps. He had broached the subject of Jan and the journey to the frontier while he was sitting with the Lapps in a tent which was full of women and children; and the Lapps had simply refused to say yes or no. They were friendly, as Lapps always are, but they would not give the least sign of whether they might be willing, or even whether they really understood what they were being asked to do. People who knew the Lapps well, being wise after the event, said they would never commit themselves to any decision while their families were listening.

Certainly the mental processes of Lapps are very strange. They do not seem to grasp the idea of expressing an opinion. On a matter of fact which is within their own experience they will be quite dogmatic and clear-headed; but their minds do not work in terms of probabilities, and if they are asked whether something is likely to happen, they are genuinely puzzled and think the question is foolish. People tell the story of a Norwegian tourist who wanted to fish for salmon and asked a Lapp if he thought he would be able to get one in a particular local river; and the Lapp, who knew him well, shook his head with a sigh, and answered: "Really, I sometimes think you Norwegians are crazy. How could I answer a question like that? Of course there are plenty of salmon in the river, but why should you think I can tell if you can catch them?"

This curious limitation naturally makes it difficult for a Lapp to make up his mind what he is going to do. When there is a question of immediate action, provided it is something to do with reindeer or the technique of wresting a living from the arctic, he may be a shrewder man than anyone; and he can think ahead in terms of the unalterable cycles of nature, the rising and setting of the sun, the seasons and the movements of the deer. But in other matters, he is no good at all at planning things far ahead.

So the question which was put to the Kaafjord Lapps was one which they were probably incapable of answering. The ski-runner did not ask them to come at once, because he knew they could not leave their reindeer, and the herds could not be hurried. The question was whether they would help Jan when they arrived with the herds at Kaafjord, and this was too far ahead for them to contemplate. It probably bogged their minds in impossible speculations. Endless imponderable ideas would have upset them and confused them: their reindeer might be sick, the weather might be bad, they might be sick themselves: anything might happen. Nobody, in fact, could have promised more at that moment than that he would do his best when the time came, and a Lapp either cannot think in such vague terms or cannot express them in language. His answer must be precise and literal. A Lapp could only say, quite definitely: "When I get to Kaafjord, I will take a man to Sweden"; and to say a thing like that would be absurd. After all, a Lapp would reason, by that time the man might be dead; and then, if he had said he was going to take him to Sweden, he would look ridiculous.

So for the present this scheme was at a standstill. The people in Kaafjord still hoped that when the first Lapps actually arrived there, they would be able to persuade them to do the job. But the migration was late already, and the blizzard would hold it up still further. None of the herds would get there for three or four days, at least, after the weather improved. The Mandal people thought this was too long to wait, especially on the mere chance that any Lapps would agree.

The blizzard, in fact, began to moderate on the day after Marius and Agnethe made their expedition, and on the following night a third party of volunteers made the ascent of Kjerringdal. They took with them everything they could muster for a long journey, but nobody in Mandal possessed the proper equipment for a winter encampment on the plateau. The Lapps, primitive though they are, would have been far more suitably fitted out, with tents of hide, and clothes of reindeer skin with the hair left on, and with centuries of experience of going to ground when the arctic weather was at its worst. In fact, the most elaborate civilised camping outfit would be less suited to those arctic uplands than the Lapps' equipment, which is entirely home-made of various parts of reindeer; and the best which could be found in Mandal was far from elaborate. Nobody even had a tent, or a stove which would burn in a wind, because nobody in living memory had ever needed to make such a winter journey. But in a place like Mandal, people never waste time in wishing for things which they have not got; they make do with what comes to hand. They could only hope the weather would not be bad.

As soon as they got within sight of the meeting-place that night, they saw the flag. They hurried down towards it on their skis, shouting the password, "Hallo, gentleman!" For the first time, Jan heard this joyful and comic greeting, and he shouted "Hallo, there!" in reply; and in a minute his solitary grave was surrounded by helpful strangers who hacked away its walls and dragged him bodily out on the sledge to the world which he had not seen for a week and had not expected ever to see again.

Those of the men who had been there on either of the earlier climbs were amazed that they had not found him. They thought they had actually skied over the top of him while he was buried there; and this is not impossible, even though he never heard them, because four feet of snow absorbs a lot of sound, and his senses were probably not so acute as he may have thought they were.

Without wasting more time than it took to explain to him what they were doing, they lashed him to the sledge again and started off on their desperate bid to cross the plateau on the way to the Swedish border. When they climbed out of the valley, their hopes were high, because they had found him without the delay of searching. Even Jan, who had learnt not to hope for much, was cautiously happy to be on the move again, and could not help thinking how few were the miles between himself and Sweden.

But from the beginning, their progress was very slow. The plateau is much more difficult ground for man-hauling a sledge than the flat ice-fields of the Arctic and Antarctic. None of the plateau is flat. It is covered all over with miniature hills and valleys. Hardly any of the hills are more than one or two hundred feet above the valleys, but one is always going either uphill or down. This is no obstacle to a skier, because the time which he loses in climbing is made up on the free runs down. But the sledge could never be allowed to run. Hauling it up the hills was slow, and going down again it always had to be checked so that it did not get out of control. Both were equally tiring. Once, the sledge did get away on a downward slope, and Jan careered madly down the hill, feet first, lashed down and helpless. But luckily the slope was smooth and the sledge did not overturn, but came to rest on a level snowfield at the bottom, with the breathless skiers chasing close behind it.

The maze of little hills, jumbled together without any form or pattern, also destroys any sense of direction. It is impossible to keep a straight compass course. Probably the best way to steer is by the sun, but when the sky is heavily overcast, as it was on that day, one has to stop every few minutes to take bearings. In normally open country, one can take a bearing of a landmark two or three miles away, and then make towards it. But on the plateau, one can seldom see far ahead and there are seldom any recognisable landmarks. If one happens from one hilltop to sight a conspicuous rock on a distant skyline, one loses it again in the valleys, and before one has reached it it seems to have disappeared. There is only one way to avoid making useless deviations, and that is to stop at the top of each tiny hill or ridge and take a bearing of some stone or fold in the snow on the next, which may be only a hundred yards away. It takes time, and a lot of patience.

As the four men, with Jan's helpless body dragging through the snow, crept farther and farther into this wilderness, steering south towards Sweden, the endless hills which were still ahead of them, with their endless petty checks and obstacles, began to seem like an impenetrable web. In forcing a way through them, they were not limited by the mountaineer's usual worry of being benighted. There was still a fortnight before the sun would actually be above the horizon night and day, but it was quite light enough for the party to keep moving through the night. The only limit to the journey was their own endurance. A time would come when they would have to try to sleep, and they were so poorly equipped that they could not expect to sleep soundly enough to restore their strength to normal. After a sleep, the second stage would be slower and shorter than the first; and the first was being so desperately slow that a new danger began to loom ahead: the danger of reaching the point of exhaustion before they came to Sweden, and after they had gone too far to be able to get home again.

So as they went on, their hopeful spirit faded, and gave way to a growing fear that they were trying something entirely beyond their powers. None of them wanted to be the first to admit defeat, and they went on a long way after it was hopeless. What finally turned the doubt into despair was the weather. During the morning the wind had sprung up again, and the snowclouds began to pile up and darken the southern sky. It looked as if the improvement in the night had only been a lull, and as if the blizzard was going to start again, as furiously as ever. They halted on top of a hill. They had been hauling the sledge for six hours then, apart from the four hours' climb up Kjerringdal. None of them knew how far they had come, but there was certainly a long way still to go. It was the sort of unwelcome decision which nobody needs to discuss. With hardly a word between them, they turned the sledge round and started back towards Mandal.

During the long weary hopeless journey back, the blizzard did come on again in earnest, and proved the decision was right. Going back, the wind was almost behind them; they could never have made any progress going south against it.

When at last they got back to the steep edge of Mandal, they found they were some distance farther up the valley than the point they had started from. This was simply due to the difficulty of setting a course on the plateau, but it had some advantages. To climb straight down into the valley from where they were would avoid Kjerringdal, which was certain to avalanche at any minute. There was no point in going all the way back to the place where Jan had been lying when they found him.

The question arose again of what to do with Jan. Remembering the experience of being hauled up the mountain, he was still very reluctant to go down again. Apart from the pain of it, it would have been such a depressing step in the wrong

direction. Besides, he could see that the Mandal men were
dog-tired. They had been at full stretch for something like
sixteen hours, and for tired men to try to lower him down to
the valley in the blizzard had obvious risks for them all. They
themselves thought that if he could face another few days on
the plateau, he would really be safer there. He decided to stay.

They found him another rock which would serve as a landmark, and dragged him to the foot of it. They untied him from
the sledge, and stowed their spare food beside him, and then
they built a low wall of snow to shelter him from the wind.
This was all they could do for him, and in fact it was all he
wanted. When it was finished, and they had promised to come
up again, they turned downhill for home, and all vanished
into the mist of snow, and left him alone again. For all the
day's journeying, he was about two miles nearer Sweden than
when he started.

CHAPTER FIFTEEN

THE LAST DUTY

HE LAY between the snow wall and the rock for nearly three weeks. In some ways it was better than the grave: he could see rather more of the sky, although he could not see round him beyond the wall; and there was enough room to move about so far as he was able. But in other ways it was worse: it was more exposed to the wind and weather, and it was much more affected by the change in temperature between night and day. In the grave, it had always been a bit below freezing point. In the open, whenever the sun broke through the clouds it melted his sleeping-bag and the snow around him till he was soaked; and when the sun dipped down at night towards the north horizon, his blankets and clothes froze solid. But although this was extremely uncomfortable it never made him ill. In conditions which were more than enough to give a man pneumonia, he never even caught a cold, because there are no germs of such human diseases on the plateau.

He was well stocked with food when they left him there, and different parties of men came up from the valley every three or four days to keep him supplied. None of it struck him as very nice to eat, especially after it had been thawed and frozen several times, and he had nothing to cook with. But still, one can live without such refinements as cookery and he was grateful for it. There was dried fish, and cod liver oil, and bread. It was a question whether the bread was worse to eat when it was wet or when it was frozen. There was also some powdered milk which had to be mixed with water. It occupied him for long hours to melt the snow between his hands so that it dripped into the cup he had been given, and then to stir the powder into it. Later on, when the thaw began in earnest, an icicle on the rock beside him began to drip. At the full stretch of his arm, he could just reach out to put the cup under the drip, and then he would lie and watch it, counting the slow drops as they fell, and waiting in suspense as each one trembled glistening on the tip. Sometimes when the cup had a little water in the bottom, the drops splashed out and half of each one was lost. When he was feeling weak, this seemed a disaster, and he would swear feebly to himself in vexation. But in the end he invented the idea of putting a lump of snow on top of the cup, so that the drops fell through it without splashing. It took hours to fill the cup. The end result, with the milk powder mixed in it cold, was a horrible drink, but it helped to keep his strength up, and he drank it as a duty.

Sometimes in those solitary days, between the chores which always kept him busy, he still had the strength of mind to laugh at the contrast between himself as he used to be and his present state of elementary existence. Looking back, his life before the war, and even in the army, seemed prim and over-fastidious. There was a certain kind of humour in the thought that he had once taken some pride in his appearance, chosen ties as if they were important, pressed his trousers, kept his hair cut, and even manicured his nails. Grubbing about in the snow for a crust of bread reminded him of a time he had had to complain in an Oslo restaurant because there was a coffee stain on the tablecloth, and of how apologetic the waiter had been when he changed it for a clean one. It had seemed important; in fact, it had been important to him as he was in those days. If the man he had then been could have seen the man he was now, the sight would have made him sick. He had not washed or shaved or combed his hair for weeks, or taken off his clothes. He had reached that stage of filth when one's clothes seem to be part of one's body, and he smelt. But, luckily, what had happened to him in the last few weeks had changed him, and he did not mind his dirt. It had changed him more fundamentally than merely by making him dirty and ill and emaciated and crippling his legs. It had changed him so that it was quite difficult for him to recognise the spark of life which still lingered inside that feeble disgusting body as himself. He knew already that if he lived through it all he would never be the same person again. He would have lost his feet, he supposed, but he would have grown in experience. He felt he would never dare to be impatient again, that he would always be placid and tolerant, and that none of the irritations of civilised life would have the power to annoy him any more. Travel broadens the mind, he thought, and laughed out loud because the plateau was so damnably silent.

When he fell into a doze during those days, he often dreamed of wolves. This was a fear he had been spared during his first week on the plateau, because nobody had told him there were wolves up there; but there are. They sometimes attack the reindeer herds, and the Lapps on skis fight running battles with them. They seldom, if ever, attack a man, even if he is alone; but nobody could say for certain whether they would attack a helpless man if they were hungry, as they often are in the time of the early spring. The Mandal men had taken the danger seriously enough to warn Jan about it and give him a stick to defend himself. Later, when they realised that a stick was no good because he had not enough strength to beat off a rabbit with it, they brought up brushwood and paraffin so that he could fire it if the wolves closed in on him. Of course he had a pistol; but it only had three rounds left in it, and he said he wanted to keep them for bigger game than wolves. Jan felt it was silly to be afraid of an animal, or even a pack of them, which had never actually been known to kill a man, so far as anyone could tell him. Yet the thought of it worked on his nerves. Until he was told of the wolves, he had only the inanimate forces of the plateau to contend with. He had relied on his solitude, feeling as safe from a sudden intrusion as he would in a house with the doors and windows locked. With all the dangers that surrounded him, at least he had not had to keep alert for any sudden crisis. But now, as he lay behind his wall of snow, unable to see what was happening on the snowfield around him, helplessly wrapped in his sleeping-bag, he knew he might see the sharp teeth and the pointed muzzle at any moment within a yard of him, or feel the hot breath on his face when he was sleeping, or hear the baying and know they were watching him and waiting. This, more than any-thing, made him feel his loneliness.

In the comparatively roomy space behind the snow wall, he could wriggle one leg at a time out of the sleeping-bag and look carefully at his feet, which he had never been able to do inside the grave. They were a very disgusting sight. His toes were still worse than anything else, but the whole of each foot was so bad that it was frost-bitten right through from one side to the other between the Achilles tendon and the bone. All the way up to his knees there were patches of black and grey. He had quite given up thinking of ever being able to walk on them again. As soon as he got to a hospital, he supposed, some-body would put him straight on an operating table and cut off his feet without thinking twice about it. He was resigned to that, but he still very much wanted not to lose his legs. Apart from the problems of keeping himself alive, he had thought more about his legs than anything else, wondering whether there was anything he could do to help to save them. He had made up his mind some time before about one drastic course of action, but in the grave there had not been enough room to put it into effect. He was still under the impression, rightly or wrongly, that gangrene would go on spreading, unless one got rid of it, like dry rot in a house. The source of it all was his toes. They were not part of him any more, although they were still attached to him, and it seemed only common sense that he would be better without them. There was nobody he could expect to help him; but now the time and the chance had come, and he made his preparations to cut off his toes himself.

He still had his pocket-knife, and he still had some brandy. With the brandy as anæsthetic, and the knife as a scalpel, lying curled up on his side in the snow with his leg drawn up so that he could reach it, he began carefully to dissect them one by one.

It would have been best to get it all over quickly, but apart from the pain and the sickening repulsion, it was difficult to cut them; more difficult than he had expected. He had to find the joints. His hands were rather clumsy and very weak, because there had been some frostbite in his fingers too, and the knife was not so sharp as it had been. He grimly persevered, and slowly succeeded. As each one was finally severed, he laid it on a small ledge of rock above him where he could not see it, because he no longer had strength to throw it far away. After each one he had to stop, to get over the nausea and dope himself with brandy. Someone had brought him some cod liver oil ointment, and he smeared a thick slab of it on each wound and tied it in place with a strip of blanket.

This grisly operation was spread out over nearly three days. At the end of it, there were nine toes on the ledge. The little toe on his left foot did not seem so bad as the others, so he kept it. When he had finished, he felt very much better in his mind. Of course, there was no immediate improvement in his legs, but it gave him some satisfaction to have done something which he hoped would help to save them; it was better to know that the rotten revolting things were gone and could not poison him any more. It made him feel cleaner.

After it was all done, he went back with relief to the simple routine of his daily life: feeding himself, collecting ice-water, mixing milk, trying to clean his pistol; once in a while, as seldom as he could, rolling a cigarette with infinite care and finding the box of matches which he kept inside his underclothes next to his skin; trying to put ointment on the sores on his back without getting too cold; sometimes treating himself to a sip of brandy; and always keeping on the watch for new attacks of frostbite. It was terribly difficult not to lie there listening, imagining the sound of skis or the distant snarl of wolves. Sometimes he stopped up his ears to keep out the ghastly silence, and sometimes he talked to himself so that there was something to listen to. When people did come from Mandal, shouting "Hallo, gentleman," from far off, the sudden disturbance of the silence was a shock, and often it took him some time to find his voice to answer.

They paid him faithful visits all those weeks, toiling up the long climb every third or fourth night. When they came, they always brought fresh food, and usually some dry wood to make a fire to heat a drink for him; but lighting fires always made them uneasy in case the smoke or the light was seen. Whenever he heard them coming, he pulled himself together and tried to look as alive as he could, because he had a fear at the back of his mind that they might get depressed and give him up as a bad job and stop coming any more. On their side, they felt they had to cheer him up, so that the meetings were usually happy, although the happiness was forced. Sometimes there was even something to laugh at, like the time when one man forgot the password. The story of how Jan had shot the Gestapo officer had got around, and he had the reputation in Mandal of being trigger-conscious and a deadly shot. So when this man found that the words "Hallo, gentleman" had quite escaped his mind at the critical moment, he hurriedly dropped on his hands and knees and crawled up to Jan on his stomach, keeping well under cover till he was close enough to talk to him and make perfectly certain that there would not be any unfortunate misunderstanding.

On one of their visits, Jan asked them for something to read. What he really wanted was an English thriller or a French one, because during the last couple of years he had got more used to reading foreign languages than his own. But nobody knew of anything like that in Mandal, and the man he happened to ask could only offer him religious works in Norwegian. He declined that offer, but afterwards the man remembered an annual edition of a weekly magazine which he could borrow. Jan thanked him, and the heavy volume was carried up the mountain. But as a matter of fact, Jan did not read very much of it. He never seemed to have time.

Somebody had the brilliant idea, when Jan had been up there for some time, of bringing up a roll of the kind of thick paper which is used for insulating buildings. They bent this over Jan in an arch, like a miniature Nissen hut, and covered it over with snow, and blocked up one end with a snow wall. It was just big enough for Jan to lie in, and it protected him quite well. In fact, it sometimes seemed warm inside. But it had its drawbacks; whenever it seemed to be going to get tolerably warm, the snow on top of it melted and dripped through on him mercilessly, and made him even wetter than before.

Sometimes his visitors came with high hopes, but more often the news they brought him from the valley was disappointing. On one night soon after they left him there, two men came up full of excitement to say that a Lapp had arrived in Kaafjord and promised to take him either that night or the next, and they waited all night to help Jan when he came. But the morning came without any sign of him. For the next three successive nights men came from the valley to wait with Jan for the Lapp's arrival, and to make sure he did not miss the place. They kept watch for him hour by hour; but no movement broke the skylines of the plateau. On the fourth day they heard that the Lapp had changed his mind because of a rumour that the Germans had sent out ski patrols on the frontier.

During the next few days this rumour was confirmed from a good many different sources. Recently, everyone had been so completely absorbed by the problems of Jan's health, and the weather, and the journey across the plateau, that they were well on the way to forgetting about the Germans. It was a long time since the garrison had come to Mandal, and that had been the last German move, so far as anyone knew, which had seemed at the time to be part of a deliberate search. The Mandal men had got used to the garrison and begun to despise it. But now it began to look as if the Germans were still on the hunt for Jan and even had a rough idea of where he was. When Jan was told about it, he reflected that the Germans had got a jump ahead of him for the first time in his flight. In the early days, when he was on the move, they had never done more than bark at his heels; but now, it seemed, they had thrown out a patrol line right on the part of the frontier which one day he would have to cross; and unless he crossed it within a few days, he would have to do it in daylight. If only he had been fit, both he and the Mandal men would have treated the patrol as a joke, because like all Norwegians they had a profound contempt, which may not have been justified, for the Germans' skill on skis. Even as things were, nobody except the Lapp was deterred by this extra danger. If they could only get to the frontier, they were sure they would get across somehow.

But soon after this rumour started, there was an extraordinary event on the plateau which really did make them take the danger of Germans more seriously. The most remarkable thing about life on the plateau had always been that nothing happened whatever. Day after day could pass without any event, even of the most trivial kind; and Jan discovered that most of the events which he seemed to remember were really things he had dreamed or imagined. His commonest dream or hallucination was that he heard someone coming. One day, when he was dozing, he heard voices approaching. It had often happened before; but this time, as they came near him, he realised that they were speaking German. He could not understand what they were saying, and they soon faded away again; and when he was fully awake, he thought no more of what seemed a slight variation of his old familiar dream. But the next night, when a party from Mandal came up to see him, they arrived in consternation, because there were two sets of ski tracks which passed thirty yards from the place where Jan was lying, and none of the Mandal men had made them.

It was one of those utterly mysterious things which start endless speculation. Up till then, they had always regarded the plateau as a sanctuary from the Germans, partly because they had never thought the Germans would venture to go up there, and partly because the job of looking for one man in all those hundreds of miles of snow was so hopeless that they had been sure that the Germans would not waste time in trying it. Nobody could imagine where the small party of men who had made the tracks could have come from, or where they had been going, or what they had meant to do. They were not from the Mandal garrison, because that was always kept under observation, and the place was more than a day's journey from any other German post. They could not have been part of a frontier patrol, because it was much too far from the frontier. Yet if they were searching for Jan, it seemed an incredible coincidence that they should have passed so near him, unless there were hundreds of patrols all over the plateau, or unless they had a very good idea of where he was. Besides, to search in that secretive way was un-German. If they did know where he was, they would know he could not be living up there unless Mandal was looking after him, and their reaction to that would certainly be to use threats and arrests in Mandal in the hope of finding someone who would give him away and save them losing face by having to scour the mountains.

They argued round and round the mystery for a long time on the plateau that night, with a new feeling of insecurity and apprehension. It had been pure luck that the Germans, whatever they were doing, had not seen Jan when they passed him. There had been a snowfall earlier in the day which had covered the trampled snow around his lair and all the old ski tracks which led up to it from Mandal. But if they came back again, they would find the new tracks and follow them straight to the spot. Altogether, it was alarming, and the only comforting suggestion that anybody thought of was that the tracks might possibly have been made by German deserters trying to get to Sweden. Nobody ever found out the truth of it. Those voices in the night remained a vague menace in the background ever after.

When the Lapp lost courage and changed his mind, it was only the first of a series of disappointments. Hopeful stories of reindeer sledges expected at any moment kept coming in from Kaafjord and other valleys in the district; but every time the hope was doomed to die. After a fortnight in which all their plans were frustrated and came to nothing, the Mandal men got desperate. Every time they went up to look at Jan they found him a little weaker. He seemed to be dying by very slow degrees. Besides that, the spring thaw was beginning in earnest, and with every day the crossing of the plateau and even the climb out of the valley were getting more difficult. The snow was rotten and sticky already on the southern slopes, and the next week or two would see the last chance of a sledge journey before the following winter. During the thaw every year the plateau becomes a bog, criss-crossed by swollen streams, and nobody can cross it; and after the thaw, when the snow is all gone, the only way to move a helpless man would be to carry him, which would be even slower and more laborious than dragging him on a sledge.

So they decided to make a final attempt to man-haul the sledge to Sweden while there was still time, using a larger party which could work in relays. Accordingly, six men went up on the night of the ninth of May, and dragged Jan out of the paper tent and started off again to the southward. But this attempt achieved nothing except to raise false hopes once more. They had only covered a mile or two when clouds came down so thickly that they could only see a few feet ahead of them. They could not steer a course in those conditions, so they turned round and followed their own tracks back to where they had started, and put Jan into the paper tent again.

After this failure, Jan really began to get despondent. He never lost faith in the Mandal men, and still believed they would get him to Sweden somehow if they went on trying long enough; but he began to doubt if it was worth it. Nobody had told him much about what was going on, but he could see for himself what an enormous effort Mandal and the surrounding district were making on his behalf. So many different men had come up from the valley by then that he had lost count of them, and he had some vague idea of the organisation which must lie behind such frequent visits. As time went on, it seemed more and more fantastic that the German garrison could go on living down there in the valley, in the midst of all this hectic activity, and remain in happy ignorance of what was happening. Every new man who came up to help him meant a new family more or less involved in his affairs, so that the longer Mandal had to go on looking after him the more awful would be the disaster in the valley if the Germans did find out about it. Jan knew, and so did the Mandal men, the results of the uncontrolled anger of Germans when they found out that a whole community had deceived them. It had happened on the west coast, and villages had been systematically burnt, all the men in them shipped to Germany and the women and children herded into concentration camps in Norway. There was no doubt this might happen to Mandal, now that so many people were involved, and Jan had to ask himself what the reward of running this risk would be. To save his life was the only objective. When he looked at it coolly, it seemed a very bad bargain. There was no patriotic motive in it any more, no idea of saving a trained soldier to fight again;

looking at his legs, and the wasted remains of what had once been such a healthy body, he did not think he would be any use as a soldier any more. If he died, he thought, it would be no loss to the army: he was a dead loss anyway. And it was not as if he were married, or even engaged. Nobody depended entirely on him for their happiness or livelihood. His father had another son and daughter: his brother Nils would be quite grown up by now: and even Bitten, his young sister whom he had loved so much, must have learned, he supposed, to get on without him, and perhaps would never depend on him again as much as he had always imagined. He wondered whether they had all given him up for dead already, and whether he would ever see them again even if he did live on. As for his war-time friends of the last two years in England, he knew they would all have assumed he was dead if they knew where he was at all.

This idea only came to him slowly, in the course of about ten lonely days after the last abortive journey. It took him a long time to come to a firm conclusion, because by nature he had such a very strong instinct to live. But inevitably the time came, in the end, when he unwillingly saw one duty left before him. His own life was not of any overriding value to anyone but himself; and to himself, life only meant a few more weeks of suffering and a hideous death, or at best, he believed, a future as a more or less useless cripple. The life of any one of his many helpers, healthy and perhaps the focus and support of a family, outweighed it in the balance. He saw quite clearly that he ought not to let them run any more risks for him, and he knew there was only one way he could possibly stop them. His last duty was to die.

To decide to commit suicide when one's instinct is utterly against it argues great strength of mind. Jan's mind was still active and clear, but his decision had come too late. By the time he reached it, his body was too weak to carry it out. He still had his loaded pistol. Lying alone in his sleeping-bag among the wastes of snow, he dragged it out of its holster and held it in his hands. He had used it to save his life already, and he meant to use it again to end it. Until the last week he had always looked after it with the love he had always had for fine mechanism, but lately he had begun to neglect it, and it grieved him to find it was rusty. He held it in the old familiar grip, to cock it for a final shot, but it was stiff and his fingers were very weak. He struggled feebly with the simple action he had been trained to do in a fraction of a second, but it was not the slightest use. He no longer had the strength in his hands to pull back against the spring. He felt a friend had failed him.

Afterwards he tried to think of other ways of doing away with himself. If he could have got out of the sleeping-bag and crawled away into the snow, he could have let the frost finish the work it had begun. But it was a long time then, over a week, since he had had enough strength to disentangle himself from the blankets or move his body more than an inch or two. He thought of his knife too, and tried its edge; but it had not been sharp when he cut off his toes, and now it was rustier and blunter, and the thought of trying to saw at his own throat or the arteries in his wrists was so horrible that his resolution wavered, and he feebly relaxed and tried to make up his mind anew.

It was absurd really. He felt he had made a fool of himself. He had struggled so long to preserve his own life that now he had not enough strength in his fingers to kill himself. If he had not felt ashamed, he would have laughed.

CHAPTER SIXTEEN

THE SANDS RUN OUT

WHEN JAN came to this mental crisis, the men who came up to see him noticed the difference. Up to then, he had always seemed cheerful, and none of them knew what this appearance had sometimes cost him. But now there was no humour left in him, and he would hardly speak to them. In fact, up to then the occasional visits of strangers had been all he had had to look forward to, but now he was almost resentful when he heard "Hallo, gentleman," because it meant that he had to make an effort when he wanted to lie in peace. He did not tell them till later about the conclusion he had come to. It simply seemed to them that he had lost heart. They went down and told Herr Nordnes that he was dying at last.

It had never occurred to them, as it had to Jan, that what they were doing might not be worth the risk, and if he had died up there on the plateau, after all the effort they had put into trying to save him, they would have been very much disappointed and almost angry with him. But they were certainly right in their fears. The weeks of exposure had really worn him down to the point when his life might quietly end without any further warning. Only one course was left to them, since they never considered just letting him die in peace. They would have to carry him down to the valley again, and try to fatten him up and build up his strength till he was fit for another attempt on Sweden.

There were the Germans to think of. No house in the place was free of the risk of a sudden search. At night, by that time, there was no darkness left at all, and it would have been taking too much of a chance to have carried him all the way down to the inhabited part of the valley in broad daylight. But the valley extends for ten miles beyond the last of the houses, and all of it is more sheltered than the open plateau, and a few degrees warmer. Somebody remembered a cave right up at the head of the valley. There was a meeting in the school-house, and it was agreed that the only hope of spinning out his life was to cut their losses, bring him down and install him in the cave, and begin all over again.

This was a hard decision for them all, and especially for Jan when they told him what they thought. It meant going back to the stage of the journey he had reached when he was first carried into the hut at Revdal nearly six weeks before. It meant that everything he had suffered since then had been wasted. And it also meant, above all, that before he could ever hope to reach Sweden he would have to go through the ordeal of being hauled up the mountain again.

However, he was too far gone to care, and the Mandal men assured him there was nothing else for it; so he let himself be pulled out of the paper tent and lashed yet again to the sledge. Six men lowered him laboriously down to the bed of the valley, throwing away the height and the distance which the past weeks had so painfully won.

While this party was bringing him down, another was preparing the cave, by laying a bed of birch branches and grass inside it. When they got him there and pushed him inside and finally left him, he was in a state of luxury which he had not enjoyed since Marius's barn. They had taken him off the sledge, and after its wooden slats the birch bed was wonder-

fully soft. He slowly got dry, for the first time in a month;
and when his clothes had dried out he even began to get warm,
a sensation which seemed an entirely novel experience; and
when he was warm he fell at long last into a dreamless sleep.

He lay in the cave for four days, sleeping most of the time.
When he did wake he lay staring at the roof which was only a
couple of feet above his head, enjoying the gloom after the
snow-glare of the plateau. The roof was damp, and there were
sometimes drips on it. He found them fascinating to watch and
study. When one of them was just about to fall, he would draw
a trail with his finger on the slimy rock so that the drop slid
down it and fell clear of his body. When he rolled a cigarette
he prepared for it by laying trails for all the ripening drops
which he could see, so that he could be sure to have his smoke
in peace. During those days, he discovered anew the pleasures
of the very simplest things; the delight of sleep, the joy of an-
ticipating eating, the unutterable luxury of yawning.

The mouth of the cave was often darkened as a visitor
crawled in beside him to feed him with the best that Mandal
could afford and to attend so far as possible to any wish that
he expressed. The visitors sat and gossiped when he was awake,
and left him alone when he was sleepy. One day, they brought
him the news that one of the German soldiers in their garrison
had run away to Sweden, which gave them all a quite dispro-
portionate happiness. Every day, whoever had come to him
talked about the Lapps, who were now arriving in great numbers in Kaafjord and the other neighbouring valleys and were
being coaxed and offered rewards by the local members of
the organisation in the hope that sooner or later one of them
would make up his mind to help. But Jan had stopped pinning
much faith in Lapps. The only plan he had was to sleep till
he really felt he had slept enough. By then, he thought, he

would be stronger, and that would be soon enough to think about the future. Then he would decide whether to go on leaning on the kindness of the Mandal folk still longer, right through the summer perhaps, or whether to put an end to it all as soon as his fingers could cock the pistol.

But suddenly, on his fourth or fifth day in the cave, a whole deputation arrived in excitement, to say that at last a Lapp had made a firm promise. He had demanded brandy, blankets, coffee and tobacco, which were all the most difficult and expensive things to get, but the organisation was sure to be able to find enough to satisfy him, and people who knew him said he was a reliable character who would not change his mind. But his reindeer were still up on the plateau, and he did not want to bring them down and then have to take them up again. So to make sure of not missing the chance, Jan would have to be moved straight away and hauled up to the plateau to meet the Lapp and his herd.

Jan was not really ready to leave the comfortable cave. A little more rest would have made him fitter to start the struggle again. But he could not refuse to fall in with a plan which had raised the hopes of the Mandal men so high; and although he had been disappointed too often, it did seem that this might be the opportunity they had all been waiting for. He tried to show more enthusiasm than he felt, and they pulled him out into the glaring daylight and tied him down to the familiar slats of the sledge again.

A large party of men assembled for the climb out of the valley. Eight actually took part in it. In many ways this ascent was less arduous, at least for Jan, than the earlier one from Revdal. There were twice as many men to handle the sledge; and by then Jan was much less of a load to carry. His weight ultimately fell to 78 pounds, which was less than half what he weighed when he left the Shetland Islands.

The eight men were therefore able to carry him bodily for a lot of the way, and he was not so often left hanging feet downwards or upside down. But the ascent lasted no less than thirteen hours, and by the time they got him to the top Jan was exhausted, and the good effect of his rest in the cave had been undone. After these hours of rough handling, he got angry for the first time in all those weeks, and in his weakness he forgot that he owed absolutely everything to the men who were carrying him. One of them had promised to bring tobacco for him, and in the excitement it had been forgotten. When Jan heard of this, it seemed for some reason the last straw. The prospect of even a day or two on the plateau without a cigarette was too much for him, and he snapped irritably: "You would go and forget the most important thing of the lot." It was an absurdly ungrateful thing to say, especially when tobacco was so rare and expensive that almost everyone in Mandal had had to give up smoking. But none of them took any notice, because they could see he had been pushed almost beyond endurance and was not really aware any more of what he was saying.

As a matter of fact, the organisation in Mandal and Kaafjord was being remarkably thoughtful and efficient, as it had been throughout the operation. When the climbing party got Jan to the new rendezvous on the plateau where he was to meet the Lapp, two men from Kaafjord had already arrived there. They had been detailed to relieve the climbers by taking over Jan and looking after him until the Lapp arrived, and they had been chosen as Lapp interpreters. The Lappish language is said to have no relation to any other language in the world except Hungarian, and there are very few people except

the Lapps who understand it. Most of the Lapps themselves
can also speak one or another of the languages of the countries they live in, either Swedish, Norwegian or Finnish, but
the man who was expected that night was a Finnish Lapp, and
so he and Jan would not have a single word in common.

The men who had brought him up were tired out when
they got to the meeting place, so they handed Jan over to the
Kaafjord men and retreated to the valley without any further
delay. These two stayed with him to keep him company all
through the following night. But events began to take a course
which was terribly familiar. Jan lay passively on the sledge
while the chill of the night froze the dampness of the day in his
clothes. The men who were guarding him watched the snow-
bound horizon patiently hour by hour. But no sign of the Lapp
was seen, and nothing stirred. In the early morning, the men
had to go down to their daily work, and Jan was abandoned
again to his solitude.

The vigil began again with all its rigour and discomfort and
the same hopeless dreariness. He was in a different place on
the plateau, but it looked almost exactly the same. There was
no rock with icicles to fill his cup, and there was no snow wall
or paper tent. The snow immediately round him was clean and
fresh, and not stained and foul by weeks of improvised existence. But the low hills and the dead shallow valleys within his
vision could hardly be distinguished from any others, and
the familiar numbing cold, the snow-glare and the silence
made the days in the cave appear like a half-remembered
dream which had done nothing but give a fleeting glimpse of
comfort and so emphasise the misery of the plateau. He lay
dazed, floating into and out of coma, and he began to listen
again. The thin wind sighed on a distant hill, and stirred the
loose snow in feeble eddies with an infinitesimal rustle, and

died to silence again. In his moments of clarity he knew these soft sibilant sounds threatened another blizzard. When his mind lost its grip on reality, he heard the wolves again padding secretively round him. He began once more to start into wakefulness when he imagined voices or the hiss of skis.

The next night two more interpreters came to stand by him. One speaks of night and day, but by then the midnight sun was up. It was broad daylight all the time, and night only meant that the shadows on the plateau were longer and that when they lengthened the air became more chill. Throughout this brilliant, glaring, frosty night the men watched over him. But nobody came. Jan had made up his mind that the Lapp would never come. The sun passed across the north horizon and climbed again into the east. The men had to give up waiting, and went away, and left him to face another glaring day.

Four days and nights dragged by before they broke it to him that this Lapp had also changed his mind and made the excuse that he was ill. It was no surprise. Jan knew it before they told him. This time, nobody could think of any alternative. To take Jan down to the valley again in the quickly melting snow was a final admission of defeat, because they could never get him up again over naked rock. Down in the valley, there was nothing they could do except feed him till the Germans found him and took them all. To leave him where he was only condemned him to a quicker, kinder death. It seemed to them all, and to Jan too, that they had reached the end. For the first time, they had no plans whatever for the future, no hopes to offer him, nothing to say which would encourage him. The only thing they could have done in mercy would have been to deny him the food which had served to spin out his existence, and to let him fade out as quickly as possible and in peace. Whatever they did, they knew it would not be long. It was useless even to promise to come to see him again. When they left him they gave him food, but they made him no promise. They expected to come again, twice; once to find his body and protect it from the birds and wolves, and again, when the snow was gone and the earth was thawed, to bury him.

When their voices had faded and the last of them had gone, Jan lay quite still. The doleful wind ruffled his hair and sifted a little snow across his face. His mind was at rest in the peace which sometimes follows the final acceptance of death.

CHAPTER SEVENTEEN

REINDEER

WHEN HE opened his eyes there was a man standing looking at him.

Jan had never seen a Lapp before, except in pictures. The man stood there on skis, silent and perfectly motionless, leaning on his ski-sticks. He was very small. He had a lean swarthy face and narrow eyes with a slant. He was wearing a long tunic of dark blue embroidered with red and yellow, and leather leggings, and embroidered boots of hairy reindeer skin with turned-up pointed toes. He had a wide leather belt with two sheath-knives hanging from it. He was wearing it loosely round his hips, not round his waist, so that he looked all body and no legs, like a gnome. Jan had not heard him coming. He was simply there.

They stared at each other for a long time before Jan could speak. His brain was slow to readjust itself, and his memory was muddled. Had someone told him this man was coming? Had he dreamed it was all over? Was this a dream? At last, with supreme inadequacy, he said: "Good morning." The Lapp did not move or answer, but he gave a grunt, and Jan dimly remembered then that he probably could not understand a word he said. He shut his eyes again because he was too tired to make any effort to think what to say or do.

He had an uneasy feeling that he ought to know who the man was and where he had come from. There had been a lot

South towards the frontier: the plateau at the head of Mandal

Lapp sledges, on the Swedish side of the frontier *Arvid Moberg*

Jan with the King of Norway at an inspection after his return

of talk about Lapps coming to help him, he could remember that; but it had all been a long time ago, and it had all come to nothing in the end. They had given it up as a bad job. He could not think of any sense or reason in a Lapp being there on the plateau all alone. He looked again to make sure if he had seen what he thought he had seen, and the man was still standing there just the same, with his ski-sticks tucked under his armpits and no expression whatever on his face.

Jan could not rest with the feeling whenever he shut his eyes that someone was silently staring at him. He could not even tell if the stare was friendly or hostile, if the extraordinary creature he had seen was wanting to help him or fingering the long knives at the belt. He wished he would go away. It seemed to him that the man stood there for hours and did not move or speak or change his curious stooped position. But then, without any sound the man had gone. Jan was relieved, and sank back into the daze which this sudden apparition had disturbed.

In fact, this was one of the Lapps whom the ski-runner from Kaafjord had gone to see on his journey a month before. He had just arrived with his herds and his tents and family in the mountains at the head of Kaafjord, and he must have been thinking over the message all that time. When he had first been asked, the whole matter was in the vague imponderable future. Now it was in the present, and the first thing he had done when he got to Kaafjord had been to find out where Jan was lying, and then to go himself to see whether the story was true. He did stand looking at Jan for three or four hours. He was making up his mind. As soon as he had done so, he went down into the valley and announced that he was going to the frontier. Immediately the gifts which had been prepared for the Lapps who had defaulted were pressed upon him; the blankets, coffee, brandy, and tobacco which had been bought here and there at enormous prices and carefully hoarded for this purpose.

The next thing that brought Jan to his senses was a sound of snorting and shuffling unlike anything he had ever heard before, hoarse shouts, the clanging of bells and a peculiar acrid animal smell, and when he opened his eyes the barren snow-field round him which had been empty for weeks was teeming with hundreds upon hundreds of reindeer milling round him in an unending horde, and he was lying flat on the ground among all their trampling feet. Then two Lapps were stand-ing over him talking their strange incomprehensible tongue. They both bent down and picked him bodily up, talking all the time, but not to him. For a moment he could not imagine what they were going to do; but then he understood he was being moved from his own sledge to a larger one. They muffled him up to his eyes in blankets and skins, and stowed packages and bundles on top of him and around him and lashed him and everything down with thongs of reindeer hide and sinew. There was a jerk, and the sledge began to move.

This had all happened so fast that Jan was bewildered. A few minutes before he had been lying torpid and alone; now he was being dragged feet first at increasing speed in the middle of a wild tumult, and nobody had given him a word of explanation. He squinted along his body, and saw the hind-quarters of a deer which was harnessed to the sledge. A Lapp on skis was leading it. It was one of the bell deer of the herd, and as it snorted and pawed the snow and the sledge got under way and the bell on its neck began a rhythmic clang, the herd fell in behind it, five hundred strong, anxiously padding along in its wake. From the corner of his eye he could see a few dozen of the leaders, jostling for position. The mass of deer flowed on

behind; it streamed out in a hurrying narrow column when
the sledge flew fast on the level snow, and when the sledge was
checked the herd surged round it and also halted. Sometimes
in these involuntary halts Jan found himself looking up from
where he lay on his back a foot above the ground at the un-
gainly heads and large mournful eyes and snuffling nostrils
immediately above him. But when this happened, one or the
other of the two Lapps appeared, urging on the draught deer
which pulled the sledge, and sometimes giving the sledge a
heave himself till the obstacle was passed and the rumble of
hoofs began again, and the snow-hiss beneath the runners.

All day the enormous mass of beasts swept on across the
plateau, cutting a wide swath of trampled snow which hid the
tracks of the sledge which carried Jan: the most strange and
majestic escort ever offered to a fugitive in war. Jan lay on the
sledge feeling that events had got beyond him; but he was
content to let them take their course, because he had seen the
position of the sun and knew that at last, whatever happened
next, he was on his way towards the south and towards the
border.

Some time in the evening they halted. The two Lapps gave
him some dried reindeer meat and some reindeer milk to
drink, and then he saw them pitching a little tent made of
skins. The reindeer were wandering aimlessly round and
digging in the snow with their forelegs to look for the moss on
the rocks far down below. Jan was left lying on the sledge. On
the whole he was glad of this, because the tent was certainly
only made for two; but when he was left alone among the deer
he still found them alarming. They came and sniffed at him,
most obviously wondering whether he was fit to eat, and Jan,
who knew very little about the tastes of reindeer, was not sure

if he was or not. If ever he shut his eyes, hot breath and wet hairy muzzles woke him.

After the Lapps had disappeared inside the tent, a most peculiar noise began to come out of it: a monotonous kind of chant which rose to howls and died away to moaning. When the first eerie shrieks rolled out across the plateau Jan thought they must be fighting, and when one of them burst out of the tent after a little while and staggered through the snow towards him with the knives dangling at his belt, he thought an entirely unexpected death was in store for him. But the Lapp stooped over him and a waft of his breath explained the whole fearsome interlude. The Lapps were drunk, and they were singing. They had been getting to work on the brandy which had been given to them as a reward, and one had come reeling forth on his short bow legs with no more evil intention than to offer Jan a swig at the bottle. It came back to Jan then that years before he had either read or been told about Lappish singing. It is called yoicking. It is said to be a kind of ballad which tells stories of heroic Lappish deeds, but it is not in the least like the usual conception of music, and to people who have not been instructed in its arts it is apt to seem no more than a mournful wail, like a dog's howling at the moon, but somewhat sadder.

The day's sudden journey had revived Jan's interest in life, and when the Lapp thrust the brandy bottle at him he laughed: for a moment, with the wry humour which never left him except on the verge of death, he had had a glimpse of the ludicrous indignity, after all that had happened before, of being slaughtered by a drunken Lapp on the very last stage of the way to the frontier. He took a small sip from the bottle and was glad of it, but the Lapp began to talk. Not a single word he said conveyed anything to Jan, but the general meaning was clear enough. He was pressing Jan to drink more, with the embarrassing hospitality of drunk people of any nation, and he was going to be offended if Jan refused. But Jan knew from the experience of the last few weeks that one sip was enough to make him feel better, and that two might make him a great deal worse. So he smiled and shut his eyes and shammed unconscious, and after a while the Lapp finished the bottle himself and wandered back to the tent to start yoicking again.

It was a good thing to be relieved of the expectation of being murdered, but the situation was alarming still. As the lugubrious sounds of revelry rolled out again, Jan thought of the German voices he had heard in the night, and of the ski patrols which were said to be out on the frontier. He had no idea how far he was from the frontier, but the dreadful noise in the quiet frosty air sounded as if a patrol might hear it miles away. It made him nervous and there was no possible way he could hope to persuade them to stop it.

From time to time the Lapps made further sorties to offer him drinks or merely to look at him. Sometimes the bottles they brought were full, and sometimes nearly empty. He wondered how many bottles the organisation had bought, and how long it would be before the two men got over this rare and splendid orgy and were fit to go on with the journey again. He was so helplessly in their hands. He felt as a passenger in an aeroplane might feel if he discovered the pilot and crew were very far from sober. All in all, he spent an anxious night.

But during the night the singing slowly flagged and gave place to a blessed silence, and some time in the morning the tent shook and the Lapps emerged, apparently none the worse, and immediately set about striking the tent and harnessing the reindeer. They seemed as brisk as ever. He thought they must have remarkable constitutions. Soon the herd was rounded up, the sledge started, and the headlong rush of hoofs began again.

On this second day Jan lost the last of his sense of position and direction. He did not know where he was being taken, and he could not ask what plans the Lapps had made, or try to change them whatever they might be. But simply because there was something happening, some positive action going on at last, he had roused himself out of his mental apathy, and even felt physically better than he had when all hope had seemed to have come to an end. The lurching and swaying of the sledge and its sudden stops and starts were sickening and tiring, but he summoned up every bit of strength which he still possessed, inspired if not by hope, at least by curiosity. He wanted to see what was going to happen next. This wish in itself must have helped him to keep alive.

Everything happened, very quickly. The sledge lurched to a halt, perhaps for the hundredth time. The herd, swept on by its own momentum, came milling all round him again. Then he found that both the Lapps were trying to tell him something. They were pointing with their ski-sticks. He tried to look in the direction they showed him but he could not see very much between the hundreds of legs of deer. He listened to what they were saying, but it meant nothing to him at all. And then he caught a single word, the first word they had ever said which he understood. It was "Kilpisjarvi," and he remembered it. It is the name of a lake. He looked again, with a sudden uncontrollable excitement, and caught a glimpse of a steep slope which fell away from where the herd was standing, and down below, at the foot of the slope, an enormous expanse of smooth unsullied snow. It was the frozen lake, in sight; and he had remembered that the frontier runs across the middle of it. The low banks of snow on the other side were Sweden. Slowly there dawned the wild incredible hope that he was going to win.

The Lapps were still talking. He shut his mind to that blinding blaze of hope, and tried to attend to them. They picked up handfuls of sodden snow and squeezed it so that the water ran down, pointed again to the lake and shook their heads. That was it: they were trying to tell him that the thaw had gone too far and the ice of the lake was rotten and unsafe. He looked down at the lake again, and then he saw here and there the greenish translucent patches which showed where the ice was melting.

He remembered Kilpisjarvi on the map. It was miles long, seven or eight at least, and the head of it was near the summer road, where there was sure to be a guard post. At the other end there must be a river. It came back to him: there was a river, and the frontier ran down it. But if the lake was melting, the river ice would surely be broken up and the river in spate and uncrossable. They must cross the lake: they must chance it: he had to make them try. Stop the herd, let him try it alone on the sledge: one man on skis, one deer and the sledge. But he could not explain it. He started to say it in Norwegian but their faces were blank and he stopped in an agony of frustration, and began again to try to control his impatience and to think of a way to make it all clear to them by dumb show. If only he had a pencil and paper to draw maps and pictures—

There was a crack, the unmistakable lash of a bullet overhead and then the report of a rifle. The deer froze where they stood and raised their heads, scenting danger. The Lapps froze, silent and staring. Jan struggled to raise his head. There were six skiers on the crest of another hill. One of them was kneeling with a rifle, and in the split second while Jan glanced at them another shot went over and he saw three of the men turn down off the crest and come fast towards the herd.

After seconds of stunned silence the Lapps started talking in shrill excited voices. Jan found he was shouting, "Get on, Get on! Across the lake!" The deer moved nervously, running together in groups, stopping to sniff the wind. The Lapps glanced at him and back at the patrol, the picture of indecision. The patrol was down off the hill, racing across the flats. In an access of frenzied strength Jan half raised his head and shoulders from the sledge, forgetting that words were useless, shouting, "They're out of range! For God's sake move! Move!" One of the Lapps shouted back a quick meaningless answer. The other waved both hands towards the rifleman as if he was begging him not to shoot. In an inspiration Jan fumbled in his jacket and drew his useless automatic and brandished it at the Lapps. They stared at it aghast: heaven knows what they thought, whether Jan was meaning to threaten them or defend them. With a final glance at the skiers approaching, one jumped to the head of the deer which pulled the sledge. The other shouted and suddenly, like a flood released, the herd poured over the edge of the hill and down the steep slope towards the lake, the sledge rocking and careering down among them, snow flying from the pounding hoofs, rifle shots whining past and over, across the frozen beach, out in a mad stampede on to the slushy groaning ice and away full tilt towards the Swedish shore.

EPILOGUE

ESCAPE STORIES end when freedom and safety are reached, but this story can hardly be ended without telling what happened to the people in it after it was all over.

Jan and Marius and the Mandal men had dreamed so long of the Swedish frontier that they had never thought much about what would happen on the other side of it. Of course they all knew it was a very long way from the border to a town or hospital, but to travel in a country where there were no Germans seemed so absurdly easy that none of them worried about the distance.

But as it turned out it was quite a long time after the hectic dash across the lake before Jan was put to bed in a Swedish hospital. Once the tension was over, his memory went to pieces. He remembers a day which he spent in a hut with a lot of Lapps, and another day in a canoe going down a fast river of which one bank was Finland and therefore controlled by the Germans, and the other Sweden. Eventually the river led to a telegraph station, where the operator sent an urgent message to the Swedish Red Cross.

That excellent organisation sent an ambulance seaplane, which made a perilous landing on a stretch of the river where the ice was still breaking up. Before the plane could take off again, a squad of men had to break more of the ice to give it a longer run. The take-off was the last of the experiences which Jan recollects as having scared him out of his wits. After it, he had a complete blank in his memory until a doctor told him he had been in hospital for a week.

In hospital, he had the very unusual satisfaction of being asked what surgeon had amputated his toes, and of saying with a casual air that he had done it himself; and later he had a satisfaction which was even greater, when he was told that his operation had saved his feet. The decision about his feet remained in the balance for a long time. He very nearly lost them when the doctors first unwrapped them; but they called in a specialist who decided to try to redeem them, and after three months' treatment they were declared to be safe.

As soon as he woke up in hospital, he began to try to get a confidential report of what had happened through to London. It was not very easy. As Sweden was neutral, there were naturally Germans and German agents around, and if his report had got into the wrong hands, of course it would have been a death warrant for the people in Norway who had helped him. He was worried too by the recollection that the Swedes had only let him out of prison three years before on condition that he left the country, so that they had every right to put him in again. But some of his story had filtered across the border, and no doubt the Swedes who heard rumours of it felt he had earned the best treatment they could give him. They let him get into touch with a secretary in the Norwegian embassy, and to her he dictated all that he could remember of the story.

In England, we already knew, of course, that the expedition had come to grief, and vague reports had come through of what had happened to the *Brattholm*. There had been a long, sarcastic and gloating story in the *Deutsche Zeitung* about the brave and ever-vigilant defenders who had won the

battle of Toftefjord, and this German view of the affair had
even been quoted in brief in the London papers in early June,
while Jan was still lying unconscious. But Jan's report gave the
first news of the unlucky chance which had betrayed the landing, and it was also the first indication we had that one of the
twelve men who had sailed from Shetland had survived.

Jan himself flew back to England in the autumn, after being away from his unit for seven months. In some ways, his return to war-time London must have been a disappointment to
him after he had dreamed of it for so long. When the welcom-
ing drinks and the official compliments were over, there was
hardly anyone he wanted to talk to about what had happened
to him. The Linge Company in which he had been trained
was a company of adventurers, and nobody in it talked much
about personal experience: for one thing, everybody in it was
waiting his own call to go to Norway and knew it was best not
to be burdened with other people's secrets. The few staff officers to whom Jan could talk freely had already seen his report and were busy with other plans, and anyhow were sated
with stories of desperate adventure. There was nobody who
could share the pictures which were still so vivid in his own
mind: pictures of the endless snow, the cold, the glaring
nights, the procession of faces of people who had offered their
lives for his and whose names he had never known, the sound
and smells of the northern wastelands, the solitude and hope-
lessness and pain. In the busy, grey autumnal streets of London, these things began to seem like a private dream: a dream
which was overcast and darkened by anxiety, because he did
not know what had happened in those desolate valleys after he
got away, so that he was haunted, for the whole of the rest of
the war, by the thought that his own life might have been
bought at the cost of appalling reprisals. To help himself to

live with this burden of worry, he threw all his energy into the routine of army life, and into training himself to walk and run without losing his balance, and getting himself fit again in the hope that he would be allowed to go back to Norway.

But if nobody in England could share in Jan's anxiety, it had its counterpart in arctic Norway. For month after month, in Furuflaten and Lyngseidet and Mandal, Kaafjord and Tromsö and the islands, all the people who had helped to save him went about their daily business in the constant fear that something would still be found out which would give them away to the Germans. But time passed and nothing disastrous happened, and the fear very slowly faded; and in fact the Germans never discovered anything, and nobody was ever punished for Jan's escape. Furuflaten and Lyngseidet survived the war intact, but Mandal, on the other side of the fjord, was the very last of the places which the Germans destroyed in a futile "scorched earth" policy when their retreat began. The people were driven out and every house was burnt to the ground. For a long time the valley was deserted. But now, it has spacious new houses and its people have returned. The valley is still as remote as ever: it still has no road: but its placid life has begun again, and Herr Nordnes has a new generation of pupils in a new school, the sons and daughters of the men who went up to the plateau.

As I write, the midwife of Ringvassöy is still at work; the same people live in the cottage in Toftefjord; and old Bernhard Sörensen, who rowed Jan across the sound among the searchlights, still thinks nothing of getting his feet wet at 82. But his son Einar died some years ago, and the two grandsons who made Jan tell them a story are grown up and have gone to work in town, so that Bjorneskar is a lonely place for the old man and his wife.

The village of Furuflaten is very prosperous. Marius has formed a partnership with three other local men, one of whom is Alvin Larsen, who was with him that awful night when they dragged the sledge up Revdal. They are building contractors, and they have also put up a factory in the village, just by the place where they hauled Jan across the road below the school-house. In the factory they make concrete blocks, and a special kind of arctic prefabricated house, and, most unexpectedly, ready-made trousers. The business is growing: they are starting on jackets to match the trousers, and there is no end to their plans.

Marius, I am glad to say, married Agnethe Lanes, whom he treated so roughly on the night they climbed up to the plateau. They are bringing up a family in a new house they have built beside the log cabin where Jan stumbled in at the door. Marius is beginning to worry about his figure, but he still has his quiet irresistible chuckle, and I think he always will have.

As for Jan, he got his own way in the end and was sent over again to Norway as an agent, sailing once more from the base in the Shetland Islands. So it happened that he was on active service there when the capitulation came. In the midst of the national rejoicing and the hectic work of accepting the surrender of the Germans, he picked up the telephone and asked for his father's number, and heard at last that his family were safe and well. When he was free to go to Oslo to meet them, his schoolgirl sister, Bitten, for whom he had worried so long, astonished him by being twenty and having grown up very well, as he saw at a glance, without the benefit of his brotherly hand to guide her.

Jan is a married man now. His wife Evie is American. Jan and his father work together again, importing mathematical and surveying instruments from abroad. To meet Jan, absorbed in theodolites and his family affairs, in his house in the pinewoods in the outskirts of Oslo, you would never guess the story which he remembers. But you would see for yourself that it has a happy ending.

APPENDIX I

CHRONOLOGICAL TABLE

March 24 *Brattholm* sailed from Shetland.

29 Landfall off Senja.

30 The fight in Toftefjord.

31 Jan in Ringvassöy at the midwife's house.

April 3 Reached Bjorneskar.

4 Rowed across sound.

5 To Kjosen by motor boat: through Lyngseidet at dawn.

5 to 8. Lost in Lyngen Alps.

8 Found Marius's farm at Furuflaten.

12 Across Lyngenfjord to Revdal.

12 to 25. In the hut at Revdal.

25 Ascent of Revdal.

25 to May 2. In the snow grave.

May 1 Marius and Agnethe climb the plateau.

2 Mandal men arrive: first attempt on frontier.

9 Second attempt on frontier.

22 Carried down to cave in Mandal.

26 Carried up to plateau again.

June 1 Crossed the Swedish border.

APPENDIX II

A German newspaper account of the "Brattholm" incident
taken from "Deutsche Zeitung," 8th June, 1943

FISHING BOAT WITH STRANGE CARGO

British sabotage group rendered harmless on Norwegian Coast

IN THE twilight of a spring evening a large seaworthy fishing-boat
steams slowly out of a little harbour in the Shetland Islands. In the
light breeze which blows in from the sea, flutters the Norwegian
military flag—it has only been hoisted as the ship left port. No
security measures were to be neglected. Even before sailing, everything had been done to prevent unwanted people approaching
the boat or her crew. After all, even in England it is not every day
that a fishing-boat is made ready for a trip to Norway. No wonder
the greatest pains were taken to get the enterprise off to a good
start.

Twelve men comprise the crew of this boat as it sails towards the
east. Anyone who overheard them would soon be able to establish
that all the men were talking Norwegian. A certain Sigurd Eske-
sund is leader of the expedition. He was born on a mountain range
in Norway, but his parents died prematurely when he was young,
and so he left his native country and made his way, as so many did
at that time, to the United States. For years in America he fought
starvation, tried his luck here and there, until at last he found food

228

and shelter and the necessities of life on a farm. When war broke out, unemployment threatened again. Then one day he was urged to go to England to join the Norwegian legion. For two days he thought the matter over. But time had helped him to make a decision. The spectre of being without food hung over him again, and moreover he was being accused again of being a foreigner. And so he reported himself to the recruiting centre. A little later, he arrived in England. There he underwent his military training, and also attended a sabotage school and was taught to be a paratrooper. Months passed, months that were used in London and in Scotland to forge plans—not for the daring invasion that was always being talked about, but merely plans to decide where and how and when the Norwegian sabotage troops could be utilised. And now at last such an enterprise was under way.

Four days passed. Three men stand on the upper deck of the Norwegian boat and look eastwards. To-day they are wearing—according to orders—civilian clothing. They are the three men of the sabotage party. The real crew are no longer allowed to show themselves. Once again, to the best of their knowledge, all precautionary measures have been taken. I hope, said one of the men, Harald, that behind this fog bank there lies our coast. For it was about time. Engine trouble yesterday had forced them to slow down.

They sail on to a small outlying island which is only inhabited by a few fisher folk. This really ought to be an ideal hide-out. They hope it will be, for none of them feel happy on their lame vessel any longer—especially since a German reconnaissance plane continually swoops over the boat. In the faces of these twelve men on the fishing boat *Bariholm* there is consternation: have we been recognised? It is true the Norwegian battle flag has now been hauled down, but there is still the danger that the German is not quite satisfied.

For all three members of the sabotage party one thing is certain: as soon as they get ashore they will set up their radio and send this report to London—that the German air reconnaissance and coastal guard are very strong indeed. There is no way of slipping in unobserved. Not even a chance for a cleverly disguised fishing-boat—though God knows there are plenty of herring barrels on board to disguise her. All one has to do is to take them to bits, without any fear that salt water will pour over one's sea-boots, or that twitching fish will wriggle and slither away. No, all that has to be done is to open these barrels and there are wonderful well-oiled machine-guns. And it is the same with the fish boxes, only they contain hand grenades.

Now the coast looms up out of the fog. A small bay is selected as it has high rocks to protect it. Here the boat will probably be well concealed. Somewhat reassured by this, but none the less anxious and nervous, the sabotage party paddles ashore in a dinghy. It is a fair distance they have to cover. So they are glad when at last they touch land and jump out on to the beach. After long years they have Norwegian soil under their feet again!

They set off in a direction where they can see smoke. An old woman comes towards them—the first Norwegian in their own homeland! What greeting and reception will they get on this far-flung islet? They begin to ask her questions. They ask for someone who understands engines and can help them to repair the engine of their boat. But the woman will not help them. Next they meet a boy. Yes, he says, he will fetch his father who is a fisherman. They seldom see foreigners there, he says. Harald looks at Sigurd. But Sigurd behaves as if he has not heard what the boy said. He tries to do business with the fisherman. No, says he, he can give them no advice. In their short talk he has already summed up these intruders. What is the meaning of it all, Sigurd wonders.

They go on and on, like spurned beggars in a foreign land. Again and again they are told with a shrug that no help can be given. So the three offer first money, and then food which had been specially issued to them for bribery. But even that is useless.

Their task unaccomplished, they can only go back, grumbling

and tired, to the hideout of their boat. Damn it, what is to be done now? Over here the boat is no further use to them. They must bury its valuable cargo. A thousand kilograms of dynamite are stowed in the hold. Where to put it? First of all let's get back, says Sigurd, to look at the maps on board and think it over! Little do they imagine what surprise awaits them.

Downcast by their cool reception in their one-time homeland, by the unsuccessful pleading and attempts at bribery, they push off again in their dinghy. Hardly have they come in sight of their boat when close by they see a German warship. They turn towards land again, there is yet one more chance—escape! But they hear the shout of "Halt!" The three of them row with all their might. A burst of machine-gun fire from the warship sweeps over the water. Onward! shouts Sigurd. A fresh wave of machine-gun bullets smashes the side of the boat. The water begins to rise in it. There is nothing for it but to swim for shore. And now they see that two boats have cast off from the German warship. They are trying to cut off their escape. It is a matter of life and death! The water is cold, it grips the heart.

When finally they get to land, a party of German soldiers and sailors is waiting to receive them. The long swim in the cold water, the strong current, and perhaps also their experience ashore, have taken more toll of their strength than they realised. Helpless, shivering with cold, with no will-power left, they drag themselves up the stone quay—and give themselves up as prisoners. Sabotage operation "M" is broken up. Norwegians, who once believed they were helping to free their country, have once again been cynically and uselessly sacrificed by England. When their countrymen who had taken part in the capture heard the Wehrmacht communiqué, they expressed their verdict in a single word: "Misled."

THE
LAST CATHOLIC
IN AMERICA

THE
LAST CATHOLIC
IN AMERICA

A Fictionalized Memoir

JOHN R. POWERS

Saturday Review Press

NEW YORK

Published simultaneously in Canada by
Doubleday Canada Ltd., Toronto.

Library of Congress Catalog Card Number: 72-88664

ISBN 0-8415-0218-8

Saturday Review Press
380 Madison Avenue
New York, New York 10017

Printed in the United States of America

Design by Tere LoPrete

Portions of this book have appeared in slightly different form in *Chicago*
magazine, the *Chicago Tribune Sunday Magazine*, *Scouting* magazine,
and the *Houston Post*, in 1970, 1971, and 1972.

To my parents, June R. and John F. Powers, without whose love I would not have been possible

Acknowledgments

Randy. Margo Powers, for that night at the roller rink. Gay and Dr. Joseph V. Gioioso for their contributions. Dr. Martin J. Maloney of Northwestern University, John Fink of the *Chicago Tribune Magazine*, and Bill Wright for both their professional and personal assistance.

Contents

THE
LAST CATHOLIC
IN AMERICA

I / Because

Q. 150.   Why did God make you?
A. God made me to know Him, to love Him and to
   serve Him in this world, and to be happy with Him
   for ever in the next.

> Question 150 from the
> Baltimore Catechism

Morning flight. Cross-country from New York with but one
thought in mind: to sell a few million paper cups to a lavatory
firm in Los Angeles.

Talking to the fellow next to me, a law student from Harvard University. It is the usual pitter-patter conversation that

often ferments between passengers of adjoining seats: dribblings of dialogue spaced by half hours of silent negligence.

I ask him where he's from.

"Pittsburgh," he replies.

"Oh," I say. That's all I can think of to say about Pittsburgh. "Oh." But it's the type of inquiry that must be reciprocated. He complies somewhat blandly.

"And you?"

"Chicago."

"Oh." He knows as much about Chicago as I do about Pittsburgh.

I ask him if he knows anyone from Chicago. I say it as if I'm on a first-name basis with all four million of the city's inhabitants.

"Only one person," he says, "a gentleman who used to be a night security guard at my father's department store. His name was . . . ah . . . ." He looks up at the ceiling of the plane for the answer. "Ah, Alex Rummersfold, I believe."

"Alex Rummersfold! I know him!" I am almost shouting. Whenever I get excited, I always talk louder than I should. The Harvard law student, who is sitting next to the window, kind of turns his back on me and begins looking out at the cloudless sky.

A stewardess walking by is somewhat startled by my verbal explosion. She stares at me vacantly for a moment, then smiles weakly and moves on. I'm sure that if my head had just fallen off, she would have done the same thing. Stewardesses are like that.

"Alex Rummersfold," I say quietly to myself, "Jesus Christ, I forgot all about him." I turn in my seat toward the Harvard law student. "He's a short, squatty guy with huge shoulder blades, right?"

The Harvard law student continues to gaze out the window. "Yes, as I recall," he says.

"And he had a very odd, disgusting odor about him, right?"

That brings the Harvard law student away from his window. "Why yes, yes he did."

"That's because he has overdeveloped armpits. He's always smelled like that. He even smelled like that on his first day of school. He was the only six-year-old I knew who had fully matured sweat glands. He was an altar boy, too. Used to serve Friday night novenas all the time."

I relate the facts of Alex Rummersfold smugly. It's always a pleasure to drop a little history on the ignorant.

The Harvard law student isn't impressed. He goes back to staring out the window.

Thirty thousand feet over Ohio and thoughts of Alex Rummersfold don't mix very well in one's head so I try to think of other things. But it doesn't work. My mind keeps drifting back to Alex Rummersfold, hundreds of other people as weird as him including me, and that world we all shared together.

By the time the plane reaches Chicago for a stopover, I am more interested in tracing my umbilical cord back to its origin than in sticking some guy in Los Angeles with two million four-ounce paper cups.

Taking a cab from O'Hare Airport to the far South Side of Chicago. The cab is approaching a small hill that is topped by cemeteries on either side of the street. As the cab begins crawling up the hill, I yell at the cab driver to stop.

"Right here?" he asks.

"Right here." I hand him the fare, climb out of the cab, and begin walking up the remainder of the hill. I don't dare go into my old neighborhood in a cab. In all the years I lived there, I never once saw a cab on one of its streets.

It is a good day to be alive in Chicago. I have never been a big fan of Chicago's weather. The city's winters are unbelievably cold and piled with snow. Between the frigidity of winter and the torrid heat of summer are two days called spring. But

Chicago's autumns make up for all of it. They are cool days with clear complexions, flavored by crispy brown leaves and mellowed by a summer-aged sun. Today is such a day.

Looking through the wrought-iron fence as I approach the top of the hill. Grave markers and ground alike are speckled with leaves, many turned brown by the eons of summer.

There are a few newly dug graves. One is so fresh that leaves have yet to fall upon it.

An older friend of mine once told me that although you may live in many places, "home" will always be the one you grew up in. As I reach the top of the hill, I realize that he is right. Below me lies the main street of my old neighborhood.

It's a different neighborhood than most, if for no other reason than the fact that more than half of its inhabitants are dead and have been for years. Although the neighborhood is legally part of Chicago, it is isolated from the rest of the city by grave markers and evergreens. The area is entirely surrounded by cemeteries, seven of them to be exact. The neighborhood is named after the largest of these cemeteries, Seven Holy Tombs.

Seven Holy Tombs was originally a small town that was annexed into the city of Chicago sometime during the 1920s. The founder of Seven Holy Tombs was supposedly a gravedigger. But it wasn't until the late 1940s and early 1950s that the area really began to grow.

The men who came to Seven Holy Tombs were those who had fought, and won, World War II and who had used the G.I. Bill to buy their homes. Their wives were girls who had spent a few years after high school working for the telephone company and were now content to grind out the rest of their existences as mothers and housewives.

During those years, the white frame two-flats and chocolate brown brick bungalows of Seven Holy Tombs supported two

V.F.W. halls, a Moose lodge, a Knights of Columbus chapter, seven music stores all of which exclusively specialized in teaching the accordion, a three-story hobby shop, four dime stores, two custard stands, the world's largest Little League organization, a dozen gas stations, and about four thousand corner food stores.

Although most of the men of Seven Holy Tombs worked in other parts of Chicago, the vast majority of residents thought you needed a visa in order to get out of the neighborhood for more than one day at a time. It was customary for the natives, upon reaching puberty, to marry the girl next door and then move two blocks away. We children of Seven Holy Tombs believed that the edge of the earth lay two blocks beyond the cemeteries. Most of the adults felt that it was somewhat farther than that.

The young couples who had come to Seven Holy Tombs in the late 1940s and early 1950s were part of the fuse that ignited the postwar baby boom. Long engagements were their only form of birth control and that didn't always prove successful either. Through their endeavors, Seven Holy Tombs became the fastest-growing community in the country. It was during this time of her adolescence that I, and thousands like me, were born and grew older in Seven Holy Tombs.

Then, there were two major religions in the world, Catholic and "Public." Catholics went to St. Bastion Grammar School, had longer summer vacations, had to get off the sidewalks when a Public kid told them to since the sidewalks belonged to the Publics, and were constantly yelled at by adults who would say, "I expected better behavior from you Catholic kids, with all those nuns watching over you."

Publics went to Seven Holy Tombs Public School, had shorter summer vacations, were often subjected to "what can you expect from Public school kids" glares from adults, and went to a number of different churches in the neighborhood, which, according to the Catholics, were all the same anyway.

I notice few changes as I walk down the main street. It's a quarter to one. Almost the end of lunch period. Kids are streaming out of the various dime stores, their arms loaded down with packs of loose-leaf paper, pencil sharpeners, and new, unblemished notebooks.

In many of the boys' eyes, you can see that good old September enthusiasm. "Yes sir, this year is going to be different. I'm going to do my homework every day as soon as I get home from school. And no goofing around either. This is the year I show them what kind of student I can really be." Such enthusiasm inevitably dies within two weeks of the current campaign.

Some of their faces look familiar. Probably younger brothers and sisters of kids I grew up with.

Since I'm heading in the same direction, I walk along with them, but my step is not as fast as theirs. I don't have to be in my classroom before the bell rings.

With their accelerated pace, they shortly desert me. By the time I reach the St. Bastion parish complex, which includes the school, convent, the old church, which has been converted into classrooms, the new church, and the rectory, the school bell has rung. The playground is clear. The streets are no longer soaked with sound.

Directly across from St. Bastion is the neighborhood's major park, named quite appropriately Seven Holy Tombs Park. Being a baseball fanatic, I spent a good part of my youth chasing grounders and fly balls, most of which evaded me, across its various diamonds. With the kids in school, the park is virtually empty except for an occasional young mother pushing a baby carriage and a few old men cluttering up some of the park benches.

I get a long drink of water from the fountain, then pick out an empty bench that overlooks the park. Resting my arms along the back of the bench and stretching my crossed legs, getting all the wrinkles out. Relaxing while my body saturates the easy breathing of Seven Holy Tombs. Thinking.

II / *According to My Permanent Records*

I didn't say good-bye to all my imaginary friends or do anything stupid like that before I went off to my first day of school. Not that I didn't have imaginary friends. At that time I had two, Joe Brown and Pete Brown. By the time I was fifteen, I had forty imaginary friends. I still hang around with a few of them.

Joe Brown was the bartender in the upstairs bathroom. Joe was the owner and Pete was his assistant. Pete Brown got his own place when we put in a bathroom downstairs.

The only place I ever sat long enough to do any serious thinking was in the bathroom. Sometimes it's easier to do serious thinking if you have someone to talk things over with. Not all the time because it's nice to be alone, too. But sometimes.

After watching all those Sunday afternoon Westerns with their sympathetic bartenders, more and more often Joe Brown would just happen to be in my bathroom when I was there. Sometime later, Pete Brown started coming around to help Joe out. After a while, I started running into Joe Brown and Pete Brown all over the house. Gradually, more imaginary friends kept coming to stay. "Friends" really isn't the proper word to use. I didn't like all of them. Bill Doodle, for instance, was a very tough guy to get to know and an impossible person to get along with. Most of them were okay, though.

It was kind of nice having all those people around. The house was like a town in itself. The upstairs hall was sometimes a street and sometimes the hallway of the hotel many of us lived in. The stairs emptied out into the living room, which, with the dining room, was the rest of the neighborhood. The kitchen wasn't anything because one of my parents or my older sister was in there most of the time. Imaginary friends and family don't mix.

I would have never considered saying good-bye to my imaginary friends before I went to school that first morning. They were adults and so was I. Like any kid I might be a cowboy one day and the next day be a major-league ballplayer and they would change right along with me. But we were always adults. So why the hell would a bartender like Joe Brown care about some kid starting school?

With a quart of hair oil seeping through my fifty-cent haircut from Angelo's Barbershop, the clip-on bow tie gouging my Adam's apple with every swallow, the suspenders constantly slipping off the three-dollar corduroy pants that scraped and scratched with every step, three unsharpened pencils wrapped in my fist, and my feet encased in Buster Brown shoes "Made Just for You," I stumbled along the streets of Seven Holy Tombs, following the early morning school crowd to St. Bastion Catholic Grammar School, wondering what God had in store for me.

St. Bastion school had no guidance counselors, televisions, gym, school nurse, faculty room, cafeteria, or field trips. St. Bastion's had classrooms. Lots of them. And each classroom had kids. Lots of them. Through the combined efforts of the parents of St. Bastion's, the parish had the largest student body of any elementary school in the city of Chicago.

A nun stood in front of the large red double doors, her arms folded and her eyes peering down at me as I cautiously began to climb, for the first of many thousands of times, the steps of St. Bastion school.

I had met nuns a few times before when I had gone to Sunday mass with my parents. The nuns were sweet to me, then. Hugging me and saying what a sweet little fellow I was and all of that. They probably just said that because I was with my parents. Nuns are always very nice to you when you're with your parents. But if you're alone, look out.

"You, what grade you in?"

"I'm not in any grade, Str, I'm just starting school today."

"Hey, what are you? Some kind of wise guy? Downstairs in the basement with the other first graders."

The walls of the school basement were lined with smooth yellow brick. At the back of the basement was a stage with the curtain closed. The curtain was crowded with squares of advertisements advocating the patronage of local businesses. "Georgi's Jewelry Shop—When you think of Mother, your priceless jewel, think of Georgi, he's a real gem, too." "Don's Donut Shop, food good for the HOLE family." "Everrest Cemetery, We care. Free water cans."

A couple of hundred wooden and metal folding chairs had been set up in front of the stage with a space left in the center of them for an aisle. All the boys were on one side and all the girls were on the other. Angelo the barber had done a good week's business. He had even got some of the girls.

Everyone was sitting as if they had been painted into their folding chairs. The nuns swished along in their black and white habits, patrolling the outskirts of the chairs. No one talked.

A few minutes later, all the nuns began mumbling, "Good morning Father, good morning Father, good morning Father." Down the center aisle came a huge, balding, black-cassocked priest with a bloated belly so big it was outdistancing his head to the stage by two or three feet. His hands clasped each other behind his back, in silent agreement that there wasn't enough room for them up front with all that abdominal flesh.

He didn't answer the nuns but simply nodded in their direction as he inched up the aisle, slowly shifting the weight from one foot to the other. The nod seemed to be enough for the nuns. They went nuts over it.

If it had been a Bing Crosby movie, the priest would have been smiling and he would have said, "Greetings, children. It's certainly nice to see all your happy faces today. My name is Father O'Reilly and I would like to welcome you to St. Bastion Grammar School. We have a lovely school here, which I'm sure you will enjoy. We at St. Bastion's believe that children should study hard, pray hard, and play hard, though not necessarily in that order." Then he'd throw in a few phony "heh heh heh's" and we'd all phony "heh heh heh" him right back. Then he'd say, "I'm sure if you listen to the good sisters, obey the rules, and cooperate with your classmates, you will come to love St. Bastion school almost as much as it loves you."

That's not the way it was. Father O'Reilly didn't introduce himself. He didn't have to. Through his years of self-sacrifice, hard work, determination, Hell-preaching, and pure intimidation, parishioners had come to fear Father O'Reilly even more than they feared God. Although we first graders believed there was a God, we KNEW there was a Father O'Reilly.

He didn't smile. He didn't "heh heh heh" us and we didn't "heh heh heh" him back. His actual talk took about three dozen words and lasted less than thirty seconds.

First, Father O'Reilly led us through about ten minutes of prayers, "Hail Marys," "Our Fathers," "Glory Be's," the usual stuff. Then he said to us, "Obey the nuns and you won't get into any trouble. Now, I don't want to hear a sound when you leave this basement. And remember, from now on, everything you do for the rest of your life goes down on your permanent records."

After another ten minutes of prayers, we lined up, boys on the right side, girls on the left, and filed out of the basement to our classroom upstairs. Without making a sound.

My first-grade classroom had eighty-five kids in it. The nun, Sister Eleanor, spent half that first day bragging how she had over ninety kids the year before. Since at the time I couldn't count past four, neither number impressed me.

Sister Eleanor repeated Father O'Reilly's warning: everything that we did from this day forward would be etched eternally in our permanent records. She told us about how some former graduate of St. Bastion Grammar School had applied for a very important job in a steel company somewhere downtown. Sister Eleanor said that the prospective employer called the school and asked the principal to check the guy's permanent records and see how well the guy did in first grade, especially in Reading. We believed her.

Sister Eleanor also informed us that God did not like people who chewed gum in school, talked in line, or who insisted on going to the bathroom more than five times a day.

There were two other first-grade classrooms but the one I was in was a split classroom, half first graders and half second graders. In a few weeks it became apparent that Sister Eleanor felt the world of academia lay in rows four through eight, the rows of the second grade. She was always yelling at more of us than of them and she was always slugging more of us than them.

It must be admitted that, in fact, the second graders did have a lot of class. Sister Eleanor would tell them to take out their English workbooks and they would know which book to take out. She'd tell them to take out their catechisms and they'd know which book that was, too. Instead of buckles, many of them wore tie shoes. They had to be taken to the washroom only four times a day. Vomiting among the second graders was a rarity.

On the first-grade side of the room, someone was always goofing it up. We'd be lucky if we got through morning prayers without one of us getting clouted. Richard Dumple most often messed things up.

At the beginning of morning prayers, when he began making the sign of the cross, his finger tips stood a fifty-fifty chance of landing either on his forehead or in his eyes.

Usually a kid who constantly gets in trouble goes out of his way for it, at least in the beginning. Not Richard Dumple. He was different from the rest of us kids and we knew it, though we weren't quite sure in what way. He was very hairy. A few years later, he would be the only fourth grader with a five o'clock shadow.

In a class of only thirty or forty kids, you'll usually find a couple who are social outcasts and have no friends for one reason or another. But in a class of eighty-five, there are so many kids that even the weirdos have other weirdos to hang around with. But no one was as weird as Richard Dumple so he always ate his lunch alone, walked home alone, or did whatever he was doing, alone.

It wasn't until I was in high school that I realized the reason Richard Dumple was different from the rest of us kids was that he was emotionally disturbed. And it wasn't until a few years later that I realized it was the other way around.

In Catechism class we memorized the answers to such questions as "Who is God?" "Who made the world?" and "What is man?" We were learning to "defend" our faith though no one ever bothered to tell us who was attacking it.

The answer to the question "Where is God?" was "Everywhere." Sister Eleanor, my first-grade nun, loved to remind us of the fact.

"You may be able to fool your parents," she'd tell us, "and sometimes even the good sisters. But never God. He is everywhere. He sees everything. He hears everything. No matter where you go, God is watching you. Remember, children, you can never put anything over on God because HE is everywhere, everywhere, everywhere."

Besides being under God's constant surveillance, Sister Eleanor told the class that each one of us had his own personal guardian angel who had been assigned by God to do nothing but watch every move that was made by the kid whom he was told to guard. I already had double coverage and I hadn't even reached the age of reason yet.

On the days that Sister Eleanor was feeling a little fruity, she'd tell us to sit on one side of our desk seats so that our guardian angels would have room to sit down. We'd do it, too. We were as crazy as she was.

Life at St. Bastion Grammar School quickly settled into a routine that varied little for the eight years I was there. The mornings would start off with Catechism followed by Math, more commonly called Arithmetic. Then English, Reading, and right before lunch, Spelling. Spelling period was held just before lunch because it wasn't that important so we could always cut it short if the necessity arose. History and Geography were in the afternoon.

We didn't have all those subjects in the first grade, of course. All we did that year was try to remember how to get back and forth to school.

Reading period at St. Bastion's was always good for a fair amount of groin-tugging. I groin-tugged a lot during Reading period mainly because the nuns would never let you know exactly when you were going to be called on.

Normally a nun would tell a kid to stand and read a few lines from his reader out loud. After he finished, she'd ask the next kid in the row to do the same thing and so on down the row.

On occasion, however, the nun would suddenly ask a kid on the other side of the room to start reading, hoping she'd discover that he wasn't paying attention and had lost his place.

Actually, it wasn't a case of not paying attention that would cause you to lose your place but the fact that even the dumbest person could read faster silently than the kid who was standing up and reading out loud. To protect yourself from being caught off guard, you would teach your finger to read. As the kid read out loud, your finger would travel along the page of the book at the appropriate speed, underlining the words that were being read. Meanwhile, your eyes could race ahead a few pages to reveal the end of the story. If you were suddenly called on to read, your finger would save you.

The nuns always aimed such unexpected maneuvers at certain kids and never at a sugar cube such as Mary Kenny.

Mary Kenny was the top bootlicker in my class, managing to hold the title against all sorts of competition for the entire duration of grammar school. When attendance was taken each morning, she was the one who would answer "present" instead of "here." There were other teacher's pets but she was *the* teacher's pet. Mary Kenny had such a nauseating smile that she could turn your mouth inside out with disgust. Mary Kenny always sat in the front seat nearest the door, ostensibly because she was short (most bootlickers are short) and had to sit in a front-row seat in order to see the blackboard. The real reason was because, sitting in the seat closest to the door, Mary Kenny was the "natural" one to send on all errands. And if there was a fire, she could be the first one out the door. St. Bastion's could afford to lose a few ordinary kids. The school had too many anyway. But you could never have too many Mary Kennys.

All the bootlickers were like Mary Kenny. Girls, short, with very soft voices. I felt sorry for this one girl, Alice Blazer. You could tell she wanted to be a teacher's pet. Most of the girls did. But Alice Blazer was a very tall girl. She never had a chance. She was just too tall to put in a front seat.

About every two months we spent an hour in the afternoon doing Art or Music. It wouldn't have bothered me if we never had Art or Music. I never liked Art. During Art class, I always ended up sitting next to Virginia Leer, who ate her crayons and then got the runs in four different colors.

I like to sing but not the songs we sang at St. Bastion's. All we ever sang about was the Virgin Mary, except around Christmas when we sang about the Infant Jesus, too. We used to sing songs like "Queen of the May." "O Mary we crown thee with blossoms today, queen of the angels, queen of the May. . . ." Singing that kind of stuff for eight successive years can get to you.

Singing, like most things at St. Bastion's, was for the girls. The nuns always sang the songs at least twelve octaves too high for any boy. Whenever we boys tried to sing that high, it sounded like a hoe was being dragged across our throats. The major cause of hernias at St. Bastion's was "Queen of the May."

St. Bastion's believed in lines. In the morning, we came into school in a line and in the afternoon we left school in a line. We went to the washrooms, the playground, the coatroom, and up to the blackboard in line. If you felt like throwing up, there was a line for that, too. One was rarely allowed to walk around unless he was looking at the back of someone else's head. There were patrol boys stationed every ten feet who made sure we stayed in line and there were always the nuns hanging over us, daring us not to stay in line.

Lines were usually made up of double rows that were segregated: boys on the right side, girls on the left. It was considered capital punishment to put a person in the row of the opposite sex.

St. Bastion Grammar School was eight years of meandering through workbooks, praying, writing English essays that no one read, listening to the Pope on the radio, praying, standing up and telling the nun why you didn't do your homework, the excuse usually falling into one of five categories: "I forgot what the assignment was," "I left it at home," "My little brother ate it," "I can't find it," and "Uh," doing arithmetic on the blackboard and trying not to screech the chalk or trying to screech the chalk depending on the situation, coming up with nickels of mission money, praying, raising your hand to go to the washroom even though you didn't have to go—you just wanted to get out of your lousy desk for a while—making a hurried sign of the cross under orders of your nun because an ambulance siren wailed by the school, praying, reading from your book out loud to the class, praying, and watching the clock crawl around to three o'clock and summer. All of it, we were warned, went on our permanent records.

One day in the first months of first grade, I was walking home from school with Mike Depki. Depki was the only kid in the first grade who wore his hair in a "Detroit," a crew cut on top and long hair combed back on the sides. He lived at the end of my block in a large, clumsy brown frame house that looked like an old farmhouse. According to the neighborhood oral tradition, that's exactly what it was at one time, a farmhouse. Supposedly, the Depki family owned the entire neighborhood when it was still farmland. The only reason, claimed the oral tradition, that the Depki family didn't become wealthy after selling all the land for development was that they drank up all the profits. Since Seven Holy Tombs has never been worth more than a six-pack, it wouldn't have taken much drinking.

There were dozens of people in the Depki family, maybe even hundreds. They all lived in that one farmhouse. No one knew how many Depkis there actually were because the family was never seen together. Since there were so many of them living in the old farmhouse, they had to do everything in shifts.

At different times of the day, certain Depkis would be in the house eating and sleeping while other Depkis would be outside working or doing whatever they did. On blistering August afternoons, when the air was too hot even to breathe, Mike Depki would be the only kid on the street simply because it was his shift not to be in the house.

Mike Depki lived on Pepsis and Hostess Twinkies. He was every mother's example to her child of what not to eat. Yet Depki was the strongest kid in the neighborhood. And that was before the sixteen-ounce bottle.

No one in the Depki family had ever finished high school. An upper-grade nun told Mr. Depki, at the only parent-teacher conference that he had ever shown up for, that she was sorry to tell him that she thought he had a socially maladjusted child in his family. Mr. Depki said he thought so, too. He asked her if she knew which one it was.

Mike Depki had a very logical mind, which was one reason why he did so poorly in school. He was one of those guys who in class was a nominal nitwit but the moment he cleared the school door, he became the neighborhood Nietzsche.

On this particular afternoon, both Depki and I had been kept after school. I for not doing my homework and Depki for being Depki. He was telling me about the conversation he had had with one of his older brothers—the one who worked as a butcher during the day and as a bail bondsman at night.

"My brother says that the first four years of grammar school are a waste of time," said Depki. "All they teach you to do is to read and write and do arithmetic. According to my brother, you don't need any of that stuff until you're at least ten. Right?" Depki looked at me for confirmation.

"Right, Mike," I said. I didn't know what he was driving at, but I wasn't about to disagree with him. As I have mentioned, Mike Depki was the strongest kid in the neighborhood and like most intellectuals, he didn't tolerate dissent from his views. Depki continued.

"Remember how Eleanor tried to tell us if we studied hard we'd be able to read street signs, be able to count our change from the store, and be able to write letters to our friends."

"Yeah, I remember that, Mike."

"It kinda made sense to me at the time. But last night I told my brother what she said and he said that was a lot of shit."

That Depki sure was intelligent. He talked just like my father.

" 'Look, Mike,' my brother says to me, 'you know the names of the streets for four blocks in each direction and that's as far as you're allowed to go anyway. After that, you deserve to get lost. And what change do you have to count from the store? Twinkies and Pepsis are a dime each. You don't have to count a dime. You see a dime. And as far as writing letters to your friends, that's a lot of shit, kid. You haven't got a friend that lives more than five doors away. Why the hell would you want to write them a letter.' Then my brother puts his arm around my shoulder and he.says to me, 'Mike, why don't you skip school until you're ten and then see if it's any use to you. Speaking from my own personal experience,.I really can't see why you need those first four years.' You see, Ryan," Depki said to me, "these first four years are a waste of time."

It was the only instance I can recall where Mike Depki's mind went astray. The first four years of grammar school weren't a waste of time. The first eight were.

According to my permanent records.

III / Confession

It was in second grade that Father O'Reilly, the pastor of St. Bastion Church, came into our classroom to tell us about Confession. We knew something unusual was about to happen. Father O'Reilly was always the bearer of extraordinary news.

"You are now," he began, "seven years old and have reached the age of reason. Before you reached this age of reason, you were incapable of committing sin. Now, at the age of seven, you can totally comprehend right from wrong. You are capable of committing any and all kinds of sins. The week after next, you will be receiving the sacrament of Penance, which is another word for Confession. The following Sunday, you will make your First Holy Communion. Sister here will instruct you as to how to conduct yourself in Confession and Holy Communion. You better not make any mistakes."

Our nun first told us that there were two kinds of sin: Venial and Mortal. A venial sin was a minor offense against God and included such things as disobeying your parents, lying, stealing an item of small worth, deliberately not doing your homework, or not brushing after meals.

Although venial sins didn't have to be told in Confession, it was a very good idea to do so because by confessing them in Confession, we'd cut down the time we'd have to spend in Purgatory for them.

Venial sins, Sister said, were like nails in our souls. Confession pulled the nails out but there were still holes left in our souls. Purgatory took care of the holes. But if we didn't confess the venial sins in Confession, we'd have to spend an even longer time in Purgatory while the nails were being taken care of.

Then there was Mortal Sin. A mortal sin was a very serious offense against God and included such actions as missing mass on Sunday, swearing, stealing something of extreme value, divorce, murder, and eating meat on Friday.

Although it was a good idea to tell our venial sins in Confession as it would cut down our time in Purgatory, it wasn't absolutely necessary. Venial sins alone couldn't send us to Hell. But if we died with just one unconfessed mortal sin on our souls, that was the ball game. We'd go straight to Hell.

The confessional, said Sister, consisted of three attached closetlike rooms, all in a row. The middle closet, where the priest sat and listened to our sins, had a window on each side that opened into each of the closets next to it. The reason there were closets on both sides of the priest's closet was because one person could be telling his sins to the priest while the person in the other closet could be organizing his sins in order to be ready for the priest when the priest came to his window.

There was no light in the confessionals. We would be able

to see nothing except perhaps the small crucifix that would be hanging above the window. Neither we nor the priest would be able to see through the window as there was a darkened screen across it. We would be able to hear only one another.

The priest would slide a wooden panel across one window in order to guarantee privacy to the person at the other window who was about to begin confessing his sins. When we heard the wooden panel sliding back from our window, we were to begin telling the priest our sins.

He would listen, talk to us for a few moments, ask us if we were sorry for our sins, and then give us absolution for our sins and a penance that usually consisted of a few prayers, "Hail Marys," "Our Fathers," stuff like that, which we were to say in church immediately after leaving the confessional.

"Of course," said the nun, "you aren't really telling the priest your sins. When the priest is in the confessional, he is acting only as God's ears. A priest can never repeat anything he's heard in the confessional. Many priests throughout history have chosen to die rather than violate the secrecy of the confessional."

I imagined Father O'Reilly standing in front of some nebulous king, choosing to die rather than tell the king I had disobeyed my parents twice the previous week.

Sister told us that she knew people who had never committed even one mortal sin in their entire lives. If we ever did, she said, we'd never forget the first time. Sister said that if she ever committed a mortal sin, she'd be afraid to cross the street for fear someone would run her over and she'd go straight to Hell.

"Believe it or not," she said, "sisters can be sent to Hell. I would even suspect," said our nun, who was now almost whispering, "that somewhere in Hell there may be a priest." The last four words sped out of her mouth lest the crucifix on the wall overhear.

No, we didn't believe it. And no, we didn't believe that either.

After school, a group of us guys were playing softball in the vacant lot next door to Depki's house. The Depki family owned half the lot. They hadn't drunk that up yet. No one knew who owned the other half of the lot. Not much softball actually got played in Depki's field because of the sour apple tree in the middle of the field. There were about a million rules covering what happened when the softball went into the tree so we spent most of our time arguing about what branch the ball hit. Usually we played softball on the street but the neighborhood police were on another crime-prevention kick and were chasing us off before we could even get the game started.

Depki was both happy and angry about all the Confession news. He was happy because he had been told by Father O'Reilly that he now had a clean slate when he had already presumed it had been pretty well banged up.

"All this time," Depki said, "my old lady's been telling me about how I'm gonna hafta spend a lot of time in Hell for being such a jerk and here all the time I hadn't even reached the age of reason yet. Didn't even know I was doing wrong. What a fantastic deal. I just wish they had told me about this age of reason stuff sooner so I could have made more of it. Now, it's too late."

Johnny Hellger was there that day, too. Johnny was the number-one man on that infamous list of guys I wasn't supposed to hang around with. He was always causing trouble but he rarely got caught in it himself. I guess it was because he was a very calculating type of guy. When Johnny Hellger reached into a box of candy for a chocolate cream, he got a chocolate cream.

Hellger said that he was going to commit a mortal sin the first chance he got. He figured that, sooner or later, he was going to anyway so he might as well get the first one out of the way.

I myself was overawed with this new power of being able to do something as horrendous as a mortal sin. Not that I'd ever commit one. Never. But just having the power within me to condemn myself to Hell. It was very impressive in a lousy sort of way.

Tom Lanner, who was a tall, blond-haired, easygoing friend of mine, kind of agreed with everyone. He always did. Not that he was terribly wishy-washy or anything like that. He was just very agreeable. That's all.

I felt kind of sorry for Lanner. He lived with his mother and sister in one of the few buildings in the neighborhood that could qualify as a bona fide shack. His father was dead, I guess.

Like Depki, Lanner wished he had learned about "the age of reason" earlier. Like myself, he was overawed with this new-found power of self-condemnation. And in a way, Lanner thought the same as Johnny Hellger. Lanner also felt that he would probably commit a mortal sin fairly soon. Not that Lanner wanted to commit one. He just figured that, with his lousy luck, he'd inevitably fall into one.

For the next few weeks, our nun conducted mock confessions during Catechism class. She would call on someone and he would stand up and say, "Bless me father for I have sinned. It has been one week since my last confession. I lied six times, disobeyed my parents three times, and didn't do my home-work once."

As part of the mock confession, our nun would ask the kid if he was sorry for his sins just as the priest would do in the real thing. In the spirit of the mock, the kid would reply that he was and she'd give him a mock absolution for his sins and a mock penance of three "Our Fathers" and three "Hail Marys." The only kid who goofed up the dry runs was Richard Dumple, who actually told his sins, with explicit detail, in front of the room's eighty-four other kids.

The nun had us say "one week since my last confession" in the dry runs so we'd get into the habit of telling the priest how long it had been since our last confession even though we were supposed to say "this is my first confession" the first time we went.

On Friday afternoon, our nun told us to start keeping track of our sins because the following Thursday we were going to go to Confession for the first time. The Sunday after that, we would make our First Holy Communion.

First Confession and First Holy Communion were usually made a few days apart. Although Confession required a lot more training, First Holy Communion was considered the more important of the two sacraments. In Confession, our souls were cleansed of our sins. But in Holy Communion we received the actual body and blood of Christ.

Making First Holy Communion was one of the three high points in one's life, the other two being the sacrament of Confirmation, which came somewhere around fifth grade, the exact time being dependent on when the bishop could get to the parish, and Graduation Day, which, logically enough, came at the end of eighth grade.

Each of these occasions was commemorated at home by a Saturday of cleaning the basement, returning empty pop bottles, getting more ice from the store and more folding chairs from the neighbors. Then a Sunday of open house, three-dollar envelopes from relatives, a one-inch-high, one-yard-square white frosting cherry vanilla cake with CONGRATULATIONS TO
. . . fill in the appropriate name . . . ON THIS MOST HOLY AND HAPPY DAY scribbled on top in red icing. And wondering on Monday morning which uncle left all the half-drunk beer cans in the dining room.

On First Holy Communion Sunday, the girls wore white

lace dresses and veils, white socks, and white patent leather shoes. The girls got to keep their outfits. The boys dressed in white suits too, but rented their outfits from Silverstein Formal Wear, whose advertisement could be found in the highest box on the left side of the stage curtain in the school basement. For such major social functions, girls always kept, boys always rented.

On Thursday morning, my First Confession Day, my class solemnly and silently filed into the basement church and formed lines at the different confessionals, girls on the left side of the confessionals, boys on the right side.

St. Bastion Parish actually had two churches in one building. The upstairs church was for the adults while the church in the basement was for the kids.

Standing ten kids back in line, I was slowly being towed toward the confessional door as it continually opened and closed, sucking in one kid as it spat out another. Now I was at the front of the line, waiting for the kid in the confessional to tell his sins so I could take his place in the conscience cleaner.

Fortunately, at that time, my sins fell into two major categories: disobeying my parents and lying. During the past week I had meticulously recorded each of my sins, under the proper heading, in a brown memo notebook. Through careful tabulations on my way to school that morning, I had determined that I had disobeyed my parents three times and had lied five times during the previous week. I assigned the responsibility of remembering how many times I disobeyed my parents to my left hand, which hung innocently at my side with three fingers open. My right hand, assigned to keep track of lies, hung at my side with all five fingers open. I considered myself extremely fortunate that for this first time, when the least little forgotten detail could screw up the whole thing, my sins had not outnumbered my fingers.

As I mentally reviewed the classroom mock confessions in

my mind, I could hear Depki, who was standing in line behind
me, mumbling to himself. Man, he was talking double figures.
Even Johnny Hellger, who was right behind Depki, wasn't
goofing around as much as he usually was. At least I couldn't
hear him.

The confessional door eased open in front of me. One of my
classmates came out, gave me a guilty look, and slipped into
one of the pews to say his penance. I stepped into the black cubicle, quickly pulling the door closed behind me.

Kneeling in front of the window, I felt my knee caps rising
and falling among the pitted crevices of the kneelers. A crucifix hung over the window. It was just He and me. My mind
started rattling off a lot of silent "Our Fathers" and "Hail
Marys" while constantly interspersing between them, "Left-
hand fingers, disobeying my parents, right-hand fingers,
lying." Mumblings came from the other side of the window.
The confession of the kid from the other side. I silently started
praying faster to get my mind off the mumblings. We had
been warned that we'd burn plenty for listening to someone
else's confession.

The mumbling stopped. I heard the wooden panel slide back
from my window. This was it.

"Bless me father for I have sinned. It's been one week since
my last confession."

The voice behind the screen said, "I thought this was your
first confession." I recognized the voice as that of the young,
newly ordained priest who had just recently been assigned to
St. Bastion Parish, Father Krowley.

"That's right, Father. Bless me father for I have sinned. It's
been one week . . . this is my first confession. I . . ." left
hand, three fingers . . . "lied three times . . ." count the
fingers on the right hand . . . "disobeyed my parents five
times."

The voice behind the screen started giving me a pep talk.

"You realize, of course, that when you lie to others you are really telling them that you have little faith in yourself as a human being and you have little faith in your God. Further, you should always try to obey your parents for they have devoted their lives to raising you in the image and likeness of God."

He went on and on. First Confession and I had to have the luck of drawing a dedicated priest. I could feel my knee caps beginning to crack from the pressure of the kneeler. I kept replying, "Yes Father, yes Father, yes Father," hoping he'd stop. But the words kept right on coming.

What were those kids who were waiting in line outside the door thinking? Hellger's probably mumbling to Depki, "Christ, that Ryan must have done some beauts. He's been in there a couple of hours already."

And still the priest talked. "Yes Father, yes Father, yes Father. A . . . Father, I have to go to the bathroom." I really did, too.

"Oh, yes, why of course, son. Are you sorry for your sins?"

"Yes, Father."

"For your penance then, say two 'Our Fathers' and two 'Hail Marys.' Now go in peace and God bless you."

As I stepped out of the confessional door, I heard Hellger whisper at me from behind Depki. "Hey, Ryan, who did you murder?" After I finished saying my penance, it was lunchtime and since only half of the class had gone to Confession, we were told to go home for lunch and meet back in the church basement at one o'clock.

On the way home, Johnny Hellger was still giving it to me about spending so much time in the confessional. He was trying to get Depki to razz me too, but Depki's mind seemed to be on other things. Johnny Hellger wasn't bothering me. I was too busy going over in my mind the details of that First Confession.

Things had gone surprisingly well. The only minor slipup had been the pep talk by the priest and that could hardly have been my fault. I had performed admirably. I had committed a proper variety of sins, just about the same kind that our nun had used in the dry runs. About the right number, too. Not so few that it would have seemed I had added wrong nor so many that I couldn't keep track of them with my fingers. I had handled myself well as a sinner.

At that time, when I was seven, there were two women whom I very much liked. I dreamed of them often. Whoever was starring in a particular dream would find me late at night, alone on the street. An orphan, lost, bewildered, sad-faced. She would pick me up, hug me tightly, and then take me home with her where she would rock me to sleep in her arms after having fed me milk and Campbell's Chicken Noodle Soup. Those two women were Dinah Shore and the Blessed Virgin Mary.

I had developed an intense liking for Dinah Shore through watching her fifteen-minute television program, which was on every Tuesday and Thursday night. At St. Bastion's, we were constantly told that the Blessed Virgin Mary was the second most important person in the world, second only to her son, Jesus Christ. There were a lot of statues and pictures of the Blessed Virgin Mary around St. Bastion school, which showed how pretty she was. Of course, she was always dressed in those long gowns but you could still tell that she was a nice-looking woman.

Lunch wasn't quite ready when I got home so I decided to spend a few minutes relaxing in my little red rocker. Mom was making Campbell's Chicken Noodle Soup for lunch. The aroma of the soup drifted into my nostrils. My mind on Confession already, I naturally looked up at the ceiling and began thinking about how proud the Blessed Virgin Mary must be in Heaven after seeing the brilliant way I handled myself in my

First Confession. Now she knew my love was sincere and that I was a faithful apostle of her son.

With my red-rocker world rolling so smoothly over the living room rug, I decided to relive once more in my mind my First Confession so that I could again feel the exhilaration of knowing how well I had handled myself in this first venture into the world of organized sin. My mind had instant replay long before CBS.

I pulled the brown memo notebook out of my pocket and once again went over my sin tabulations.

LIES

Friday	Lied to Dad when he asked me if I had used his hammer.
Saturday	Lied to Mom when she asked me if I had broken Linda's roller skates.
Saturday	Lied to Mom when she asked me if I had taken out the dog.
Tuesday	Lied to Depki when he asked me if I had a dime he could borrow.
	Total lies for the week: three.

I knew I didn't have to count the lie I told Depki because he wasn't an adult or a member of the family. Then I again went over the list of the times I had disobeyed my parents.

DISOBEYING MY PARENTS

Friday	When Dad told me to take out the garbage *now*.
Saturday	When Mom asked me to straighten out my room.
Sunday	When Mom asked me to turn down the television.

Sunday   When Dad told me to stop crying after
                Mom hit me for not turning down the tel-
                evision.
Tuesday   When Dad told me to put away my base-
                ball stuff in the basement.
Wednesday   When Dad told me to go out and close the
                garage door.

                Total disobeyings for the week: five.

I added them up again just to make sure. I shouldn't have.
When I did, I got six disobediences instead of five. I added the
disobediences up again and I got six instead of five again. I
added them up a third time and got six for the third time.
Good God! I had told the priest in Confession that I had disobeyed my parents five times and here I had disobeyed six
times.

I brought my little red rocker to a fast halt, slamming both
feet to the floor. My tongue was running around collecting sa-
liva, slapping it up against the roof of my mouth, and sliding it
down to my throat, which was gulping spasmodically.

The Blessed Virgin Mary was looking down on me all right.
Looking down and thinking what a rat I was. I went over my
column of lies again to see if I had also made a mistake there.
Then I realized that if I had lied in Confession about how
many times I had disobeyed, that was another lie for the week,
which meant that I was wrong in the lying category, too. So
when I told the priest how many times I had lied during the
week, I had lied again. My mind was becoming engulfed in an
infinity of lies. As close as I could figure, my First Confession
was off by at least one disobedience and two lies.

Neither Father O'Reilly nor my classroom nun had told us
what happened to someone who lied in Confession. Probably
no one had ever done it before so there wasn't even a rule to
cover it.

The phone rang. My mother came in from the kitchen to answer it. I knew it had to be the priest who had heard my confession. He had just found out that I had lied in Confession and was calling my mother to tell her that I was being expelled from St. Bastion school and excommunicated from the Church . . . and the country, just for starters.

"Hello? Oh, hello, Aunt Margaret. Could I call you back? The kids are home from school for lunch right now."

Aunt Margaret, who, every time she came over to the house, told me I behaved like a bed wetter. I hated her, until that phone call. She was okay in my book now. Aunt Margaret had come through when it counted.

Campbell's Chicken Noodle Soup and milk were my favorite lunchtime combination. One is very hot and the other is very cold. If I alternated them properly, I could get my teeth to feel like they were jiggling. It was a cheap but very enjoyable thrill.

But that lunchtime, I was not concerned with cheap thrills. As I sat at the lunch table, the Blessed Virgin Mary stared down at me, intoning, "How could you? How could you? How could you?" Then, for the first and one of the few times in my life, my mind reasoned out a solution.

Lying in Confession is a sin, right? Right. And you're supposed to tell your sins in Confession, right? Right. So this afternoon, when your class meets in the basement church in order for the other half of the class to go to Confession, you go to Confession again and tell the priest about the sins you committed in your First Confession.

"That's it!"

"That's what?" asked my mother. "Is the soup too hot?"

"No, Mom. The soup's perfect." The rest of the lunch was spent in cheap thrills.

That afternoon, when we met in church, Sister said, "Those of you who have already gone to Confession, kneel in one of the pews and say some extra prayers. The rest of you who still have to go to Confession, line up at the confessional doors like the other children did this morning."

Nobody noticed I was in the confessional line for the second time until Johnny Hellger turned around in his pew and saw me. He was really impressed. Johnny Hellger had always more or less taken me for a chump. Now it was apparent that I was so rotten I had to go to Confession twice a day.

"For Christ's sake, Ryan," Johnny Hellger whispered, "what do you do during lunchtime?"

In the black cubicle, listening for the sliding wooden panel.

"Bless me father for I have sinned. It has been one hour and ten minutes since my last confession."

Twenty seconds later I was free from sin, free from sin, free from sin. When I went to sleep that night, the Blessed Virgin Mary once more found me alone on the street. An orphan. Lost, bewildered, sad-faced. She picked me up, hugged me tightly, and took me home with her where she rocked me to sleep in her arms after having fed me milk and Campbell's Chicken Noodle Soup. Never again did I dream of Dinah Shore.

Confession gradually became as much a routine in my life as mass on Sunday and no meat on Fridays. The categories of sin increased as did the number of sins in the categories. The holes in my soul or the nails of Venial Sin that caused them no longer gnawed at my conscience with the same vitality that they had only a couple of years earlier. The increase was gradual so I didn't notice it that much. Committing more sins seemed to be another inevitable cost of growing up, like getting more homework. Besides, venial sins were insignificant. No matter how many I committed, they couldn't send me to Hell. Mortal Sin was where the action was.

In third and fourth grade, I spent most of my time hanging around with Johnny Hellger, who by then had become THE kid in the neighborhood to hang around with. Hellger's popularity was based on the fact that his life-style closely resembled that of the neighborhood's hero. Bugs Bunny.

The easiest way to find out what heroes are popular in a particular neighborhood is to check out the lunch boxes. But the lunch boxes carried by the kids of St. Bastion Parish weren't smothered with the faces of Gene Autry, Roy Rogers, the Blue Fairy, or any of the other big names. Most of our lunch boxes were colored gunmetal gray with nothing but "Made in U.S.A. by Union Workers" stamped on the bottom of them. Bugs Bunny didn't pedal lunch boxes. He was above all that.

Johnny Hellger, like every other kid in Seven Holy Tombs, was a punk. But unlike most of us run-of-the-mill punks, Johnny Hellger actually won. He would steal and not get caught. He'd lie and no one would care. He would disobey and everyone would forget. Johnny Hellger was indeed a proficient protégé of Bugs Bunny, that most professional of punks.

Today, Bugs Bunny would be called an antiestablishment figure. Then, he was just a punk. But unlike us punks in the St. Bastion world of everyday reality, Bugs Bunny always won. He'd sucker Elmer Fudd into catastrophes almost at will and not once did Bugs ever lose a round to Yosemite Sam.

Bugs Bunny was a punk's punk. But since he didn't live in the neighborhood, the kids of Seven Holy Tombs sought out the next best thing, the company of Johnny Hellger. I was one of the few chosen from the many.

Johnny Hellger and I did all sorts of rotten things together. We climbed people's garages, cut across their yards, stomped through their bushes, rang their doorbells and ran, played in construction areas, pitched pennies on the sidewalk, and went over to Seven Holy Tombs Public School and yelled "sucker" outside the school's windows on days that St. Bastion's had off and the public schools didn't.

Johnny Hellger also used to steal candy bars from the grocery stores. I never did any of that, though. Climbing people's garages seemed fair. Stealing candy bars didn't. Besides, I was too chicken.

I did swipe some Baker's chocolate from my mother's cabinet once, but that didn't work out too well. Pure Baker's chocolate tastes something like brown sand.

Like most bad habits, it took a lot of money to keep up with Johnny Hellger. On my twenty-five-cent-a-week allowance, it simply couldn't be done, legitimately. So I began pilfering nickels and dimes from around the house. After a while I moved up to quarters and on occasion even snatched half-dollars.

I wasn't in danger of committing Mortal Sin, though. I had checked it out right at the beginning of the school year with my nun during a Catechism class.

The four questions we had had to memorize for that morning's lesson were on Mortal Sin. I raised my hand and, in an extremely objective tone of voice so as not to cast any shadow of suspicion on myself, asked Sister a question.

"Str, how much money would someone have to steal in order for it to be a mortal sin?"

"Oh, it would have to be quite a lot of money," she said. Generalities wouldn't do. I needed specifics.

"How much, Str?"

"A dollar, I'd say."

She had taken the vow of poverty, all right. But it seemed a logical enough line of division to me. Change couldn't have been too big a thing. I handled it all the time myself: going to the store, buying school supplies, getting stuff at the dime store. I rarely got to touch paper money. A dollar sounded just about right for a mortal sin.

A few days after I found out what it cost to commit a mortal sin, Johnny Hellger asked me to go to Woolworth's with him to buy some French fries. I was tempted to steal four quarters from the house to finance the venture, but I didn't. It wouldn't have really been a mortal sin since it wasn't actually a dollar. But I knew four quarters would more likely be missed by one of my parents than even a dollar so I didn't take them.

On Sunday morning, Johnny Hellger called me up and asked me if I wanted to go to the show with him that afternoon. The show was quite a distance from Seven Holy Tombs, a thirty-minute bus ride and you had to transfer buses twice. At that time I was allowed to go only with my older sister and then only rarely. For one thing, such an expedition took a tremendous amount of money. At least a dollar seventy-five.

I scrounged around my bedroom and could come up with only eighty cents. On the way to the breakfast table I saw it, a crumpled-up dollar underneath the dining room table center-piece, an orange fruit bowl devoid of fruit.

I knew Johnny Hellger would be unmerciful in his derision of me if I failed to go to the show with him. He'd presume that the reason I wouldn't go was that I was afraid to disobey my parents and leave the neighborhood without my sister. Hardly an acceptable excuse.

I decided to have breakfast first. Maybe the dollar would be gone when I finished. It wasn't. Standing in the dining room and staring at the crumpled-up dollar bill for minutes. What the heck, there was no rush. I didn't have to tell Hellger whether I was going to the show or not until one o'clock.

I went outside and played baseball for a few hours, hoping the dollar bill would disappear by the time I got back to the house.

Saying silent prayers as I hurried through the dining room with my baseball equipment. A momentary weakness. A glance. It was still there. Stopping. Many times in the past few months I had almost stolen a dollar. Somehow, I knew this time would be more than a temptation. I recalled the words of my nun, who had told of the deadliness of Mortal Sin.

"If you commit a mortal sin, you are spiritually dead in the eyes of God. And if you die with it on your soul before you get a chance to tell it in Confession, you go straight to Hell. The only thing that can save you between the time you commit the mortal sin and the time you go to Confession is saying a perfect act of contrition to God. But a perfect act of contrition is actually a perfect prayer of love to God. Very few people are holy enough to make a perfect act of contrition. And since those people love God so much, they never commit mortal sins anyway. Yes, children, I'm afraid that perfect acts of contrition are very hard to come by."

I thought of that bald, bulgy-faced cowboy who always played the leader of the bad guys on television. I saw him handing a gun to one of his cronies, who always called him boss, and saying to him, "Don't worry, Louie, your first murder's always the toughest." It was the same for Mortal Sin.

Who am I kidding? I said to myself. Last Wednesday I almost decided to steal a dollar. The week before that I almost did, too. If I don't steal a dollar today, I'll probably steal one tomorrow or the next day so I might as well steal it when I need it.

But my conscience wouldn't quit. It kept yelling, "Damned for eternity. Spiritually dead." I knew that if I kept listening to my conscience, I'd be out a dollar. I had to act fast. Grabbed. The act was committed. I was in the state of Mortal Sin.

My first compulsion was to spend it. I was afraid I'd put the dollar back and then not only would I be in the state of Mortal Sin but I'd also be out the dollar as well.

I raced outside, hopped on my bike, and went to four neighborhood grocery stores and bought a quarter's worth of candy at each. I couldn't buy a dollar's worth at any one of them. Such a large purchase would have aroused suspicions in the owner, which would have been reported back to my parents.

The autumn afternoon was already dying when I began home, walking my bike down the cinder alley that ran along the back of my block and behind my house. Half of the candy was souring in my stomach, the remainder of it lay in a brown paper bag clenched in my fist. As I shoved the bike wheels through the loose cinders, I flipped the bag into a neighbor's uncovered garbage can.

Already spiritual rigor mortis was beginning to set in. Spiritually dead. I couldn't even go to Holy Communion because one of the rules stated that if a person had a mortal sin on his soul, he couldn't receive any of the other sacraments or he'd be committing another mortal sin.

Damned for eternity. If I died between now and the time I went to Confession, I would go to Hell for a dollar.

I suddenly realized that I had indeed picked a bad time to commit a mortal sin: Sunday afternoon. St. Bastion Church didn't hold any confessions until the following Saturday afternoon. I was eternally damned for at least a week.

I was dying by the time I got home. The consumed candy, which I thought had gone to my stomach, had instead coagulated in the middle of my throat, refusing to budge.

"Johnny Hellger called you this afternoon while you were out," my mother said. "He mentioned something about you going to the show. You weren't planning on going to the show with him, were you?"

"Of course not." I choked out the words around the glop of goo in my throat. "Even if I was allowed to go that far by myself, I don't have any money."

"I told him he must be mistaken," my mother said. "You

know your father and I don't like you hanging around with that boy. Why, his own mother doesn't even know where he is half of the time."

I was going to say, "Neither does Hellger," but that would have just prolonged the conversation and I didn't feel much like talking.

It wasn't until the next morning that I decided God had allowed that dollar to be placed in my path as a test because He was planning on having me die that week and wanted to see if I deserved to go to Heaven or Hell. His conclusions were all too apparent to me. I convinced myself that perhaps if I was real careful and didn't expose myself to any unnecessary dangers, God would let me live another week until I had time to go to Confession on Saturday afternoon.

I faked being sick on Monday so I could stay in the safety of my house. During the rest of the week, when I walked to and from school, I constantly watched for cars to swerve out of control to try and run me over on the sidewalk. I didn't play outside. My mother had told me once about a kid who had died while playing outside. At night, I stayed awake as long as possible. If I was going to die, I wanted to be around when it happened. Saturday took years to come.

Confessions at St. Bastion's were held from three to five o'clock on Saturday afternoons. I got to the church around two-thirty and waited around outside in front of the building until about three-thirty. I wanted to give the priests a chance to get into their confessionals so they wouldn't see me when I came in.

As soon as I got into church, I knelt down in the last pew and pretended to pray. Actually, I was trying to figure out which of the six confessionals was the safest to enter. In those days, there were no names on the outside of the confessionals identifying the priest who was inside. You had to gamble if you wanted your sins forgiven.

There were two priests I could not afford to get: Father O'Reilly and Father Luvan.

Whenever I had gone to Confession to Father O'Reilly, he had always seemed reluctant to forgive me for my sins. And those were only venial sins. I was afraid he might not even forgive a mortal sin even though I knew he was supposed to.

Father Luvan was a very nice priest but he was deaf. Anyone who went to Father Luvan for Confession had to shout their sins all over the church.

The ideal priest to get would have been Father Lupienski, a Hungarian priest who had been in this country for only a few months. Father Lupienski was a very friendly guy who smiled and said hello to everyone he met, although he never stopped to talk to any of the parishioners.

Depki told me that he had gone to Confession four weeks in a row to Father Lupienski and no matter what sins Depki told him, Father Lupienski always gave him the same penance, three "Our Fathers" and three "Hail Marys."

Depki suspected. The next time Depki got Father Lupienski in Confession, he told him that he had lied thirty-eight thousand times to his parents.

"Are you sorry for your sins?" asked Father Lupienski.

"Yes, Father," said Depki.

"Then for your penance, say three 'Our Fathers' and three 'Hail Marys.'"

It was apparent, said Depki, that although Father Lupienski had memorized a few lines of it, he neither spoke nor understood any English.

For an hour I knelt in the last pew of St. Bastion Church, trying to tell by the length of the lines who was controlling what confessionals. It didn't take a line to tell me what confessional Father Luvan was in. I could hear him shouting all over the church. "Tell me your sins again and louder please, I can't hear you." There was no line at all forming at confessional number three. The word had passed. Father O'Reilly was lurking there.

As long as I knew where those two were, I was okay. It really didn't matter that much who I got as long as the priest was halfway human. I was hoping I'd get Father Lupienski but it wasn't absolutely necessary.

I got in line over at confessional number five. I wasn't worried about dying anymore; even if God grabbed me right there I was sure he'd give me some credit for at least being in church. The line moved along quickly. In a few moments I was kneeling down in the confessional.

While I waited for the priest to come to my side of the confessional, I practiced whispering in a phony voice so he wouldn't be able to recognize me if he ever heard me outside the confessional. Not that I was worried he'd tell anyone about my mortal sin. I just didn't like the idea of him knowing who did it.

Hearing the wooden panel slide back from my confessional window. I waited for the priest to ask me to begin because then I'd know who he was. I knew the voices of all the St. Bastion priests.

"Yes," he said, "please begin." It was the voice of Father Durlin, the young assistant priest.

"Bless me father for I have sinned. It has been one week since my last confession. I have committed the mortal sin of stealing." I had forgotten to use my phony voice. It was too late now.

"What did you steal?"

"I stole a dollar."

"That's not a mortal sin."

"It's not?"

"No, it's not. Who told you stealing a dollar is a mortal sin?"

"The sister in school."

"Well, she's wrong."

"She's wrong?"

"She's wrong. Stealing a dollar is not enough to constitute a mortal sin. Did you commit any other sins this past week?"

"Uh, yes, Father, but I can't remember them right now."

"No other mortal sins?"

"Oh no, Father, no other mortal sins."

"Fine. When you remember your other sins, tell them in your next confession. Now for your penance, I want you to say a decade of the rosary and while you're saying it I want you to think about Christ and how He suffered and died on the cross for your sins. Now go in peace and God bless you."

I burst out of the confessional door, slid into an empty pew, and said two quick decades of the rosary, the extra one for God allowing me to live long enough to get to Confession. Then a quick genuflection, a two-finger dip in the holy water as I shot by the door, and I was out.

What a fantastic feeling! To come back from the spiritually dead. To be free from sin! free from sin! free from sin! As I walked through the neighborhood, brown igloos of raked leaves smoldered lazily, scenting the air with their familiar fall fragrance. The world fit so comfortably around me that everything I saw and heard seemed as if it had just been given, as I had, a brand new shot at life. Even Billy Schmidt, a kid with whom I shared a mutual hate, looked good to me as I passed him on the street. I said hello to him and he was so shocked that he said hello back. When I got home, my favorite dinner, fried chicken, was already on the table. The Jackie Gleason show was on at 6:30 and Mom even said we could eat on trays in the living room.

I can remember my most amusing confession. I was in college and I had stopped in a small-town church on my way into

Chicago one Friday afternoon. A nun had a class of children going to Confession. I simply got in line with them.

In the confessional, I recited my sins. After I finished, there was a long pause followed by an old, tired voice.

"Those are some sins for a fifth grader."

And I remember the last one. Kneeling in a confessional in some city's cathedral. When the priest asked me if I was sorry for my sins, in a moment of indifference, I gave him an honest answer. He shouted. I left. By then, there was more than a darkened window separating us.

Down the steps of the cathedral knowing, no, hoping in my mind that I was right yet realizing I was never again to feel that resurgence of faith in my own and the world's immortality. Never again to experience the exhilaration of rising from the spiritually dead. Never again to be free from sin, free from sin, free from sin.

IV / Father O'Reilly

Father O'Reilly, pastor of St. Bastion Parish, was a priest who took a totally Old Testament attitude toward the souls God had entrusted to him. He was strictly a company man. Either you played according to the rules of the Catholic Church or he told you to go to Hell. He was our shepherd and we were his sheep. And if a sheep got out of line, Father O'Reilly cut his head off.

He was the one-man Mafia of Seven Holy Tombs. Father O'Reilly controlled the entire neighborhood, everyone and everything in it, with simple brute force. He was worse than the Mafia for he had God on his side.

If a Catholic kid was picked up by the police in Seven Holy

Tombs, he was given the choice of being taken to either the police station or to St. Bastion's Rectory and Father O'Reilly. Most made the wise choice of the police station.

Like many men of power, Father O'Reilly was a financial wizard. He had come to Seven Holy Tombs and founded St. Bastion Parish in the early 1920s, when the parish was little more than a few scattered farms. The first parish church was a deserted barn. By the late 1920s, when the depression struck, the town of Seven Holy Tombs numbered a few thousand.

During those depression years, Father O'Reilly kept the parish going by selling chickens door to door. No one knew where the chickens came from. They were Round Neck chickens, a breed of chicken rarely found in this country. Some of the early parishioners who survived the depression with him claimed that if it hadn't been for Father O'Reilly and his Round Neck chickens, they would have lost their homes.

It was also during the depression that Father O'Reilly began his greatest commercial coup, the legendary St. Bastion Carnival. Although its beginnings were probably humble, by the early 1950s it had mushroomed into a fantastic financial four-day kill.

As is true of most monetary geniuses, Father O'Reilly diversified his financial interests. There was the annual chancebook crusade, two cents a chance, a dollar for a book. A member of the clergy almost always won the grand-prize Ford Thunderbird. There were pantry showers for the nuns, bake sales, mission money drives, and of course the traditional Sunday mass pass-the-basket collections. But the biggest event was the yearly St. Bastion Carnival.

One day, at the beginning of the school year, we kids would look out the school windows and see five or six wooden braces standing on the playground. They had been set up the night before by some men of the parish. The braces would have multiplied themselves by the time we came back to school the next day. By Thursday, the entire school yard would be a field of beam stalks. On Thursday night, we'd go back to the playground and, while whispering speculations to one another about the wooden crates of prizes and carnival counters that were being carted in, watch the parish men roll the green canvas across the braces.

There were at least forty or fifty booths under the green canvas. There were dart booths, ringlet booths, ball-and-metal-milk-bottle booths, guess-your-weight-within-five-pounds booths, and just plain reach-in-the-jar-and-try-and-pull-out-a-winning-number booths.

In the center of the playground was the major attraction—the bingo game. It was formed by about two dozen metal-top folding tables arranged in a large square, marking the boundaries of the game. Each table was armed with a number of ashtrays filled with corn kernels, the ashtrays courtesy of "Smiling Sam, he's a Gas, Service Station."

In the middle of the bingo square piled high on wooden racks were the prizes: blankets, five-dollar dinnerware, stuffed animals, religious statues and ukuleles. In front of the prizes was the revolving wire barrel that spat out an appropriately marked poker chip on every third hand-turned revolution.

"Are you ready, ladies and gentlemen?" Father O'Reilly's voice would wrinkle through the static-filled public-address system. Parish men hustled by the bingo tables, their coin-crammed hardware-store aprons looped under their navels, snatching dimes and quarters from fingers while simultaneously retrieving old bingo cards that had failed to win and dispensing new hopefuls.

Players' hands scooped up kernels of corn from "Smiling Sam, he's a Gas, Service Station" ashtrays and wrapped the kernels into fists. The corn kernels were allowed to drip out until the weight of the fist was just right. Then one kernel would pry itself loose from the others and work its way up until it nudged itself comfortably between the thumb and index finger. The fist would slowly settle onto the bingo card. Ready.

"I 17," Father O'Reilly's voice would bellow through the canvas-covered playground. The first four numbers were swiftly called. It takes five to win in bingo. But beginning with the fifth call, Father O'Reilly's words ventured out cautiously.

"G 28," he'd rasp into the microphone. If the next few seconds passed unmolested, a united sigh of relief would shiver through the silence. Father O'Reilly would whisper the next number, "O 17." Inevitably a voice would tear through the tension, hysterically screaming BINGO. Around the bingo tables some of the Ten Commandments would fall to the mumblings of the losers.

Bingo could have been fun if it hadn't been for Mrs. Murphy. Like all old ladies, Mrs. Murphy had natural bingo ability. But even taking into consideration Mrs. Murphy's advantage of being an old lady, she was exceptionally good, winning almost every game she played. People came away from the bingo tables repeating the word "bingo" to themselves just to see if their lips could really form the word.

Mrs. Murphy died a few years ago. It would be nice to report that she had a nephew with a sense of humor who had Mrs. Murphy's tombstone inscribed solely with her favorite word. That's the way it should have been, but it wasn't.

Among us kids, the most popular booth was the goldfish-bowl booth. A regulation goldfish-bowl booth consisted of a wooden railing, a table twelve feet beyond covered with small round goldfish bowls, two goldfish to a bowl, and lots of Ping-Pong balls.

It cost ten cents to toss three Ping-Pong balls at the table, no reaching over the railing. If you landed a Ping-Pong ball into a goldfish bowl, you won.

Rare was the kid in my parish who went through eight years of grammar school without winning a goldfish bowl. Rarer still was a goldfish from my parish who lived longer than a week.

I was in third grade when I won my goldfish bowl. I had spent the better part of the previous three days practicing in the bathroom by standing in a corner of the tub, in order to get the proper distance, and pitching wads of paper into the toilet.

Upon arriving at the carnival that Sunday afternoon, it took me four Ping-Pong balls to discover that toilets and goldfish bowls don't have a lot in common. The fifth Ping-Pong ball hit a rim of one of the goldfish bowls. But instead of ricocheting off the table as most Ping-Pong balls would have done, it went straight up and came down in a goldfish bowl. I was delirious. It was the first time in my life I had gotten something in life that I had wanted and didn't deserve to get. I named my two goldfish Bill and Fred.

When I got Bill and Fred home, I was shocked at my parents' indifferent attitude toward my victorious return. Here I had left only three hours earlier with nothing but sixty-five cents in my pocket and a little hope that I might somehow break even with Father O'Reilly's carnival. Now I had scored big and still had fifteen cents left. I hadn't won a lousy stuffed animal or some plastic toy donated by Woolworth's, I had won two goldfish and a bowl. I went to put Bill and Fred on top of the television.

"Don't put them there," my father said, "they'll interfere with the reception."

"Okay, I'll put them on the kitchen counter. That way they'll be close to fresh running water."

"Fine, fine," he said and went back to reading his newspaper.

While I was getting Bill and Fred situated on the kitchen counter, my mother was rinsing off potatoes in the sink for supper.

"I'm going to have to go out and buy Bill and Fred a big tank tomorrow and some goldfish food too," I said. "And then I'll teach them a lot of tricks."

"You don't have to buy them food," my mother said. "They can eat small pieces of bread. And you can't teach them any tricks. Goldfish don't do tricks."

"What do you mean goldfish don't do tricks?"

"I mean," she was putting weight behind her words now, "that goldfish don't do tricks. They just swim around."

"That's not much," I said.

"It is if you're a goldfish."

By Tuesday, Bill was swimming on his side and Fred was beginning to do the same thing. I thought maybe the Ping-Pong balls had managed to plunk both of them in the head so instead of just serving them pieces of bread, I put butter on the bread first. Bill and Fred looked like they could use the extra nourishment.

When I got home from school on Thursday, the goldfish bowl was on the counter, empty and smelly.

"Where are my goldfish?"

"I flushed them down the toilet," my mother said.

"Why did you do that?"

"Because they were dead."

That came as no shock to me. On the way home from school, Depki had warned me about the usual life expectancy of a carnival-won goldfish. But flushing them down the toilet?

"Why didn't you bury them?" I asked. "I thought Catholics buried things when they died." When mad, go after a person's jugular vein, their religion.

"We do, but not goldfish. The goldfish weren't Catholic."

"How do you know? They came from a Catholic carnival, didn't they?"

My mother turned around and gave me a look that said the conversation was over.

I went upstairs and peered into the toilet. Nothing. Bill and Fred were now forever in that world where all things dropped into the toilet go.

I went over to Depki's house and told him about my goldfish. He wasn't surprised. "That's the same thing my old lady did, except she flushed them down the toilet the next day. I don't even think they were dead. You know what they oughta do at that carnival."

"What's that?"

"They oughta give away dogs. You can't flush a dog down a toilet."

While the carnival was being held on the playground, a spaghetti dinner was being served in the school basement. Six rows of tables ran across the entire length of the basement from the entrance doors right up to the base of the stage.

A whisper could be whipped into locomotive strength by the acoustics of the school basement. The noise of a St. Bastion Carnival dinner crowd would assault the walls with such intensity that sound would be sucked dry before it could travel even a few feet. Everyone talked but no one heard.

The spaghetti dinner without meatballs was a dollar. You could eat as much as you liked but you normally learned your lesson after the first plateful. Dessert was from the tray of donated delicacies at the end of the table.

On the following Monday, all the leftover spaghetti became macaroni and was served to the school children at ten cents a plate. The next day, approximately 20 percent of the school population would contract the twenty-four-hour crippler commonly known as Carnival Cramps.

As an added enticement to attending the carnival, the name of a different parishioner would be announced over the public-address system every hour. If the parishioner reported to the bingo booth in the following five minutes, he got five dollars. If he wasn't around, another name was announced. Father O'Reilly didn't believe in living room winners.

Father O'Reilly's carnival would begin in the early evening hours of Friday night and rage right through the weekend until the early hours of Monday morning snuffed it out. For those three days, St. Bastion Parish whirled around like an unknotted balloon. But by Monday morning, the air had passed. The balloon was flat.

As we'd pass the school playground on the way to our classrooms, we'd see the green canvas lying exhausted across the braces, waiting for the men of the parish to get home from work so they could come and take her down. All the prizes would be gone from beneath her, even the metal milk bottles would already have been packed away for another year. All that would remain would be the hollow booths surrounded by scattered ticket stubs discarded by sweaty hands that had hoped in vain for a winner. What a miserable day to be alive. But the postcarnival Monday morning of fourth grade was the most miserable of them all.

Depki and I used to meet at seven-thirty in the morning on the corner and walk to school together. The first thing he said that Monday morning was, "Hey, Ryan, what are you going to do with that five dollars you won?"

"What five dollars?"

"The five dollars you won at the carnival yesterday. You mean you weren't there when your name was called?"

"My name wasn't called, Depki. Who're you kidding."

He insisted it was. When we met Johnny Hellger on the way to school, I went through the same routine with him. I figured that Depki and Hellger had got together the day before and had set me up for it.

I was getting worried when Tom Lanner asked me the same thing as I was hanging up my jacket in the coatroom. By morning prayers, it was a confirmed catastrophe. I had blown five dollars by being in the wrong place at the wrong time.

The nun spent twenty minutes in front of the class asking me how I felt and what I would have done with all of that money if I had won it. Those nuns were beautiful. When you were down, could they kick.

Father O'Reilly could always be found at a St. Bastion Carnival just as he could be found at any church function, whether it was midnight mass or a janitors' meeting. He'd stand there in his seamy, shiny black cassock, his hands clasped behind his back, his eyes peering out beyond the precipice of his stomach. His whole frame would gently rise and fall as his feet rocked from heel to toe.

Father O'Reilly would spend his time talking to a few parishioners or standing in the background. He never acted as if he was running things even though everyone knew that he was. Father O'Reilly was happy to limit his performances to twice a week: Friday night novena and the Sunday morning eight o'clock mass.

Besides being Seven Holy Tombs's one-man Mafia, Father O'Reilly was also its one-man Inquisition. The Friday night novena often served as a launching pad for one of his neighborhood raids.

He'd come out on the altar after the service and his words would growl out over the gravel in his voice to that multitude of old ladies, simple-minded men, and young married couples who thought the Friday night novena was a "night out."

"There are," Father O'Reilly would wait for his first words to engulf the church, "dirty books in Delvin's Drugstore." Father O'Reilly would wave his arm in the general direction of Delvin Drugs even though everyone in the church knew where Delvin Drugs was since it was the only drugstore in the neighborhood.

"We are not going to allow our children to be exposed to that kind of trash. We are not going to allow Delvin's Drugstore to make money on dirty books."

Then Father O'Reilly would march down 138th Street with the Friday night novena crowd right behind him and into Delvin's Drugstore where he would tell Mr. Delvin to get the dirty books off the shelves.

Since the neighborhood was mostly Catholic, Father O'Reilly could have used financial threats, but he didn't. Neither did he threaten physical violence. Father O'Reilly never hit anyone his own size. Father O'Reilly would simply tell Mr. Delvin to take the dirty books off the shelves and Mr. Delvin, like all residents of Seven Holy Tombs, would obey.

Unlike the Supreme Court, Father O'Reilly had no difficulty in determining what was a dirty book. A dirty book looked like a dirty book. You could tell a book by its cover.

Father O'Reilly never bothered to lead a raid on Dirty Shirt Andy's store even though that store was a block closer than Delvin's. It was more than rumored that Dirty Shirt Andy also had some dirty books rotting somewhere among his shelves.

Dirty Shirt Andy was simply too undependable. Father O'Reilly knew that Dirty Shirt might not be open when he got there. Sometimes you could go by Dirty Shirt Andy's store at three in the morning, look in, and see him sitting behind his Butternut Bread counter, his arms dangling over the counter, right above the "B" in the Butternut, his eyes staring past you into the darkness. Other times, the store would be closed for weeks, even though Dirty Shirt Andy lived right behind it. One of the advantages of having no business is that you don't have to worry about not being there when your customers don't show up.

Although the American Pharmaceutical Association was acutely aware of Father O'Reilly's Friday night novena raids, the average citizen of Seven Holy Tombs wasn't. The raids

occurred only as the necessity arose. Father O'Reilly also realized that a lot of the old ladies couldn't stand the five-block
walk to Delvin's Drugstore more than once every three
months. In short, the raids were a sometime thing. But like all
great geysers, Father O'Reilly had to spout off regularly and
the Sunday morning eight o'clock mass was his place of burst.

Father O'Reilly, blessed with a tongue that could cut rock,
believed that the best way to get people to Heaven was to scare
the Hell out of them. There was plenty of weeping and gnash-
ing of teeth when Father O'Reilly talked from the pulpit. His
words rolled like a roller coaster as he sought to save your soul
and have you see the light.

He'd start out slowly, calmly, nonchalantly dragging you up
toward that first big dip. Even though you'd been on this ride
before and knew that dip was coming, you were already getting scared. He'd work you right up to the very peak of serenity, pause a moment, and then plunge you straight down as
your stomach shot up to your head. A straightaway of sheer
fright and speed. Then another climb, dip, climb, dip. There
wasn't a deodorant made that didn't fail a Father O'Reilly sermon.

Oddly enough, Father O'Reilly's enthusiasm encouraged a
lot of people to commit Mortal Sin. He was constantly telling
them to take advantage of the opportunity to go to Holy Communion at his mass as they might be dead the next day.

In order to go to Holy Communion, you had to fast from
midnight and be in the "state of grace," in other words, have
no unconfessed mortal sins on your soul. If you didn't fast and
you weren't in the state of grace but you went ahead and received Holy Communion anyway, you committed another
mortal sin.

It required a person with a lot of moxie to remain in his
place while the rest of the people in his pew clumped by him to
go to the Communion rail. You could always claim you had ac-

cidentally broken your fast but then, you knew what you'd be thinking if someone else had remained in his pew.

The kids' eight o'clock mass in the basement church always ended before Father O'Reilly's mass, which was going on in the upstairs church for the adults. During our mass, we would hear his thunder overhead and would wonder what it was like to be so close to lightning. After our mass, some of us would wait around in front of the church for our parents to get out. A few minutes later, we would see them teetering through the pine doors, giddy, numb, dazed, sick to their stomachs, thankful to be off the roller coaster for another seven days.

One early morning in April the nuns lined us up in front of the basement church doors and told us that since the basement church had got some rain the night before, we were going to have to stand in the back of the upstairs church and attend the adult eight o'clock mass.

What a break! It was like my mother running out of milk and asking me if I'd mind having beer with my peanut butter and jelly sandwich. Father O'Reilly's eight o'clock mass sermons were, like drinking and smoking, only for those of legal age or older. We were, in effect, being handed a visa to the adult world.

The first part of the mass was uneventful. No one came in late, of course, just as no one would try and sneak out of mass early. Such attempts were stopped by Father O'Reilly, who, upon seeing the aspiring escapee trying to crawl out of church, would yell at him from the altar. "Can't even give God an hour of your time, huh. He gives you a life and you can't even give Him an hour a week."

The altar boys stepped cautiously as they moved about the altar. Serving mass for Father O'Reilly was considered slightly more difficult than walking on water. Some of those altar boys would grow up and spend the better part of their adulthood in neighborhood taverns sopping up free drinks and reliving heroic moments of Father O'Reilly masses while a few of the faithful would gather around the barstool and shake their heads in affirmative disbelief.

When it came time for the sermon, Father O'Reilly casually walked over and leaned his huge bulk against the lectern, flopping his flabby arms on top of it. He paused a moment, making sure all eyes in the church were riveted on him, before he began. His first words came matter-of-factly, almost in a whisper, as if he were presenting a commentary on the ten o'clock news.

"Saw Ed Connery at this mass last Sunday morning. He was sitting in the third pew right over there. He was on time for mass, paid attention. Went to Holy Communion. Then he went home and had breakfast with his wife and six kids. Decided to go into the living room and watch a little television. Ed Connery turned the set on and went to sit in his easy chair. He was dead before he got there." PAUSE. THINK ABOUT THAT YOU BASTARDS. "We buried Ed on Tuesday morning.

"Ed was sitting here with us last Sunday morning, a healthy man, younger than most of you." The roller coaster words of Father O'Reilly began to CLIMB CLIMB CLIMB. "Had a beautiful family, except for the second youngest, who did poorly in school, had a good job, nice home," CLIMB CLIMB CLIMB, "yet God decided that Ed Connery's time had come."

Like all great roller coasters, Father O'Reilly paused a moment before the big plunge. And then, THE PLUNGE. "Maybe we'll be burying You next Tuesday." Once again, Father O'Reilly ripped into a straightaway.

"Are you ready to die this very instant? Were you on time for mass this morning? Have you been paying attention every moment to what has been going on up at this altar? Have you been keeping God's laws? Have you been saying your morning and evening prayers? Have you been taking care of your family? Have you been going to Confession every week? Have you have you have you?" Out of the straightaway and climbing again.

"Sometimes you just can't get a man to come to church and when you finally do, it takes six men to get him through the door. We're all going to die, you know. And in a very short time." CLIMB CLIMB CLIMB "We live sixty, seventy, eighty years at the most. It's not a very long time." CLIMB CLIMB CLIMB "Ask someone who's that old. He'll tell you. It just didn't seem to take him that long to get old." CLIMB CLIMB CLIMB "This life is just a testing period. A time for God to see . . ." CLIMB CLIMB CLIMB "if we deserve to spend eternity with Him, to be forever in the presence of His . . ." CLIMB CLIMB CLIMB "beatific vision, to be with Him forever in the happiness of Heaven or . . ." PLUNGE "to be damned for eternity in the everlasting fires of Hell." As we continued to roll on with Father O'Reilly, heads began turning purple from the rapid changes in altitude.

On the way home from mass, Depki stopped in at Marty's Food Shop for his usual entrée of Pepsi and Hostess Twinkies. Lanner, awed by the horrors of the ride his soul had just taken, had stayed for another mass. Even Johnny Hellger, whose mouth normally observed no Sunday blue laws, was unusually quiet. I kept catching my tongue saying silent "Hail Marys." I was going to ask Depki for one of his Twinkies, but I didn't think it would mix too well with the ashes of Hell that were still smoldering in my mouth.

"You know," said Depki as he popped the Pepsi bottle from his mouth, "what if Father O'Reilly's wrong?"

"What do you mean?" I asked.

"What if he's wrong about the whole thing?"

"I don't follow you," I said. Depki shrugged and took another bite of his Twinkie.

"Yeah," said Johnny Hellger, "but what if he's right."

St. Bastion Parish was long overdue for a new church when, at one of his eight o'clock masses, Father O'Reilly announced that the building of a new one was to begin in six weeks. Anyone who was interested in the details was to come to a parish meeting in the school basement the following Tuesday night. Father O'Reilly never discussed money matters from the altar. That's what parish meetings were for.

At the meeting, most of the questions about the new church were asked by the younger couples who had been in St. Bastion Parish for only a few years. The older couples had learned long ago that Father O'Reilly either did things very right or very wrong and that he was little influenced by what anyone else thought. They were just there to offer their help.

"Where do you plan on putting the new church, Father?" asked a thirty-three-year-old insurance man who felt that being active in one's parish was important to the well-being of one's soul, family, community, and insurance accounts.

"Over on 111th Street," said Father O'Reilly. "It's the only vacant piece of property the church owns. The old church is going to be turned into classrooms, which we badly need."

"Then I presume," said the insurance man, "that you have already started legal proceedings to buy the brown-shingled two-flat on the corner." The insurance man began to sit down.

"You presume wrong," said Father O'Reilly, and the insurance man began to stand up while he was still beginning to sit down.

"You mean," said the insurance man, "she refuses to sell."

"I wouldn't know," said Father O'Reilly. "I haven't asked."

"You mean to tell us, Father, that you plan on building our two-million-dollar church next to that two-flat shanty? Why that place doesn't even have indoor plumbing."

Father Verga, who was standing at a safe distance behind Father O'Reilly, replied, "Our church will have two bathrooms so you don't have to worry about having to run next door."

No one laughed. Father Verga didn't expect anyone to. Father O'Reilly turned around and glared at him. Father Verga's eyes refused to accept the challenge and skipped about the room as if totally unaware of the crime just committed by the mouth below.

Father Verga knew he had sinned grievously. First of all, for attempting to be funny. With Father O'Reilly, God and laughter never mixed. And secondly, for discussing matters of sex, i.e., bathroom, in a mixed group. Father Verga knew he was going to Hell and prayed every night that he'd burn for a better reason than the sins he had committed that day.

Father O'Reilly turned his attention back to the audience.

"That building and its occupant have been there on that corner for a long time. Even before St. Bastion Parish. No one's ever been bothered by it. I doubt if anyone ever will be. Now, as far as I'm concerned, the matter is closed."

"Well, it's not closed as far as we're concerned," said the insurance man. "We're not having our church built next door to Garbage Lady Annie's house." His mouth had said the words "Garbage Lady Annie" before his mind had had time to censor them. Embarrassed at having said a name that only the children of the neighborhood normally vocalized, it was considered beneath the dignity of an adult to say the old lady's name out loud, the insurance man grabbed his wife's hand and bounded out of the basement hall. About twenty other young couples got up and followed him out.

Father O'Reilly watched them leave and then looked at the older couples who had remained. "Now, where were we?" It was the first time that Garbage Lady Annie made the minutes of a St. Bastion Parish meeting.

Garbage Lady Annie was a little dented and demented old lady who dressed in tennis sneakers and old babushkas and dresses that she picked out of people's garbage cans. If it hadn't been for the dresses and babushkas, she could have just as easily been thought of as an old man. Garbage Lady Annie had long ago ceased to appear as, or cared about being, a member of either sex.

Garbage Lady Annie's house resembled a shoebox on its side: long, narrow, porchless, and even with the street level. The building leaned eastward or westward, depending on which way the wind was blowing. Garbage Lady Annie supposedly lived on the first floor because there was a For Rent sign, turned yellow with age, in a window of the second floor. Next to the house was a black dirt yard enclosed by a fence made out of the sides of crates. The yard was loaded with the neighborhood's refuse: piles of newspapers, broken dolls, mismatched boots. Each commodity was neatly stacked in a section of the yard.

No one had ever actually been in Garbage Lady Annie's house. Theories of its contents ranged from more neatly stacked garbage to millions of dollars being stashed in the furniture and linings of the walls. Garbage Lady Annie herself was never actually seen going into or coming out of her house. She did, I'm sure, but no one ever saw her.

Garbage Lady Annie could be seen in only one of two places: in the alleys looking for garbage or in the last pew of St. Bastion Church.

She was strictly a seasonal Catholic. The colder it got, the more of a churchgoer she became. In the worst winter months, Garbage Lady Annie became so religious that she'd often attend all six Sunday masses. You always knew when Garbage Lady Annie was in church because she'd park her red coaster wagon, which she constantly dragged behind her, outside on the church steps.

Many of the women in St. Bastion Parish wished that Garbage Lady Annie had been a little more nonreligious. There was the Sunday morning Garbage Lady Annie showed up for mass in an old dress that belonged to Depki's mother. Garbage Lady Annie had apparently picked it out of the Depki garbage can. Depki said that for years afterwards, every time his mother wore a new dress, she kept imagining that she was hearing people say, "Yes, yes, that's a very nice dress. I'm sure Garbage Lady Annie will like it."

Most adults thought that Garbage Lady Annie was nuts. I liked her, especially when I was a little kid. Most of the little kids did. She was the only adult we knew who spent most of her time in alleys. As any kid knows, alleys are the best part of a neighborhood.

The dogs of Seven Holy Tombs hated her. Being typical middle-class dogs, they had little to justify their existence. So whenever Garbage Lady Annie started picking in the family garbage can—which was usually located a few feet outside the fence in the alley—the resident dog felt obliged to leap up against the fence and carry on like he'd really bite her if he got the chance. I doubt if there was a dog in the neighborhood who would have risked his health by biting Garbage Lady Annie.

The only dog around who didn't bother Garbage Lady Annie was Blink, a brown lump of matted fur who wandered around the neighborhood. No one knew, or cared, where Blink came from.

Blink could always be found at some neighborhood sporting event: a street-corner softball game, a football game at the park, or a game of marbles being played on a curb. Blink would never bark, run after the ball, or in any other way annoy those around him. He would simply do what he had come to do: watch.

According to Depki, Blink was the great neighborhood protector who regularly ate up other dogs and cats that were mean and kept the neighborhood free of bullies. Depki watched too many Rin Tin Tin movies. I never knew Blink to show any emotion whatsoever. As far as bullies were concerned, the neighborhood was overrun with them. Everyone was bullying somebody.

Although Blink had four legs and a tail and looked exactly like a dog, he wasn't actually considered a dog. You would never walk up to Blink and pat him on the head or say something stupid to him like, "Here Blink, boy." People would have thought you were crazy.

Blink had no yard to "protect," no family to impress. He never bothered Garbage Lady Annie for they were two of a kind.

Garbage Lady Annie was a fixture of the neighborhood just as much as the traffic lights on 111th Street and she warranted about as much attention until the site of the new church was announced.

The insurance man and his followers formed an organization, gave it a sincere title, something like "Concerned Parents for a Better St. Bastion Parish," and set out to denude Garbage Lady Annie of her shanty.

They asked the Chicago Board of Health to force Garbage Lady Annie off her property. The board said there were no legal grounds under which condemnation proceedings could begin. They asked the city Building Commission to condemn the building. The commission told them that Garbage Lady Annie's house had passed a city inspection the previous year. The insurance man and his followers circulated a petition stating that Garbage Lady Annie and her garbage-picking habits were a health hazard to the neighborhood. The petition got "lost" in City Hall. Apparently, the insurance man and his followers had underestimated Garbage Lady Annie's political clout.

They were getting desperate, so desperate they were willing to try anything. They went to talk to Garbage Lady Annie herself.

With his followers standing a safe distance behind him, the insurance man walked up to Garbage Lady Annie's house and gingerly knocked on the front door. It was perhaps the first knock ever laid on Garbage Lady Annie's door. But there was no answer.

They found her picking garbage in the Larding Street alley. There, they asked her if she would like to sell her house. They told her they planned on raising the money for the purchase by holding a cookie drive. Garbage Lady Annie thought they were nuts.

By now the church was finished. A husky red brick bastion with a muscular marble interior. Plain but strong. Though few were overawed by it, everyone seemed to like it. Even the insurance man and his followers agreed that the new church was quite good enough. Garbage Lady Annie was sufficiently impressed. That year, she was seen attending mass as late in the cold season as the last week of March.

Then, there was a fine Catholic tradition, at least on the South Side of Chicago, that after a pastor had completed such a tremendous task as building a new church, he would die shortly thereafter, supposedly because he had worked himself to death completing the job. Father O'Reilly, who was never one to buck tradition, promptly died two months after the new church was completed.

Garbage Lady Annie lived five more years. They found her one Sunday afternoon after the twelve o'clock mass, hunched over in the last pew. The ushers had become suspicious because the day was warming up.

The insurance man and his followers volunteered to examine and dispose of Garbage Lady Annie's house. The insurance man was the first to step inside it. Today, his name is better known in Seven Holy Tombs than is Neil Armstrong's.

On the first and second floors were a few pieces of old furniture and some piles of junk, neatly arranged, just as there were in the yard. But in the basement, they found a number of large chicken coops filled with chickens. The farmer who came to take the chickens away said that they were Round Neck chickens, a breed of chicken rarely found in this country.

V / Some Great Moments in Sloppy Scouting

Contrary to popular folklore, Cub Scouts do not spend all their time helping old ladies cross the street. In my neighborhood, they couldn't have. There weren't enough old ladies to go around. Larry Gogel, who lived a few doors down from me, owned one. She was his grandmother, I think. All she ever did was sit in the kitchen. She had no desire to cross the living room much less the street.

In the neighborhood of Seven Holy Tombs, Cub Scouting was a lot more than simply collecting bundles of old newspapers on Saturday mornings. It was the training wheels of life and was as much a part of growing up as breaking bones and getting pimples. There was something wrong with a boy's glands if he didn't become a Cub Scout. Boys who didn't join Scouting seemed to grow up strangely. But then, how can you expect a kid to mature properly when he's never dressed like an Indian?

It was Sunday afternoon and my eighth birthday, the age when one normally joins the Cub Scouts. I was due to be initiated into the Scouts the following day. As I walked through the kitchen, my mother told me that my father, who was outside in the backyard painting the fence, wanted to see me.

The first eight years of my life had been somewhat less than impressive. In school, I had started out in the highest reading group, the Robins, but was quickly demoted to the Sparrows. My nun once remarked that she was thinking of creating a new group just for me called the Droppings. My mother made me quit the Pee Wee Baseball League because I kept getting lost on the way home from the park. I even got the feeling that some of my imaginary friends considered me a loser.

When I got to the backyard, my father was squatting next to the fence, painting the pickets.

"You wanted to see me, Dad?" He didn't look up. He just kept painting.

"Yes, son," he said. "Tomorrow is a real big day in your life, as you know. Tomorrow night, you'll wear the blue and gold uniform of a Cub Scout. Your mother and I feel this is a very important step in your life. It's a sign that you're maturing, that you're growing up. You know what I mean, son?"

"Yeah, Dad, I know what you mean." I leaned on the fence.

"I realize that things in the past have not always worked out for you," my father said as he continued to paint the fence, "but I'm sure that as a Cub Scout, you're going to make everyone very proud of you." He looked up from the picket he was painting and saw me leaning on the fence.

"Hey, get your hand off the fence. I just painted there."

I jerked my arm away and looked at my hand. It was loaded with paint. "Sorry, Dad."

He mumbled something about illegitimacy and went back to painting the pickets.

My father was right. I had blown the first eight years of my life. It was time to grow up. I went next door to find out from Demented David, who had already been a Cub Scout for two years, how one went about making it big in the Scouts.

"Nothin' to it," Demented David told me. "All you have to do to impress your parents is to get Mr. Barnum, the pack leader, to think you're a hotshot. Do a nice job in something, like singing or hiking. If Mr. Barnum notices you, at the next pack meeting he'll lead the whole pack in giving you three cheers." Demented David demonstrated, flinging his fist into the air each time he yelled, "Hip hip hurrah, hip hip hurrah, hip hip hurrah. Most of the parents go to the pack meeting," Demented David continued, "and when they hear their kid getting hip hip hurrahed, they go wild."

"What's a pack?" I asked.

"All the Cub Scouts in each neighborhood make up a 'pack,' which has as its name a four-digit number," Demented David said. "Then each pack is divided into a number of dens made up of nine or ten guys and a den mother."

"And all I have to do to get hip hip hurrahed at a pack meeting is to have Mr. Barnum notice me doing a nice job in something?"

"That's all," said Demented David.

The pack meeting that Monday night was held in the park-house. The meeting began with the Pledge of Allegiance and then Mr. Barnum handed out badges to about twenty different Cub Scouts. After each Cub Scout received his badge, Mr. Barnum would yell, "How about three cheers for . . ." (whoever it was) and while punching our fists into the air, we'd all yell, "Hip hip hurrah, hip hip hurrah, hip hip hurrah." After about forty thousand "hip hip hurrahs," Mr. Barnum welcomed us new Cub Scouts.

"As Cub Scouts, boys," said Mr. Barnum, "you will acquire many new skills that you, as an adult, will need later on in life. You'll be taught to make model airplanes, shoeshine kits, and Mother's Day cards. You will learn how to survive in the wilderness with nothing but two sticks and a Clark Bar."

Mr. Barnum went on to teach us the Cub Scout pledge, sign, handshake, and the secret writing. Mr. Barnum also told us about the three Cub Scout books: the *Wolf Book*, the *Bear Book*, and the *Lion Book*. We would receive badges for completing the exercises and challenges in each book, Mr. Barnum said. Actually, the books sounded like parents between covers.

Mr. Barnum also informed the new members of Pack 3838 that the key word in Cub Scouting was "akela," which was the "secret" word used to refer to a good leader. A good leader included Mr. Barnum, den mothers, parents, and basically anyone taller than a Cub Scout.

"Of course," said Mr. Barnum, "as Cub Scouts you will be trained to be good followers. Good leaders," said Mr. Barnum, "are good followers."

Later in life, I discovered that statement to be untrue. Good leaders are rotten followers because they're always gunning to be leaders.

"Now," said Mr. Barnum, "we're going to do something that all Cub Scouts love to do, sing." He held up his hands as if he were allowing them to drip dry. "And remember, men, use those hands to express the words of the song."

This was what I had been waiting for: an area of skill in which I could immediately establish my supremacy. I limbered up my fingers, ready to perform to perfection the dictations of the song.

Mr. Barnum started us off. "One, two, three . . ."

Do your ears hang low,
Do they wobble to and fro,
Can you tie them in a knot,
Can you tie them in a bow.
Can you throw them over your shoulders
like a Continental soldier, do your ears hang low.

That is not an easy song in which to excel. At first I was
panic-stricken. I couldn't do any of the things the song said.
My ears didn't hang low, they didn't wobble to and fro. I
couldn't tie them in a knot or tie them in a bow. I looked
around at the other Cub Scouts. They weren't doing any of
those things either. They were just waving their hands around
their ears as Mr. Barnum was doing up in front of us.

The next song consumed by our lungs was the national anthem of all Cub Scouts, the "Itsy Bitsy Spider" song.

The itsy bitsy spider ran up the water spout,
Down came the rain and washed the spider out.
Up came the sun and dried up all the rain,
And the itsy bitsy spider crawled up the spout again.

We sang the "Itsy Bitsy Spider" song about fourteen times,
each round faster than the previous one. This entire song is accompanied by intricate finger movements, none of them obscene. Such intricate finger movements are not learned in one
night of "Itsy Bitsy Spider" singing. Considering I was a nov-
ice, I did fairly well except when "the itsy bitsy spider ran up
the water spout." I almost broke my thumb. You do not get
cheered for that, not even in the Cub Scouts.

I was assigned to Mrs. Dunnewater's den and a week later
attended my first den meeting.

Mrs. Dunnewater was perhaps the only woman in the world

to ever earn a double-figure income as a crossing guard. She had a habit of throwing herself in front of cars and collecting the insurance money. People became suspicious when she managed to get herself run over on a Saturday afternoon. After suddenly finding herself retired from the crossing-guard force, Mrs. Dunnewater, her fortune made, turned philanthropist and became a den mother for Pack 3838.

Demented David was in my den. He was convinced that the Cub Scouts were destined to become a military power and, marching to the "Itsy Bitsy Spider" song, go off and totally annihilate the Girl Scouts from the face of the earth, among them Demented David's older sister, who, I admit, deserved to be annihilated. Two other members of the den were Bobby Felgen, a massive piece of flesh whose personality was very much like those who leave money under your pillow when you lose a tooth, and Anthony Trielli, who wanted nothing more out of life than to be vice-president of the United States.

At the den meeting, Mrs. Dunnewater announced that Pack 3838's candy drive was beginning. We could pick up our boxes of candy at the next meeting.

This was my chance. I would become a super salesman and lead the pack in selling Cub Scout candy. No doubt I would be rewarded by a standing ovation of three cheers at the next pack meeting. I realized that this would be no minor achievement as Cub Scout candy tasted like chocolate-covered grease. But I knew I could do it. Besides, I had a lot of relatives living in the neighborhood.

On the way home from the meeting, I told Demented David of my plans.

"Forget it," he said, "you'll never beat Alex Schietzer."

"Why? Does he have that many relatives in the neighborhood?"

"No," Demented David said, "he can actually sell the stuff

to total strangers. Really, I've seen him. He gets this sappy look on his face and just about cries on the front porch if someone says no to him."

It wasn't even close. Alex beat me by forty-seven boxes and three hip hip hurrahs.

Demented David told me that occasionally Pack 3838 gave three cheers to a kid who behaved particularly well on a field trip. Three weeks later, I had my opportunity when Pack 3838 visited Lincoln Park Zoo.

I had never been to a zoo. The only animals I was familiar with were dogs, cats, and squirrels from a distance. At Lincoln Park Zoo, I discovered just how messy real animals could be about themselves. I spent the entire day holding my nose and/or stomach. Still, I might have had a chance to impress Mr. Barnum with my excellent behavior if I hadn't been given Charley Goodwell as my "buddy."

Any time that Cub Scouts venture out into the world, they are always paired off into groups of twos, or "buddies." Scout leaders will tell you that the idea behind it is for each kid to keep track of his "buddy" and therefore increase the chances of getting everybody home alive. But a Scout leader I knew in my later years told me the true reason. Like all organizations that wear uniforms, the Cub Scouts want to be well organized and keep everything neat and orderly. With the "buddy" system, they figure if one kid gets killed or lost so will his "buddy" so there'll still be even lines on the way home.

Charley Goodwell, being my "buddy," had to sit next to me on the bus as we started home from Lincoln Park Zoo. As will happen on any bus that is loaded with Cub Scouts, some weirdo started singing "100 Bottles of Beer on the Wall" and the rest of us picked it up. As usual, by the time the song got to the low eighties, everyone had quit. Everyone but Charley Goodwell. Charley had only one virtue, persistence. When Charley Goodwell started "100 Bottles of Beer on the Wall,"

Charley Goodwell finished "100 Bottles of Beer on the Wall."
Somewhere around "28 bottles of beer on the wall . . ." I
tried to strangle him. At the next pack meeting, I did not receive three cheers for my efforts. Charley Goodwell did for
being the most enthusiastic Cub Scout on the field trip. Hip
hip hurrah, hip hip hurrah, hip hip hurrah.

Every year, Pack 3838 marched in the Fourth of July parade. Mr. Barnum always gave an award, and three cheers, to
the Cub Scout who was the best marcher or, as Mr. Barnum
said, "demonstrated the best cadence." That year, I was determined to win it. I needed the three cheers.

For an entire week before the parade, I practiced marching
in the backyard. In order to simulate the actual marching conditions of a parade, I got up early one morning before school
and marched in the deserted street in front of my house. I was
unable, however, to simulate the marching conditions created
by walking directly behind an elephant, which was where I
marched that Fourth of July. Marching elephants have a way
of destroying one's cadence. Fortunately, at the next pack
meeting, the elephant did not receive three cheers for his
efforts. Unfortunately, neither did I.

In late August, Pack 3838 held its annual Pow Wow
Weekend. Pow Wow Weekend was a time when all good
Cub Scouts and their parents left the comfort of their homes to
dress up like Indians and spend two days in a flat-chested,
pock-marked forest preserve. It was forty-eight hours of dodging falling tent poles and two-hundred-pound mosquitoes
while consuming metallic well water, warm pop, cold hot dogs,
and charcoal-coated hamburgers.

During Pow Wow Weekend, there were two excellent op-
portunities to earn three cheers. The first was in the softball
game against another Cub Scout pack, Pack 3841. The second
opportunity came at the very end of the Pow Wow Weekend,
when the Indian-dancing contest was held.

There was little chance to grab glory in the softball game. Our pack leader, Mr. Barnum, didn't believe in having anyone ride the bench, so he played everyone in the pack for the entire game. Instead of nine men on the field, we had seventy-five. In the first inning, thirty others and I were standing in left field. A fly ball was hit right at me. As is customary in the softball world, I yelled, "I've got it," so that no one would run into me. Simultaneously, I heard seventy-four other guys rushing at me yelling, "I've got it." No one got it.

I didn't get to bat. With seventy-five kids in the lineup, the average player got to swing a bat for Pack 3838 once every two years.

We lost, 33 to 12, a relatively tight game by Cub Scout standards. Naturally, we gave the other team three cheers for beating us to death. Hip hip hurrah, hip hip hurrah, hip hip hurrah.

The softball game was played on Friday night. Saturday and Sunday of Pow Wow Weekend progressed smoothly. Only three kids had to be carried off by ambulance. Two of them ran into trees and the third kid managed to swallow the apple during the apple-bobbing contest.

All kinds of things went on during those two days: gunny-sack races, pie-baking contests, tugs-of-war. But I was after bigger things. I spent the two days inside my tent practicing my Indian dancing in preparation for the Indian-dancing championship that was to be held Sunday night at the close of the Pow Wow Weekend.

A rigid training schedule was followed. First, I would spend twenty minutes Indian dancing: my body crouched appropriately, the head bobbing, the tails of the Indian headdress weaving behind my back, the mouth producing perfect Indian grunts as my hand rhythmically shuttered over it, and the gym shoes shuffling smoothly under my body. The next twenty minutes would be spent doing push-ups and running around the tent. Conditioning is very important in Indian dancing.

Jerome Bizybinski had won the Indian-dancing championship for the past two years. It wasn't a case of Jerome being so good as it was of Jerome's competition being so bad. Kids who had seen both of us dance said that I definitely had Jerome outclassed. Already I could hear Mr. Barnum announcing me as the new Indian-dancing champion, followed by three lusty cheers from my fellow Cub Scouts. Hip hip hurrah, hip hip hurrah, hip hip hurrah.

I wasted no time during the Pow Wow Weekend going to the outhouse. Unlike the bathroom at home, the outhouse didn't smell of Lysol. Besides the odor, there were hundreds of flies around the outhouse. Most of the guys who used the outhouse held their breaths the whole time they were in there. I couldn't hold my breath that long so I figured I'd just skip the whole process until I got back home.

Demented David warned me that it wasn't a good idea to do that. He had done the same thing the previous year and had gotten a case of constipation that crippled him for two weeks.

The Indian-dancing contest was the climax of the Pow Wow Weekend. After dark, a big bonfire would be built and all the members of the pack would sit in a large circle around it. Each contestant would then stand up and do his stuff. After the winner was announced, the entire pack would Indiandance around the bonfire. It was a very impressive sight.

The first five contestants were strictly passé. Then Jerome Bizybinski came on. Jerome's dancing was good. Not great, but good. He had a few cute twirls and he kept his head bobbing nicely. But his dance fell far below the routine I was about to unravel around that campfire.

As I was watching Bizybinski dance, I suddenly realized that my legs were turning to concrete. Gastric pains were spreading from the base of my neck to my ankles. My mouth was dehydrating.

Jerome Bizybinski finished dancing and received healthy applause from the circle around the campfire. I tried to stand up but the pain in my stomach forced me into a crouch. Fortunately, a good Indian dancer performs in a crouch so this was no problem. As I shuffled toward the campfire, I noticed the hungry look of anticipation on my fellow Scouts' faces. Word of my skill had spread. They were waiting to witness an upset.

I slowly began dancing. My feet were hardly leaving the ground. I was afraid that if I bobbed my head, it would fall off. There was stunned silence. This was the man who was going to replace Jerome Bizybinski as the Indian-dancing champion of Pack 3838?

Mr. Barnum coughed nervously, stood up, and said mechanically, "Very very good. Now, Scouts, let's sing a few songs around the campfire while the judges decide who is going to be the new Indian-dancing champion of Pack 3838."

A few speckles of applause bid me farewell as I crawled through the circle of singing Cub Scouts and into my tent. I lay coiled on the ground, my Indian headdress hovering over my forehead. Through the blur of agony I could hear them chant.

"The itsy bitsy spider ran up the water spout, down came the rain and washed the spider out, up came the sun and . . . Let's have three cheers for Jerome Bizybinski! Hip hip hurrah, hip hip hurrah, hip hip hurrah."

VI / The Nuns

Many people think of a nun as a shy, petite little thing with a sunshine face pushing out of a habit, playing opposite Bing Crosby in a 1940s movie. In fact, nuns are generally sullen, suspicious cynics with a strong streak of savagery. They aren't at all human. At least not any of the nuns I knew at St. Bastion school.

The St. Bastion nuns couldn't have been human. In my eight years of grammar school, I never saw a nun take a drink of water, go into a washroom except maybe to chase after some kid but never for her own satisfaction, or eat something. As far as I could tell, the nuns were totally devoid of biological functions.

The nuns at St. Bastion school had one goal in life: to get out of it and into Heaven. When they first became nuns, they took three vows that were designed to accomplish this goal: the vows of Poverty, Chastity, and Obedience.

The first vow was easy enough to keep, not only for the nuns but for anyone in St. Bastion Parish. And considering what most of the nuns looked like, Chastity offered no formidable challenge either. The vow of Obedience simply meant that the nuns had to worship the ground the priests walked on, which the nuns did with absolute relish.

By taking these three vows, the nuns at St. Bastion school were among the few souls in the world who knew they were going straight to Heaven. Unfortunately for us kids at St. Bastion's, we weren't a necessary part of their master plan to attain the Eternal Reward. We were simply annoyances strewn along the path to Heaven and were treated as such.

Like most average St. Bastion students, I was absolutely terrified of nuns. Hearing the rattle of the oversized rosary beads hanging from their belts and the stomp of their 1890 black-laced, ankle-high stubby-stacked shoes clapping down the hallway hollowed me with fear. The nuns also had a very strange odor about them, something like kitchen cleanser, that upon entering the nostrils, immediately immobilized one's central nervous system.

You could tell if a nun didn't especially approve of your being alive. She'd address you as "Mr." instead of by your first name. I was always "Mr." Ryan.

A nun didn't like you walking on the stairs at the same time as her. She considered such an act disrespectful and if you forgot and did it, she'd probably knock you around.

The term "kid" was despised by the nuns. I don't know why. Say you found something on the playground, like a glove, and you went into a classroom to try and find the owner. As soon as you held up the glove and asked, "Any kid in here lose this?" the nun would interrupt you. "I'm sorry," she'd say, "but we don't have any 'kids' in here. Just children. Only goats have 'kids.' "

Some of those nuns thought that one-liner was a riot. I guess when you're a nun, it doesn't take too much to amuse you.

The nuns were very smart and very dumb. They were smart in making it a point to know who hung around with whom. At the beginning of a school year, the nuns who were teaching a particular grade would get together and make sure that good friends who were troublemakers would not be in the same classroom.

The nuns were extremely sophisticated when it came to surveillance. If a nun had to leave the class unattended for a few moments, she'd give us some work to do and warn us that while she was gone we had better do the work and not goof around as God, who was everywhere, would be watching. The nun would further inform us that, just in case God missed something, the principal would be listening in on us through the classroom's public-address system.

Maybe God did report back to the nuns. The nuns knew about everything that happened in the neighborhood, which was rather weird since the nuns were never seen anywhere but in the school, the church, or the convent. If you punched a kid in the head on a Saturday afternoon, every nun in the school would know about it by Monday morning.

But in other ways, the nuns were really dumb. Once, when I was in second grade, a nun who was walking by on the playground heard me say "shut up" to some kid. The nun really slapped me around for it, telling me how shocked she was that I'd use such foul language. "Shut up" is just not that big of a deal. Even then, I knew that, and I was only in the second grade.

The nuns also had a dumb habit of presuming that if the first kid in the family who went to school was stupid or smart, then all his brothers and sisters who followed him in school were the same. My older sister had been at St. Bastion Grammar School for two years before I started first grade. She was an excellent student, got good grades, and never misbehaved. She was always helping my mother around the house, wouldn't think of talking back to my parents, was kind to animals, and had won three cooking awards in the Girl Scouts. Naturally, I hated her.

My older sister's reckless behavior had created a family mold that I was constantly failing to fill in the minds of the nuns. They simply refused to admit that glass slippers can't always be passed from one family member to another.

Girls were never bothered by the nuns. I can't recall a girl ever being hit by a nun. The worst that could happen to a girl was to be grabbed by the shoulder and even that was done very gently.

Boys were fair game. Nuns hated boys. Even the couple of nuns who said they liked boys more than girls really didn't. They may have liked boys as much as girls, but not more. The St. Bastion nuns, like most grammar school teachers, were female chauvinist pigs.

In fourth grade, during the first week of school, we had to write essays about what we did during the summer. It was kind of a tough assignment because most of us didn't do anything during the summer. But Mike Depki, who did even less during the summer than most of us, wrote a really good story about what he didn't do during the summer. He told how he hadn't killed anyone or stolen anything, how he didn't get run over by a car, and how he didn't go to Africa. Stuff like that. It was good. I actually enjoyed reading it. It was way long enough, too. Depki's essay covered both sides of a sheet of loose-leaf paper.

I also read Mary Kenny's essay about how she helped her

mother during the summer. It was lousy. Mary Kenny got an A, Depki got an F.

First of all, Mary Kenny had a lot of things underlined in red. Nuns love to see things underlined in red. I knew only a couple of guys who underlined things in red and they didn't use a ruler so it looked sloppy anyway.

Mary Kenny also had the initials "J.M.J.," which stood for "Jesus, Mary, and Joseph," on the top of her paper. Nuns expected that. Mike Depki used to put "M.A.D." on the top of his papers until he got knocked around a few times for it. Those were his initials: "Michael Anthony Depki." I have to admit that Mary Kenny's paper wasn't quite as wrinkled as Mike Depki's but his essay sure was a lot better. The truth is that Mary Kenny got an A because she was a girl and Depki got an F because he was a boy.

Although most of us boys got clouted regularly, there were some, usually five or six guys in the classroom, that caught more than their share from the nuns. If, in the first grade, you were identified as "one of those," you were stuck with the label for the duration of your grammar school career. No matter how you tried to change the course of human events, you remained in that category. Mike Depki was in that select slime. So was Johnny Hellger. Lanner and I were borderline cases.

The nuns were always after Johnny Hellger for one reason or another. But having the inside of his desk messy was the thing that most often got him in trouble. All the boys had messy desks. Even some of the girls did. But Johnny Hellger was the only kid who ever got clobbered for it.

We'd be studying for something and the nun, having nothing better to do, would walk over to Johnny Hellger's desk, would lean over, and would look inside to see all the crumpled papers stuck between, on top of, and under the textbooks and workbooks that were piled incoherently in his desk. She'd rip out everything and while Johnny Hellger was trying to pick up all the stuff off the floor, she'd be yelling at him and beating him over the head with one of his own books. Then the nun would warn the rest of the class.

"If anyone else has a sloppy desk, they're going to get the same thing. You've got ten minutes to get those desks cleaned out."

The nun would then send one of her bootlickers up and down the aisles with a wastepaper basket, and as he walked by, everyone would throw in the garbage they had hastily retrieved from their desks.

Those desk-cleaning sessions occurred about once every six weeks, but they never started without the ritual of roughing up Johnny Hellger first.

Among the faculty at St. Bastion Grammar School was Sister Diane, "Dynamite Diane," so called because of her pestilent impatience. Before coming to St. Bastion's, she had taught at a school for truants in Brooklyn for ten years. Strangely, it wasn't a school for truants when Dynamite Diane began teaching there but quickly became one after she'd been around for only a few months.

Dynamite Diane was six feet three inches tall and had such a small neck that her face seemed to peek like a half-risen sun over the horizon of her massive shoulders. Living proof that even Catholics evolved from apes.

Unlike other nuns who would simply grab a kid by the shoulders and wildly shake him for a few moments, Dynamite Diane would pick up the kid, and the desk if he happened to be in one, and shake until either the victim's head was a virtual satellite orbiting around his neck or he simply fell apart.

Years later, at a cocktail party, I saw two strangers discover that they had both been taught by Dynamite Diane. The two of them slinked off into a corner, survivors of a common campaign, gesturing to one another and chittering in glee at atrocities of Dynamite Diane they thought they had long forgotten.

There were others. Cyril the Savage, who, with either hand, could throw an eraser with speed and accuracy the length of a classroom. She had three basic pitches: a curve, a slider, and a fast eraser, all of them impossible to avoid.

It was a common occurrence for a nun who was teaching us something on the blackboard to suddenly whip around and rifle an eraser at some kid she suspected of not paying attention. It was not a common occurrence for a nun to hit who she was aiming at, the eraser usually pinging an innocent kid. Cyril the Savage, however, was more sportsmanlike than the others, and a better aim. She would always yell a warning at the intended target, knowing full well that the warning would do no good.

Although I never had Cyril the Savage for a regular teacher, she substituted a number of times for my third-grade nun, who was always catching colds in her teeth. When Cyril the Savage was in charge of the room, about every half hour a kid's name would be called out, followed by a quick zip and bonk.

Boom Boom Bernadine liked to grab kids by the ears and bang their heads against the wall whenever they annoyed her. Fortunately for Boom Boom, most of the kids at St. Bastion Grammar School weren't too bright to begin with so if there was any brain damage, it was years before anyone realized it. At the peak of her career, Boom Boom Bernadine got overzealous and ripped an arm muscle while bashing some head against a banister. Never again were her hands to crunch a set of ear lobes. The arm muscle refused to heal. For Boom Boom Bernadine, banging heads against walls was what being a nun was all about. She left the school, never to be seen or heard from again, though there are some graduates of St. Bastion's who still hear her name whenever they brush their hair or otherwise touch their heads.

But all the greats, Dynamite Diane, Cyril the Savage, Boom Boom Bernadine, were strictly minor league when compared to Sister Lee. She had no nickname. None would have done her justice. Sister Lee was ninety years old when I began first grade and she didn't decide to die until I was nearly twenty.

Sister Lee, who taught sixth grade, was smaller than most of her students. She looked about only three feet tall. It was difficult to tell exactly how tall she was because her head was always leaning way over to one side as if her ear was trying to hear what her shoulder had to say.

Lee's body was abnormal not only in its durability and decrepity but also in its appetite for violence, which, even among the nuns, was considered unusually large.

Every summer at the Sunday masses, the priests would ask everyone to pray for Sister Lee because she was dying of a serious disease. It was kind of a stupid thing to say since most people don't die of "nonserious" diseases. Anyway, he'd ask us to pray that Sister Lee had a speedy recovery or a happy death. Each summer, every kid in the parish would pray that she had a happy death and each summer Sister Lee would have a speedy recovery.

In the autumn, Lee would come back to St. Bastion school, her BB eyes zipping back and forth between the corners of the sockets, peering out of that wrinkled face, her tawny lips jibbering to one another with no words coming through the mouth to interrupt them, the fingers of one warped hand rubbing the rosary beads that hung from her belt, and the ear on her bent-over head listening to her shoulder.

The souls of St. Bastion Parish, the nuns, the kids, the parents, the priests, were all bluffers. If you were goofing around in class or something, the nun might say, "You do that again and I'm going to put your head right through the top of your desk." You knew damn well that if you did it again she wasn't going to put your head right through the top of your desk. The nun might give it a half-hearted try but she wasn't really going to do it. She was bluffing. Or when parents came home from a parent-teacher conference in their usual ranting rage and yelled, "You stupid bum. No more watching television until you're thirty and from now on you can go out to play only twice a year." The clampdown usually lasted for about a week. They were bluffing. Although the kids in the neighborhood fought a lot, punches rarely landed. Each guy would do a lot of jumping around, throw a couple hundred punches, miss with all of them, and end up yelling obscenities at the other guy. They were bluffing.

Everyone sort of became conditioned to this barrage of bluffing that constantly went on. We were all little traffic lights watching the signals of the other fellow. "Green," and everything was okay. "Yellow" meant caution; the bluff was on. "Red," which rarely flashed, meant that someone, somehow, was going to be destroyed. The trouble with Sister Lee was that she had no yellow light. She went straight from green to red, catching her victim totally unprepared. Sister Lee figured that if you killed someone, there was no need to caution him "not to do it again."

Most of us kids would spend the first eleven years of our lives worrying about whether we would get Sister Lee in the sixth grade. St. Bastion's was such a large school that there were four rooms of sixth grade, so the odds were with you. As early as second grade, I remember playing baseball at the park and looking around at my friends, wondering which ones were marked to get Lee. But the summer months immediately preceding sixth grade were the roughest.

I would lie in my room late at night, trying to get to sleep, listening to the summer sounds drifting through my window. I could hear the voices of kids, like Depki and Johnny Hellger, who were allowed to stay out later than me, playing hide-and-seek around the street light. Convertibles with their radios wailing would be riddling down the street while adult conversations floated up from front porches. The day's sun-worn air would linger in my room; the sheets would cling to my skin and I would try to think of a time that I had really ticked off God—an annoyance so immense that it would justify His condemning me to Lee.

But when that September came neither I, nor any of my friends, got Lee. Two weeks after the school year began, though, at Sunday mass, Sister Lee almost got me.

The mass that Sunday morning had started out well enough. I had managed to get a seat at the end of the pew. I love being on the ends of things. In line, I always tried to be either the first or the last kid. And I always hoped I'd get a desk at the end of a row. The big advantage of sitting in the end seat of a pew is that you get a much better view of things, especially if you're sitting on the end near the center aisle.

During a mass, the nuns would walk up and down the aisles, searching for troublemakers or rear-enders, kids who were kneeling but at the same time resting their rear ends on the seat of the pew. When a nun tired of searching, she'd sit down in an end seat of a pew while her eyes would continue to scan the tops of the heads around her.

If a troublemaker or rear-ender was spotted, the nun would leap out of her pew, rush up to the aisle where the offender was harbored, and yell out a threat about how she was going to take care of him the first thing Monday morning when he came back to school. The chances were that she wouldn't since she had yelled threats to at least twenty other kids during the mass and it was impossible for her to remember all of them the next day. But such a threat certainly messed up a guy's Sunday afternoon just worrying about it.

That particular Sunday morning, I was enjoying my terrific view from the end seat of the pew when Sister Lee came up to me and said, "Move it over." I moved it over. She plopped it down.

Masses have always seemed long to me but that was the first one that lasted over a year. Never before had I been that close to any nun, much less Lee, for that long. I was actually sitting right next to her.

I stared straight ahead at the altar. Like most terrified animals, I was seeking safety by hoping that my body would seep innocuously into my surroundings. I didn't dare look in Lee's direction. That would have really been asking for it.

As the rituals of the mass slowly inched onward, I began wincing every time I heard Lee's rosary beads rattle because I thought she was about to slug me for doing something wrong. I was blinking my eyes too fast. I was positive she was about to punch me for blinking my eyes too fast. I tried not to blink them at all but then my eyes started melting down my cheeks. So I tried squinting them to help clear out the water and then, oh my God, she was going to say something about me squinting.

My hands had become slick with sweat. I looked at them and realized that they were doing nothing but looking back. One must never have hands in church that are doing nothing but looking back. I folded them over one another. I sensed that Lee was about to jab me for the way I had my hands folded. Some nuns are very dogmatic about the way they think your hands should be folded in church. So I folded my hands eight different ways. I knew it. Lee was becoming enraged with me for playing with my hands. At least I thought that she was becoming enraged. Of course I hadn't looked in her direction since she had knelt down. I waited. Nothing happened. Lee hadn't noticed me playing with my hands.

Lee's nunnish odor began scratching through my nostrils. It triggered within me an uncontrollable urge to scratch my nose.

I have never been much of a nose scratcher. I have dabbled in it occasionally but it has never become a habit. But at that moment, I had to scratch my nose or go out of my mind. Lee would kill me if I touched my nose. Nuns go crazy when someone starts fooling around with his nose. They get upset if they even see your hand anywhere in the general area of your nose.

I tried scrunching up my face. That only made my nose itch more. There was no sneaky way to do it. If I was three or four kids down the pew from Lee, I might've been able to get away with scratching my nose, but not sitting right next to her.

The itch had tired of waiting for me to relieve it and had begun traveling up through my nostrils, heading straight for my brain. That agitated, unscratched itch was going to kill me right in the middle of mass. There was no choice. I had to scratch fast or that itch was going to blow my brains out.

My left eye rolled to the far corner of its cage, toward where Lee sat next to me. Perhaps I'd get a real break and she'd be looking at someone else for a second before returning to me. My eye strained around my cheek bone. It could see nothing. I angled my head oh so slightly to the left.

Lee was gone. I looked around the church. She wasn't even in sight. I felt the empty seat. Not even warm. My nose didn't itch anymore.

A few minutes later I saw Sister Lee hobbling along, patrolling the center aisle. Two kids over from me knelt Paul Logan, a bit of a savage himself. He had a very bad habit of running up behind people he didn't like and hitting them in the head with a house brick. Outside of that, he was a pretty nice guy. He was one of those whose face naturally fell into a smile. He was even smiling when he was hitting someone in the head with a house brick.

During the Offertory of the mass, when we were kneeling, Logan began kicking the underside of the pew with his feet.

Every time Lee would sliver by, looking for the origin of the thump thump thump, Logan would quit doing it. So it went.

After mass, we lined up in the center aisle, girls on the left side, boys on the right, and began filing out of the basement church.

The March morning had been damp and cloudy on my way to church. But upon walking out of the basement door, I saw that the day had contracted a premature case of spring fever, the sun having arrived and cured the sky of its blemishes.

Paul Logan was on the second step of the basement staircase when it happened. A black blur suddenly stung him on top of the head. He stopped, momentarily stunned. Logan's right foot hadn't yet gotten word of the attack and was already heading toward the next step. The black blur struck at him again, catching him in the back of the shoulder. Logan staggered forward on the basement stairs, his hands clutching for the top step.

I was two people behind Logan in line. I looked up. Above the stairwell, on street level, stood Lee, her right hand holding her closed black umbrella at the wrong end, putting the walnut hooked handle on the hitting end. Her left hand was fingering the rosary that hung down from her belt.

Paul Logan was on his feet now, having managed to completely navigate the church basement stairs. Lee shuffled over to him and started jabbing the umbrella's walnut hooked handle into every part of his anatomy.

"So you don't like praying to God, do you," Lee said as she jabbed. "Didn't want to tell Him that you were sorry for all the sins you've committed against Him in the past week. No, you wanted to annoy all the people around you while they were trying to pray to God, thanking Him for all He's done for them. But you were too important to pay attention to God. You had better things to do." All the while, Lee kept jabbing jabbing jabbing.

By this time, Logan's face was red from crying. Lee kept telling him how he should ask God's forgiveness for what he had done and how God was all-forgiving and merciful in His love for His children. Sister Lee continued jabbing jabbing jabbing.

Finally, she stopped. Her bent head peeked over her shoulder and the perpetually jibbering lips spat a final sneer at Logan, who had, by now, virtually collapsed to the sidewalk. Lee turned and headed for her Sunday morning breakfast over at the convent.

Walking home with Logan, very slowly as he was still in a daze.

"Why couldn't it have rained?" he said. "Then she would have had to use the umbrella to cover her lousy head. Why couldn't it have rained?" That's all he kept saying to me. Why couldn't it have rained.

And on Sister Lee's breakfast table was Wheaties, the "Breakfast of Champions."

VII / Lent

In Catholicism, the name of the game is pain. The more one suffers, the higher he gets in Heaven. After all, Christ, who began the whole thing, was a great gourmet of pain. He started off by being born Jewish. That, in the eyes of most Catholics, is a fair amount of pain right there.

Christ went through life socially humiliated because no one would believe He was the Son of God and could change water into wine and raise people from the dead. Even in His Crucifixion, His grand finale of frustration, Christ actually lost more followers than He gained. When He rose from the dead, few of His fellow Jews were really impressed.

Christ led the life of a loser. It was an existence of persistent, pounding, pugnacious, penetrating pain. He was the first Catholic and we all faithfully followed in His footsteps.

St. Bastion parishioners suffered constantly and loved every second of it. Stubbed toes, deaths in the family, cars that wouldn't start, ruptured appendixes, rainy weekends, and scraped knees were all moments of misery that were succulently savored.

According to the rules, the more suffering you did on earth for your sins, the less you would have to do in Purgatory. There were, however, two reserve clauses to this system.

First, the pain experienced must have been beyond one's control. You could not sit around all day banging your head against the wall and expect to get to Heaven. Nor could you get credit for the pain experienced by a bad report card since, supposedly, you had control over what went on it.

The second reserve clause stated that the individual must immediately offer up the pain to God. Say you accidentally hit your fingers with a hammer. While the tips of your fingers were still in the process of being pulverized by the head of the hammer, you had to say to yourself, "I offer up this suffering to God." You couldn't swear for two or three minutes and then say, "I offer it up to God." Expediency of intention was of major importance.

Although pain was a year-round pastime in St. Bastion Parish, the apex of agony was those forty days before Easter: the nine hundred and sixty hours of Lent when the pain of simply surviving in St. Bastion's fell far short of the sacrifices necessary for Salvation.

Where the idea of Lent came from, I don't exactly know. It had something to do with Christ having spent forty days in the desert. Fortunately, there were no deserts in Seven Holy Tombs.

Lent was a time of "give ups." At the beginning of the forty days, fathers would give up smoking and swearing, mothers would give up nagging, and children would give up sweets. A few more weeks and we'd all give up.

It was forty days of smiles shrinking into frowns, shortened tempers, and lengthened glares. A time when the tightrope of life became traumatically taut.

About the only people who kind of looked forward to Lent were the fat Catholics. Throughout the Lenten period, everyone between the ages of twenty-one and fifty-nine was allowed to eat meat only once a day. Snacks between meals were also prohibited. In addition, two of the three daily meals could not equal in size the main daily meal. Of course, if you ate like a madman at your main meal, you could still manage, within the rules, to gorge yourself two more times a day and still remain in good standing with the Church.

During Lent, we kids at St. Bastion school had to attend the eight o'clock mass every morning before going to class. On Wednesday and Friday afternoons, we had to go back to church after school and sit through an hour-long Lenten service.

The month of March always managed to fall into Lent. It was a lousy month to exist on the South Side of Chicago anyway, so it was just as well. March was the final fart of winter. It would rain on us one day, freeze us the second day, and on the third day blow us off our feet. By the end of the month, we were globs of wind-wracked ice. In March we would go to school, and the Lenten services that followed, dressed in fur-lined raincoats, cleated shoes guaranteed not to slide on ice-glazed sidewalks, and bricks in our lunch boxes so we wouldn't blow away.

Latin incantations and burning incense would fill the air of those Lenten services as we knelt on the unpadded kneelers, our knees dripping blood, our bodies sweltering inside our March suits, and our twenty thousand toes squiggling to get out. We would be kneeling so erect that our spines would be constantly threatening to snap in the middle. But there was no way to take a break. It was impossible to rear-end it through a fur-lined raincoat.

A St. Bastion after-school Lenten service included, among other things, a journey through the "Stations of the Cross." A Stations of the Cross consisted of fourteen illustrations depicting the story of Christ's Crucifixion, from His agony in the garden to the time His body was placed in the tomb.

According to the rules, there had to be a Stations of the Cross in every church. They could be in the form of plaques along the walls of either side of the church, in paintings on the walls, or even depicted in the stained glass windows, but they had to be there.

During the Lenten services, as the priest made the Stations of the Cross, he would stop and stand in front of each station, holding a cross that was mounted on a staff. An altar boy, holding a candle, would stand on either side of him.

The priest's words would meander through our muddled minds as he explained a particular station of the cross, his voice giving emphasis to the pain points. He didn't make any of this stuff up. He read it all out of a little blood-red pamphlet. Each kid in the church also had a little blood-red pamphlet so we could all read and shudder along with him.

I found the story of the Crucifixion an interesting one. Even after hearing it a few thousand times, I still listened to most of it. But after the priest finished telling us what was going on in that particular station, he would then explain why it was going on. That was not so interesting.

"We adore Thee O Christ and we bless Thee," the priest would chant as he quickly genuflected.

"Because by Thy Holy Cross Thou has redeemed the world," we'd all drone in reply as we, too, dropped to one knee.

"The Eleventh Station of the Cross," the priest would cry

out as he began reading from the blood-red pamphlet. "Jesus is nailed to the cross. Mary, Holy Mother of Jesus, is pierced anew, as she sees wells of her Son's redeeming blood dug in His hands and feet by the nails of the cross. O Mary, through Jesus' wounds, help me renew my baptismal vows and with those nails bind me to Jesus forever.

"Forgive me O Jesus," the priest would continue to read from the pamphlet, "for I know that it is my sins that have put you on that cross. I realize, Dear Jesus, that each time I disobey my parents, each time I lie, each time I don't listen to the good sisters and priests, I am driving the nails deeper into Your hands and feet."

Besides being held personally responsible for Christ being crucified twice a week, Wednesday and Friday afternoons at three o'clock, each kid at St. Bastion's was expected to "give up" something for Lent: not watching a favorite television show, giving up desserts, or, the perennial favorite, candy.

A day or so before Lent would start, our classroom nun would ask each one of us what we planned on "giving up" for Lent. You'd have to stand up in front of the entire class and tell them what your "give up" was going to be.

In the third grade, the "give ups" were running particularly strong. In the fifth row alone, one kid vowed he would not watch any television during the Lenten period. The kid behind him boldly announced to the class that he was abstaining from desserts at both lunch and supper for the entire duration. It was going to be tough to keep up with "give ups" of that caliber. The dismissal bell rang before the nun got to my row.

"I think," the nun said to us as we began getting ready to go home, "that you should all give up something of real importance for Lent this year to show God how sorry you are for the sins you've committed against Him. Remember, it's your sins that put Christ up on that cross." She looked solemnly up at the crucifix that hung high on the classroom wall and then back to us. "Tomorrow is Ash Wednesday, the beginning of Lent, so tonight is your last chance to tell God what you're going to give up for Him during Lent." The meaning of her words was clear. Don't goof it up.

On the way home from school, I asked myself, Could I give it up for forty days? I looked down at it. My mother had been after me to quit. My father had warned me that if I didn't break the habit I'd be socially retarded, whatever that was. Our family doctor insisted that it was loaded with germs and that I'd ruin my health. My dentist said I'd get buck teeth. But I liked it. It was an inexpensive, convenient, and tasty habit. I thoroughly enjoyed sucking my thumb.

Today, I know my dentist was wrong. My teeth turned out fairly normal. If I hadn't sucked my thumb for all those years, my front teeth would, by now, probably be touching my tonsils.

Most people would say that third graders don't suck their thumbs because they're too old for that kind of stuff and have long ago outgrown such habits. Which is true, for most third graders.

I thought of those Wednesday and Friday afternoon Lenten services, the Stations of the Cross, Christ's Crucifixion, and the blood on my hands. If I gave up sucking my thumb for Lent, I would not only be erasing some of my Purgatory time but I would also be doing my part in getting Christ off the cross, not to mention all the germs I'd be avoiding. The decision was made. The impossible would be attempted. I would "give up" sucking my thumb for Lent.

On the morning of Ash Wednesday, the first day of Lent, the priest placed ashes on my forehead and as he made the sign of the cross with them he said, "Remember man, that you are dust and unto dust you shall return." I presumed that statement included my thumb. It wasn't hard to keep it out of my mouth that day.

Four days into Lent, the imbecilic giddiness characteristic of all new crusaders had been consumed by the panic of withdrawal symptoms. I'd normally spend a few minutes sitting in my little red rocker and sucking my thumb before heading off to school. But without my thumb in my mouth, the little red rocker just didn't seem to rock as smoothly as it had before.

The school day was no problem because, of course, I didn't suck my thumb in public. I wasn't a complete moron. But if it was raining after school and I ended up watching some television, by the third commercial I'd have to sit on my hands to stop my thumb from arching toward my mouth.

After dinner was a tough time, too. There is nothing like following up a good meal with a good thumb-sucking. But the toughest times were at the beginning and end of each day. I always loved to suck my thumb right before I went to sleep and in the first awakening moment of the morning.

I hung on for the first week, though. Not once did I suck my thumb. Those seven days had to have wiped out all of my Purgatory time and then some.

Elation over my total victory of the first week breezed me right through the second week. Then came the third.

I couldn't sleep. My food was tasteless. In school, I had trouble remembering my Catechism questions and I lost my spelling book. The Wednesday and Friday afternoon Lenten services were beginning to get to me. Big Deal. Being crucified. We all have our crosses to bear. I couldn't suck my thumb, for God's sake.

I tried to think about other things. There wasn't anything else to think about. I tried giving myself pep talks. I had heard somewhere that Notre Dame won a lot of football games because they kept telling their players that any man who played football for Notre Dame had too much pride to allow himself to lose. So I tried that approach. "Come on, kid, you've got what it takes to lay off that thumb until Lent's over. Pride, man, Pride. You've got only three more weeks to go. You can do it, kid. You can do it. Remember Pride, Pride. You said you were going to give up sucking your thumb for Lent and you're too proud to quit. Pride. Pride." Obviously, winning football games was easier than quitting the thumb-sucking habit.

One afternoon after school, I was over at Depki's house while his mother was really giving it to him about never remembering to take out the garbage. She told Depki about how her brother, Depki's uncle, never remembered to take out the garbage when he was young either. It was the only thing her brother had to do when he was a kid, Depki's mother said, but he could never discipline himself to doing it. One thing led to another and now he was living on skid row, drinking out of dirty wine bottles, smoking cigarette butts that he picked off the street, and sleeping in doorways. All because he couldn't discipline himself to taking out the garbage when he was a kid.

It seemed to me that as far as self-discipline was concerned, thumb-sucking and taking out the garbage weren't that different. I convinced myself that if I failed to keep my promise of not sucking my thumb, it would be the first step toward ending up on skid row. It wasn't the idea of skid row that bothered me, I didn't really know what skid row was. But smoking cigarette butts off the street . . .

I was down to the last week of Lent. The first three days of the week had gone by quickly. For one thing, we had the last two days of the week, Holy Thursday and Good Friday, off from school. Having the last part of the week off always makes the first part of the week go faster.

Holy Thursday was just another free day and, like most, was spent in the pursuit of pleasure: a few hours of street softball in the morning and an afternoon of rolling down dirt hills at a nearby construction site, followed by a leisurely game of marbles. Then came Good Friday.

Good Friday wasn't a good Friday at all. Actually, it was a

very lousy one. Since the Chicago public schools were also closed on that day, we Catholic kids couldn't even get the satisfaction of being able to go over and stand outside the public school windows and yell "suckers" to the public school kids inside.

On Good Friday morning, I'd have to go to church and sit with my class for an hour. It was called an "Hour of Devotion." We were supposed to kneel there and think about Christ's suffering and death on the cross.

I'd think about that for the first few minutes but you can't think of that kind of stuff for an entire hour. What I'd actually do is spend a good part of the time staring at the statues with the purple bags over their heads.

At the beginning of Holy Week, the week before Easter Sunday, purple bags would be placed over the heads of all the statues in the church. Why, I don't know. But that really fascinated me. The only time I'd ever look at those statues would be during Holy Week when they had the purple bags over their heads.

Like most Catholic kids at St. Bastion's, I wasn't allowed outside to play on Good Friday between noon and three o'clock, the hours that Christ was being crucified. We were supposed to sit around the house and think about how Christ was suffering and dying for our sins.

My mother had told my sister and me that her grandmother had told her that anyone who said a thousand "Hail Marys" on Good Friday before three o'clock would be granted any three wishes within one year of the said one thousand "Hail Marys." I actually made the thousand "Hail Marys" a few times though on most of the Good Fridays I rarely got past a hundred.

Today, such superstitions don't make any sense. But in those years of blind faith, very little made sense. On the Good Fridays when I said the one thousand "Hail Marys," all my wishes came true.

The only wish I can remember now is when I wished for a new bike. At the time it seemed like a rather outrageous request since my father had already informed me, as only he could, that there was no possible way for me to get a new bike until my sister got one first. Her bike was in much worse shape than mine. Yet, less than three months after the Good Friday on which I had said my thousand "Hail Marys" and wished for a new bike, my father met a friend of his who had a brand-new twenty-four-inch bike that he couldn't use and was willing to sell to my father for half price.

On Holy Thursday, the day before Good Friday, I would make up a list of seven or eight wishes that had been kicking around in my head for the past few months. I would then eliminate all wishes that could wait until the next Good Friday or that I might get even if I didn't pray for them. That would usually get me down to three or four wishes. If one of the remaining wishes was one of mutual interest and benefit, say for the family to take a summer vacation in Indiana, I would ask my sister to wish it for me. She always made her one thousand "Hail Marys." But like most older sisters, she was seldom interested in wishes of mutual benefit. So normally I would just forget about two or three of the wishes on my list.

Although I was entitled to three wishes, I really only took two. I figured these one thousand "Hail Marys" were being answered by the Blessed Virgin Mary herself rather than by her son, Jesus Christ. It being Good Friday, Christ must have been reminiscing about His Crucifixion up in Heaven just as we were doing down on earth. He'd hardly be in the mood to listen to some kid's three wishes. Besides, "Hail Marys" were always more or less presumed to go directly to the Blessed Virgin Mary.

So only two of the wishes were legitimate. That is, the primary beneficiary was me. The third was the sugar coating, designed to make the other two more palatable. That one went something like, "Help me be a better person," or "help me get better grades in school." Something far-out like that. Although I realized that once having said my thousand "Hail Marys" before three o'clock on Good Friday, I was entitled to my three wishes, I didn't want to ruin a good thing by getting obnoxious with my requests. I knew that if the Blessed Virgin Mary was anything like my mother, she'd appreciate such a gesture.

In a further attempt to avoid ruining a good thing, I never wished for anything that clearly fell into the category of a miracle. If you think about it, asking for a miracle implies that you're good enough to get a miracle. Christ and the Blessed Virgin Mary might have thought that I was an egomaniac or something if I had made a wish like that and might not have granted me any of my three wishes just to spite me. So although many of my wishes were improbable, none of them was impossible.

I didn't tell any of my friends about the thousand "Hail Marys" and three-wishes routine. I didn't tell Depki because I didn't think he'd believe it. Johnny Hellger might not have believed it either. If he did, he would have taken advantage of it. Johnny Hellger would have done something like using his third wish to wish for three more wishes and just keep it going like that. I might have told Tom Lanner. I don't remember.

One reason I often didn't make my thousand "Hail Marys" on Good Friday was that I would spend a lot of time between noon and three o'clock staring out the living room window at the non-Catholics, watching them playing outside and having a good time. Even some Catholic kids would be out there. Johnny Hellger was. But he was always where he shouldn't have been. Sometimes Depki was, too. But then, it might have been his shift to be on the street so he had no choice.

Besides working on my thousand "Hail Marys," I also used to pray that it would rain between noon and three o'clock so that all those kids would have to run and sit inside like me. It happened only once and then it rained only for twenty minutes. It was a spring thunder shower that sneaked up quietly on the neighborhood. As the rain poured down on my street, I patiently waited for the lightning to strike one of the non-Catholics as he streaked for his house. The lightning only struck two trees and they belonged to a Catholic.'

According to Catholic tradition, it was supposed to rain on Good Friday while Easter Sunday was always supposed to be sunny and warm. But in Seven Holy Tombs, Good Friday was always a beautiful day and it always rained on Easter Sunday. One year the devil outdid himself and we got two feet of snow. It was very strange. Seven Holy Tombs was mostly a Catholic neighborhood, but we always got Protestant weather.

On that Good Friday in third grade, between watching the non-Catholics playing outside and trying to get my thousand "Hail Marys" in, I had no problem avoiding my thumb.

Holy Saturday. The finish line was in sight. In a few hours, it would be Easter Sunday morning and Lent would be over. I was proud of myself and had every right to be. I had met me and I had won. Even then, I realized that victories over such a formidable opponent were going to be rare so I relished it while I had the chance.

I looked down disdainfully at my thumb. Of course, I would continue to suck it after Lent was over, but the forty-day abstinence had proven that I was master. Thumb-sucking would be a pleasure now, not a passion.

Pride. No wonder Notre Dame won so many football games. Pride. I walked around the house with my convex chest and casually mentioned to my mother that she and Dad needn't hide any eggs around the house tonight as I was fully aware that there was, in fact, no Easter Bunny. I had told her the same thing the previous year but she had hidden the eggs anyway and I had searched the house for them anyway. But this year was different. I had now acquired a sense of maturity, a sense of Pride. With such self-discipline, the world was mine and I knew it. I was tempted to take out my school books and do a little homework. A Saturday first. But, I figured, why overdo it.

After supper, my mother began boiling eggs while my father took out the food colorings and started mixing them in four or five different coffee cups. My sister started spreading newspapers over the kitchen table in preparation for the Easter Saturday night ritual of egg coloring.

I viewed the proceedings with an air of distinguished disinterest and only after my sister had messed up half of the eggs did I relent and, balancing the egg on the wire egg holder, dip it slowly into the coffee cup filled with orange food coloring. I have always had a weakness for orange.

I decided that I would lay awake in bed until midnight when Lent officially ended and suck my thumb for the first time in forty days. Once again I would feel my index finger stroking my nose and my tongue rolling around my thumb. But I fell asleep.

Easter Sunday morning. The purple bags were off. The days of "give ups" were over. For those who had given up on their "give ups" midway through Lent, Easter Sunday morning was a time of endless regret. "Why did I quit?" they'd ask themselves. "Why couldn't I have stuck it out just a little longer? Here it is, Easter Sunday morning already." They would spend the rest of Easter Sunday deriding themselves, calling themselves lazy slobs, sinners, spineless, all of which were most likely true. But for those who had not given up on their "give ups," Easter Sunday morning was indeed a delicacy.

I woke up and looked out the window. It was raining. Naturally. Then I remembered. I could suck my thumb. With no qualms of conscience whatsoever, I could suck it. Christ had risen from the dead. We were all free.

I jammed it in. Yech! It tasted like a foul-smelling, fat, fleshy fist. I yanked my thumb out and looked at it. There was nothing on it. I stuck it in again and sucked harder. It tasted worse. It didn't even seem to fit right in my mouth. I yanked it out again and stared at it. This couldn't be my hand. This time I tried sticking my thumb in very slowly and then I realized. By winning, I had lost.

Going downstairs and looking through the house for the orange-colored eggs. Wondering why I hadn't heard the Easter Bunny hiding them.

VIII / Bapa and the New York Yankees

I saw it turn into our street. As that black dot in the distance grew into a 1948 black Plymouth coupe, I knew it was him and I knew what he was doing here. Bapa had come to take me to the Promised Land, Comiskey Park, for a Yankee doubleheader.

It is a fine tradition in this country to name grandparents after idiotic babblings of their grandchildren. I don't know which one of us grandchildren had the distinction of sticking him with the slur, but "Bapa" was the only name I knew the man by.

He was a typical easygoing, cigar-smoking, I'll-give-you-anything-you-want type grandfather. On Saturday afternoons, he'd come over, dragging half of the world behind him. Ice cream, candy, toys, and best of all, piles of unused transfers that he brought from work. Bapa drove a city bus. For the money, not for a living. His living, he said, was done at the ball park and not on the city streets.

You see, my grandfather was a member of a species now almost extinct. He was a baseball fanatic.

Bapa had played some baseball when he was a kid. By his own admission he was not too good and eventually he ran out of teams to get bounced off of. Besides, World War I had come along and tied him up for a couple of years. After he got out, he made the fatal mistake of marrying someone who was not a baseball fanatic. So for the next thirty years or so, Bapa had to be content with simply listening to the ball game on the radio and only very rarely slipping away to Comiskey Park, the cathedral of the White Sox sect, where he was a member.

Although he was upset about Grandma's death, Bapa wasn't so shaken as to miss the afternoon game at Comiskey Park on the day of her funeral. "After all," he commented, "it isn't every day Whitey Ford pitches against the White Sox." My family was pretty concerned about his behavior but I wasn't. Now if it had been the Cleveland Indians playing the White Sox, I could have seen some reason for them getting so worried about him. But the New York Yankees? Who could cast a stone?

No one else in the family particularly liked baseball so as soon as I was old enough to stand and hold a hot dog in one hand without having its weight pull me over, throw out obscenities at the correct time, and learn the proper use of the bathroom, Bapa hauled me off to the ball park.

One Tuesday afternoon, Bapa called me up.

"I've got great news for you, Eddie, can you guess what it is?"

"We're going to a Yankee ball game this weekend."

"Better news than that."

"We're going to a Yankee doubleheader this weekend."

"Even better than that."

"What's better than a Yankee doubleheader?"

"Come on, think."

"I've got it. We're going to a twilight Yankee double-header!"

"Right. This Friday night. I'll be by about four-thirty. Make sure you tell your mother you won't be home for supper."

Although Bapa and I had seen a lot of ball games together, we had never managed to catch the almighty New York Yankees in town. Now I was going to see my White Sox go up against them in a nighttime doubleheader. It was too much.

We got to Comiskey Park at about six-thirty, but there was such a large crowd that we didn't get to our seats until after seven o'clock. Batting practice was over and the starting lineups of the two teams were about to be announced over the public-address system. I could see Casey Stengel handing the starting-lineup card to the home plate umpire and then shuffling back to the dugout, his hands in his back pockets.

"And now," boomed the voice of the public-address system, "the starting lineup for the New York Yankees." Such names as Bill "Moose" Skowron, Yogi Berra, Mickey Mantle, Tony Kubek, Hank Bauer, and Clete Boyer echoed and reechoed through every niche in the ball park. The crowd just sat in a dazed silence as those Yankee names badgered their ears and ascended into the night air.

Then the public address announced the White Sox lineup. The only three names I can remember are Sherm Lollar, Nellie Fox, and Minnie Minoso. It was certainly a night of David and Goliath.

The square blobs of lights, stilted high above the ball park, were strewing their brazen yellow offspring over the entire arena, encasing the park in a soft aroma of yellow glow as if the scene were a dream and not real at all.

The White Sox came running out of the dugout to take their positions. Bapa balanced a beer on his knee and while gazing at the field, mumbled through his half-eaten hot dog, "This may be as close to Heaven as I get."

The first Yankee up slammed Bapa and me back to reality as he promptly put the first pitch into the center-field stands. The White Sox were starting some rookie pitcher and it was a pure case of genocide. The Yanks got to the White Sox for three runs in the first inning, one each in the second, third, and fourth innings, three in the seventh, and one in the ninth inning.

The only exciting part of the game was in the fifth inning when, I think, Hank Bauer of the Yankees hit one that was headed straight for the box seats in left field. It was obvious to everyone in the park that it was a home run. Everyone, that is, except Minnie Minoso, the White Sox left fielder, who specialized in crashing into brick walls.

Minnie went racing back toward the left-field wall as if he actually had a chance of catching that ball. He didn't. He barreled into the wall in full stride, making a deadening thud that few actually heard but everyone else imagined. When they carried Minnie off on a stretcher, the crowd gave him a standing ovation.

Ball parks are funny places. You talk to the slob next to you as if he were your lifelong sidekick and you give a standing ovation to some maniac who runs into a wall for no other reason than to get a standing ovation.

As we were standing there applauding Minoso, the guy next to me said, "Jeezzs, that Minoso might not be the greatest ballplayer around but he's sure got a lot of guts."

"Guts maybe," said Bapa as he began sitting down, "but no

brains." Bapa was that rare combination of a man: a realistic fanatic.

"Minoso's done that quite a few times this year, hasn't he, Bapa?"

"Five to be exact." Bapa was already concentrating on the next hitter. "Six times actually, but one time Minoso was able to leave the field under his own steam so of course it doesn't count in the official record book. If he can do it twice more, he'll tie Woody 'The Wonder' Wallerson's record of seven unconscious stints set back in 1914. If it hadn't been for extenuating circumstances, Wally could have easily made ten."

"What extenuating circumstances?" I asked.

"After the seventh time, he never regained consciousness. I don't think Wally minded. He set another record doing that."

Bapa, like all baseball fanatics, had a compulsive love of statistics.

By the start of the second game, all the signs of drowsiness were fast encroaching on me. Hot dogs were being consumed in obligatory fashion rather than to quell my appetite. Even sips of beer were being passed up. My eyelids, gaining weight with every moment, fought relentlessly to stay up for it was the second game I really wanted to see. Billy Pierce, my idol supreme, was scheduled to pitch against the devil himself, Whitey Ford. It figured to be a real pitchers' duel and that's exactly what it turned out to be.

For the first seven innings, neither team scored. Then, in the bottom of the eighth inning, the White Sox stole a run.

The first man up, Nellie Fox, fouled off twenty-nine pitches before he finally got a base on balls. The second man up hit the catcher's glove when he swung the bat and got first base on an interference call. Bottleneck Boines, the next man to bat, used the old shirt-sleeve trick.

Bottleneck always wore a uniform eight sizes too large so

that if the ball came within three feet of him, it would hit the uniform and he'd get on base as a hit batter. That night, after the ball bumped Bottleneck's sleeve, he put on a stupendous performance of pain, shivering his entire body as if he were about to die of pneumonia.

The White Sox now had the bases loaded with Minnie Minoso due up.

Minnie came out of the dugout looking woozy, obviously still feeling the effects of his last crash against the wall. He played the moment for all its worth, taking his time getting into the batter's box and looking around the park to make sure that there wasn't an inattentive soul in sight. There wasn't. Satisfied that he was the center of all he surveyed, Minnie stepped into the batter's box, dug his back foot into the dirt, swung at an imaginary pitch, took his stance, and then silently defied Whitey Ford to throw one by him.

Ford reared back and fired one off. Minnie swung so hard he fell down. Strike one! The two of them went through the entire skit again. It was now a no ball, two-strike count on Minnie.

No one in the ball park was worried. Minnie still had one pitch left and that was all he needed to unleash his secret weapon. Whitey Ford wound up and let fly a fast ball. Minnie very calmly stuck his head out across the plate. Whammo! His body spun up like a tenpin, hung for a suspended moment above the plate, and then collapsed to the ground. The half-sheared ball went wobbling down the first-base line. Minnie staggered up, was almost tempted to take a bow, but instead limped down toward first base. That forced in a run and the White Sox were ahead 1 to 0.

The next three White Sox batters struck out and as the game moved into the ninth inning, we led the Yankees by a run. We were three outs away from shutting out the New

York Yankees and Whitey Ford. Could this be it? The beginning of the end?

For years I'd heard how the Yankee dynasty couldn't go on forever. But it did. Every spring, sports magazines shouted that this was the year the Yankees would fall. Opposing managers predicted it, newspaper writers hoped for it, and fans begged for it. But the Yanks went right on winning. But maybe losing this game was going to be the first step on a downward journey for the New York Yankees that would carry them from the top of the league standings to a horrendous crush of Yankee pride, ending at the bottom of the American League standings.

No maybe's about it. This was it. And I was there to see it: to witness the first crack in the Yankee fortress.

Ten minutes earlier, I couldn't keep my eyes open. Now I was jumping up and down like crazy. Everyone else was standing up, too. The guy next to me was getting so excited that he was spilling beer all over my feet. I couldn't have cared less. It felt a little sticky between the toes but, through my frequent outings to the ball park, I had become accustomed to Schlitz-scented tennis shoes.

The White Sox came on the field for the ninth inning and bedlam broke loose. The park looked like an open-air insane asylum. As Billy Pierce walked to the pitcher's mound, the fat woman behind me cupped her hands to her mouth and bellowed, "Come on, Billy boy, mow those sonofabitches down."

Bapa was just sitting there, marking something on his scorecard. I leaned down so he could hear me.

"What's the matter, Bapa, too much beer?"

"Nothing's the matter."

"Then why are you just sitting there?"

"How many innings are there in a ball game?" Bapa asked. Already I knew what was coming.

"Nine."

"And how many have they played?"

"Well, eight, but . . ."

"I'll cheer when we win."

At that moment, I realized later, Bapa displayed the exclusive badge of all professionals: that self-assured serenity that refuses to become unnecessarily excited or to take anything for granted. All professionals have it whether they be baseball fanatics or brain surgeons. Another name for it is cockiness.

The first man Billy Pierce had to face in the top of the ninth inning was Tony Kubek. On the first pitch, Kubek hit a high chopper to the White Sox second baseman, who threw him out by twenty feet. The next Yankee up, Bill Skowron, also swung at the first pitch and lined it right back to Pierce.

The White Sox were now one out away from shutting out the Yankees and Whitey Ford! One out away! One maddening out away! Just one!

Then Mickey Mantle, the cleanup hitter, drilled a single to right field. Two out, a man on first, and we still led the New York Yankees by a run. One more out and it would be all over. Just one more.

Slowly, the Yankee kneeling in the on-deck circle got up and began moving toward the plate, waving four or five bats around his head. His squatty legs had apparently forgotten to keep up with the rest of his body. His beefy shoulders almost hid his neck.

As he stepped into the batter's box, he threw four of the bats behind him and leaned the chosen one on his shoulder. Yogi Berra was ready.

Billy Pierce checked Mantle's lead over at first. Then Pierce pulled both feet together and proceeded to slowly rear back on his left foot, stretching his left arm so far behind him that he appeared as if he were going to knock the center fielder's cap off. At the peak of his windup, Pierce's body became momentarily motionless. An instant later, Pierce started leaning forward, his arm came racing over his head, and his hand released the ball as the windmill lash of his body sped it toward the plate.

The ball was coming in low and outside. Yogi Berra stood dumb. The ball was almost past him. Suddenly, the springs unleashed in Yogi's wrists, the bat ripped off his shoulder, and the smack of bat on ball migrained through the park.

Minnie Minoso was running back toward the wall in deep left field, looking up with glove outstretched. He had a few fans fooled. They actually thought he had a chance for the ball. But maybe he did. Maybe this time, Minnie Minoso really did have a chance of grabbing it. I looked down at Bapa, still sitting, quite relaxed.

"Upper deck, fifth row," he said.

I looked back toward the field. The ball was just beginning to come down. That familiar thud as Minnie went plowing into the wall and crumbled in a heap at the base of it. The ball landed in the upper deck, fifth row, seventy feet over Minnie Minoso's head. A two-run homer.

As Yogi Berra went into the dugout after rounding the bases, a few of his teammates patted him on the behind as he walked by. None of the Yanks were too terribly excited, though. Pros don't get excited.

Already the crowd was moving for the exits even though the game had a half an inning to go. Bapa wanted to wait.

"Minoso's still down there," Bapa said. "Let's see what happens. Here come the boys with the stretcher. Now we can go."

We started walking down the ramp. By the time we reached ground level, the final score was being announced: New York Yankees 2, and the White Sox 1. I felt as if I was a part of the world's largest funeral. Almost no one was talking.

"Well," said Bapa, "one more time and Minoso will tie Wallerson's record."

"Think he'll make it, Bapa?"

"Oh, I think so. Minoso's got the head for it."

IX / Dirty Shirt Andy

Dirty Shirt Andy owned what passed for a grocery store on the corner of 103rd and Allen Street. He went under a number of aliases such as "The Slob," "Fat Man Andy," and simply "The Pig." But Dirty Shirt Andy was his real name. No one could wear a shirt as dirty as Dirty Shirt Andy.

A kid never went to Dirty Shirt's unless it was to look for something that was "out." Dirty Shirt Andy always had the stuff that was "out" simply because no one went to him to buy it when it was "in."

Kites in August, marbles in October, and hockey sticks in April. That was Dirty Shirt. His store was about four months behind all the other grocery stores in the neighborhood. In toy turnover, that is.

In food turnover, he had to be at least five years behind. All the food in Dirty Shirt Andy's looked the same. There'd be a little yellow shriveled-up label on one of the shelves that would read "bread." All there would be above it would be large greenish brown humps. Then on the next shelf there'd be a label that would read "cookies" and above that would be a lot of little greenish brown humps.

The canned food looked the same, too. Silver. None of it had any labels. The only edible stuff in Dirty Shirt Andy's store was his potatoes. They were growing out of everything.

Dirty Shirt's storefront boasted the only ghetto-gray window panes in the neighborhood. Behind one of the panes was a group of ten-year-old comic books, stripped of their covers and thrown around a pile of canned Henrietta's Beets, unlabeled of course. Two of the cans were half opened and Louie Vega, the foremost beet authority in the neighborhood, said they were definitely "Henrietta's." It wasn't a matter of faith and morals, but Louie's opinion carried a lot of weight when it came to beets.

Now everyone knows there's only one source of evil in the world. It's just that no one seems to be able to agree on what that particular source is. Christians claim it's Adam and Eve while non-Christians claim it's Christians. Other speculations have included certain animals, witches, the devil, and politicians.

But in our neighborhood, there was no doubt whatsoever what that one source of evil was. It was Dirty Shirt Andy, though most adults simply referred to him as "that moron on 103rd and Allen Street."

Anything that went wrong in my neighborhood could be traced back directly to Dirty Shirt Andy. If church attendance was down, it was because people were too busy reading the dirty books they had bought at Dirty Shirt's. If a kid was late for school, he had probably stopped at Dirty Shirt's to buy some cigarettes. If a black family was seen driving around the neighborhood, it was because they were looking to buy some old food from Dirty Shirt Andy.

It was so accepted that Dirty Shirt was the one source of evil in the world that if you happened to ask someone in my neighborhood, "What is THE source of evil in the world?" they would look at you as if you had asked, "Is the sun hot?" That's just the way they would look at you.

It was the adults of the neighborhood who held that view, though, and not us kids. Most of us liked Dirty Shirt Andy because he didn't treat us like kids. Adults would like you because you were a kid or would dislike you because you were a kid. Not Dirty Shirt. He hated us because we were people. Child or adult, it made no difference to Dirty Shirt. If you showed the signs of a human being, then he hated your guts. He detested every and all, his hatred refusing to discriminate on the basis of age. Dirty Shirt Andy was truly a democratic hater.

There were a few kids who agreed with the adults that Dirty Shirt was the one source of evil but they were the same ones who took the adult line on all major issues. In short, they were the Royal Pain kids.

I, like most of my peers, was convinced that adults, not Dirty Shirt Andy, were the one source of evil. Until that moment in my seventh year of youth when I became a believer.

On that particular day, my older sister and I were going around turning in empty pop bottles that we had collected from our basement, the space underneath the kitchen sink, and neighborhood prairies. We had got rid of the Pepsis at Ed's Store, the Cokes at Ginny's Food Mart, and had even managed to unload the Nehies at the Midwest. Now we were stuck with some unmentionables such as "Loring Cherry Soda, THE PRIDE OF EAST LANSING." Where else? We headed for Dirty Shirt's.

We walked in and headed down the long aisle toward the back of the store, each of us carrying two cartons of empty pop bottles.

We had to step around Dirty Shirt's dog, a wrinkling, ratty fur slab of a nauseating hue that nobody had thought up a name for yet. Although the dog matched Andy's lust for filth, it definitely had a more pleasing personality. It slept most of the time.

We got to the end of the aisle. There, amid the growing potatoes, greenish brown humps, and old hockey sticks sat Dirty Shirt Andy with his bald head sliced by dirt-crusted wrinkles, the U-shaped frown dangling over the unshaven jaw, followed by a three-inch strip of neck. Then the grand finale. That crud-coated T-shirt vainly trying to shelter Dirty Shirt Andy's preposterous pot.

He was sitting, as usual, behind the counter with the Butternut Bread advertisement stretched across the front of it. "Tut tut nothing but . . ." The "Butternut Bread" was scratched out and an obscenity had been scribbled in.

We walked up and put the cartons on the counter. I was biting my tongue. I was, after all, standing before Dirty Shirt Andy, alias "The Slob," "Fat Man Andy," and "The Pig." But normal human beings don't go around calling people names like that. Especially when that normal human being is three feet tall and the object of his derision is one Butternut Bread counter away and would just as soon kill him as look at him.

But I could feel those words racing up my throat, slithering past my tongue, and bellowing by my teeth. Hey, Dirty Shirt, give us some money for these empty pop bottles, huh?

I didn't have to worry about saying anything wrong. My sister was already starting to speak. She was biting her tongue too, I could tell. And she was mentally checking every word before letting it out, lest she make a fatal slip.

"Hello, Andy. We were wondering if you could give us the deposit money on these empty pop bottles."

Andy began in his Mississippi, South Side of Chicago accent.

"What ya got dere?"

"Oh, we've got all kinds here, Andy."

"I know dat. I can see, ya know. How many? How many?"

"Four cartons, Andy. Twenty-four bottles."

"Forty-eight cents' worth, huh. Tell ya what, I'll make ya a deal."

"What . . . what kind of a deal?"

Dirty Shirt Andy reached down behind the counter and brought up a puppy. A black and white one. "I tell ya what, throw in fifty cents and the pop bottles and he's yours."

"All we've got are the pop bottles, Andy."

"Well . . . okay. It's against my better judgment, but I'll make ya an even trade. The dog for the bottles."

I looked down at the mongrel on the floor and then up at the puppy.

"Ya don't have to worry about that. They ain't related." Dirty Shirt tried to put on a smile but he couldn't seem to remember what one looked like.

My sister and I looked at each other. We knew a good deal when we saw one. That wasn't the problem. It was the hierarchy at home. For years we had been trying to get a dog into the house but every attempt had been smacked down by a logical no. But now we realized that life had pitched one right across the plate. Our eyes silently conferred. It was unanimous. Swing!

"Okay, Andy, it's a deal."

"Put da bottles at the end of da counter and here's your dog."

We scampered the four blocks home. The dog piddled on my sister twice and me once. I stood outside with the puppy next to the side door while my sister went in to deliver the news. Through the screen, I could hear her talking to my mother.

"I see you're home, dear. Get rid of all your bottles?"

"Yes we did, Mother."

"That's nice. How much money did you and your brother make?"

"Ninety-six cents and . . . one dog."

"Oh, that's nice. What are you going to do with . . . What dog?"

"We got a dog for some of the pop bottles."

"From who?"

"Dirty Shirt."

"Where's it at?"

"At the side door."

I heard her coming. Mom flung open the side door and looked at the puppy, which was sitting on my shoes. She stared disbelievingly, as if it were missing two of its heads or something. She knew Dirty Shirt Andy, too.

"It is kind of cute."

"Can we keep it, huh, Ma, huh, can we, huh, can we?"

"We'll see what your father says." We were in. We knew it. She knew it.

My father got home late that night.

"Hi, hon. What's for dinner?"

"Stew, dear."

"Anything new?"

"Why yes. The children got a puppy today."

"Got a what?"

"A puppy. You know, a little dog."

"I know what it is. That's just what we need around here. Four more legs. Where is it?"

"Downstairs in a corner of the basement in a little cardboard box. I gave him our alarm clock."

"Why? Does the damn thing have to get up for work? I do, you know."

"Keep your voice down. The children are listening. Why don't you go downstairs and take a look at the little thing before you get yourself so excited over it."

He walked through the kitchen, past my sister and I, mumbling about how he should have reenlisted, and headed down the stairs to the basement, closing the door behind him. The three of us listened as his feet chewed up each descending step. BAM BAM BAM BAM. My mother's brain had a built-in radar system for my father's temper. It worked on the principle of bams. Loud and slow bams were a bad sign and that was exactly the sound charging up from those stairs.

A few seconds of silence as he walked across the basement. Then, clumping, scratchy, blurry noises as if someone was madly trying to get up the stairs. We opened the door and, sure enough, that's what my father was doing: madly trying to get up the stairs. Finally he made it, slammed the door behind him, and locked it.

All we could hear now was my father's heavy breathing and the tinkling of puppy's paws as they moved up the basement stairs. Slowly, my father began to wheeze out words.

"That . . . dog . . . is . . . foaming . . . at . . . the . . . mouth."

I looked through the keyhole. He was right.

"It's . . . got . . . rabies. . . . Where . . . did . . . you get . . . that . . . dog?"

Where else?

I looked at my sister but she didn't look back. We'd been conned. In my mind, I could see Dirty Shirt Andy leaning over his Butternut Bread counter, bits of dirt crumbling off his T-shirt as it brushed against the edge, summing up the entire situation in the same word that Bugs Bunny puts it to Elmer Fudd. Sucker.

For the rest of my youth, I was a disciple of the good. And like any disciple of the good, I spent all my time telling everyone where the bad came from.

"You wanna know why our school didn't get the day off like the rest of the schools? Because Dirty Shirt Andy talked to our principal, that's why." "You know who told your mother you broke that window? Dirty Shirt Andy, that's who." "Don't you know why it's raining on Saturday? Because Dirty Shirt Andy bumped his head on the end of the bed and couldn't get up in the morning. Don't believe me, huh? Well, have you seen Dirty Shirt this morning? I didn't think so."

Within a few months, every kid in Seven Holy Tombs was converted. It seems that Dirty Shirt Andy had sold more than one foaming dog. Like typical converts, most of the kids simply took their old belief and wound it in with their new one. Adults were still, in general, believed to be the source of all evil. But THE adult source of all evil was Dirty Shirt Andy.

A few years ago, I ran into Louie Vega in downtown Chicago. He's a steelworker now. We both had a little time so we stopped in at a bar and shot the bull about the old neighborhood. Lou still lives there.

"Say, Lou, does Dirty Shirt Andy still have that store on 103rd and Allen Street?"

"No, he moved out about five years ago. The city condemned him. Not the building, just him. Someone's told me he's died since then," said Lou.

"Do you believe it?" I asked.

Lou leaned over the table and in a very hushed tone said, "There's a lot of talk about God being dead, isn't there?"

"Yes, Lou, there is."

"Now take a look around you at this world full of crime, Communists, race riots, beatnik college kids, and all the other kinds of shit that we live in."

I did, but all I saw was the inside of a cocktail lounge. Lou sat up, very satisfied with himself.

"After taking a look at this world, it's not hard to believe that God is dead, is it?"

"No, Lou, not hard at all."

"Now you and I know THE source of all this evil, don't we?"

"Yes, Lou, I guess we do."

"Now take a look at that very same world and tell me that Dirty Shirt Andy is dead."

I didn't have to. Lou was right.

"Never," I replied, "never."

X / *Felix the Filth Fiend Lindor*

Like any average human being, I received my sex education in alleys, under stairwells, on street corners, and in vacant lots. I did, however, have the privilege of studying under one of the most fabulously filthy minds of the modern era—Felix the Filth Fiend Lindor.

Felix Lindor had enough dirt in his mind to apply for statehood. He had to have gone through puberty during his preschool years because he was already a dirty old man by the time he got to the first grade. He constantly made snide remarks about "Dick and Jane," and once when we were talking about "Superman," Felix told me what *he'd* do if he had X-ray vision.

Felix the Filth Fiend knew almost everything there was to know about sex and what he didn't know, I later discovered, he made up.

No matter who in the neighborhood told you a dirty joke, you knew it originated in the muddy mouth of Felix Lindor. Felix himself told such dirty jokes that sometimes he didn't even get them. Of course, Felix never did understand jokes with double meanings. He could never find the clean one.

Although Felix was undoubtedly born with more than his share of the sex syndrome that we're all blessed with, he developed his talents with diligence and self-discipline until he drove himself to the absolute depths of depravity. For Felix the Filth Fiend Lindor, a dirty mind was a twenty-four-hour-a-day job. He could look up at any cloud and see a dirty picture.

I didn't get to know Felix Lindor really well until I was in the fifth grade. Felix lived on the other side of the neighborhood, so I never went to his house or anything like that.

There were a couple of large dirt hills, surrounded by weeds, in a prairie on Roland Avenue. In one of the hills, some kids had dug a small cave. The cave had an extremely small entrance so you really had to squeeze to get through it. The cave was pretty small inside, too. Everyone had to sit with his knees up against his chest.

It was there in that cave that Johnny Hellger, Tom Lanner, and I, and sometimes Depki, would meet Felix after school, two or three afternoons a week.

Johnny Hellger would bring cigarettes—he claimed he was already a pack-a-day man—and would give one to each of us along with a mint Life Saver to kill the tobacco smell on our breaths before we went home for supper. Johnny Hellger was intensely proud of his index and middle fingers, which had turned yellow from holding cigarettes. He often bragged about having the yellowest fingers of any fifth grader at St. Bastion's.

Johnny Hellger could also inhale the smoke, talk a few seconds, and then blow the smoke out through his nose. He could entertain you for hours with a pack of cigarettes.

Hellger never believed that stuff about smoking stunting your growth. Years later, when Johnny was full-grown, he stood just slightly taller than a king-size cigarette.

In my neighborhood you had to be careful what you said to a guy about sex. If you said something that betrayed your ignorance, you'd get pie-in-the-face laughs and be reminded of your stupidity for weeks afterward even though the guys doing the laughing may have gotten the correct information only a few hours before you talked to them. But there is little joy in knowing something unless you can laugh at someone who doesn't.

Therein lay Felix's greatness. He loved ignorance. You could ask Felix any question about sex with no danger of derision. The cruder the question, the better. This mentor of the mundane would lean back, jet-stream the cigarette smoke from his mouth, pick the pieces of tobacco from his tongue, and in his whorish voice proceed to explain, in detail, things we'd never even heard about, diagraming difficult concepts in the dirt with his finger. Felix was a multimedia man when it came to teaching.

Felix Lindor believed in using concise terminology. His definitions never contained words of more than five letters. When the lecture began to lag, Felix would throw in a dirty anecdote, using names of kids we knew. Besides teaching theory, Felix also gave us lessons in social protocol.

"When you take a piss in a girl's house," said Felix, "always bank it off the side of the toilet. Otherwise, it sounds like hell and everyone in the house can hear you taking a piss. It's also a good idea to pull the chain just as you're starting. That way, nobody can hear nothing."

Then there was the day Felix introduced us to the art of

buying a dirty book, a feat that was more easily performed then than now.

Today, there aren't many good dirty books around. Obscene ones? yes. But dirty ones? no. Great dirty books, like great lovers, always maintain a certain level of tension in the suitor that keeps him coming back. Only at closing sales should you let it all hang out.

A girl looks more enticing in a tight skirt than she does naked. The same principle holds true in books. The sex act is a rather simple biological function. Stated in clinical terms, it would make boring reading. Therefore, the secret of succulent success for a dirty book is to treat sex as if it were dirty. Lots of description and very little narration of actual sexual acts.

A good dirty book has only about three actual sex acts, each preceded by fifty pages of sensuous description, which, if the proper lines are reread twenty or thirty times, gives the reader a feeling of active participation. Once you have savored a truly dirty book, an obscene book will usually strike you as . . . well . . . obscene.

Obscene books simply, and very briefly, describe one ultimate sex act after the other, leaving nothing to the imagination. Instead of discussing sex as the dirty, disgusting, degrading debauchery that we all know and love, an obscene book talks about sex as if it were perfectly legitimate and clean. Disgusting.

A good dirty book starts off with an innocent kiss on page 3, a not so innocent touch on page 20. By page 135, the heavy action is well under way and by page 150, the details of the score are being narrated. A few pages at the end to state the "moral" of the book so it can be classified as "art" rather than pornography and that's it. The cover of a dirty book is usually simple, with perhaps just the title.

Obscene books, however, have very obscene covers. Within

the first two pages, they've done it all. Like throwing an ocean at a thirsty man. Drowning him is not the same as satisfying his thirst.

In fifth grade, when I was listening to Felix the Filth Fiend Lindor in the dirt-hill cave, there was no worry about confusing dirty books with obscene ones. Obscene books hadn't been invented yet and, thanks to Father O'Reilly, even dirty books were hard to come by in Seven Holy Tombs. But for Felix, the Marco of Porno, such logistics problems were easily solved.

After a particularly intriguing lecture in the dirt-hill cave one afternoon, Felix said to us, "If you guys wanna read some good stuff"—we certainly knew what Felix meant by "good stuff"—"you oughta buy some paperbacks at Cromie's Drugstore."

"Cromie's Drugstore? I've never heard of it, Felix," Johnny Hellger said between the circles of cigarette smoke he was haloing from his mouth.

"It's in the Seventy-ninth Street neighborhood, over by the Hollywood Theater," said Felix. "The only stores around here that have dirty books are Dirty Shirt Andy's and Devlin's Drugstore. But if you go to either of those places, you take the chance of someone you know seeing you buying dirty books. But there ain't anybody in that Seventy-ninth Street neighborhood who knows any of us."

"I've never seen Cromie's Drugstore," said Lanner, "and I was at the Hollywood Theater just last weekend." Lanner could hardly talk, his eyes were watering so badly from the smoke of the cigarette he was holding. "Hey, I think I hear something outside." Lanner crawled to the mouth of the cave and cautiously poked his head out.

Both Lanner and I worried that the cave was going to be raided some day, by whom we didn't know. I guess we worried because we knew the cave deserved to be raided.

"Lanner," yelled Felix, who was obviously annoyed by the

interruption, "will you quit your fucking around and get back in here."

Lanner resettled himself against the wall of the cave, his eyes still listening for any foreign sound in the prairie that surrounded the dirt-hill cave. "It must have been the weeds blowing around out there," said Lanner apprehensively.

"Yeah, yeah," said Felix the Filth Fiend Lindor. "Anyways, Cromie's Drugstore isn't on the same block as the Hollywood Theater. It's about a block down on Seventy-ninth Street. Say, when are you going to the show next, Lanner?"

"We're both going this Saturday afternoon, Felix," I said. "Hey, Hellger, you wanna come along, too?"

"Naw, I can't. I gotta go see my grandfather. He's dying again."

Felix leaned forward toward Lanner and me, as if the dirt walls were trying to listen. "Look you guys, I'm gonna tell you how to buy some really great dirty books. You wanna know how to buy dirty books, don't you?"

Did we want to know how to buy dirty books? Why else were we huddled in a dirt-hill cave, our eyes smarting from the cigarette smoke, the flesh on our arms being ravaged by invisible bugs, our nostrils wilting from the onslaught of Johnny Hellger's bad breath. Lanner and I certainly weren't there trying to work off Purgatory time.

"Here's what you do," said Felix. "First of all, when you get in Cromie's Drugstore, make sure there's no one in the place that knows you. That neighborhood's pretty far from here, but you never know. So check that first.

"As soon as you get in there, buy some candy bars and then go over to the magazine and book racks. Don't eat the candy bars while you're in the drugstore 'cause that gives 'em the idea that you bought the candy bars just so you could eat 'em while you're looking for dirty books.

"Now, if you walk right over to the magazine and book

racks as soon as you get in the store, without first buying some candy bars, the guy behind the counter is gonna figure you don't plan on spending any money so he might ask you to leave right away. But if you show him right off that you're a paying customer, he'll be less liable to throw you out. I know that sounds crazy to you two, but that's the way those guys think.

"When you get over to the racks, remember that you can't spend a lot of time there because if you do you're gonna get bounced.

"Forget about the magazines. No matter how dirty the covers look, they're not worth it. I spent fifty cents on one of those movie magazines once that said something on the cover about Liz and her seven lovers that she went to bed with every night. Exclusive photos, the whole bit. Her seven lovers turned out to be cats. That was fifty cents shot to hell. So remember, forget about the magazines, they're a waste of time.

"Don't bother with any of the detective paperbacks. You're lucky if you can find three dirty paragraphs in one of those books.

"If you look through a book and it seems like the writer's really trying to tell a good story, don't bother with it. If the guy's out to write a good book, he's not gonna have a lot of room for dirty stuff. And also skip over the ones that have the writer's picture on the cover. Writers don't put their pictures on the covers of dirty books.

"What I do is I usually check a few pages at the beginning, in the middle, and at the end of a book. Out of those, if I can't find at least two dirty pages, I figure the book's not worth my time.

"Another thing you can try is letting the book kinda fall open naturally in your hand. A lot of other people have looked through those books too, and maybe they've found the dirty pages already. If that's the case, the book will sometimes fall

open to the dirty pages. This trick doesn't always work, but
sometimes it does."

"Man, you sure know what you're doing, Felix," Lanner
said. Felix threw Lanner a sneer from the side of his mouth,
not recognizing Lanner's awe with even a comment.

"Oh yeah," Felix continued, "have even change for whatever books you're buying. The longer you have to stand in
front of the counter with those books, the more likely the guy
behind the counter will give you a hard time, like asking you
how old you are and shit like that. And after you've paid, wait
long enough for him to give you a bag to carry the books in.
You wouldn't want to be seen on the bus carrying them. You
guys got all that?"

"What's in it for you, Felix?" I asked. I wasn't quite as naïve
as Tom Lanner. For one thing, I hung around with Johnny
Hellger a lot more than Lanner did.

"All I ask," said Felix, "is that I get to read the books after
you're through with them."

"Me too," said Johnny Hellger.

"Oh no you don't, Hellger," I said. "If you can't come
along with Lanner and me to help buy them, you can't help us
read them either."

"For Christ's sake, that's not fair. I told you I gotta go visit
my grandfather this weekend. He's dying, for Christ's sake."

"He's been dying for the last three years. How long does he
plan on taking?"

"You knocking my grandfather, Ryan?" Johnny Hellger
started getting up but when his head hit the dirt ceiling, he remembered that he was in the cave. "I dare you to say that
again, Ryan. I double dare you to say that again."

"Double darers go first," I began to reply, but Felix cut
short my legal retort.

"All right, all right you guys, let's cut out all this arguing
crap. Now, I think you guys agree that it's fair I not pay any-

thing. I've done my share by telling you guys all this stuff. Agreed? Okay, Lanner and Ryan, you guys should buy one book each. They usually cost about thirty-five cents apiece. Since we're all in this together, I think Hellger should be allowed to read the books after you guys get done with them if he pays a third of the cost." Felix looked over at me. "Fair enough, Ryan?"

"Fair enough."

"That okay with you?" Felix nodded toward Lanner.

"Yeah, okay."

"We'll meet back here Monday after school," Felix said. "You two make sure you have the books with you. Now let's get the hell out of here. I'm getting bitten all over the goddamn place."

About an hour later, Tom Lanner and I were parking our bikes in front of "Mary's" Delicatessen.

"You know, Eddie," said Lanner as we entered the store, "I don't like the idea of going to Cromie's Drugstore tomorrow. That's a rough neighborhood. Usually when we go to the Hollywood Theater, we get off at the bus stop in front of the place and walk right into the show. But Felix said Cromie's is at least a block away. I'm not looking forward to walking around there."

"I don't like the idea either, Tom. But I don't see any way out of it."

"There's a good show at the Hollywood Theater tomorrow, too," Lanner lamented, "*Savage Sundown*. And we won't be able to see it because we'll be spending all our time getting those books."

I was now standing over "Mary's" Delicatessen's freezer chest, searching under the frozen packages for a couple of ice cream cones.

"You wanna go tell Felix that we're gonna back out of it?" I asked.

"Not me, man, How about you, Eddie?"

"Chocolate or vanilla, Lanner?"

"Chocolate."

In big black letters, the marquee of the Hollywood Theater announced *Savage Sundown*, starring some people whose names I don't remember. I could see the same actor three weeks in a row and still not be aware of his real name. Sometimes I couldn't even tell whether the guy on the screen was the same guy I'd seen in a different movie the previous week. I'm still that way.

As Lanner and I got off the bus, Lanner looked up at the marquee and said, "Why don't we tell Felix we lost the money?"

"He'd never believe us, Lanner. Come on, let's get it over with."

I was beginning to feel lousy about the whole situation. For one thing, I really enjoyed going to the movies with Lanner. He saw more than most people did. Six months later, he could recall almost every scene in a movie. I couldn't do that the next day. In horror pictures, though, Lanner hardly saw anything at all.

Whenever a scary part came on, Lanner would simply get up and walk out into the lobby, coming back to his seat only when he was sure the scary scene was over. He was the only kid I knew who had enough guts to do that.

Johnny Hellger would run out into the lobby, too. But he was always making up excuses, like he had to go to the washroom or get some candy. A lot of kids pulled that "excuses" stuff. Not Lanner. If he was scared, he'd tell you so.

I myself was never much impressed by horror pictures. Everything else in life terrified me, but not horror pictures.

As soon as Lanner and I turned the corner, I spotted a Prescription Drugs sign hanging over the sidewalk at the far end of the street.

"That Prescription Drugs sign must be Cromie's, huh, Tom?"

"Yeah, I guess so."

The Seventy-ninth Street neighborhood, occupied mostly by feeble red stone apartment buildings, was a much older neighborhood than Seven Holy Tombs. Seventy-ninth and Kenian, the street that the Hollywood Theater was on, was a nice-looking street. But the same could not be said for the street on which Lanner and I were looking for Cromie's Drugstore.

Little shops with slimy windows seemed to shove at you as you walked by them. The curbs were crummy with garbage while used chewing gum soured the sidewalks and obscenities sprawled across boarded store windows. The people walking by didn't look so hot either.

"I sure wish Cromie's wasn't way the heck on the other end of the street," said Lanner.

"So do I, Tom, so do I."

We walked hurriedly toward the Prescription Drugs sign, our feet automatically weaving through the used gum on the sidewalk. Some old guy carrying a bottle of booze teetered up to us and mumbled something to Lanner. We couldn't understand what he said, but we sure started walking a lot faster.

As we opened the door to Cromie's, a tiny bell clanged overhead. The moment it clanged, Lanner shoved into me from behind. I yelled at him over my shoulder.

"Will you watch where you're going, Lanner. Relax, will ya."

"Sorry. Sorry."

We walked in and, as Felix had told us to do, looked around for anyone who might know us. They were all strangers.

Cromie's was a vintage drugstore complete with soda fountain and windmill fans hanging from the ceiling. Even though it was a cool May day outside, the inside of Cromie's was muggy. The fans whirled frantically above us forcing me to almost shout to Lanner, who was standing right next to me.

"Okay, Lanner," I said, "let's buy the candy bars."

The clerk behind the counter was a stocky, brutish-looking man with a square head covered by a crew cut. He was dressed in a smudgy white smock and he had pudgy meatball hands.

His mouth said nothing as he took our money for the candy bars. But his eyes were of the variety commonly worn by parents. They spoke plainly enough. "You are kids and therefore under suspicion. We will be watching you. Don't try anything."

Lanner bought two Snickers bars. I remember Lanner as being very big on Snickers. I bought a Hershey's chocolate and a Mounds bar. Then I remembered that a Mounds was a ten-cent candy bar. Since we figured this was going to be an expensive escapade into the erotic, I put the Mounds bar back and took another Hershey's.

After dropping our coins into the clerk's pudgy meatball hands, Lanner and I began unwrapping our candy bars as we pretended to head toward the door. At the last second, we nonchalantly veered right and headed straight for the paperback and magazine racks.

Although Felix the Filth Fiend Lindor had told us not to bother with the magazines, one of the covers was too tantalizing to ignore. "How Debbie Keeps Eddie Up ALL Night," the cover line read. I opened up the magazine and began looking for the article.

Lanner was already on his knees looking through the paperbacks on the bottom rung of the rack. When he saw what I was doing, he shouted something up to me. I couldn't hear him the first time because of the noise from one of the whirling windmill fans, which was hanging directly over our heads. I yelled back at him to repeat it.

"I said," bellowed Lanner, "that I thought Felix told us to forget about the magazines and to concentrate on the paperbacks."

"Yeah, he did," I shouted back. "I just wanted to check out a few of them for myself." I could tell by Lanner's look that he was irritated by my breach of self-discipline.

When I got to the article on Debbie and Eddie, I discovered that Debbie kept Eddie up all night by calling him on the phone every half hour. What a rob. Felix was right. I went over to Lanner, who was still on his knees next to the bookrack.

"Find anything good, Tom?"

"Nope. All I can see are a few cookbooks and some Spanish-English dictionaries."

I began searching out the books that were buried behind the others, figuring that maybe Cromie made it a point of hiding the dirty books so that only the people who wanted dirty books would know that Cromie was dirty enough to carry them. That's what I would have done if I owned a drugstore and sold dirty books. I wouldn't want the whole world to know I was selling dirty books. Just the people who wanted them. Of course, if I owned a drugstore, I wouldn't sell dirty books because it's a very dirty thing to do. There's a big difference between buying dirty books and selling dirty books.

Lanner and I were both flipping through the pages of different books, frantically searching for some fragments of filth. We were trying all the techniques Felix had taught us: selecting random samples from the beginning, middle, and ends of books, letting them fall open naturally in our hands, avoiding books that had the author's picture on the cover. Still nothing.

Lanner was getting nervous. He kept looking at either the Coca-Cola clock that was above the greeting card display or over at the clerk who was behind the counter.

Finally, Lanner said, "Hey, Eddie, let's get going. That clerk is beginning to look over here a lot."

"You go over and buy another candy bar," I said. "That'll keep him busy so I can keep looking. If I can't find anything by the time you get back here, we'll give up."

"Well, okay. But as soon as I buy the candy bar and get back here, we leave, right?"

"Right, Tom."

Lanner started for the counter, which was on the other side of the store.

I spotted it behind three other books. A thin, plain red-covered book with its title in gold letters: SANDRA THE SEX KITTEN, HOT FROM CINCINNATI. I didn't even bother opening it. I knew. This was the real thing.

Lanner was already on his way back from the counter with the Snickers bar in his hand.

"Hey, Tom," I yelled, "I found one."

He didn't hear me, even though he was only ten feet away, because of the loud whirring of the windmill fans dangling from the ceiling. So I said it again, only much louder. But just as I started, the engines on the fans stopped and I heard a voice shout through Cromie's Drugstore.

"Hey, Tom, I found a great dirty book."

Everyone in the store turned around and stared at me and SANDRA THE SEX KITTEN, HOT FROM CINCINNATI, which was now burning in my hand.

Tom stopped for a second, stunned by the voice, and then continued on toward the door, walking by as if he didn't know me.

I tried to reach behind my back and replace SANDRA THE SEX KITTEN, HOT FROM CINCINNATI back on the rack without being obvious. I heard it slap to the floor. I picked it up and jammed it back on the rack. As I turned around, I saw the crew-cut, square head behind the counter point a finger of his pudgy meatball fist at me.

"Hey, kid, get."

I got.

Lanner was waiting for me about a block away.

"You rat, Lanner, deserting me like that."

"What could I have done? I bet that guy behind the counter threw you out and you didn't get the book anyway."

"Well, it's pretty obvious that I didn't get the book, Lanner. Where the hell could I be hiding it? In my ear?"

"You got thrown out, didn't you."

We began walking toward the bus stop a block away.

"What are you going to tell Felix and Hellger?" Lanner asked.

"I don't know. But no matter what we tell them, we're gonna be lucky if Felix ever lets us back in the cave again."

The double-feature show was within a few minutes of ending when Lanner and I got to the bus stop in front of the Hollywood Theater. I was hoping a bus would come along before the crowd got out. It's very depressing to sit on a sunny Saturday afternoon bus and listen to a bunch of kids talk about a double feature you haven't seen, especially when the reason that you haven't seen it is because you're so stupid.

As I stared down Seventy-ninth Street, searching for a bus, I noticed Lanner looking at the glossy glass-enclosed pictures of the double feature, which hung gleaming on the front of the Hollywood Theater.

"Come on, Lanner, forget it."

"Yeah," he said, "I'll be right there." But he just kept standing there in front of the glass-enclosed pictures, awkwardly shifting his weight from one foot to the other, his hands punched deep into his pants pockets.

I looked up at the massive face of the Hollywood Theater with its marquee teeth and back down at Lanner, who was standing directly under the marquee. I imagined the Hollywood Theater's tongue rising out of the sidewalk and casually flipping Lanner through the door, gulping him down into oblivion. An amusing thought except that the Hollywood Theater was the kind of building that, if it could have done such a thing, would have.

I've always had a problem with buildings intimidating me. Not all of them. Just some. I can walk up to most buildings, jerk open their doors, and rumble through their bods with no trouble at all. They're dirt under my feet and they know it. With other buildings, it's more of a standoff.

There have been a few brick bullies that, no matter how many times I have entered them, look upon my presence as a degradation of their dignity. The Hollywood Theater was one of those.

I was six years old when I first entered the Hollywood Theater. It was on a Saturday afternoon, of course. Immediately, I realized that I was out of my league. As I walked past her massive glass-frame doors and under her multicolored embroidered ceiling, I felt my body slowly shrinking. By the time I got to the candy counter, I was less than three inches tall. The same thing happened every time I walked inside of her.

The lobby of the Hollywood Theater was about a mile long and a city block wide. If you passed through the door marked Aisle 1, you found yourself in the actual seating arena, which was surrounded by a Roman courtyard, complete with columns, windowed walls, and a real staircase that wound its way up into a cube of black.

A couple of times when the show was over, I'd try to sneak up those stairs to see what was up there. Each time, I'd get caught by the same little fat usher with the falsetto voice who kept his flashlight stuck in his belt in front of his belly. When he needed the flashlight, he'd simply turn it on and twist it around in his belt until it was pointing where he wanted it to. I was almost halfway up the stairs once when he caught me. I heard the squeaky voice, looked down, and saw the flashlight beaming at me from his navel.

"Hey, kid, get the hell out of there."

"Isn't this the way out?"

"I said, get the hell out of there."

"It's not, huh?"

It was always a clear night above the seats of the Hollywood Theater. Where the ceiling should have been was a black sky speckled with twinkling stars of all sizes. I thought they might have been lights stuck in the ceiling, but I really wasn't sure. Even today, there is still some doubt in my mind.

The washrooms of the Hollywood Theater had more class than my living room. And they were bigger. Rows of huge round sinks encased by marble counters. In the lobby of the washrooms was a triple mirror where I first discovered the back of my head. I used to stand in front of that triple mirror for fifteen minutes at a time, amazed at the sight of the back of my head.

For the first few years of grammar school, the only way I was allowed to go to the Hollywood Theater was if I went with my older sister. Her taste in movies was slop. Doris Day musicals and Lucille Ball stuff. I spent most of my time then looking up at the stars, taking walks in the lobby, or staring at the back of my head in the washroom. Sometimes I'd stand in front of the candy counter and watch the caramel corn being made.

The Hollywood Theater caramel corn was made in a large steel pot behind the popcorn counter by a pimply-faced, stringy-haired, flat-chested high school dropout who had chewed-up dirt under her fingernails. Her personality was no bargain, either. But she sure could make caramel corn.

She'd shovel some corn from a cardboard barrel into the steel pot. Then she'd open a large jar of caramel and hold it upside down over the steel pot. The caramel would slowly ooze out. GLOP GLOP GLOP. Sometimes it would take as long as five minutes for the caramel jar to empty out. It was at such times that the pimply-faced, stringy-haired, flat-chested high school dropout chose to display her Seventy-ninth Street vocabulary.

After the caramel was in the steel pot, she'd take her two forty-five-pound hands, wrap them around a wooden oar, and stir that pot of caramel and corn as smooth and fast as if it were empty. Her arms moved so frantically that her feet used to float a few inches off the floor. If there was a dull show running, she'd sometimes have as many kids in the lobby watching her as were inside watching the show.

After the stirring and twenty minutes to let it dry—caramel corn must dry you know—she'd start scooping it out with popcorn boxes, filling and flapping them closed, all performed in one easy, fluid motion. That girl had a great pair of hands. If she hadn't been a female, and so ugly besides, she would have made a great second baseman.

Within minutes, caramel-corn boxes would fill the counter. Two other fairly normal-looking girls, who also worked the popcorn counter, did the actual selling. The supply of caramel corn would be quickly depleted and the pimply-faced, stringy-haired, flat-chested high school dropout would once again start the steel-pot procedure.

Like all great caramel corn, a box of the Hollywood Theater's caramel corn could never be completely consumed. The first fistful would be ecstatic. The second, delicious. The third, fair. Then you'd feel that blob of caramel corn swelling in your stomach and you'd know that one more gulp of it would ignite the blob and send it rocketing up through your throat, knocking your head off.

By the fifth grade, I was allowed to go to the Hollywood

Theater without the moral support of my sister. Lanner was the guy I most enjoyed going to the show with, but he rarely had enough money. So I usually ended up going with Johnny Hellger.

He had a mind almost as dirty as Felix the Filth Fiend Lindor's except that whenever Felix talked about sex he would do it in a normal tone of voice while Johnny Hellger's voice always dropped to an almost inaudible whisper, interspersed with a lot of low-throated chuckles. Although Johnny Hellger's mind wasn't quite as filthy as Felix's, it was certainly a lot moldier.

Johnny Hellger always had to get a receipt from the cashier to prove to his mother that he had in fact gone to the Hollywood Theater instead of to the Cosmo Theater across the street. Johnny Hellger's mother, like mine, was a firm follower of the Catholic Legion of Decency ratings. The Hollywood showed only A-I pictures. The Cosmo wasn't as inhibited.

A few times, Johnny Hellger had managed to slip over there and catch some A-III and B movies. He claimed he saw a C (for condemned) movie once. Johnny Hellger tried to tell me about it but I wouldn't listen. You can go to Hell for just hearing about a C movie.

Once Johnny Hellger had gotten past the cashier, he would head up the stairs that led to the balcony. You had to be fourteen years old or older to sit up there. Although Johnny Hellger was only ten years old, he seemed to look at least twenty years older every time he stepped into the Hollywood Theater. I had to be contented with the first-floor routine.

Besides being closer to the stars up there, Johnny Hellger could also get his cheap thrills watching the high school kids make out. During intermission, he'd meet me in the lobby. There, over a package of M&M's, Johnny Hellger would tell me, in an almost inaudible whisper spiced with low-voiced chuckles, the sex scenes he had witnessed.

"Come on, Lanner," I yelled, "there's a bus coming." Lanner took one last look at a glass-enclosed picture that featured a scene from *Savage Sundown*, turned, and reluctantly began shuffling toward me. Too late. The Saturday afternoon double feature had apparently ended. Already, kids were beginning to explode out of the doors of the Hollywood Theater.

I knew how they felt. If the two movies were good, you'd sit through four hours of almost total darkness, the only light coming from the stars overhead and a few exit signs that you could see speckled along the edges of the dark. You'd sit there so long you'd actually forget that it wasn't nighttime.

After the show, you'd walk through the lobby feeling tired and lousy, like you'd been in school all day. It wasn't until you made the turn around the popcorn machine and saw the daylight through the front doors that you realized it was light out. Like finding a few hours of sunshine you'd thought you'd already lived through. It felt good to discover that sunlight and it really excited you. That's why people exploded out of the Hollywood Theater instead of just walking out.

The bus ride home was a classic. A real classic. All these kids around Lanner and me talking about two movies that neither of us had seen. They talked about different scenes, why they thought the Range Rider left the girl behind at the ranch before going into town. How Driman, the crooked bank owner who was secretly the leader of the gang, got killed. And how the ending was so terrific. Stuff like that. It was very depressing.

Two kids, sitting behind Lanner and me, were eating Hollywood Theater caramel corn. The sounds of their caramel corn crackled in my ear lobes, slid down through my inner ear, and right into my mouth. And all I had to chew on were my cheeks.

The Saturday afternoon had diluted into dusk by the time

the bus reached Seven Holy Tombs and our block. Hopping
off the bus and heading home.

"Wanna get together tomorrow after mass and play some
baseball?" I asked.

"Can't. Gotta do work around the house tomorrow. Did
you think of something to say to Felix in the cave after school
Monday?"

"No, I haven't. Have you?"

"No."

We were standing in front of Lanner's house now.

"Well," said Lanner, "I'd better get in, dinner's probably
on the table."

"Yeah, see you later."

I started trotting down the street. I didn't want to be late, either. My mother made a big deal out of Saturday night sup-
pers. I began thinking about the whole afternoon. Cromie's
Drugstore, SANDRA THE SEX KITTEN, HOT FROM CINCINNATI,
and how I'd never know the ecstasy contained between her
covers. The Hollywood Theater and how I'd never again get a
chance to see those two movies. I thought about having to meet
Felix in the dirt-hill cave on Monday after school with the
story of my failure.

I slowed down my trotting to a walk. Sometimes you just
don't feel like running to get where you're going.

"Yo, Eddie." It was 3:30, Monday afternoon and I was
changing into my after-school clothes when I heard Lanner
calling for me at the side door of my house. In my neighborhood, no kid ever knocked on the door for you. He simply
stood at the side door and shouted, "Yo . . ." whatever your
name was.

On the way over to the dirt-hill cave, Lanner and I tried to
decide on a story to tell Felix. We tested and rejected numerous accounts. In desperation, we agreed to tell Felix the truth.

Neither of us felt comfortable with it, but it seemed like the only thing to do. We were walking so slowly that we were a half hour late by the time we got to the prairie.

Lanner and I squiggled through the high weeds, which had by now totally eclipsed the dirt-hill cave from street view. We were only a few feet away from the cave, but were still among the weeds when we saw him standing just outside the cave entrance: that brutish-looking man with the pudgy meatball hands and the square head covered by the crew cut. The clerk from Cromie's Drugstore.

He was listening intently to the conversation going on inside the cave but Lanner and I were too far away to hear what either Felix or Johnny Hellger was saying.

Suddenly the clerk from Cromie's Drugstore became enraged at something he apparently overheard. He stooped down and stuck his arm into the entrance of the cave, yelling for whoever was in there to come out.

Johnny Hellger came running out, barely avoiding the grasp of the man, and ran into the weeds, heading straight for us. Felix the Filth Fiend wasn't so lucky. As he came out of the dirt-hill cave, the clerk from Cromie's Drugstore snared him by the arm and started dragging him toward a blue sedan that was parked in an alley behind the prairie.

"Oh my God!" yelled Lanner, "the cave's being raided."

Lanner and I grabbed Johnny Hellger as he started to run past us through the weeds. At first, not realizing who had grabbed him, his body flinched statically from our touch. Then Johnny Hellger saw who it was.

"Let go of me you guys," he said. "I gotta get the hell out of here."

"Don't you know who that guy is?" I asked. "We gotta help Felix."

Johnny Hellger ripped away from Lanner and me, and

began once again to skitter through the weeds. He yelled back at us.

"You're goddamn right I know who he is. And I'm not going back to help Felix. I've never seen old man Lindor so mad."

XI / Blah on the Altar Boys

Deborah came to St. Bastion's fifth grade in October. She was a transfer student. The nun put her in the double seat next to me. Deborah was pure class. She wore rings on her fingers, her dress came to only an inch below her knees, and she had a terrific build on the days that she wore it.

As soon as Deborah would finish her English workbook assignment, she'd take a green hard-covered book out of her desk. On its cover was a young couple holding hands while walking by some tall, overhanging trees. Deborah would often read the same page two or three times.

Once I asked her what the book was about. "It's about love," she sighed. "About love." Man, the way she said it, that word "love" just hung between us right through spelling period.

A few weeks after she arrived, Deborah caught me in the most embarrassing situation possible: she saw me with my parents. Our family had gone out to buy some shoes and we were walking back to our car, which was parked about a block away from the store, when Deborah and a few of her girl friends walked by. She smiled and said hello. I mumbled something back. My father grinned and started teasing me about having a girl friend. He was weird that way. Deborah actually saw me with my parents. I felt like a real jerk.

For the first few weeks, I tried engaging Deborah in some casual conversation. But it was no go. I'd do all the talking and she wouldn't do any of the listening. It was almost unnatural. People in double seats always talked to one another. Sharing double seats was almost like being related.

I asked Depki to find out what the trouble was. Talking to Deborah, he quickly discovered the problem.

"She thinks you're a very nice guy, but that's about it," said Depki.

"What does that mean?" I asked.

"It means she thinks you're blah."

"Blah?"

"Blah," Depki repeated emphatically. "You gotta realize, Ryan," he said, "that there are two kinds of kids in this school —those who are 'in' and those who are 'out.' The kids who are 'in' are the ones who get noticed by everybody else. Now to get noticed, you usually gotta be real good at something, like say sports, or say you're real smart in school. Or you're really stupid. Real stupid kids get noticed, too. You gotta be something really different, you know."

"Where did you learn all this?" I asked.

"From my older brother," said Depki. "He knows all kinds of things about what it takes for somebody to be a hotshot.

When he was telling me about this stuff, he says to me, 'Mike, what do you notice about a train when you're standing up at 103rd and Langlen waitin' for it to go by?' And I says, 'I don't know. The whole train, I guess.' My older brother says, 'No you don't, Mike. The only thing you remember about that train is the engine and the caboose. All the regular cars just rumble by without you ever really seeing them. That's the way life is too, Mike,' says my brother. 'If you wanna be a hot-shot, you gotta be either an engine or a caboose.'

"Another thing my older brother told me," said Depki, "is that 'in' people don't mix with 'out' people very much."

Depki didn't have to say any more. We both knew. I didn't cut it. I was brilliantly blah in everything I did.

Not Deborah. She was probably the greatest volleyball player in the history of the St. Bastion volleyball team. She had a fantastic personality, too. Everyone liked her except for a few girls who were jealous of her. And brains? I can't think of a page in her workbook that wasn't done.

One afternoon, right before dismissal, we were handing in our arithmetic homework. Actually, I never handed in any arithmetic homework in fifth grade. What I did was hand in all my fourth-grade arithmetic papers that I had left over from the previous year. They all look pretty much the same. The first time I tried it, I had that day's homework done so if the nun noticed my fourth-grade paper, I could just claim that I had accidentally handed in the wrong paper. But she didn't notice. So every day after that, I'd hand in a fourth-grade arithmetic paper. I guess the nun didn't check them because she never did catch on. The kid who came down the row to collect them never noticed the difference either. I was very proud of myself, outmaneuvering a nun.

Anyway, that afternoon, right after handing in my arithmetic homework, I whispered to Lanner, who sat four desks behind me, "Want to goof around together after school?"

"Naw," said Lanner, "I can't. Got to go over to church."

"Church? On a Tuesday afternoon?"

"Yeah, Father Durkin's holding a meeting for all the fifth-grade boys who want to become altar boys. Didn't you hear Sister announce that this morning?"

"Yeah, sure I did," I said. "But why do you want to become an altar boy?"

Lanner laughed. "Gee, I don't know. I just think I'd like it. Why don't you come along with me?"

"I don't think so, Tom. I'd like to, but I gotta goof around this afternoon." And then I heard voices in my head.

"You mean, Deborah, that you sit in a double seat with Eddie Ryan! Why, he's the greatest altar boy in the entire school. The greatest!"

Lanner was getting his books ready to go home.

"Hey, Lanner," I whispered, "I'll go with you." The nun had spotted me.

"Mr. Ryan, were you talking? Come up here to the front of the room."

Later that day, as I contemplated the life of an altar boy, I thought to myself that perhaps this was the opportunity that God was waiting for to single me out as someone special. Naturally, I was quite familiar with the stories about God appearing to different saints. Quite a few of them were children, like the kid at Lourdes and the three kids who were involved with "Our Lady of Fatima." Not that I thought I was a saint. But I bet a lot of those people might not have been saints either until God appeared to them. And what better time was there for God to appear to me than when I was running around as an altar boy. I knew there wasn't much possibility of such a thing happening but that didn't stop me from thinking about it. Sort of like a Catholic's dream of making it big in Hollywood.

Becoming an altar boy was easy enough. All you had to do was memorize some Latin and know how to move around the altar. I didn't even bother learning the Latin. I'd just put my head down and mumble nonsense syllables. A lot of the other altar boys did that, too, I think.

But getting to be known around school as the best altar boy at St. Bastion's wasn't going to be as easy as I had planned. I had figured that a lot of other blah guys like myself would be joining the altar boys, looking for their place in the sun, and I was right about that. But according to most of the pew population, Bobby Bracken had just about claimed the title of the greatest altar boy at St. Bastion's, a title left vacant by the graduation of Sam "The Saint" Simpson, who had insisted that Christ had made numerous appearances to him in the coatroom.

There is a Bobby Bracken in every parish. The kid who seems to hold all patent rights on piety. Before he is even out of the womb, his mother is telling him, and all of her friends, that he is going into the priesthood. The nuns adore him, the parish priests patronize him, and his father doesn't know him. He's the kid who tells anyone who will listen that he is going to become a priest and never even considers being a policeman. The worst part is that he usually does become a priest.

Years later, Bobby Bracken would, in his sophomore year, be thrown out of St. Philip's Seminary after being caught in an empty classroom "saying mass" while using sugar wafers for Holy Communion. From there, Bobby Bracken would move on to a notorious career in homosexuality. But in the fifth grade, he was still a formidable power.

The sure sign of being a great altar boy was getting a lot of wedding assignments from Father Durkin, who was in charge of the altar boys. It was customary for the bridegroom to tip the altar boys a few bucks for their efforts. Thus, an altar boy, like most professionals, was judged not by his actual performance but by the size of his bankroll.

According to Father Durkin, the reason that Bobby Bracken

got so many weddings to serve was because Bobby Bracken was constantly filling in for guys who failed to show up for their assignments. For instance, if an altar boy didn't show up for one of the daily masses, say the six o'clock mass, Father Durkin claimed he would call up Bobby Bracken, who would come over to church and take the absent kid's place.

Bobby Bracken was supposedly called because he lived only a half a block from church. A lot of kids lived just as close to church as Bobby Bracken, but none of them were ever called. I doubt if Bobby Bracken was ever called that much, either. I think Father Durkin just said that. Maybe Bobby Bracken was called once or twice, but that was about it.

"The reason," said Depki, who quit the altar boys after a week, "that Bobby Bracken gets all those weddings is because he's a sticky sweet sonofabitch who's constantly going around telling everyone how he's going to be a missionary in Africa and that dummy Father Durkin eats up that kind of shit." I think Depki was right.

Lanner and I, who were usually assigned to serve together, had had only one wedding by the end of November. Right in the middle of the ceremony, I somehow managed to drop the tray with the wedding bands on it. All over the church, you could hear them bonking along the floor. We didn't make any money on that one.

Next in importance to the weddings was the children's eight o'clock mass in the basement church, because of the prestige of performing in front of the entire school. Father Durkin was fair about that. He assigned different kids each week to serve it so that all of us got our chance to be holy hotshots in front of the student body. At one of the weekly Monday afternoon altar-boy meetings, Father Durkin announced that on the following Sunday, the children's eight o'clock mass would be served by Bobby Bracken, Tom Lanner, and myself. It was the only mass that I know, for a fact, God did not attend.

I went to bed early that Saturday night. At that age, I still believed all the garbage people told me about having to have a lot of rest if I wanted to do something well. Of course since then, I've discovered that the exact opposite is true, having enjoyed some of my greatest days while being virtually totally asleep.

That night, I dreamed of Deborah. She was so impressed with the way I served the eight o'clock mass that she bragged me to her girl friends all the way home from church. The following Monday morning, she stared at me constantly as we sat in our double seats, and laughed hysterically at anything I said. I asked the nun if I could go back to the coatroom to get a pen that I had left in my jacket pocket, I looked up and saw Deborah standing a few feet away from me. Deborah and I, alone in the coatroom, her lips gently floated into a gentle smile, her arms began extending toward me. . . .

I abruptly awoke to the clattering of ice chips bouncing off my bedroom window. For a split second, I vainly hoped that this was a dream and that the reality was Deborah and I in the coatroom. But the clattering of the ice chips continued.

I pulled up the window shade and saw the early morning sky retching rain and snow. Everything below the window, tree branches, sidewalks, cars, was glossy with ice. As I climbed out of bed, I realized that I had a headache and my stomach hurt. My mouth felt like I hadn't brushed my teeth in eight years. If it hadn't been a Sunday, I would have thought it was a report-card day. My mouth always felt like I hadn't brushed my teeth in eight years on report-card days.

A few minutes later, my legs moving in robot fashion, I inched across the icy sidewalk toward St. Bastion Church. Ankles remained rigid as each foot slowly plopped down. The body, constantly wary of the foot losing its grip, would cautiously shift its weight onto it. Once secure, the body would swing out the other foot and the procedure would repeat itself.

My eyes were concentrating so intently on this plodding procession of my feet that my unguided head ran straight into a wall of St. Bastion Church.

After going down the basement steps and into the church sacristy, I went into the altar boys' closet and tried to find a cassock my size. There weren't any. The nuns, who each Saturday night took half the cassocks over to the convent to be cleaned, had apparently managed to grab all the cassocks that were even near my size. The closest I could get was one cassock that came to an inch above my knees and another that ended two feet beyond my shoes. I put on the one that was two feet too long. Father Durkin would give you a very hard time if you tried to wear a cassock that was too short.

As I finished buttoning it, I stood in front of the full-length mirror that hung on the back door of the closet. The cassock had swallowed me whole. I was afraid that when Deborah saw me in that cassock, she was going to think she was sharing her double seat with a dwarf.

Lanner came walking into the sacristy. He looked at my cassock, the bottom of which lay in folds around my feet.

"Say, Ryan, did you take a bath last night? You look like you've shrunk."

"That's very funny, Lanner. But I'm afraid that you're not going to be quite so amused when you look in the closet and discover that you're going to have to wear the same thing." Lanner was about the same size that I was.

He started looking around at the different cassocks in the closet. "Where are all the normal-size ones? There's nothing here but longs and shorts." Lanner started putting on a cassock even longer than mine.

"I don't know," I said. "All I know is I'm having trouble keeping my hands free with these crazy sleeves drooping over them."

Just then, Bobby Bracken glided into the sacristy, a cassock, encased in a plastic cleaning bag, slung over his shoulder.

"Good morning, fellas! Say, what's with the long cassocks?"

"Where did you get that cassock, Bracken?" I demanded.

"Oh, this is my own cassock."

"Your own cassock?"

"That's right. Father Durkin told me that since I was serving so many masses I should have my own cassock. This way, my mother can keep it nice and clean and it won't get dirty by hanging in the closet with all the other cassocks."

Lanner muttered something about how this mass might turn into a funeral mass but Bobby Bracken didn't seem to hear him.

"Hey, Ryan, which one of us is going to sit on the side?" Bobby Bracken asked me as he was putting on his cassock.

It took only two altar boys to serve a mass. But Father Durkin had to assign three altar boys to each Sunday mass because so many people attended mass on Sunday. At Communion time, a couple of priests would have to come over from the rectory and help out the priest who was saying the mass serve Holy Communion. Each priest needed an altar boy to assist him.

As the priest would place a host of the Holy Communion on the tongue of the communicant, the altar boy would hold a paten, a metal disk with a handle attached, under the chin of the recipient. This was done, not so much because of the danger of the host, or the Eucharist as it is also called, falling off the person's tongue, although that possibility existed, but because microscopic crumbs of the host supposedly fell from the priest's fingers when he handled it. Since Catholics believe that the Holy Eucharist is the actual body and blood of Christ, it's vital that no part of it ever hit the floor. After the Communion part of the mass, the priest would wipe the paten off into the chalice, the gold cup where the Holy Eucharist was kept.

So although three altar boys were needed for a Sunday mass, only two of them actually served it. The third altar boy knelt at a kneeler, which was to one side of the altar, until Communion time when he was needed to help one of the priests serve Holy Communion.

As I said before, Depki was right about Bobby Bracken. Bobby Bracken was what being a sonofabitch is all about. He always went around telling people how he couldn't wait to become a missionary and start saving souls for Christ. And how if he was real lucky he might get a chance to become a martyr for Christ.

All of us, during our more pious moments, thought stuff like that. But we didn't go around telling everybody mainly because we knew, once we'd gotten out of the mood, we'd regret that we had shot off our mouths.

Not Bobby Bracken. He was a real weirdo. I met his mother a few times and she was even weirder than Bobby. It was probably her fault that her kid was so strange. Or maybe it was the other way around.

Bobby Bracken was very friendly toward everyone. I have to admit that. I'm not saying he was not a royal pain in the ass. He was. And he probably figured that being nice to people was part of the game when you were planning on becoming a missionary for Christ. Still, he was pretty nice toward people. So when he asked me which guy was going to sit on the side, I didn't feel like telling him that Lanner and I wanted to serve the mass and have him sit it out. Of course, I knew that if I could convince Bobby Bracken to sit on the side, it would look to a lot of the kids like Lanner and I were better servers than Bobby Bracken since we were serving the mass and he wasn't.

"What do you feel like doing, Bobby?" I asked.

"I feel like serving this morning," said Bobby Bracken, the tips of his phony smile almost touching his ear lobes.

"I'll sit on the side," said Lanner.

"You don't have to do that, Tom," I said. "Why don't we all flip coins and the odd man sits out."

But as soon as Bobby Bracken heard Lanner's words, he started heading down the narrow passageway that ran behind the altar and over to the priests' sacristy, leaving Lanner and I alone.

"Look, Tom," I said, "you don't have to take that kind of stuff from Bracken. We'll just tell him we're going to serve the mass and that'll be it. He won't be able to do anything about it. We probably won't get the chance to serve this eight o'clock mass again for the rest of the year. Bracken gets it a couple of times a month."

I didn't really think Bobby Bracken got the eight o'clock mass that much but that's what I told Lanner.

"That's okay, Eddie. I don't feel like serving today, anyway. You serve it with Bobby. I'd just as soon sit on the side. I got up this morning feeling kind of sick."

"Yeah, so did I, Tom. It must be the weather or something."

Lanner walked over to the sacristy window and looked out at the swirling, icy snow. You could still hear it clattering against the window. "Boy, it sure is lousy outside," he said.

"Come on, Tom, let's get over to the priests' sacristy."

"You go on, Eddie. I'm gonna stand here and look out the window for a few minutes."

When I got over to the priests' sacristy, Father Durkin was putting on his vestments, assisted by Bobby Bracken, of course.

"Good morning, Father."

"Good morning, uh . . ."

"Ryan, Father."

"That's right. Of course. Ryan, Ryan," he mumbled.

Father Durkin was putting on the last of his vestments. "Where's the other altar boy?" he asked.

"Here he comes now, Father," I said. Lanner was just emerging from the passageway.

"Good morning, Father," Lanner said.

"Good morning, uh . . ."

"Lanner, Father."

"That's right. Lanner, Lanner," Father Durkin mumbled.

The St. Bastion bells, dangling in the tiny tower atop the church, began counting out the hour in their low, monotonous groan as the four of us slowly swished out onto the altar. Without actually tilting my head from its straight-on stare, all great altar boys constantly stare straight on, I managed to sneak a glance over at the girls' side of the church.

There was Deborah, in the third row, looking very surprised that it was I, her own double-seat partner, who was serving the eight o'clock mass. I was determined that I was going to turn this ordinary children's eight o'clock basement mass into a brilliant performance. One that would have the entire school talking about it. And Deborah would casually mention to her volleyball teammates, "My double-seat partner is Eddie Ryan, you know. The best altar boy in St. Bastion's."

Bobby Bracken and I genuflected together at the base of the steps, in the center of the altar, and turned our backs on one another as we moved to our respective positions, the opposite corners of the first altar step.

I was within a foot of my position when I felt a tug. I tried taking a step, but it was no go. I looked over my shoulder and saw Bobby Bracken standing a few feet behind me and staring up at the altar as if he was in a trance or something. He was standing on the bottom of my oversized cassock. Still facing the other way, I tried whispering to him.

"Bracken, will you get off my cassock." I tried moving forward again. He was still on it. I gave a tug on the cassock. No reaction. A harder tug. Again no reaction. I had no choice. I turned around and walked up to Bobby Bracken, who still appeared as if he was in some kind of a trance, just staring up at the altar.

"Bracken, you're standing on my cassock."

His head slowly turned and gazed at me, his eyes glazed even more than usual. He suddenly seemed to snap out of it. "Oh," he said mechanically as he calmly removed his feet from the bottom of my cassock.

"Thanks a lot," I whispered. I nodded my head sarcastically and tried to sound sarcastic, too. But that's very hard to do when you're whispering.

I began heading back toward my position at the corner of the bottom altar step, head bowed, my eyes fixed on my feet. All humble people go around with their heads bowed. In order to be a great altar boy, one must be humble.

My bow-bent head bumped into something. It was Father Durkin coming down the altar steps to begin the prayers at the foot of the altar.

"What are you doing? Uh . . . uh . . . Ryan, isn't it?"

"Sorry, Father." I quickly stepped around him.

Five minutes later, when I had to move the missal from one side of the altar to the other, the book stand collapsed. Bobby Bracken was delighted. Being a future missionary of Christ, he refused to outwardly show it, but I could tell anyway.

In a certain part of the mass, the altar boy rings a small bell three times, very loudly. Each time the bell is rung, everyone in the church bows his head and thumps his chest with his fist. The reasons for all of this are very complicated and you probably wouldn't believe them even if I told you. But that's the way it is. The signal for the altar boy to ring the bell is when the priest puts his hands, palms down, out over the chalice.

I was grinding my teeth, thinking about the book-stand collapse, when Bobby Bracken whispered to me.

"Hey, Ryan! . . . Ryan!"

Regaining consciousness, I looked up and thought I saw Father Durkin's hands over the chalice. I grabbed the little bell from the step in front of me and began frantically shaking it.

The sound of fists pounding into chests could be heard throughout the church. THUMP THUMP THUMP THUMP THUMP THUMP. I rang the bell a second time. There were thumps, but not as many as the first time. The third time, I heard only one thump and that was my own.

Father Durkin looked over his shoulder at me from the top of the altar, started to say something, and then just slowly shook his head and went back to what he was doing. "Nice going, Ryan," Bobby Bracken whispered, "you just rang the bell five minutes ahead of time."

"What were you whispering at me for, then?"

"I was trying to tell you that you've got your cassock on in-side out."

I felt for the label behind my neck. It was on the outside. Bobby Bracken was saying something else but I didn't hear him. I was no longer thinking of how I was going to impress the whole school or fascinate Deborah with my holy moves. My mind held but one thought, survival.

Praying to God to turn me into a turtle, I pulled my head down as deep as I could into my oversized cassock. It was dark and warm inside my shell and no world existed outside of it. But still I heard the bell ringing and the thump thump thumps.

One knocked-down candle and dropped paten later, the mass was over. My only consolation was that the mass moved from a one-ring circus to a three-ring circus. During Communion time, Bobby Bracken got careless with the paten and chopped it into some kid's Adam's apple. The kid almost strangled to death right at the Communion rail. Lanner got caught in a rundown.

Father Durkin believed that in order for one to be close to God and a good altar boy, one had to move slowly while on the altar. So we altar boys had to walk with baby steps whenever Father Durkin was around. Father Boyle, however, who was one of the priests who came over from the rectory to help hand out Communion, believed in speed. Especially on Sunday mornings when he was in a big rush to get the mass over with so he could talk and goof around with the parishioners as they came out of the church.

Father Boyle was working out of one of the side altars, which was around the corner from the main altar. Lanner, who had to go over to the side altar to assist Father Boyle in serving Communion, had to crawl until he got to the corner and then, once he was out of sight of Father Durkin and in view of Father Boyle, had to almost run across the altar, spurred on by Father Boyle's encouraging whispers. "Come on, will ya. We haven't got all day, you know."

Lanner spent the entire Communion time either sprinting or braking, depending on who was watching him. To the kids in the pews, Lanner probably looked like he was going crazy.

After mass, when we had gotten back into the priests' sacristy, Father Durkin had things to say.

"Look at you two guys," Father Durkin said to Lanner and me. Bobby Bracken was quietly putting Father's vestments away. The bastard. "How you two guys managed to become altar boys, I don't know. Look at you. Your cassocks are three feet too long and Ryan, you even have yours on backward. Lanner, I've never seen an altar boy handle himself as poorly as you."

Lanner. I couldn't believe it. Father Durkin was going after Lanner. I had damn near single-handedly brought down a two-thousand-year-old institution and Father Durkin was going after Lanner.

"I want a twenty-five-hundred-word essay from you by next Friday on how to be a good altar boy, Lanner," said Father Durkin. "Either do the essay or quit the altar boys."

As the two of us turned and headed toward the altar boys'

sacristy, we heard Father Durkin saying, "Nice mass, Bobby, nice mass."

"That Durkin's crazy," I said to Lanner as we took off our cassocks in the altar boys' closet. "Bobby Bracken goofed up the mass more than you did and I messed up ten times more than both of you guys put together."

"Don't worry about it, Eddie," Lanner said. "Durkin's an asshole, so what can you expect."

"You're not going to do the penalty, are you?"

"I don't know what I'm going to do yet," he said as he hung his three-feet-too-long cassock up on a closet hook.

The following Friday, Lanner handed in his twenty-five-hundred-word essay to Father Durkin and then quit the altar boys.

As I walked home from mass, the rain-speckled snow was still coming down. But now, instead of icing everything, it was simply self-destructing into slush. I thought about Lanner and the rotten deal he had gotten from Father Durkin. And I wondered why it always seemed to be Lanner who got rotten deals. I thought about Deborah, too. About how I'd be lucky now if she didn't ask the nun to change her seat. But I thought mostly about Lanner.

The next morning, I got into my double seat just before the bell rang. Deborah was reading her green book with the lovers on the cover.

"Can I borrow a sheet of paper?" I asked. I had tons of paper. I just wanted to see if she'd even talk to me.

Deborah reached inside her desk. "Here, take five sheets. I have plenty. There's a volleyball game this afternoon, you know."

"Oh, there is?"

"Over at Crest Hill Park. I never see you at the games. How come you never go?"

"Oh, I'm pretty busy being an altar boy, you know."

"You! Why, you're the worst altar boy in the school. On the way home from mass yesterday, all my girl friends were saying how funny and cute you looked up there on the altar. Are you going to go to the volleyball game this afternoon?" The bell rang and we had to stand for prayers.

I don't remember praying, though. All I could see was a freight train rumbling by and everyone straining to see if the caboose was in sight yet.

XII / Sister Edna

Sister Edna, my seventh-grade nun, was a huge woman with freckled hands. On her desk could be found the usual pile of garbage that nuns accumulate: corrected papers, grade books, paper clips, staples, and confiscated contraband.

In addition, Sister Edna also kept seven small plastic statues, one for each day of the week she said, and, in the upper right-hand corner of the desk, the only item that was never subjected to being moved or used: a twelve-hundred-page book of *Louis, King of France*. Even its bookmark, a Saint Joseph holy card, was immune to movement, always seemingly wedged between the same pages.

Whenever Sister Edna got mad, she'd make a gun out of her

hand and wave the barrel finger right in your face as she bawled you out or just before she slugged you.

She was kind of an old nun, Sister Edna. Not real old, but kind of. I liked her. She didn't do a lot of terrifically kind things for me or any of that other Mr. Chips bullshit. There were over seventy kids in my seventh-grade classroom. Like any nun, Sister Edna spent most of her time just thinking up things for us to do. But she never went out of her way to make life miserable for anyone. For that reason alone, I liked her. She didn't make school fun. That would have been preposterous. But she did make it tolerable.

Sister Edna did do me a favor once, though. It was no big deal but it did give me an idea of what Sister Edna was all about. It was almost time for dismissal and she had given the class a few minutes to start on their English homework that was due the next day.

"Mr. Ryan, come up here to my desk." Sister Edna said it matter-of-factly so I wasn't too worried. I figured she wanted to see me about some routine paper work. I thought maybe I had forgotten to pay my milk money for that month.

"Wait out in the hall for me," Sister Edna said as I came up to her desk. I was shocked. Normally you heard the words "Wait out in the hall for me" only when you were about to receive such violent retribution for a previous escapade that it was going to be too gory for the rest of the class to witness.

As I walked toward the door, a few heads in the front row bobbed up from their work and grabbed a glance of me as I went by. Their faces had a tinge of sympathy diluted by a lot of self-satisfaction. Something like that gave everyone, with the exception of the kid who had to go out in the hall, a bright new outlook on life. "Things could be a lot worse," they'd tell themselves. "I could have been the guy out in the hall today."

As I stood out in the hallway, the only thing that I could think of that I had done wrong recently was I had been chewing on my pencil eraser when Sister Edna had called me up to her desk. Hardly cause for violent retribution, even for a nun.

I didn't have much time to worry about it because I was in the hall only a few seconds when Sister Edna came out to me, closing the classroom door behind her.

"Do you brush your teeth?" she asked. It was not the type of question I was expecting. Besides, even then, I realized it was a very personal one. But Sister Edna didn't ask me in a sarcastic tone of voice, as if she already knew the answer and just wanted to see if I'd lie. She asked like she really wanted to know. So I told her.

"Yes, Str. I brush them every morning." That wasn't exactly true. I didn't brush my teeth every morning. But I did brush them four or five times a week.

"Well, Eddie," Sister Edna said, "your breath is bad. It doesn't smell very good at all. It would help, I think, if you could brush harder and more often."

"Yes, Str, I will."

"Fine. Fine." Sister Edna opened the classroom door and went back to her desk and I went back to my seat. Heads popped up as Sister Edna and I came back into the room, disappointed, for they had heard no sounds of violence volume from the hallway.

It was no big deal. I wasn't embarrassed having Sister Edna tell me I had bad breath. That room was loaded with kids who had bad breath. Actually, I thought it was really nice that Sister Edna had even bothered to tell me. She didn't have to. I wasn't breathing around her all the time. She could have let me go through life with bad breath. What did it matter to her?

Most nuns wouldn't have bothered to tell me. Or if they had, they would have done it in front of the entire class and in a demeaning way, as if to say, "Hey, slob, have you got bad breath! Yech!"

But Sister Edna pointed it out to me as if she were telling me about an untied shoe. No moral connotation. She simply told me I had it and suggested a remedy to cure it. It was very unusual for anyone, especially a nun, to notice something wrong with you and not presume it was your fault. Very unusual.

By some divine decree, Lanner and I shared the same double seat for the entire seventh-grade year in Sister Edna's room. It was an unheard-of phenomenon at St. Bastion school that two good friends would end up sharing the same double seat. The nuns kept close track of who hung around with who and made it a point to keep at least four rows between good friends. But that year, their surveillance system slipped up and there in the seventh grade sat Lanner and I, together in a double seat.

I have always felt that it is the moral obligation of an occupant of a double seat to entertain and be entertained by his partner. Lanner totally agreed with my philosophy. We both considered ourselves superb exponents of the one-liner and it was during history period, when Sister Edna asked the class questions, that our hackneyed humor reached its heights.

For instance, Sister Edna would call on some kid and ask him in what year Lincoln was shot. While the kid was standing up and "uuhhhing," Lanner would point at his ear and whisper to me, "The left ear." Stuff like that killed me. I whispered equally inane comments to him.

They don't seem very funny now. They wouldn't have seemed very funny then if they had been told anywhere but in the classroom. But I'm the sort of person who's most easily provoked into laughter when he's in a place where he has no business even smiling. A joke that would bore me on a street corner would break me up in a library. Lanner was that kind of jerk, too.

It was during these seventh-grade history periods that I developed an art that was to serve me well, not only in school, but as the years passed, through hundreds of hours of funerals, dull parties, and after-dinner speeches: the silent laugh.

At St. Bastion school, even smiling was suspect. Only troublemakers and kids who were enjoying themselves smiled. And at St. Bastion school, the only kids who enjoyed themselves *were* the troublemakers. So for those interested in self-preservation, smiling, much less actual laughing, was strictly out.

Normally, a laugh starts jelling in the stomach, springs through the throat, and ha's out the mouth. Like most things that shoot out the mouth, a laugh comes on an exhale. It's impossible, for instance, to talk and be breathing in at the same time.

The secret of the silent laugh is that just as the laugh is springing through the throat, you cut off your exhale stroke. The stomach vibrates slightly. Faint pitting sounds emit from the throat, but that's about it. In extreme cases, a great one-liner, well-timed, may cause the eyes to water and the stomach to experience minor muscle spasms. But even if a nun was looking right at you, the worse she could think was that you were going through a mild seizure of the dry heaves.

Unfortunately, Tom Lanner never mastered the silent laugh. His laughter always fell out in lopsided chunks. He was often caught, although even I was nabbed a few times.

Whether it was Lanner or I, or anyone else for that matter, who was detected, the procedure was the same. Sister Edna would call the culprit up to the front of the room.

"Were you talking?"

"Yes, Str."

Wham!

Sister Edna ran a very pleasant room. If you got caught, you got slugged. She didn't lecture you or say the words that every kid who's gone to school and laughed at a whispered comment has heard, "Well, if it's that funny, why don't you share it with all of us." Sister Edna didn't keep you after school or mete out punishments according to her daily temperament. One detectable laugh simply received one detectable slug.

The part of the day that Sister Edna enjoyed most was Catechism class when she would talk about the "poor souls of Purgatory."

"We must remember, children, each day to pray for the poor souls in Purgatory. It's too late for them to pray for themselves so we are their only hope of shortening their Purgatory time. We must keep in mind that we, too, will some day be poor souls in Purgatory. If we're lucky."

Sister Edna would then tell us about indulgences even though she knew we had been told about them for the past six years. An indulgence was something you could do that would take off Purgatory time either for you or for someone who was already in Purgatory. You could apply an indulgence to whomever you wanted.

Just about everything Catholic could earn you an indulgence. Saying the rosary, making the Stations of the Cross, going to Friday night novena, fasting, and kissing a bishop's ring were just a few of the activities that had indulgences attached to them.

The rules were quite specific about how much indulgence you would get for each activity. Making the sign of the cross, for instance, was good for 150 days off of your, or someone else's, Purgatory time. However, the sign of the cross was worth 300 days if it was made with holy water, a bonus of 150 days just for the holy water.

I once picked up an easy 500 days by kissing a saint's relic. I can't remember now who it was. The relic was a tiny piece of the saint's bone, about the size of a pin head. It was enframed by a purple cloth inside a small plastic case. All I had to do was kiss the plastic case. I felt pretty stupid, but 500 days is 500 days.

The super day for indulgences was All Souls' Day, which fell on November 2. On that day alone, for each set of ten "Our Fathers," "Hail Marys," and "Glory Be's" you said in church, a soul was freed from Purgatory. You could, however, save only one soul per church visitation so you had to step outside of church for a moment in between each set of prayers so it would be considered a separate visitation to church.

On All Souls' Day in sixth grade, Bobby Bracken claimed to have saved over two hundred people. Of course, he lived very close to church. I was never that successful but I did manage to pull quite a few souls out of the fires of Purgatory.

Sister Edna also enjoyed talking about "fallen-away Catholics." "Yes, children, a fallen-away Catholic has lost the gift of faith. He has turned his back on God, and, by his actions, has told God that he does not want to spend eternity with Him in Heaven. A fallen-away Catholic can receive none of the sacraments and therefore stands little chance of ever gaining Heaven.

"Usually, fallen-away Catholics just don't decide one day that they no longer want to be Catholics. It's a gradual thing. They begin skipping their morning prayers. They stop going to Confession every week. They no longer say their rosaries.

"Then, sooner or later," Sister Edna continued to tell us, "weakened by their lack of prayer, they fall into a mortal sin: they deliberately eat meat on Friday or, for no good reason, they skip mass on Sunday.

"After the first few mortal sins, they'll go to Confession to have them forgiven. But after a while, they become hardened to the damning effects of Mortal Sin. They become indifferent to the saving graces that God is sending to them. Eventually, their love of God becomes a forgotten thing.

"I know it's hard for some of you to believe this now, but even among the people in this class, there are probably a few

who will eventually lose their faith and become fallen-away
Catholics."

Whenever Sister Edna said that, we'd stare at her eyes to
see who they were looking at, but they'd always start skipping
around, unwilling to tell us who they thought the future in-
fidels might be.

Those Catechism classes were about the only times that Sister Edna's words didn't make too much sense. Who could become hardened to the damning effects of Mortal Sin?

In the middle of the year, Sister Edna started leaving the
classroom about every hour for a minute or two. It was very
unusual behavior for a St. Bastion nun. They rarely left their
classrooms and when they did, they'd normally put their number-one bootlicker in front of the class to take down the names
of any kids who looked the wrong way. Sister Edna didn't
bother doing that. She didn't have a number-one bootlicker
and besides, she wasn't gone for more than a minute or two so
there wasn't enough time for any real kind of trouble to start.

Most of us figured she was going to the drinking fountain.
There wasn't enough time for her to be going anywhere else.
But that didn't make sense, either. The nuns never used the
school's drinking fountains. I don't know why. They just
never did.

It was a few months after Christmas, in the early part of
March, I think. As we came into class that morning, Sister
Edna was standing behind her desk, her hands clutching her
black knit shawl, which hung loosely from her shoulders.
Standing next to Sister Edna was a young nun who had a face
that was almost attractive. The young nun certainly came as
close to looking good as any nun I've ever seen.

Sister Edna's seven saints, one for each day of the week,
were gone from her desk, presumably tucked away in the
black briefcase that stood open-mouthed at her feet. The top of

the desk was nude save for the twelve-hundred-page book of *Louis, King of France*, which, along with its Saint Joseph holy-card bookmark, appeared unmoved.

Sister Edna was busy talking to the young nun. Every now and then, Sister Edna would illustrate a point in her conversation by waving to the blackboards, the window shades, her desk, the coatroom, or by taking out one of the workbooks from her shelf and opening it to a particular page.

Although I couldn't actually hear the conversation that was going on between Sister Edna and the younger nun, I could easily imagine what was being said.

"The blackboards are cleaned every third day, Sister. The girls in each row take turns doing that. . . . I usually pull the window shades down at about two o'clock, especially if I plan on putting any geography questions on the blackboard. Even with the shades down, some of the children can't see the blackboard because of the glare. . . . Each row goes to the coatroom separately and the next row isn't called until the previous one is back and sitting in its seats. . . . Because of the holidays, we're two units behind in our Spelling, but if you take five extra words a week, you should be caught up by the middle of April. . . ." Our class was undergoing a changing of the guard.

I had seen all of this happen twice before, once in second grade and the other time in sixth grade. It was a case of the nun simply not being able to go the distance and having to get relief help. The nun would be out of school for five or six weeks and then come back with her vicious vitality fully restored.

Usually, the nun who was leaving wouldn't say anything to the class before she left. If some kid asked the new nun where the regular nun went, the new nun would give an answer like, "Sister's gone away to take a little rest," or "Sister hasn't been feeling too well lately so she's gone to stay at our motherhouse for a while to get well," or "None of your business."

After morning prayers, though, Sister Edna did speak to us. "Children, I'm going away for a while and I want you to pray for me while I'm gone." Spoken like a true nun. All nuns want you to pray for them while they're gone. They must think that if you're doing that, you won't have as much time to get in trouble.

"Of course," Sister Edna continued, "I will remember you in my morning and evening prayers and throughout the day." Sister Edna motioned toward the young nun. "This is Sister Gregory, who will be teaching you until I get back. I'm sure you will cooperate with Sister Gregory and make me proud of you."

A girl in one of the front desks raised her hand. She had, through seven years of grammar school, established herself as one of the school's finer bootlickers. As I have mentioned, Sister Edna didn't have any bootlickers but if she did, this girl would have been one of them.

"Sister," the girl asked, "you are coming back, aren't you?"

"I certainly hope so," Sister Edna laughed. "Why? Do you want to get rid of me?"

"Oh, no, Sister," the girl said, "I didn't mean that."

"Does Sister Gregory here look that mean?"

"Oh, no, Sister. . . ."

Sister Edna was just kidding around with her but I don't think the old bootlicker realized it. Sister Edna sure had that kid going.

We all stood and said a "Hail Mary" and an "Our Father" together and then Sister Edna left.

"Man," I thought to myself, "that girl sure did ask a stupid question. Would Sister Edna be back. Was that a stupid question. They all came back.

But Sister Edna didn't. In a month she was dead.

Walking with Lanner through the school yard late at night. Coming back from St. Bastion Church where Sister Edna was being waked. We were almost out of the school yard when I motioned toward one of the concrete blocks.

"Hey, Tom, wanna sit down and shoot the bull for a while?"

"Yeah, sure," he said absentmindedly.

We sat and stared silently at St. Bastion school as she lay anchored on the other side of the school yard. That night, she didn't look like the same overseer who daily sucked me through her doors. Rather, she appeared almost dignified as she floated in the nebulousness of the night, lapping up the wet early spring breeze, her temper cooled by the melancholy mood of the April night.

Lanner and I had spent the past hour kneeling in front of the open coffin, praying for Sister Edna. The thoughts that had been born there live now in the school yard on the concrete car block.

Neither of us talked but simply sat there, our arms laying across our knees, which were propped up in our faces, each of us tinkering with his own thoughts.

For the first time in its life, my mind began taking a look around: over my shoulder to where I had been, scanning the perimeter to see where I was, glancing ahead to where I might be going.

I had been told before. Hundreds of times. But I never believed it. That night, my mind did reluctantly admit the possibility of its truth. Perhaps I would not be in grammar school forever, I would not be a child, forever. I would not be, forever.

Death. Never before had it burned so closely. Sister Edna was dead. Sister Edna was dead and in that world Father O'Reilly had raved about, that my parents and the nuns had repeatedly told me about, that I had so often thought about.

That world of precision judgment and infinite rewards and punishments, of Heaven and the eternal fires of Hell.

The young nun had been called out of our classroom the previous Friday afternoon right after she had handed out the *Young Catholic People's Gazette*. All of us were in our usual Friday afternoon mood, delirious with joy about being within an hour of a weekend.

The *Young Catholic People's Gazette* was a regular part of the Friday afternoon festivities. It was a miniature six-page newspaper, which contained such literary lures as a "Current News" column, a feature story on the "Saint of the Week," two jokes written in dialogue between "Al" and "Nel," a "to be continued" story about either basketball or horses, and an "Open Letters to Father John" column, which contained such Ann Landers questions as "What special graces can I obtain by saying a decade of the rosary before bedtime?"

Since the *Young Catholic People's Gazette* was always handed out on Friday afternoons, it had become the Pavlov bell announcing the weekend. My mouth was already tasting the three o'clock dismissal bell when the young nun came back into the classroom.

There were tears in her eyes. I was fascinated by the phenomenon. I had always thought nuns were limited to two emotions: anger and, more infrequently, sadistic humor. This tear thing was something new altogether. Everyone in the class seemed to be staring in amazement at the young nun.

"Sister Edna," the young nun began speaking sporadically, "passed away this morning at the motherhouse. Her cause of death was bone cancer."

The young nun was speaking so softly that she could hardly be heard. She pulled out a small white-laced handkerchief and began dabbing it around her eyes and nose.

"Sister Edna knew for the past six months that she was not going to live. When the doctors informed her of her condition,

Sister Edna simply replied that she was glad it was she and not somebody else who wasn't ready to die."

The young nun continued to talk about Sister Edna, telling us to pray for Sister Edna's soul even though the young nun was sure that Sister Edna was already in the arms of God. I tried to imagine that scene, Sister Edna in the arms of God, but I couldn't. It was just too strange.

After the young nun had finished talking, she walked out of the classroom without saying a word. The room was perfectly still. Not a sound. I looked down at my *Young Catholic People's Gazette*, which was pinned to the top of the desk by my elbows. I had been halfway through the "Open Letters to Father John" column when the new nun had made the announcement about Sister Edna. I closed the gazette, stuck it in my desk, and put my head down on top of my arms.

Eyelids squashed my eyeballs as I attempted to permanently etch Sister Edna's image in my mind. She was a part of my life that was over and I was afraid that if I forgot what Sister Edna looked like, it would be as if I had never lived that part of my life at all.

The sanctity of the night was shattered by some kids as they walked past St. Bastion school, yelling obscenities at one another. I looked over at Lanner sitting motionless at the other end of the concrete car block.

"What are you thinking about, Tom?"

"Nothing. A lot of stuff."

"About Edna?"

"Yeah," Tom said.

"Me, too," I said. "Don't you wonder where she's at and what she's doing right now and whether she's watching us down here and stuff like that?"

"You know what I think," said Lanner.

"No, what?"

"I think she's watching us and listening to every word we

say. And I think she can watch every kid in our class at the same time if she wants to, even if they're all in different places."

"Why do you think she can hear and see us right now?" I asked.

"I don't know. I just kind of think so."

"You mean you sort of feel it, Tom?"

"No, I can't really say that. I just think that's the way it is, I guess."

Silence for a few moments and then.

"I sure wonder what it's like, don't you, Tom?"

"Yeah. We'll find out eventually, that's for sure."

"True enough," I said. "Ever think there might not be a God?"

"Sort of," Tom said. "Yeah, sometimes. You?"

"Sometimes. It must really be something, though. Dying and meeting God, face to face. Having Him talk to you."

"Think you'll get to Heaven, Eddie?" Lanner asked.

"Yeah, I think so. I bet I'll probably have to spend a lot of time in Purgatory, though."

Lanner laughed. "I know what you mean. I don't think I'll be catching the express train, either."

Slivers of rain began slipping from the sky.

"Is it raining?" Lanner held out his hand for a moment and then answered his own question. "Yeah, it is." Neither of us made any attempt to move. "Bone cancer. That's a lousy way to go," Lanner said. "My aunt says you suffer like hell with that."

"You know," I said, "I don't think I would have been able to say 'I'm glad it's me instead of some guy who's not ready to die.' I know I couldn't have said that. I could give a shit for the other guy. Hell, I'll never be that ready."

"Did you see all those five- and ten-dollar mass cards next to Edna's casket?" Lanner asked.

"Yeah. I guess you can take it with you," I said. "Now, what's to stop a guy from stealing millions of dollars and investing them in masses to be said for his soul after he dies? You could steal your way right into Heaven."

"I don't think you could get away with that," said Lanner.

"Why not?"

"I don't know. I just don't think you could."

The rain was gaining strength. "We better get going," said Lanner. "I've got some arithmetic homework I've got to do before I go to bed tonight."

"Think we'll get Wednesday off for her funeral?" I asked Lanner as I stood up. My rear end hurt from sitting on the concrete block for so long.

"I don't know," said Lanner. "But even if we do get the day off, we'll have to blow the morning going to her funeral mass because we were in her class."

"You're right, Tom. I never thought of that. But I wouldn't worry about getting that arithmetic homework done tonight. Just tell Sister Gregory that you went to the wake tonight. She won't keep you after school with an excuse like that."

"You're right," Lanner said. "If I tell her that, she won't even have me make it up."

Running home. Watching the rain turn the sidewalks tan beneath our feet. Getting out of breath and slowing to a walk as we come to a corner.

"You know, Tom, I kind of liked Edna. She was all right."

"Yeah," said Lanner in between breaths as we crossed the street, "she was all right."

The beginning of a new block. Once again, running toward home.

XIII / Eighth Grade: Top of the Bottom

For seven long years, we had heard about it. Older brothers and sisters had told us of its power, its privileges, its pageantry. It was, they said, a year of carefree contentment, chic cosmopolitanism, continuous carousing, and chauvinistic comradeship.

Once you reach it, they said, you will find your tongues speaking a language that only others like you will comprehend. Those younger than you will not understand your ways, for they have not been there. And most of those older than you will have long forgotten that they, too, once walked through the Promised Land.

Depki's older brother, in one of his rare poetic moments,

told us just before we began the year, "Never again will so
many of you be so goddamn high for·so goddamn long." A
tear came to his eye as he recalled a personal moment when he
was at the peak.

Those older kids were wrong, of course. But after all, they
were only finite human beings with limited means of communication. They couldn't help but vastly underestimate the
magic of those months that made up the eighth grade.

Like all eighth graders everywhere, we at St. Bastion's were
a privileged minority, enjoying a virtual monopoly on all the
prestigious positions in the school. The eighth-grade girls mon-
itored the classrooms during lunchtime, ran the school library,
and controlled the candy room in the school basement. The
eighth-grade boys filled most of the positions on the St. Bastion's football and basketball teams, cleaned the classrooms
after school, and were the school's patrol boys.

Every eighth grader, of course, was a school hotshot simply
by the fact that he was an eighth grader. But in order to be a
hotshot among the hotshots, you had to hold down one of those
prestigious positions. In September of eighth grade, it looked
fairly certain that God had indeed not chosen me to be a hotshot among the hotshots.

I had absolutely no chance of getting on the football team.
To make the St. Bastion football team, you had to have hair on
your chest, blood in your eyes, and space in your head.

Father LaBlanca, who coached the team, was a cross between Knute Rockne and King Kong, with a touch of Bishop
Sheen that surfaced at after-dinner speeches. Father LaBlanca
consistently produced the best and meanest grammar school
football team on Chicago's South Side. Opponents considered
it a successful day if they went home alive.

The best way to make the team was to get the word around
the neighborhood that you were a stupid, selfish, but savage

sonofabitch. Beating up four or five kids right before tryouts would naturally enhance your chances of making the squad. More than one star of Father LaBlanca's was literally snatched from the road that led to the state reformatory.

I was too small to play football for Father LaBlanca. I weighed only about a hundred pounds when I was in eighth grade. Some of Father LaBlanca's players had fingers that weighed more than that. Besides, I was too weak. I never in my life beat up anybody although, throughout my younger years, I was pulverized almost weekly by numerous adversaries. Some of the finest fists in St. Bastion's have pushed through my face.

I could never play basketball very well so I didn't even have to worry about whether I could make that team or not.

Couldn't clean classrooms, either. I'm allergic to dust. Not all dust, just the dust on St. Bastion's floors. Every time I got near that dust, my eyes would swell up like tangerines. I tried sweeping a classroom once and I spent the next three days trying to see through my eyelids.

The only position of power that I was qualified for was patrol boy. Unfortunately, the nun in charge of patrol boys that year was Sister Triona. I had had Sister Triona in sixth grade. On the second day of class, she decided that out of all the seventy-four kids sitting in front of her, she hated me the most. She spent the rest of the year proving it. The next year, Sister Triona was transferred up to the eighth grade and put in charge of the patrol boys.

Being a patrol boy was as close to becoming an adult as you could get. If you were a patrol boy and you said a kid was talking in line, then he was talking in line. If you said a kid was walking too fast, then he was walking too fast. If a kid really annoyed you, you could "bring him up" to the principal, which was something like arresting him. She'd really chew him out or give him a penalty. Sometimes both. Your word was never questioned. It was a great way of life, having absolute power over your peers.

Most of the patrol boys were picked in their last month of seventh grade so that when school opened the following September, they would already know their duties and there would be no confusion. Very few kids were picked for patrol boys once they actually got into eighth grade.

This passing of power from the present eighth graders to the future eighth graders was a gradual process. I remember, in my last month of seventh grade, I would be marching along in line through the halls, or outside on the way to dismissal, or crossing a guarded street corner. I would look up, and instead of seeing the eighth-grade patrol boy, I would see one of my own seventh-grade classmates wearing the same granite face of authority and the same white patrol belt as his eighth-grade predecessor.

It was humiliating to realize that he and I were the same age, had identical educational and religious backgrounds, and yet now he was a shepherd while I was still just another lamb among the sheep.

You could tell what television cowboy series a patrol boy watched most often by how he stood on patrol. Back straight, feet far apart was a Gene Autry fan. Thumbs hitched in the belt and head cocked slightly to the left was Roy Rogers. Bow-bent back and drooping arms was the Range Rider. When Bobby Bracken, who was a patrol boy, naturally, stood on patrol, he reminded you of Dale Evans.

Like all figures of authority, the St. Bastion patrol boys had a system whereby they could always, whether on patrol or not, be quickly identified as persons not to be messed with. With Chicago cops, it's the Police Association sticker on the windshield. With the St. Bastion patrol boys, it was a wad of white dangling from their waists. After patrol duty, they would roll up their patrol belts into little squares, which they would hang from their pants' belts.

Many were the backs punched in washroom lines. When the victim turned around to retaliate, he would be totally disarmed by a smug smile and a white rolled-up patrol belt dangling from the midsection.

"Blessings often come in strange packages," my mother would frequently tell me. Since it was my mother who told me, I didn't believe it. But she was right. For in eighth grade, I received a blessing in the guise of the worst case of dandruff the world has ever seen.

I don't know where it came from or why, but by the first week of October I had one huge case of dandruff. I tried washing my hair three times a day. It got worse. I tried not washing my hair at all. It got worse. My mother took me to a scalp specialist. "This child has a severe case of dandruff. That will be ten dollars." My dandruff got worse. It got so bad that wherever I walked, it looked like I was leaving a trail of bread crumbs behind me.

"Why don't you get a crew cut," my mother suggested to me one night at the supper table. She had been after me for years to get a crew cut because she thought a crew cut made a kid look clean-cut, neat, and athletic, which were the same reasons why I didn't want to get a crew cut.

There was another reason. I have a very high forehead. If I drew a line across the top of my head from one ear to the other, the line would fall on my forehead. Therefore, I have always combed my hair forward until it's hanging around my nose. It doesn't fool all of the people all of the time but it fools enough of the people enough of the time. With a crew cut, I would be able to fool no one any of the time.

"I don't know, Ma, I don't think I'd like a crew cut," I said as I grabbed for my glass of milk.

"It would allow a lot of fresh air to get to your scalp," my father said to me through the Irish stew in his mouth, "and that's what you need to cure that dandruff. A lot of fresh air up there."

When it came to medicine, my father was a naturalist. By this time I was getting desperate so I reluctantly agreed to get a crew cut.

The next day after school, I got fifty cents from my mother and headed over to Angelo's Barbershop on the corner of 109th and Wendell Avenue.

Neighborhood rumor insisted that Angelo the barber had formerly worked as a hired killer for the Mafia but was forced into retirement when his eyes started going and he began shooting the wrong people. Knowing that Angelo couldn't be happy in a profession where he wasn't drawing blood, his Mafia friends set him up in the barbering business in Seven Holy Tombs.

The tiny silver bell coughed overhead as I pushed open the door to Angelo's barbershop and cautiously walked over to one of his red-vinyl, steel-rimmed chairs. I sat down and began flipping through one of his five-year-old *National Geographic*s, hoping to find some naked breasts even though I knew the odds were against me since I had already gone through each magazine a couple of hundred times.

Angelo had a little body topped by a massive head with ears so large they seemed to stretch out past his shoulder blades. His thick eyebrows hung like awnings over his tiny squinted eyes.

There were about twelve kids ahead of me. Adults never went to Angelo, not even before the holidays. A customer toppled out of the barber's chair, still swooning from Angelo's talcum powder pounding. Angelo pointed to a little kid sitting in one of the red-vinyl, steel-rimmed chairs and, in the same tone of voice that the guard on death row probably uses, said, "You're next."

After the little kid climbed in, his head was about a foot

below the back of the barber's chair, so Angelo put in a booster chair. Then Angelo pumped up the barber's chair. Finally, the little kid was sitting high enough for his noggin to be attacked by Angelo.

"Say, how old are you?" Angelo said.

The little kid just hunched his shoulders and sniffled loudly.

"Come on, kid. Are you over fourteen years old? You know if you are, you gotta pay the adult price. Come on kid, how old are ya?"

The little kid held up four fingers. "I'm this old."

"You sure you're not fourteen, uh, kid?"

The little kid nodded his head and then shook it negatively. Angelo grunted and reached for the white sheet, the ends of which he promptly wrung around the little kid's neck.

Angelo then grabbed his electric pearl-handle shears from the shelf behind the barber's chair, threw the button to "on," and swept the shears around the sides of the little kid's head.

Back to the shelf where the electric shears were exchanged for the scissors. A few seconds later, the scissors had completed their assault.

Angelo sprinkled some water on the little kid's head, knocked the little kid's hair down with a comb, made a crooked part, grabbed a large white-fibered shaving brush, threw some talcum powder on it, banged the brush around the little kid's head and face, whipped off the white sheet, let down the chair, tapped the little kid on the head, and said, "Out. Fifty cents."

The elapsed time from the moment of sit-down was slightly under two minutes.

Angelo pointed to another kid and announced, "You're next."

The little kid was still wobbling from the effects of his fast descent in the barber's chair when Angelo walked up to him.

"Fifty cents, kid. Come on."

The little kid jammed his fist into his pocket and fumbled around a moment before yanking the fist out. He slowly opened it, exposing the two quarters on his palm.

Angelo stared at them for a second and then snatched them up. He walked over to the cash register and dropped in the two coins. "A great haircut like that and you don't even tip the barber."

"Huh?" said the little kid.

"Go on. Get going, kid. No loitering around here." Angelo pointed to the No Loitering sign on the wall. "Can't you read?"

"Huh?"

As I sat there in Angelo's red-vinyl, steel-rimmed chair, I tried to convince myself that getting a crew cut was a sane idea. "Well, at least it will cure the dandruff." "I've never had a crew cut before, maybe it will look good." "I guess I haven't got *that* high of a forehead." "What the hell, even if the crew cut does look real bad, my hair grows back pretty fast."

I was so busy talking to myself that I wasn't even concentrating on looking for naked breasts in *National Geographics*.

"You're next, kid." I looked up and saw Angelo pointing at me. Now it was my turn to take that long walk to the barber's chair.

As I hopped up into the chair, Angelo asked, "How old are you, kid?"

"Thirteen, Angelo."

"You look fourteen to me."

I took out a copy of my birth certificate and handed it to Angelo. We had been going through this routine for years. He studied it for a few moments, probably looking for the word "legitimate." Angelo was that kind of guy. He grunted as he handed it back to me.

"Give me a crew cut today, Angelo." I said the words quickly as if speed would make their delivery easier.

Angelo didn't even bother answering. He just reached for his pearl-handle shears. Angelo was basically a one-bowl barber who produced only one style of haircut, the divot. If he left the hair on top of your head long enough to comb, then it was called a "regular" haircut. If it was too short to comb, then it was a crew cut.

Angelo liked crew cuts almost as much as my mother did. Occasionally, Angelo would get complaints from parents. Too much off the top. Not enough off the top. But there were never any complaints about crew cuts. A few lawsuits perhaps, but no complaints. With crew cuts, Angelo just kept shaving until he hit skin.

As I heard the shears revving up, I said to Angelo, "Make it about an inch high." I indicated the desired height of my crew cut between my index finger and thumb.

ZIP. "Sure, kid, sure," Angelo mumbled as he passed the shears over my head. Ten zips, one water sprinkling, and a talcum powder pounding later, came the tap on the head.

"Out. Fifty cents."

As I slid out of Angelo's chair, I noticed that my head felt decidedly lighter. Angelo didn't have any mirrors in his shop. He figured they might hurt business. Just as well. I didn't trust myself. I was afraid that if I saw what my crew cut looked like in Angelo's barbershop, and I didn't like what I saw, I would either cry in front of Angelo or beat him to death with his own talcum-powdered shaving brush. Neither one would have helped the situation any.

After handing Angelo half a dollar and listening to him complain about the lack of a tip, I took the red knit cap out of my pocket, which had been brought along for the specific purpose of covering up the crew cut on the home flight, and jammed it on my head.

A few times on the way home, I reached under the red knit cap and touched it. It felt kind of fuzzy and certainly not an inch high. Once, when I reached under and felt it, an old lady was walking by me. She gave me a very weird look.

I wasn't even home yet and already I was beginning to regret the debauchery of my scalp. I could hear my fellow eighth graders exclaiming to one another tomorrow morning when I walked into the classroom. "Gee, I never knew he had *that* high of a forehead."

The girls would shun me and the boys would snicker. Johnny Hellger would make obscene remarks and Lanner would feel sorry for me. And Depki would wonder how I could have been so stupid as to get one in the first place.

As soon as I got into the house I went upstairs to the bathroom mirror and pulled off the red knit cap. My head looked worse than it felt. Angelo had cut my head so close that it looked like it was covered by a thin layer of swirling dust. Now I knew why my father was so sure that a crew cut would cure my dandruff. You can't have dandruff on a bald head.

My forehead looked big enough to roller skate on. There must have been a foot of skin between my eyes and my hairline. I tried squinching my face to see if I could pull my hairline down any. It helped a little, but not much. I was both enraged and crying at the same time. I went down to the basement to see my mother, who was working on the wash.

From past experience, I knew that if my mother said a haircut looked good, then it looked bad and if she said it looked bad, then it looked good. Her standard of judgment was based on one criteria: length. The shorter it was, the more she liked it. That day I was hoping she'd admit the error of her ways and agree that Angelo had, in ten zips, created a hideous holocaust on my head.

"Hey, Mom, look at my haircut."

"It looks nice, dear."

"Nice! Look at my forehead."

"What's the matter with your forehead?"

"Well, for one thing, there's an awful lot of it, wouldn't you say."

"What are you talking about?"

Just then, I heard my father come in from work. He came down the basement stairs, took a look at my head, and said, "Well, I see you didn't get a crew cut."

"I didn't?"

My mother was waving her hand at him to shut up but he hadn't seen the signal in time and now it was too late.

"If this isn't a crew cut, Dad, then what is it?"

"It's a baldy sour."

"A baldy sour?"

"Yeah, it's the kind of haircut they give you when you go into the army. It's much shorter than a crew cut. It looks pretty good on you." He went upstairs into the living room to hang up his coat.

Baldy sour. It even sounded disgusting.

I got up at about five o'clock the next morning and began dressing for school. I planned on getting to school and into my classroom before anyone else and then hiding my head under my workbooks all day. Then I was going to stay after school and not come home until the entire neighborhood was busy eating supper.

It was still dark when I arrived at St. Bastion school. I pulled on the handles of the big red doors. They were locked. A long time later, as the sun was beginning to trickle over the horizon, came the sounds of someone unlocking the doors. As one of the big doors cautiously cracked open, the head of Sister Triona, the nun who was in charge of the patrol boys, peaked from behind it.

"Mr. Ryan? What are you doing here so early?"

"Nothing, Str. I just wanted to be on time for school this morning."

She pushed open the door a little farther and gestured emphatically with her hand for me to pass by her.

"Come on, come on," she said, "I haven't got all day."

I hurried through the door, past the landing where Sister Triona stood, and began climbing up the school's main steps, which directly faced the big red doors. My feet had eaten up about four steps when Sister Triona's voice froze me from behind.

"Mr. Ryan, come back down here a moment."

I came back down the stairs and stood in front of Sister Triona.

"Something looks different about you this morning," she said. "Did you get your hair cut?"

"Yes, Str."

"That's a baldy sour, isn't it?"

"Yes, Str."

"I haven't seen a boy wearing a baldy sour in a long long time." Sister Triona glanced up at the ceiling and made a hasty sign of the cross. "My brother, God rest his soul, wore a baldy sour when he was your age. He was a good athlete, you know. Most good athletes wear baldy sours, you know. It makes a man look so clean-cut and healthy, you know."

"Yes, Str."

Sister Triona's mind suddenly came down from the ceiling. "That'll be all, Mr. Ryan."

"Yes, Str." Once again I began climbing up the main stairs and, once again, my ascension was stopped by the voice of Sister Triona.

"Mr. Ryan, come back down here again."

I was in big trouble now. There was no other reason she'd call me back. I must have made too much noise going up the stairs.

Standing in front of Sister Triona, fully expecting to get clouted.

"How would you like to become a patrol boy?"

"Yes, Str, I'd like that." Inwardly I was ecstatic, but outwardly I maintained the same blank expression on my face that one always presents to nuns. It's never a good idea to let a nun know that she's actually communicating with you.

"Go upstairs to my classroom and get one of the patrol belts that are on my desk. Then come down here with it."

Up two flights of stairs and into Sister Triona's classroom, looking for the patrol belts. As I walked into the classroom, my nostrils were immediately infiltrated by that smothered chalk odor that hangs in all cubicles of learning. On her desk were the patrol belts, each one tightly rolled into itself.

I picked up one of the wrapped patrol belts and squeezed it tightly in my hand. Then I tossed the patrol belt up a few inches and let its authoritative weight fall back against my fingers. Symbols of power are always heavy.

When I got back downstairs, Sister Triona was still floating around behind the big red doors, occasionally poking her head out to see if any more students had arrived.

I walked up behind her. "I have a patrol belt now, Str." I held out the patrol belt as evidence.

Her head snapped around to face me. "Well, put it on, put it on."

I unraveled the patrol belt, placed one length of it over my head and the other section around my waist, buckled the belt with its metal clamps, and then pulled on the clamps to make sure they were locked.

Sister Triona gestured toward the top of the stairs. "This morning, you'll stand up there. James Gilmore, who usually has that post, will be absent today. Tomorrow, I'll give you your own assignment."

She began climbing the stairs, taking full advantage of the support provided by the railing. When she reached the first floor, her head turned and squawked over her shoulder, "If any children come while I'm gone, tell them to go directly to their rooms and take out a workbook." Then Sister Triona disappeared down the hallway.

With back arched, I slowly began walking up the stairs, deliberately dropping each footstep and waiting for the ensuing thud to die in the stairwell before dropping another.

Upon reaching the first-floor level, I spun around and stood straight, feet braced far apart, hands clasped behind my back, facing the school's big red double doors, which stood at attention at the base of the stairs.

I had made it. Eddie Ryan, notorious nobody, had become a patrol boy. I silently practiced snapping out orders. Hey, you, quiet. Stay in line. No talking. Pick up those feet. No noise on the stairway.

The first thing that every kid would see when he came into St. Bastion school that morning would be me and my power, my prestige, my . . . baldy sour! I had forgotten all about it.

It was a long morning. Twenty-two hundred came through those big red double doors; twenty-two hundred pairs of eyes bloated in amazement. Twenty-two hundred jaws dropped in awe. And twenty-two hundred minds silently asked, "Who's the forehead at the top of the stairs?"

The next day, Sister Triona put me on the bicycle patrol. It wasn't the greatest assignment in the world but it wasn't the worst, either.

About two hundred kids a day took their bikes to school except when there was heavy snow on the ground. Then the number would drop to one, me. On such mornings, my "snow" tires would swell to five feet in diameter by the time I got to school.

It was my job to make sure kids locked their bikes, didn't talk, and parked them in the right grade section.

Sister Triona said that since I was in charge of the bikes, I should ride a bike to school myself. My own bike had been stolen the year before when I left it at the park so I had to use my sister's bike.

It was a real beauty, with a blue body and all-chrome fenders. My father never walked into a store and bought anything so none of us knew where it came from. He always had a friend who knew of a friend who knew of a friend who knew . . . My father claimed that it was the only bike ever made with pure chrome fenders. I myself have never seen another bike with pure chrome fenders.

Unfortunately, my sister didn't like them. One afternoon, she decided she'd cover them with some orange paint that she had found in the garage. But the paint she had grabbed from the garage shelf was gutter paint, which gets sticky and runs every time it rains. Thereafter, whenever the bike was ridden in the rain, little blips of orange would trail behind it. That orange paint never totally dried.

Being a patrol boy has been one of the few jobs in my life that I have handled professionally. Only one minor incident marred an otherwise flawless performance. On Halloween day of that year, I almost killed a first grader.

It was during lunchtime and, since it was Halloween, I was in a big rush to get home, eat lunch, and get back to school for the Halloween party in the afternoon.

At St. Bastion school, you couldn't dress up like a witch or goblin or anything like that. You had to dress up like one of the saints. I wanted to go to my class's Halloween party dressed as St. Joseph but my mother wouldn't trust me with a hammer. So I went as St. Christopher. You can't do much damage with a globe.

Rushing anywhere on my sister's orange-gutter-painted bike was no minor achievement. It took approximately a thousand pounds of pressure per pedal to get the bike going over three miles an hour.

Racing home to lunch that day, I was doing the best I could.

My legs pistoned the pedals as calf muscles ripped away from bone. My tongue, dehydrated from lung exhaust, hung limp from my mouth as perspiring hands slid around the handlebars.

About a half a block ahead of me, I saw a first grader trying to cross the street. First graders are easily recognizable. They are the only ones who have mittens clipped to their coats in October.

As his mother told him to, he was crossing at the corner and was looking in each direction for oncoming cars. He was within seconds of discovering that his mother didn't warn him about everything.

I was about fifty feet away from him when he started to cross. I began to brake. He saw me coming and stopped. I saw him stop and I started pedaling again. He saw me stop and he began walking again. I started. He stopped. I stopped. He started. I started. He stopped. And then one of my starts hit one of his stops.

I saw him go down in front of my bent bicycle basket. PLUMPLUMP. I got him with both wheels. I jumped off the bike and ran back to him. He was starting to get up, which was a good sign.

"You okay, kid?"

"Sure, I'm okay." He didn't sound too sure. "Did you see my glasses?" he asked.

"Here they are, kid." I picked them off the curb and handed them to him. The lenses were dusty and all but they weren't broken.

"Where do you live, kid?" I thought I'd better walk him the rest of the way home and explain to his mother exactly what happened even though I didn't know exactly what happened.

"Over on 108th and Crandel."

"Okay. Come on, I'll walk you home. You're sure you're not hurt, now."

"Yeah, I'm sure." He sounded a little more convinced of it himself this time.

"Your back doesn't hurt, does it?"

"No."

I had heard my parents talking about how a lot of people involved in accidents liked to sue for phony back injuries so I wasn't taking any chances.

We didn't talk much as I walked him home. What does an eighth grader have to say to a first grader? Nothing. Absolutely nothing.

He was worried about a big blotch of orange gutter paint on his cheek. I told him he didn't have to worry about it because the orange gutter paint never dried, and how the fender dripped when it rained.

"Go ahead," I said, "touch one of the fenders."

"It's sticky."

"See, I told you. It never dries."

I was hoping the kid didn't have any older brothers or sisters that would spread the word in school that I had run him over. I had never heard of a kid getting run over by a bike before. I had heard of kids threatening to run over somebody, but no one actually ever did it. If the word got out that I was running over first graders with my bike, people would think I was a moron or something.

I took the kid up to his house and rang the doorbell. It didn't look like much of a house. The screen on the front door was ripped, the lawn was thinning, and the paint on the house was beginning to peel.

When his mother came to the door, she had on an old housecoat, her hair was in curlers, and she was chewing gum and smoking a Lucky Strike cigarette. Lucky Strikes have a very distinctive smell about them.

"Good afternoon, mam. This is your kid and I just ran him over with my bike."

"Oh yeah, how come?"

"It was an accident, mam."

"I didn't think you did it on purpose."

"No, I didn't, mam."

"You a patrol boy or something?"

I had forgotten about my patrol belt. I still had it on. "Yes, mam, I'm in charge of the bikes."

She took a long drag on her Lucky Strike, took two chews on her gum, and then blew the smoke through her nostrils, which sounded somewhat clogged up.

"You're in charge of the bikes, huh. And you ran over my kid with your bike. Jesus Christ, that's some school they're running over there." The kid was just standing there, listening to all this bullshit.

"I don't think he's hurt, mam."

She opened the screen door, the kid stepped in, and she put her arm around him.

"It's going to take more than being run over by a bike to slow down my Ernest. Last year he was run over by a car and all he got was a bloody nose. This summer, me and my husband took Ernest to a ball game at Comiskey Park and Ernest caught one of Nellie Fox's pop fouls right in the head. Or did Sherm Lollar hit it? Anyway, Ernest hardly missed a bite on his hot dog."

She patted Ernest on his well-worn head. "Me and my husband are very proud of Ernest. He's not very b-r-i-g-h-t but very t-o-u-g-h. Very t-o-u-g-h."

"Well, I have to get going, mam."

She looked down at Ernest again and touched his cheek. "What's this sticky orange stuff on his face?"

"Oh, that's gutter paint, mam."

"Oh."

I don't think the kid had any older brothers or sisters because I never had anyone mention the incident to me. I don't think the first grader told anyone, either. Some friend of his lived right next door to me and he never even asked me about it.

I guess that after getting hit by a car and beaned in the head by a foul ball off the bat of Nellie Fox or Sherm Lollar, getting run over by an orange-fendered bike is, at best, anticlimactic.

XIV / The Sex Talk

It is part of the American myth that the normal male in this country doesn't become interested in girls until he is well into his teens and doesn't even notice them until he is at least thirteen or fourteen. As every American male knows, such is not the case.

Being an average American male, I experienced my first love affair at the age of four. It lasted three years, one day a year. Her name was Linda Bogan and every year I saw her at the annual Knights of Columbus picnic, which my family faithfully attended.

At each yearly picnic, I would win the footrace and be re-

warded with a Sears, Roebuck ukulele and a smile from Linda.
I still have all the ukuleles, but I can't say the same for Linda's
smiles. In the fourth year, I got off to a poor start in the footrace and finished second. She would have nothing to do with
me. Linda was strictly a first-place girl.

It wasn't until eighth grade, the first week of it to be exact,
that St. Bastion Parish and I received our first sex talk. But
only years later did I realize that's what it was. During that
first sex talk, the word "sex" was never mentioned. And for
good reason; it didn't exist in St. Bastion Parish.

The nuns never mentioned it. The closest they ever got to it
was during English period when they talked about a noun's
gender. " 'He' is of the Masculine Gender, 'She' is of the Feminine Gender." The parish priests never mentioned it. Our
parents never mentioned it. The girls never mentioned it.

For eight years, the nuns and priests did tell us about the
"Immaculate Conception" of the Blessed Virgin Mary. But
like most things the nuns and priests talked about, we had no
idea what they were talking about.

Even among us boys, the word "sex" was never spoken.
How could we say it? We'd never heard of it. Felix the Filth
Fiend Lindor, who could refer to any part of the human anatomy with at least ten different dirty words, never actually used
the word "sex."

During the first few years of my existence, I didn't worry
that much about where I came from. Occasionally, I'd ask my
mother and she'd say, "Why, you came from God. Where
else could you come from?"

"How come I don't remember?" I'd ask.

"Haven't you ever noticed how little babies can't talk?"

"Sure I have."

"Well, that's because they still remember Heaven and God
doesn't want them to tell anyone about it. As a little baby

learns to talk, he gradually forgets Heaven so that by the time he can talk to anyone about Heaven, he's forgotten all about it."

That made sense.

When I got old enough to go to school, the nuns' teachings confirmed my mother's story of my origins. Question 149 of the Baltimore Catechism: WHERE DID YOU COME FROM? ANSWER: I came from God who is all kind, just and good." It was a simple answer. I had a simple mind. I was satisfied.

Eventually, I developed theories of my own that were actually little more than modifications of the original story. For instance, my search for cause and effect drove me to the conclusion that, although I had come from God, I had not come from Him directly. He had dropped me off at the hospital where my mother had to go and pick me up. Keen observation of relatives who had had babies led me to this conclusion. It wasn't until I met Felix the Filth Fiend that I learned the truth of the matter. I learned all the basics from Felix although I'm still learning the finer points.

At St. Bastion school, we could be marching along in line and if somebody got caught goofing off, the nun would take the offender by the shoulder and make him or her stand in the row of the opposite sex. Our lines were always segregated. Boys made up the right row while the girls stood in the left row.

Being placed in the opposite sex's row by a nun was supposed to cause great embarrassment in the offender. Except for a few people like Felix, who got his giggles by such misplacements, it was quite an effective punishment. Until eighth grade.

We eighth graders were a strange bunch. The girls constantly talked about boys but that was about it. They spent most of their free time watching *Bandstand* on television. Only a few of the girls really mixed with the boys, if you know what

I mean. Among us boys, there were those who would, in the same sentence, talk about their sexual achievements and the latest model airplane that they had glued together.

A few years before I started eighth grade, Father O'Reilly had died and Father Myers had been assigned to replace him as pastor of St. Bastion Parish. Father Myers was the first drip in the new wave of liberalism. According to him, you would still go straight to Hell for eating meat on Fridays, but not nearly as fast nor as far down as Father O'Reilly would have had you believe.

In line with this philosophy of liberalism, and knowing that the savage of sensuality was already pacing up and down within us, Father Myers sent Father Vendel, one of the parish's assistant priests, over to St. Bastion school to talk to us eighth graders about the "facts of life," something that had never been done during Father O'Reilly's reign.

When Father Vendel arrived, all of us eighth-grade boys were sent down to an empty first-grade classroom to do our geography homework while the girls were put in one of the eighth-grade rooms to listen to Father Vendel. After he was finished talking to the girls, we were told, he would come down to the first-grade classroom and talk to us while the girls did their geography homework up in their classroom.

As I sat wedged in that first-grade desk, trying to keep my knees out of my mouth as I fought with some fraction, I wondered what Father Vendel was going to say to us. At that point, I had no idea. As it turned out, I had even less of an idea after he said it.

I was kind of excited about just being out of my own classroom. When Father O'Reilly had been pastor, breaks in the daily routine were never tolerated. The only time you were allowed out of your classroom was to go to the principal's office, to the washroom, or for a fire drill.

We were working on our geography homework for about

half an hour when we heard the voice of the nun who was watching us boom out from the back of the room. "Close your books, fold your hands on top of the desk, and sit up straight."

Father Vendel sneaked into the classroom, coughed apologetically for being alive, and placed some loose-leaf papers neatly on the lectern that he had brought along with him. He was an old priest, built in streaks of lanky flesh, his lean head constantly hovering over his navel.

Ever since Father Myers had made Father Vendel the moderator of the newly formed Teen Club, Father Vendel had felt obligated to keep his gray hair in a crew cut and wear white socks and penny loafers that stuck out obtrusively from beneath his cassock.

Everyone liked Father Vendel because he was a pretty nice guy. I liked him because he was a very sincere guy. I can like anyone who's sincere. He always believed in whatever he was doing even though, most of the time, he didn't know what he was doing, which was another reason why I liked him. I could identify with him.

"Let's stand and say a few prayers, boys," Father Vendel said, "before we have our little talk. And considering today's topic, I think it would be a good idea if we said a few extra 'Our Fathers' and 'Hail Marys' in asking Our Lord to bless and watch over our discussion."

As we stood up, I heard Depki moan behind me. I didn't know whether he was moaning because of the extra prayers or because he had managed to rupture himself while prodding his body loose from the first-grade desk.

Ten "Our Fathers," "Hail Marys," and "Glory Be's" later, we sat down and squeezed back into the first-grade desks.

Father Vendel first gave us the usual pitch about the possibility of each of us having a "vocation." Whenever anyone at St. Bastion's talked to you about your future, they inevitably mentioned the strong chance of you having a "vocation," meaning God had chosen you to become a priest or religious brother or, if you were a girl, a nun.

Father Vendel informed us that one out of every four of us had a religious vocation and that the only reason one out of every four of us wouldn't become a priest or religious brother was that some of us just weren't listening to God.

He went on to tell us that God had, somewhere in the Gospels, personally promised priests and all other members of religious orders that they would be rewarded one hundredfold in this life, and even more in the next, for whatever sacrifices they made.

I don't think anyone was really listening to Father Vendel, except maybe for a few guys who were debating about going to a seminary high school after they graduated from St. Bastion's. Most of us had already made up our minds about it, one way or the other. We had been getting that same pitch for eight years now.

The nuns were always telling us how being a religious was a higher calling than being a parent. The single life was rarely mentioned and when it was, the nuns subtly suggested that the only ones who remained unmarried were those who refused to answer God's calling them to a "vocation" only to discover that their lives, except for an occasional Sunday dinner invitation, were totally devoid of joy.

I personally couldn't see how the nuns were collecting their one hundredfold but then I saw them only in school. When questioned, many of them insisted they were getting it.

That "vocation" stuff was a very tempting deal. I don't imagine there was ever a Catholic kid who didn't, at one time or another, think of being a priest or a nun. The other alternative, parenthood, certainly wasn't as lucrative as one hundredfold. I was around my parents a lot more than I was around the nuns and I knew, for sure, my parents weren't collecting such dividends.

After Father Vendel finished talking about our "vocations," he picked up one of the loose papers from his lectern and began reading from it.

"Boys, you are at an age when your bodies are undergoing great changes. These changes, like all beautiful and wonderful things, are being brought to you by the infinite wisdom and love of God. These changes, these beautiful gifts of God, are the first steps toward adulthood.

"But the devil, as usual, is jealous of God's gifts to you and is trying to take your souls and condemn them to the everlasting fires of Hell.

"And how is the devil going about this, boys? How is the devil trying to get you to commit a mortal sin and"—Father Vendel interrupted himself to turn to the next page of his notes—"thereby, if you die in the middle of the night without the benefit of a priest's presence, sending your soul to the deepest corners of Hell?

"I will tell you, boys." The next sentence was spoken in an odd mixture of whisper and shout. "By tempting you to commit sins of impurity."

Father Vendel leaned smugly over the lectern, waiting for our faces to blush at the use of such crude terminology. We stared back. Satisfied with himself, Father Vendel went back to reading from his papers.

"First of all, boys, sins of impurity are perhaps the most dangerous kind of sin. Almost all sins of impurity are mortal sins. It is very difficult to commit a venial sin of impurity. Therefore, it is extremely dangerous to commit any sin of impurity.

"Furthermore, boys, it has been estimated that more people go to Hell because of sins of impurity than for any other kind of sin. Perhaps as many as two out of every three people who go to Hell go there because of the sin of impurity.

"Now, boys, you may be asking yourself, 'How does the devil go about tempting me to commit these sins of impurity?'

Well, boys, one way the devil always uses is he tries to get us to have impure thoughts. Yes, boys, those impure thoughts are the devil's way of getting you to Hell.

"Remember, boys, that Christ said to His disciples, in Matthew, Chapter 5, Verse 28, 'But I say to you that anyone who so much as looks with lust at a woman has already committed adultery with her in his heart.' Which means, boys, that if you willfully have an impure thought, you are responsible not only for the intention but the act as well."

Sitting there listening to Father Vendel, I knew I was in big, big trouble. My mind spent most of its free time having impure thoughts. And if it was true, as Father Vendel said, that thinking something was as bad as doing it, then I was molesting at least eighty girls a day.

"We must be on our guard, boys, against the devil, who is forever trying to persuade us to attend 'suggestive' movies, look at 'suggestive' books, and associate with 'suggestive' people." Everybody turned around and stared at Felix the Filth Fiend Lindor, but he just maintained his eye fixation on Father Vendel.

"Boys, keep in mind that God realizes you have a lot of excess energy at this age. That is why God allows time for you to play after school, to do homework every night, to help your parents around the house. God wants you to keep busy. A busy young man or woman who is leading a full Christian life doesn't have time for impure thoughts.

"We must constantly remind ourselves that our bodies are made in the image and likeness of God Himself. We are not simply bone and flesh. Our bodies are temples of the Holy Ghost and must be treated as such. Temples of the Holy Ghost," Father Vendel sighed, "isn't that beautiful, boys, to realize that our bodies are temples of the Holy Ghost."

Father Vendel stood there behind his lectern, smiling into his chest and muttering to himself, "Temples of the Holy

Ghost, isn't that beautiful." After a few seconds, he came back down to earth, reshuffled his papers, and began reading once again.

"Another way the devil has of getting us to commit sins of impurity, boys, is by tempting us to touch the private parts of our bodies. We should never, I repeat, never never never touch the private parts of our bodies.

"It is a very serious sin, boys, to willfully place yourself in a position whereby you allow yourself to become . . . ah . . . shall we say 'aroused.'

"Sometimes though, boys, through no fault of your own, you will find yourself becoming aroused. You will find yourself having impure thoughts. When that happens, turn to God for help and think beautiful thoughts. Imagine Christ hanging on the cross, dying a torturous death for your sins. Feel the agony of the nails driven through His hands. The unbearable pain of the crown of thorns as they press into His head. Such beautiful thoughts, boys, will save you from becoming aroused and will help you in your fight against sins of impurity.

"Now, boys, I am aware that all of you know individuals who hang around the street corners who consider themselves 'experts' on the topic we have been discussing this morning." Again all our eyes turned toward Felix, giving a silent salute to his raunchiness. This time, Felix recognized our praise. His head hung low over the first-grade desk in order that Father Vendel might not see him. A smutty smile spread across Felix's face while greasy giggles gargled in his throat.

"These so-called 'experts,' " Father Vendel continued, "actually know very little of what they are talking about. Worse yet, they try, by their 'snide' and 'cute' remarks, to make the beautiful God-created relationship between man and woman a dirty and disgusting thing.

"But remember, boys, our bodies were not created to be made fun of or to be ashamed of. They are temples of the Holy

Ghost. Isn't that beautiful, boys, temples of the Holy Ghost."

Father Vendel then had a movie projector rolled into the classroom. For the next twenty minutes we were subjected to a color version of "The Life Cycle of the Polar Bear."

"Now, boys," Father Vendel shouted over the whine of the projector as it rewound the film, "are there any questions? None, uh. Well, uh . . ."

Father Vendel was just stalling around. It was customary that, after a priest had spoken to us, one of the bootlickers would ask him if he would give us his blessing. A priest considered it extremely poor taste not to be asked for his blessing.

The nun in the back of the room coughed loudly. Finally, Bobby Bracken raised his hand.

"Uh, yes? Bobby," Father Vendel said.

Bobby Bracken stood up. "Could we have your blessing, Father?"

"Why certainly. Kneel down, boys."

We pried our bodies loose from the first-grade desks and plopped to the floor on our knees. Father Vendel muttered some Latin and waved his hands over us a few times in the sign of the cross. We stood up, mumbling, "Thank you, Father," and began lining up at the door.

"Now remember, boys," Father Vendel said as we began marching out of the classroom, "your bodies are temples of the Holy Ghost."

When we got back to our own classroom, it became quickly apparent that Father Vendel had told the girls a few things that he hadn't bothered telling us boys. As we filed into the room, every girl looked up from her geography homework and gave us a facial expression normally reserved for a newly arrived pile of manure.

It seems that Father Vendel had told the girls it would be a good idea to stay away from boys since all of them, without exception, had very dirty minds.

XV / *Finale*

Then came the month of June and God handed us a deed to the world. Every song that was played on the radio seemed to be written for us, the eighth graders of St. Bastion's. When adults met, they spoke only of us. Every story line of every television show had only us in mind. The sun rose only to shine on our heads.

The latest dance step bounced from our feet, graduation ribbons flowed from our chests, dry wit dripped from our mouths, and visions of the future glistened in our eyes. We were, in the words of Felix the Filth Fiend, truly hot shit.

St. Bastion school continued to exist, of course, but only for our glorification. We were positive that the school would disintegrate behind us once we had stepped out its doors for the final time. Our days of diagraming sentences were indeed just about over.

That June, we went through our last year-end Workbook Push. In all my years of grammar school, no nun ever managed to pace her class fast enough to get all their workbook pages done by the end of the school year. So during the last few days of school, the nun would have us do nothing but workbook pages for five hours a day. As soon as all the workbooks were completed, they'd be put into stacks and carried down to the principal's office by some of us boys.

The nun would always tell us that we wouldn't be able to go on to the next grade the following September unless we finished all our pages. She'd also inform us that the principal would spend all summer going over every page of every workbook of every kid in the entire school.

It was an established fact, however, that as soon as we kids left the school on the final day of class, all the nuns would go to the principal's office and carry all the stacks of workbooks down to the school basement where they were then promptly thrown into the school furnace and burned.

During our final days of eighth grade, the nuns would try to burst the bubble with the infamous comment, "You may be at the top of the pile now, but just wait until next year when you get to high school. You'll be right at the bottom of the heap again."

"Next year." They had to be kidding. No eighth grader ever thought of "next year."

On Graduation Day, the nuns turned away four girls who showed up for the ceremony in sleeveless dresses. For the next three months, Bobby Bracken insisted that sexual intercourse had something to do with a girl's biceps.

Our class behaved in the traditional Graduation Day manner. The girls cried while the boys laughed like madmen.

A couple of weeks before we were to graduate, Johnny Hellger, Tom Lanner, and a few other guys were caught stealing out of the Church's poor box. I'm sure Johnny Hellger talked Lanner into it. All of them caught royal hell. The fact that there wasn't a kid in the parish who had more of a claim to some of that money than Lanner never entered into it.

The weeks following Graduation Day contained the filet of the eighth-grade finale: the graduation parties. Such parties couldn't be held before graduation because the nuns wouldn't allow it. They defined an orgy as any social gathering where both sexes attended.

Teddy Baskin's party was a good one. Teddy was built like a half-melted ice cube. His face was smeared with freckles, his nose constantly ran, and he had a beer belly even though he didn't drink. Yet, he was the most popular boy among the eighth-grade girls.

Teddy was a devout patron of the portable radio. He had no faith in transistor radios, which were relatively new then. He spent most of his time waddling along the sidewalks of the neighborhood, his left arm wrapped around his blaring portable radio, which looked big enough to be a floor model. The fingers on Teddy's free hand snapped out the tune while his head and rear end swung in opposite directions to the beat of the music.

If you passed Teddy on the street, he'd smile and wave and you'd return the salute. No point in saying hello as Teddy had gone deaf years ago. He'd been walking around like that since third grade. For five years, he was considered nuts. But by eighth grade, he was considered "in."

With all his smiling and waving, Teddy made a lot of friends, especially among the girls, so his party was a big success.

I almost didn't go to Teddy's party. My fingers, on their usual morning pimple patrol, felt a huge one just about to surface on my chin. I couldn't quite see it yet, but I could really feel it.

Only after Johnny Hellger assured me that Teddy's basement was as dark as a dungeon did I decide to go to the party. I had a great time. But it was a good thing for me the basement was dark because it was the kind of party where a pimple would have really stuck out.

Gloria Downgill also had a good party. It could have been a lot better if she had listened to Felix Lindor. Twelve times he suggested that we play "Spin the Bottle" or "Post Office" and twelve times she pretended she didn't hear him.

Gloria Downgill was one of those girls who hits her social peak in eighth grade and then is never seen or heard of again. In seventh grade, she wore her hair short and straight. But the sheet of hair hanging off the left side of her head looked a lot longer than the sheet of hair hanging off the right side of her head. She wore her glasses crooked, too. Maybe Gloria Downgill thought that made her haircut look more balanced.

The miracle occurred right at the beginning of eighth grade. One day Gloria Downgill was ugly and the next day she was gorgeous. I don't remember exactly when it happened. But it did.

She immediately became the girl to be seen with. She formed a clique of friends that virtually monopolized the eighth-grade social scene.

Tons of kids came to her party, which roared far into the night, right up to the eleven o'clock curfew when everybody had to go home.

But within a year, the peach of St. Bastion's eighth-grade class began to rot. Two years later, she looked little better than a rusted pit.

The cycle had been completed. Not that Gloria Downgill looked the same as she had in seventh grade. But she looked just as ugly, only in a different way.

I suspect that today, somewhere, she is standing behind a sales counter or on top of two little kids in some miniature two-room apartment. And nary a day is allowed to dissipate that the mind of Gloria Downgill doesn't drift back to those ecstasies of eighth grade.

XVI / SWANK

I squint to see the dials on my watch: 4:30. Better get going if I want to catch that plane tonight. The sun is just beginning to die. I shiver from the cold death air as it settles on the day. A yellow autumn sky glows above Seven Holy Tombs Park as the sun winks over the horizon.

The young mothers with their baby carriages are home now preparing dinner. A few old men remain on the park benches but most of them, too, have surrendered the park to the neighborhood kids.

Walking down Wendell Avenue to catch a bus on the main street that will take me out of Seven Holy Tombs.

I let the first bus go by. It's an express that runs directly out of the neighborhood. Waiting for the local that winds around a few additional streets before it leaves Seven Holy Tombs. On one of those streets is a friend I'd like to catch a glimpse of before I leave.

My father wanted a pack of cigarettes. I think that's the reason we stopped. The drugstore we pulled up to was on the corner of 109th and Talson, "Sin Corner" of the world. The rest of the family was talking about the Aunt Reggie dinner they had just endured, the final point of which proved nothing but the limits some people will go to for a topic of conversation on a late Sunday afternoon.

I simply stared out the back window at a mystic structure across the street, pushed twenty feet back from the sidewalk and caught between Elmwood Cleaning on one side and Henry's Pizza House on the other. Across the top of the building was a huge metal billboard with a man and a woman skating like they do in the Olympics and above them, in blatant orange letters, was SWANK Roller Rink.

Although I had heard a lot about the SWANK I had never actually seen it. The yellow-tinged brick wall with its blob orange steel doors seemed to indicate a greater life in the thereafter but my fourth-grade mind could not even begin to comprehend what actually lay beyond. It was after Sunday closing time and the crowd had by now slithered back to their dens.

As the car pulled away, I swore to myself, "I shall return, and soon." The SWANK just sat back, looking aloof and very very tough. I was wrong. It was quite a while before I got in there.

SWANK Roller Rink, besides being the bar mitzvah of the neighborhood, was also its class structure. If you were a connoisseur of the SWANK, you were most assuredly bourgeois, but if you didn't frequent that cathedral of wooden wheels, you were strictly a peon. And I, at the age of nine, realized that I was, in fact, a peon.

Within a year, Johnny Hellger had become a frequenter of the SWANK. Not only had he become a rookie of such a place at the tender age of ten but he had also, so he claimed, skated with Pat Redglen, *the* sex symbol of all time. She had a very sinister smile that was quite appealing. I never met her but she had that smile in a picture Johnny Hellger had of her. He told us that he even went to the show with her and they kissed every time the actors did on the screen. I never wanted to do anything like that, though. With my luck, I would have gone and drawn a straight run of Bugs Bunny cartoons.

If you want to know the truth, my parents and Johnny Hellger's played in a different league. Going somewhere with Redglen was just inconceivable for me, so why dream?

He being a rookie, Johnny Hellger went only on Saturday mornings. As soon as the morning session had ended, he'd come over to the street corner where the rest of us had been playing softball. Nothing could break up a softball game faster than a Johnny Hellger fresh from the SWANK Roller Rink.

We'd stand around him while he'd tell us about the beautiful women, the flashing of the colored lights, the roar of the organ, the violence of the fox-trot. Then, all of a sudden, Johnny Hellger would say, "Hey, I've got better things to do than stand around here and shoot the bull with you guys," and he'd walk off. Man, we could just imagine the "better things" a guy like Johnny Hellger had to do.

After he had gone, the rest of us would just sit around. We wouldn't even talk or anything. I mean, here we had been knocking a stupid softball around the street while at the same time the lurid life of the SWANK was going on only a mile and a half away. Fox-trot? We didn't even know what it was.

By the time I reached the seventh grade, I had become a regular attender of the SWANK Saturday morning sessions, the first apprentice step in becoming a full journeyman of the SWANK. The simple fact that these rounds went on inside the SWANK made them mystery beads in one's rosary of life. But outside of that, they were strictly passé.

For one thing, Saturday morning sessions were overpopulated with Boy Scouts, Girl Scouts, and all other sorts of weirdos. Such organizations in my neighborhood gave out merit badges to anyone who could prove that they couldn't stand on roller skates any longer than three seconds. Their leader was always some stocky little log-legged chunk who skated like she had no knees.

Saturday morning didn't even have live organ music. It was taped. The highlight of the session came at about ten-thirty when the race was held, the prize being a ticket to the next week's morning session.

What they'd do is line up all the little guys at the starting line and then they'd take the two social retards who were obviously big and good enough to be skating at the afternoon session and put them all the way on the other side of the rink, about eighty yards behind the rest of the mob, in order to make the race fair. Sure it was.

As soon as the whistle blew, the mob inched forward, bodies self-destructing all over the place. The ones who didn't fall out of ineptness succumbed to sheer panic as they heard those two huge morons behind them building up speed like madmen. You'd look over your shaky shoulder and you'd see two low-crouched forms, arms swinging, legs pumping, eyes like laser beams heading straight for you. Swish swooish swooish Swish swooish swooish Swish swooish swooish kill! kill! kill!

Within seconds after the race began, the two morons would reach the crowd and begin playing Sherman's "March to the Sea," the first one bouncing to the floor any bodies that had managed to remain intact, the other guy cutting around the front of the pack to take the lead.

The two usually glided the last hundred yards quite nonchalantly, no longer in the crouched positions of challengers but in the upright and dignified forms of champions, readjusting the collars of their blue denim shirts like all goons after a successful hit. A few deteriorated minds would cheer them as they crossed the finish line. Probably the same ones that backed the Yankees when they came to town.

The rink was almost silent then except for an occasional moan from one of the fallen. The floor looked like a battlefield, bodies strewn all over the place. The air was thick with the odor of fresh blood and broken dreams. Why, some of the fallen had practiced hours just to get run over. No doubt about it. Boy Scouts are born losers.

The Saturday morning sessions served their purpose, though. They transformed me from a stumble-two, skate-one, love-your-mother, stay-near-the-railing, be-polite sucker to an elbows-out, shoulders-in, speeding, cutting, compulsive, get-out-of-my-way-or-I'll-skate-over-your-head, eight-wheeled maniac. I was ready for the afternoon session.

In the late 1950s, Frankie Avalon was singing "Venus, if you will, please send a little girl for me to thrill . . . ," Eisenhower had the nation safely tucked in bed, the New York Yankees and the Church were still infallible, Vietnam was the name of an Oriental dish, and I was going to the Saturday afternoon sessions at SWANK Roller Rink. Camelot it was!

To try and imagine the exhilaration of skating three hours at the SWANK on a Saturday afternoon is beyond man's mere mind. "Eyes have not seen nor ears heard . . ."

The mere physical beauty of the SWANK was overwhelming. The rink itself was made of the purest oak plywood imported from Gary, Indiana. The surface was as smooth as Lincoln's face and the entire thing was covered by a thin, yet very penetrating layer of dust so that if some ding-a-ling fell, his point of contact was marked by this indelible mist that stigmatized him for the rest of the session. It also served as ample warning to others of their fate if they chose to be clods.

In the middle of the rink an oval had been drawn. If you wanted to skate backward during an "all-skate," you had to do it inside this oval. The oval was also the home base for the SWANK guards, a group of sweat-soaked, fatty-faced bums, naturally all natives of Seven Holy Tombs, who had dropped out of school at about the third grade or as soon as they could count to eight in order to know if all their wheels were there. They weren't.

When someone would fall, one of these guys would race out of the oval with all the finesse of a jackhammer, knocking over at least a dozen people on his way to helping the poor slob who probably had been rollered to death already anyway.

Directly above the center of the rink, about fifty feet up, hung a silver sphere the size of a basketball, that constantly twirled. When the colored lights began flashing on and off, the sphere would catch flecks of them and flick the fragments across the ceiling, turning the entire SWANK into a kaleidoscope.

The colored lights, which had never been taken down from SWANK's first Christmas party, did not contain a psychedelic message but rather one of power. They were overloading SWANK's electrical system and that's why they kept flashing on and off.

The walls of SWANK were two-tone; the upper half being a Puke Purple, so called because it could cause or cover up said fact depending on whether it was instigator or victim. The lower half being Wolski Red, named after its creator, Arthur Wolski.

Running alongside the actual skating area was a skate room that was always good for a few broken kneecaps since some joker who was looking at something he really shouldn't have been looking at would inevitably skate into one of the low-lying benches.

Next door to the skate room was Sarah's Snack Bar. Sarah looked forty, acted twenty, and talked like she was ten. The rumor was that Sarah had tried to be a neighborhood whore but things hadn't gone her way. In an area of the city where 95 percent of the population was under thirteen, it wasn't hard to figure out why.

Sarah wasn't too terribly bright either. She never did learn how to mix the Coke syrup with the soda water. Her gummy Cokes would stick to your teeth like Milk Duds. There was also something very strange about her ice cream bars that I never have been able to figure out. I'd just about get the wrapping off and it would be melted all over my hand. It was very odd.

After Sarah's Snack Bar came the dance room. It was where all the "scancs" hung out. A "scanc" was a not-too-nice term to apply to a girl. Although no one could actually define a scanc, all but the simplest of souls could spot one. Her hair was ratted, she wore very tight black slacks that had creases going sideways, used makeup, and tied her babushka directly on her chin as if it were a riot helmet instead of a babushka.

They had a jukebox in the dance room and all these crazy girls would dance in there for almost the entire session. The only time they'd put on their skates would be for the "ladies only" number. Really. At about a quarter to three, ten minutes before the "ladies only" number was to come on, all these girls would start putting on their skates. They'd go out and skate the "ladies only" and then come right back and dance the rest of the afternoon. I suppose this custom worked on the same principle as closing a private road once a year that's normally used by the public. If you don't do something occasionally, people are going to think you can't do it at all.

Then there was the washroom. Anyone who used the SWANK washroom did so because of one of several reasons: he had had one too many of Sarah's Cokes; he possessed no kidneys whatsoever; he was a narcissist and had to comb his ducktail just one more time; or he had never been to the SWANK before.

The air in there was ninety proof, a mixture of Vitalis, H A Hair Arranger, Brylcreem, and Vaseline Hair Tonic for men plus a healthy dose of that gas exclusively produced by forest-preserve outhouses. It would have been a great place to train scuba divers. No one ever inhaled twice. Not twice.

To get to the SWANK washroom, you had to travel down two steps, on skates. You would have to hold on to the wall and go down them very gingerly, as if you were stepping into a pool of ice water.

Immediately after the steps, you had to make two quick ninety-degree turns. Miss the first turn and you'd cut your midsection in half on one of the sinks. Miss the second and you'd skate right into a toilet. Usually, a ten-minute wait was in order since half of the facilities were stuffed up and overflowing.

For me, it was a very nervous ten-minute wait. If I perchance bumped into one of the ducktails, he'd get very touchy about it. He had to. It was part of his code of ethics. He'd say something like, "Hey, asshole, don't you know how to skate?" I had to mumble something back. It was part of my code of ethics. I suppose I could have told the jerk the truth. "Sure I do, but not in two feet of water while holding my breath for ten minutes." Then the ducktail would say, "Okay, wise guy, see you outside after skating's over."

The rest of the afternoon would be spent in visions of being mauled in front of SWANK viewed by an audience of girls I had tried to impress during the last ten years of my life. The guy would never show up but it was certainly a wear on the nerves.

Once I dreamt that I had actually fallen in the SWANK washroom. I've never even heard of someone falling in the SWANK washroom. What would someone do who did fall in the SWANK washroom? Who would he talk to? Where would he go? How would he get home? What would he do when he got home?

The last landmarks at SWANK were the organ nest and, directly above it, a light board that flashed the name of the dance number in progress. In one corner of the board was a small red light, which beamed only when the fox-trot ritual was being performed.

The organ nest hung out like a tree branch over one corner of the rink. It was more profanely known as "Lloyd's Limb." Lloyd, the organist, had this very long vulture face, clawlike fingernails, a kind of protruding nose, and wore his hair in a style that suggested he never went to the barber his mother sent him to when he was a kid.

When you were skating around the floor, you had an instinctive aversion to going near Lloyd's Limb. You kept getting the feeling that at any moment Lloyd was going to leap off of his perch, sweep down, and grab you by his clawlike fingernails and deposit you in some ungodly place, like the washroom.

Rumor had it that Lloyd's mother suffered from delusions of grandeur. She'd figured that Lloyd was going to end up in Carnegie Hall. But one thing that worked against Lloyd's claim to fame was his ability to remember music. He couldn't. It took him literally years to get one song down. By 1958, he was just wrapping up "Paper Doll."

But Lloyd could really play the boogie-woogie, the national anthem of all roller rinks. Lloyd only played the boogie-woogie for important occasions like the fox-trot, a dance in which the guy skated as fast as he could backward while dragging a girl along with him who happened to be skating forward, if all was going well.

The fox-trot was easily the most violent moment of any session save the Saturday morning one, which didn't have any fox-trot mainly because anyone who was skating backward on Saturday morning was probably doing so involuntarily.

Although there weren't many things Lloyd could do to perfection, he could play loud and long. Loud? If Lloyd wasn't in full view, you'd swear to God he was leaping on the keys. And long? In all the years the SWANK was open, no one ever saw Lloyd not playing the organ. Put them all together and you had a very loud and long boogie-woogie.

Skate a boogie-woogie on Saturday afternoon with Lloyd at his machine and the boogie-woogie would be hanging on your ear lobes till the following Friday. There were some weekly worshipers who existed in a perpetual audio world of boogie-woogie.

Every Saturday afternoon, at a quarter to two, I'd head out for Tom Lanner's house, skates slung over my shoulder in appropriate pony express style. We'd head up the main street, past St. Bastion school, the park, through the business district, and alongside the cemetery hill, shooting the bull all the way.

The first "all-skate" of the afternoon would be spent looking for a chassis to drag around in the upcoming "couples only." As soon as an acceptable one was spotted, not so cute that she'd turn me down nor so ugly that she'd turn me off, I'd start skating within her vicinity so that once the "couples only" flashed on the big board over Lloyd's Limb and the great dome of the rink darkened, I would be able to glide up to her and garble, "Would you like to skate?"

My social consciousness extended to the point of knowing about deodorant. Mouthwash was a good year off. The only

Freudian insight I got out of such affairs was that if one goes around with an unknown girl, especially in a roller rink, his hands will get sweaty.

After the "couples only" I'd look around for Lanner and we'd slide around the rink during the "all-skate." One did not stay with a girl after a "couples only." Such was paramount to a formal proposal of marriage, or more.

As 4:30 approached, the kill-free attitude of the SWANK was slowly swallowed up by an apprehension that perhaps 4:30 would never come. Maybe it wouldn't be as great as the last one. What if the world really did end this time?

Up to 4:30, everything was strictly preliminary. "Couples only" were for kids and "waltzes" for lovers. But at 4:30 came the orgasm of the SWANK Roller Rink—the fox-trot. And that was only for the pros.

On that great board in the sky would suddenly flash those horrendous words, FOX-TROT. It was every man's high noon. Did he have what it takes to go out there, in other words no brains, or would he choose to stand along the sidelines smiling blandly and hoping everyone would think he had a bad back that he was too proud to talk about. But the fox-trot was a lot like quicksand: stand around it too long and you were bound to fall in.

The couples are out there now. A few girls, just seeing the board, realize that they are not out there for a waltz but for THE FOX-TROT and they can't get the madmen to let go of them. Old Lloyd is warming up with some 1930 tune waiting for that red light, the checkered flag of the fox-trot, to flash on.

RED! Hips jutting, skates slicing out as the couples build up speed. Boogie-woogie boogie-woogie boogie-woogie boogie-woogie. There's a couple down. Another one piles into them. A third one hits both of them. Here come two guards like Mack trucks on a puppy farm. They knock over three more couples. Boogie-woogie boogie-woogie boogie-woogie boogie-woogie. A girl passes out. Her partner keeps dragging her on. He doesn't even know it. Another couple has made the mistake of looking up at the silver sphere. Damn rookies. They're both hypnotized . . . heading straight into a . . . boogie-woogie boogie-woogie boogie-woogie boogie-woogie.

Lloyd's in the homestretch. His fingernails look as if they're going to touch the ceiling the instant before he plunges them into the keys. Lloyd's face looks like the hot end of a thermometer and the sweat's creating creases in his cheeks. The Puke Purple and Wolski Red walls balloon out with every blast and like all great outfielders reaching over the fence for the home-run ball, grab that boogie-woogie and fling it right back to Lloyd. And caught in the crossfire are those skates-screaming, torso-twitching, face-flushing, leg-lashing, sphere-spinning boogie-woogie boogie-woogie boogie-woogie boogie-woogie kids.

It stops. The Puke Purple and Wolski Red walls shudder as if suddenly conscious of what they have come through, sigh, and relax.

Lloyd has bounced into a jazz version of "Chattanoogie Shoe Shine Boy." No one's ever heard of Chattanoogie or a shoe shine boy for that matter but they know it marks the end.

The red light flickers off both on the board and in Lloyd's complexion. He looks almost normal now. As close as he'll ever get. The guards are still growling but their breathing isn't quite as heavy and their fangs are almost covered.

Still everyone skates. Admirers begin shouting from the sidelines, "It's over, it's over." But those fox-trot veterans hear only one sound in that cubicle that previously housed a mind. Boogie-woogie boogie-woogie boogie-woogie boogie-woogie.

Finally they come off the floor, disdainful of those who gather about them. Their eyes glare through these parasites with their friendly pats and hollow words of praise.

"Where were you when the big one came? Where were you when the chips were down and the boogie-woogie was up? Where were you?"

Within a few minutes, Tom Lanner and I were on our way home, our feet reluctantly readjusting to the law of gravity. It was about five-thirty now and as the sky squeezed out the sun, Tom and I would walk alongside the cemetery hill, down the main street, through the business district, and on home talking about very important things, which like all important things have long since been forgotten. We were in no big rush to get home and our pace gave evidence. Contented people don't walk very fast.

As they usually do, the years slipped between the SWANK and me until their weight wedged us apart and we went our separate ways.

I worked for a few years in downtown Chicago and every day I would drive right past the SWANK. I never thought about it much. You tend to take old friends for granted. Since then, I've heard that she's closed a few times but it didn't bother me one way or the other. Who doesn't rest when they get a little older?

Riding along in the bus, searching through my wallet for my plane reservation. The bus stutters to a stop at a corner. I look up.

She is dead. Already her left side has been leveled and where the silver sphere once hung stands a crane with its lead wrecking ball mimicking the past. Sarah's Snack Bar is where we're all heading and the organ nest is empty. Lloyd's Limb without Lloyd. Good God!

Looking at those sun-embarrassed Puke Purple–Wolski Red walls in their crippled condition empties me. I don't know why

I am so surprised. Real hearts aren't candy-shaped and rosy-colored.

Finally the bus turns and crawls through the intersection, down the main street, through the business district, and over the cemetery hill where Lanner lies.

As I jostle along in her lit-up belly, the bus's wheels seem to mumble incoherently, slowly, boogie . . . woogie . . . boogie . . . woogie . . . boogie . . . woogie.